"DON'T THANK ME, THANK YOUR RECRUITER"

"DON'T THANK ME, THANK YOUR RECRUITER"

Ken Conklin

AuthorHouse™
1663 Liberty Drive
Bloomington, IN 47403
www.authorhouse.com
Phone: 1-800-839-8640

Published by AuthorHouse 06/25/2012

ISBN: 978-1-4772-0298-2 (sc)
ISBN: 978-1-4772-0297-5 (hc)
ISBN: 978-1-4772-0296-8 (e)

Library of Congress Control Number: 2012908463

CONTENTS

This book is dedicated to my father, Ken Conklin Sr. Without him I would not be where I am today. When I was young he told me "ALWAYS SHOOT FOR THE MOON. THE WORST THAT CAN HAPPEN IS YOU FALL AMONGST THE STARS." I've never forgotten it since.

PROLOGUE

When I first came up with the idea of writing this book, I took a lot of things under consideration. First and foremost I took under consideration my own personal experiences and how I wanted to convey them to you, the reader. Also, I took under consideration the fact that there are many stories and books written by former Soldiers about their experiences. Some of these books that are out there are written by General Officers who served everywhere from the Vietnam War all the way to the halls of the Pentagon. Such examples of this are the books of General Petreaus and of Retired General Colin Powell. When I read Colin Powell's book I found myself intrigued and captivated by the various stories of this man who started off as an Infantry Officer and eventually rose in the ranks not only all the way up to becoming a General, but also eventually becoming Secretary of State under President George W. Bush. To be honest, I found his work of literature to be quite inspirational.

Other works of literature written by former or even current military personnel often include compelling stories of their experiences in various wars. There are many books written by or about individuals who fought in wars such as the Iraq War, Afghanistan, the Gulf War, Vietnam, and both World Wars to boot. Usually these stories involve Soldiers who actually did the fighting; proven infantrymen and combat vets who sacrificed all and put everything on the line for this great nation of ours. This is even done with movies as well. There are plenty of movies out there; We Were Soldiers, Black Hawk Down, and the Windtalkers just to name a few. I always remember that if it weren't for the sacrifices of the brave men and women depicted in such books and movies that the United States of America wouldn't be free, or at least would be in jeopardy of losing its freedom. The few make sacrifices so that the many can be free. There is no greater line of work than that of a Soldier in my opinion.

So you may wonder why, after reading the past few paragraphs, did I write this book? Well, the answer is simple. I wrote this book to tell a story that isn't often told: the story of a Support Soldier. I am not in any way going to discount the sacrifices made by infantrymen and Special Forces however, it is not very often that a story of a Support Soldier is told to the world. Support Soldiers still deploy to combat zones for as long as 12 to 15 months at a time, and they are still put in harm's way. For those reading this who have no real knowledge of the military, a Support Soldier is a Soldier whose main profession is simply not combat-arms related. A Support Soldier could be a medic, a cook, a legal clerk, finance, a personnel clerk, a mechanic, a supply specialist, along with a whole long list of other professions. In the Army, these professions are called your MOS, which stands for Military Occupation Specialty. There are over 200 Military Occupation Specialties in the Army, and I am willing to believe that the general public may not be aware of that. After all, when I was a kid, I thought the Army was what I saw in the movies or on television. I thought the Army was exactly what I saw on GI JOE. When I finally grew up I realized that this wasn't actually the case.

I spent 9 years, 7 months serving in the Active Army as a 42A, which is the MOS code for Human Resources Specialist, aka personnel services. In that period of time I traveled the world, in fact, I went to 14 countries total, counting countries I passed through. I served honorably. Along my journey I met a lot of people, some were great people, and some were not so great people. I met people from all walks of life. I tried my best to learn something from every person I met along the way. I feel that we take something; a lesson from every experience we encounter in life, whether it's from the places we have visited, to the people that we meet, or the jobs that we work. I feel that these lessons help shape the person that we are today. Of course, that is just my opinion and we are all entitled to our own opinions and philosophies on life. I just hope that in this writing I can simply convey my story to the world, to tell the story of my own experiences, both the good and the bad. As I stated before, I wish to take nothing away from the Infantry Corps by writing this book. I am merely here to tell you my story. This is not an autobiography of my entire life, but merely my military life. My name is Ken Conklin Jr. I am a patriot. This is my story.

CHAPTER 1

BASIC TRAINING

I first entered the United States Army on November 6, 2001. I still find it amazing that I can remember the exact date that I joined. It was nearly 2 months after the tragic attacks of September 11, 2001 which resulted of the death of thousands of Americans in the World Trade Center in New York City as well as the Pentagon. It was the most tragic day in American history. The event caused not only devastation here at home, but it also caused America to engage in the War on Terror, ultimately resulting in the United States sending troops into Afghanistan and eventually into Iraq. As a kid from a small town in upstate New York, I knew the impact of the attacks. As an American, I wanted to do whatever I could to help my nation. I love my country. Always have, always will. So, in November of 2001 I boarded a plane in Albany, NY heading south to Columbia, SC. I was scheduled to attend basic training and my advanced individual training for my MOS at Fort Jackson, South Carolina. This was my first plane trip in my entire life. I was very anxious about the journey in which I was about to embark upon. Many questions raced through my head: Would I like the Army? Would I make it in the Army? Would I make mistakes? Would I be on top of my class? What will the food be like? What about the people? Is it anything like it is on TV? Another thing going through my mind was just how much I was going to miss home. I am from a small town where everybody knows everybody. The town is called Saint Johnsville. We have one stop light in my town. Figuratively speaking, if you sneeze in my town, there's a good chance someone on the other side of town is going to know about it. When you grow up in a small town like this you tend to build closer friendships with the people that you grow up with, as opposed to if you grew up in a major city. I also knew I would miss my family. I was the oldest out of 4 kids that my father had (he would end up having one more and adopting one more later on, making a total of 6). For me, being the oldest kid in the house, the first to graduate high school and the first to leave and move out was definitely overwhelming for me. How would my brother Jason and my sisters Melissa and Jen survive without me? Of course they most certainly did survive, but when you're a young, full of yourself, 18 year old kid you almost tend to envision that it is impossible for them to survive without you. You end up learning that isn't really the case.

I arrived to Fort Jackson, South Carolina late in the evening. It turned out to be an extremely long day because we weren't permitted to sleep until around 3 am. The very first thing I can remember happening was being formed up into a formation at a place called reception battalion. Reception battalion is the in-processing center for the Army. It is the place that you go to when you first show up to receive your initial issue of your uniforms, get your first haircut, get your shots, and do your initial entry paperwork. You also get to make your first phone call to let your family know that you made it in ok and that you were safe. Throughout Basic Training you come to find out that phone privileges aren't something you take for granted. You can only use the phone to call home when the drill sergeants allow you to. Sometimes it can be weeks before you even get to call home, however they do have to give you that first phone call. Oh, and by the way, that first phone call usually lasts all of 3 minutes, if you're lucky. There's nothing quite like trying to tell your family you made it and you're safe, you're ok, and oh by the way you love them and miss them, while there are 3 to 5 screaming drill sergeants in the background. When you're an 18 year old kid who has never left New York State, it tends to be slightly overwhelming.

I can also remember many times at reception where we had to stand in formation and wait, for a very long time, for almost nothing. Or sometimes, we would be waiting for uniform issue. The big thing about reception is trying to get you into the Army mindset in just a matter of days. They make you get up early, sometimes at 3 or 4 am and go stand outside in formation to wait for breakfast at the dining facility. While standing and waiting you are either standing at the position of attention or parade rest. You're not moving, unless told to. You're not speaking, unless told to. That's how it goes. And you're standing outside at 4 am . . . but breakfast doesn't actually start until 6 am in some cases. In some ways, it is a mind game. In the Army there is a phrase "hurry up and wait." This phrase means exactly what it says. You're going to be ordered to hurry the hell up, and then, you're going to stand and wait. After that, you'll most likely wait some more. I know it may sound comical but that is how these first few days go. You are only at reception for a matter of 2 weeks, maybe less, before basic training begins. The main killer about reception is there's nothing fun about it. Perhaps you can find the fun in basic training whether you're learning to fire a rifle for the first time, or doing physical training. These are activities that one may find fun. In reception however, there is absolutely nothing fun about standing around and waiting. It gets boring and quite frankly it can be easy to lose your mind while doing this. There's just so much about reception that can be mentally taxing. There you are away from home for the first time, with nothing but a ton of time on your hands, with minimal sleep, to stand there, get yelled at, and contemplate your very existence. There's any number of thoughts that can pass through your head at this time: "Why am I here? Why am I being yelled at this time? I didn't even do anything. Oh man, the guy next to me really messed up, he's getting yelled at big time. Damn, I miss home. God I'm hungry. I'm also tired." These are just some of the thoughts that can nearly drive a Soldier insane in reception.

At the end of the first week of reception, the drill sergeants had my entire reception company in a room sitting silently waiting to do some of our initial entry paperwork. I can remember this angry drill sergeant looking at this room of young kids and yelling at us, "IS THERE ANYONE HERE THAT DOESN'T WANT TO BE HERE!?!? YOU JUST GOT HERE! IF THERES ANYONE HERE WHO DOESN'T WANT TO BE HERE, TELL US NOW AND WE WILL SEND YOU HOME, NO QUESTIONS ASKED. THIS IS YOUR FREE PASS. IF YOU DON'T WANT TO BE HERE, NOW IS THE TIME TO TELL ME. I'LL GET YOU OUT OF HERE. IF YOU WAIT TO TELL ANYONE, IT IS GOING TO BE MUCH HARDER TO GET OUT DOWN THE LINE AND YOU WILL BE STUCK HERE! WITH THAT SAID, WHO THE HELL DOESN'T WANT TO BE HERE?!?!" As intimidating as the drill sergeant was to the company, he seemed to be offering an olive branch if you will, a way out for anyone who couldn't hack it, who in those few days simply had enough and decided that the United States Army wasn't for them. Personally, I wasn't about to raise my hand; I was here for a reason, I wanted to be there. But at this moment, while I was thinking about how much I did want to be there, a young private actually stood up said, "Drill Sergeant, I do not want to be here! Please send me home." This kid was about to cry. I could hear it in his voice. I could see it in his mannerisms. What happened next I didn't expect whatsoever. The drill sergeant who made the offer got in this young private's face, along with two other drill sergeants, and they proceeded to yell and scream at this Soldier, not to mention insult him, in front of the entire room. "WHAT DO YOU MEAN YOU WANT TO GO HOME? I GOT NEWS FOR YOU! YOU AINT GOIN NOWHERE!" I thought to myself "sucks to be him!" Of course, I didn't say that aloud, for I may have reached the same fate. You have to pick your spots when you're in this type of situation and obviously this kid didn't pick the proper spot. The drill sergeants made him go to the front of the room, and proceeded to smoke this Soldier in front of the whole room. The term "smoke" or "smoking a Soldier" in the Army means that the Soldier is going to be doing an awful lot of push-ups, sit ups, and various other exercises, in front of everyone, while being yelled at and humiliated. The drill sergeant apparently tricked the Soldier, just to see who would crack. I guess in a lot of ways this can be compared to prison, like in the movie The Shawshank Redemption, when the new guys show up to prison and on their first night the other prisoners take bets to see who cracks first. It's the same thing in all reality. Only here it's the Army, and there it's prison. And for those wondering, that Soldier didn't get to go home. No, he stayed right there with the rest of us. It was at this moment in time I realized for myself that there were going to be mind games of some sort in basic training, and I needed to stay on my toes. I didn't want to end up like this guy, that's for sure.

After those 2 weeks of reception, we finally loaded up onto the bus to go to our basic training site. Basic Training was really only a 10 minute ride from the reception battalion. The drill sergeants crammed us onto this white school bus with all of our bags so it was extremely cramped. What I also found particularly funny was how the drill sergeants made us put our faces down into our bags, so we couldn't see out the windows on the way to the basic training site; as if we weren't supposed to know the way. I really did find this funny, but I did not voice this to anyone, for obvious reasons. When we got to our destination, we all went through what I like to call "the get off my fucking bus drill." Those of you reading this who were never in the military are probably wondering what exactly this is, while those of you who were in the military are probably laughing.

So, for the benefit of those who have never been in the military, I will explain: The "get off my fucking bus drill" is when you arrive to the basic training site and one drill sergeant walks onto the bus and starts angrily screaming at you, "GET OFF THE BUS! GET OFF THE BUS! WHAT, YOU DIDN'T FUCKIN HEAR ME? GET OFF THE FUCKIN BUS! YOU'RE IN THE ARMY NOW!" I apologize for the swearing but, I feel the need to include it so you, the reader, can fully grasp what is happening. Chances are, if you're reading a book about the army, than you can handle a few bad words. Anyway, it's at this moment that you as a Soldier grab your stuff and head off the bus as quickly as possible. You try to run but it's a school bus; there's only so much room and there's like 10 other dudes in front of you, and all you want to do at this point is not give the drill sergeant an excuse to make a target out of you. I remember getting off the bus, hitting the ground and there's another drill sergeant there screaming some more. In fact, that drill sergeant is also yelling "GET OFF THE BUS!" Of course, me being the self-appointed comedian that I am, I think to myself, "but I'm already off the bus." Obviously I didn't say this to the drill sergeant. That would have been a bad idea. All the Soldiers then head into a courtyard, where we are forced to dump out our things to take an inventory, despite the fact that we just did this prior to leaving reception. Seemed like a big waste of time to me, but apparently those drill sergeants really, really need to make sure that you have seven brown t-shirts and seven brown pairs of underwear, along with a Class A dress uniform and a pair of flip flops in addition to a bunch of other stuff. One thing you will not hear me say in this book is that a lot of what happens on a day to day basis in the army makes sense. Now sure, on a strategic level the army does make a lot of sense, and sometimes even on an individual level but sometimes there are just going to be those things in the army that happen that leave you scratching your head and asking why. That's how it is at all levels. It's not a perfect way of life, but then again, what in life is?

So once you get through this arrival day of basic training, the real fun begins. The actual Soldier training (which I loved) happens next. Your drill sergeant comes busting into the bay, which consists of about 40 Soldiers, and starts screaming at everyone to wake up. Of course, this all takes place at 4 am regardless of the fact that the day before you were up until midnight. Ahh yes, the good old days. They give you 15 minutes to get outside for formation to begin physical training. In these 15 minutes you have to accomplish many tasks such as making your bed, shaving (if you are a male), brushing your teeth, and getting into your physical training (PT) uniform. Once you get outside into formation, there's no talking, no moving, only silence while the drill sergeant accounts for everyone. While one drill sergeant is doing that, another is walking through the formation to verify that the males shaved. Of course if you are a male and you didn't shave, the drill sergeant is going to get on you about that. I can remember Soldiers who didn't shave would first get yelled at and forced to do push-ups. Then if they continued to mess up, the drill sergeants would make them carry out some sort of humiliating task, such as coming out to formation with their shaving razor tied to a piece of rope like a necklace. Then they would end up wearing their new little necklace for a little while as they thought about the importance of shaving. Yeah, I know it sounds messed up. From my standpoint I usually shaved regardless even while I was growing up, so it wasn't an issue to me. If I don't shave on a certain day, my face feels dirty and greasy for the rest of the day, but that's just me. Really in the Basic Training stage of the army it's all about instilling a certain amount of discipline. That's the goal, instilling a personal discipline to maintain a level of professionalism, and it all starts with appearance. If you aren't disciplined enough to maintain a nice looking uniform, a haircut, and a clean shaven face, then how can you be counted on to carry out the big missions in the army? If you can't shave when asked to, how can I ask you to pick up a weapon and go on a mission in Iraq or Afghanistan? I do understand the methods, to an extent.

Physical Training (PT) during Basic training is a journey in itself for a lot of Soldiers. A lot of Soldiers who are in basic training were not athletes in high school. Most high school athletes were most likely granted a sports scholarship by a university and ended up going to school as opposed to joining the military. It's a logical choice and by no means am I knocking it. Hey, to each their own right? As far as me, PT was never a problem for me in basic training. I spent my entire time in high school taking martial arts and lifting weights. In 2001, I traveled to Buffalo, NY with one of my History teachers who was an avid weightlifter like me to compete in a powerlifting meet. I ended up winning a U.S.P.F. (United States Powerlifting Federation) State championship for my age and weight division. I still have the trophy to this day. My history teacher also won his respective championship too. Needless to say it was a hell of an accomplishment. Not only did I have that accomplishment under my belt, but I also bought out the gym that I trained under once I graduated high school. I took the "Fire Eagle/Black Tiger Kung Fu academy/weightlifting gym" and turned it into "Ken's All American Gym." So, coming into basic training I had a ton of experience in working out and exercising as it is, and therefore when I saw a lot of Soldiers around me falling out of runs I found it heartbreaking. For me in high school, it wasn't a choice. My dad made me hit the gym. He didn't allow an option. If I refused it would have meant pissing him off, which I wouldn't ever want to do. I have the upmost respect for my father, and I love him to death, but if there was one thing I knew, it was not to ever cross him. In a fight, I knew there was no way in hell I could beat him. He used to tell me stories of how he was a moving man in Poughkeepsie, New York at a place called "Ken's Place" and he would tell his fellow co-workers who thought they were strong tough guys that he never met the man who could beat him in a fight. My father earned his black belt at Madison Square Garden in New York City. One time when my father said that he never met the man who could beat him in a fight, one guy walked up to him and said, "Hello, my name is Winkey." (Winkey of course was the guy's nickname.) My dad looked at Winkey and said, "Hello Winkey, I'm Ken, and I still haven't met the man who can beat me." Winkey shut up and walked away. Either way, I can tell you that in my 28 years of being alive on this earth that I haven't met the man who can beat my dad in a fight. So in other words, my dad did right in raising me the way he did, and he did right by making me work out because it prepared me for the greatest honor of my life; serving my country. I just wish more parents in America instilled these same values in their children, especially the fellow Soldiers I served alongside with in basic training who's high school lives apparently included an awful lot of video games.

After arriving to basic training and going through the initial few days, we were made to take our first PT Test. Only this wasn't a full record PT test, instead it was half of a PT test to see where we all stood physically. It was an important tool for the drill sergeants to use so they could assess exactly where their troops were physically. To me, it's a good training method. A normal PT test consists of 2 minutes of push-ups, 2 minutes of sit-ups, and a 2 mile run. This PT test however consisted of 1 minute of push-ups, 1 minute of sit-ups, and a 1 mile run. Like I stated, this was just to see where we were at so far. I can remember being somewhat excited because even though I knew on a personal level that I had a proven record of working out, I was still a little nervous about the idea of showing the

Army (in this case the drill sergeants) what I could do. The funny thing is my first challenge from an individual didn't come from a drill sergeant whatsoever but instead a fellow Soldier, another private who was in basic training with me. I can still remember this kid clearly today. He was a tall skinny kid named Pope. He was a high school basketball player, and for some reason he liked to make that known to the other people there in the platoon. On that morning he looked at me and said, "You don't look like you're Army material." To say that his words pissed me off would be an understatement. Honestly, I was infuriated. After all, who the hell was he? He was just a fellow private in basic training, just like me. He wasn't a drill sergeant where he would have been in a position to say something degrading to a Soldier. As far as I was concerned he was nobody, so who the hell was he to say that I, Ken Conklin, the owner of Kens all American Gym wasn't Army material? I decided to take that anger I had for this punk and channel it on the PT track. I maxed out my push-ups and sit-ups (for the halfway-watered down, 1 minute standard they were testing us with as opposed to the real PT tests we would all take later on in my career.) I was ready to get the one mile run underway and show him who was boss. After all, for a tall kid who played high school basketball, this was probably his easiest event. Maybe he would even come in first or second. I couldn't wait to knock the smug look right off of his face. Yeah, I knew that I was only 5 ft., 7 in tall, but I knew in my heart I could destroy this kid on the run. I just knew it deep down. The run started and I focused, but the only person I focused on was him. I didn't care about the other Soldiers on the track; they hadn't said anything out of line to me. Hell, I didn't even care about passing the test in general. I really just cared about beating him. What even brought this about? I didn't know this guy from Adam. Never met him before in my life, yet he thought it would be cool to go ahead and try to single me out. I ran by him and left him in the dust. Just to make sure he didn't catch up, I kept on trucking, continuing to run my hardest to the end of the track, just as hard as I did when I was home and I was preparing myself to join the Army.

I reached the finish line and sure enough I came in first place. My 1 mile time was just a few seconds over 6 minutes. (To reach a maximum score of 100 points on the real 2 mile PT test you would need to run the 2 mile run in 13 minutes flat for my age group. So a max on this test would have been 6:30.) I waited near the finish line after I was done running. Even though I had the satisfaction of coming in first, I still needed a little more personal satisfaction. Just as that kid had said something out of line to me, I felt the need to return the favor. I've often been accused of being slightly arrogant in my day; and I don't often deny it. So I continued to wait, the Soldier in second place came in; it wasn't PVT Pope. The third, fourth, fifth place Soldiers came in, all of them, were not PVT Pope. Finally, after most of the platoon came in, PVT Pope came jogging in, all winded and tired. I do not remember exactly what place he came in, but I do know he wasn't in the top ten, that's for sure. The second he came in, what do you think I began doing? Yep, you guessed it, I proceeded to start running my mouth. "Not Army material, huh? Aint that some shit! I came in first place, you staggered in here looking like shit. What's the matter, you got nothing to say? Who's not Army material now?" Pope just kept on walking. He put his hands on his head to catch his breath, and I could tell he was trying his very best to ignore me. Since he seemed to be making a profound effort to ignore me, I pressed on. He never said a word. I guess I proved him wrong. Maybe I was Army Material. And maybe, just maybe, he wasn't the great athlete that he thought he was. Looking back on it now through a more mature set of eyes I realize that maybe I was just a little wrong for continuing to provoke him. But on the other hand, he started it. All of my actions were purely a reaction to the words that he said. I'm sure nowadays I may have handled it differently, perhaps in a more mature manner, but I was an 18 year old brand new Soldier who had a lot on my mind as it was. I guess it all boils down to self-defense. When someone starts trouble do you just let them get away with it or do you take a stand and let your voice be heard? Do you send a message to the world saying that you just aren't going to take it? I would say yes. That's how I was raised. It reminds me of something else my father said to me when I was a kid. He said to me, "If you ever find yourself surrounded by a gang that wants to kick your ass, be sure to walk up to the biggest, baddest guy in the group and fight him. You may get your ass kicked, but the rest of the group is going to think twice before jumping in because you were crazy enough to start with the biggest one to begin with." I've never forgotten that advice. It makes sense, from a figurative standpoint as well as a literal standpoint. After that day, PVT Pope never said a word to me again, and no one else in basic training gave me any lip either.

Besides PT, there were a lot of other things to learn during basic training, actual Soldier skills. We did so much. The 9 weeks of basic training are designed to take an ordinary civilian and transform them into a United States Army Soldier. In basic training you learn drill and ceremony, which is more or less how to march. You learn hand to hand combat. You learn first aid, and you learn how to fire a weapon. Basic Training was actually the very first time in my life I have ever fired a weapon. Notice I use the term "weapon." Civilians will most likely call them "guns." A Soldier is taught from day one of Basic rifle marksmanship that you will not call it a gun. It is a weapon, and that is what you will call it. When a Soldier would slip up and refer to it as a gun, they would usually be forced to do push-ups. After a while, you learn. Even today as a civilian I do not call it a gun. I just can't do it. Either way, as a kid growing up I never fired a weapon. My dad didn't hunt like a lot of the other kid's fathers in upstate New York. A lot of kids in high school had fired various rifles and 12 gauge shotguns by the time they grew up and graduated high school, but not me. Sure, I knew how to use a Bo Staff and a Katana Blade but those weren't exactly the type of weapons that the US Army trains you on. So, knowing I had zero experience firing any weapons growing up I was a little nervous firing a weapon for a first time. As it turned out, that didn't matter. The drill sergeants told us right from the beginning to forget anything we had ever learned about weapons growing up, to forget what our fathers taught us, and to forget what they liked to call "Kentucky Windage." I wasn't really familiar with that term, but I was relieved to know that my lack of experience in this matter wasn't going to put me at a position of disadvantage. One main thing I noticed about the weeks that we worked on BRM (basic rifle marksmanship) is that the drill sergeants seemed to lighten up a little bit. They weren't doing as much yelling, and they weren't forcing the Soldiers to do as many push-ups for minor things. Granted, we were definitely still in basic training, but now the main focus seemed to be ensuring that we knew how to fire our rifles properly. It was genuine teaching. And if you really think about it, it makes perfect sense. Here we were in late 2001, months after the September 11th attacks. Soldiers were getting ready for combat deployments to Afghanistan. For many of us, we could potentially be sent overseas immediately following arrival to our first duty station. Learning how to fire and maintain our weapon was probably one of the most important skills that I had to learn in basic training. I remember feeling awkward doing it, and I can still remember the very first time I pulled the trigger, everything about it, the minor kickback of the rifle, the smell, everything. It ended up taking me a few tries to grasp and actually be able to qualify, but at the end of BRM I knew I had learned a very important skill. I was proud of myself. Of course once BRM was finished and we had qualified, it was back to business as usual. We couldn't have possibly thought that the drill sergeants were going to be this mellow for the rest of basic training, could we? Well, some of us did think so, but it didn't take us too long to realize.

Over the next few of weeks we continued to refine our Soldier skills. Aside from the marksmanship training and of course the PT, we spent a lot of time working on other skills as well. We focused a lot on drill and ceremony. Sometimes the drill sergeants would have us marching around over and over again in the big lot by the bay while we waited to go eat our meals. We could spend hours out there working on facing movements, counter columns, and various other drill movements. Most of all, we would work on discipline. The fundamental focus was always to ensure that you were in step with the rest of the formation, and that the rest of the formation was in step with itself. This may sound a little redundant to those of you reading this that never served in the military, but believe me it is not. Drill and ceremony is a tradition that dates all the way back to the very beginnings of our country. It is an important part of military customs and courtesy. Furthermore, it builds teamwork. One thing I have noticed about my time in the Military is that there does, (in most cases at least) seem to be a certain level of camaraderie that doesn't exist in a lot of other lines of work. It is simply the "nature of the beast" so to speak. In the civilian world, otherwise referred to as the "private sector" you may have a job where you have one or two friends there, but it doesn't compare to the level of teamwork that the US Army instills in its Soldiers. Soldiers are willing to sacrifice for each other, even going as far as to sacrifice their own lives for one another. It's another part of what makes a Soldier a Soldier. This idea, this practice, it starts all the way in basic training. You are waking up with this group of people every single day, early in the morning. You eat with all of them; you train with all of them. You get punished with all of them and you are rewarded with all of them. They are in effect your brothers and sisters in arms. That is one aspect of the military that I miss. And maybe that's why I stay in touch with a lot of my former comrades to this day, even though I am no longer in the military. You build a bond with each other that you cannot just forget and you can't erase. And in some cases on the battlefield, it's that bond you have that keeps each other alive.

As mid-December came along, a very special thing happened. The drill sergeants informed us that the Army shuts down Basic Training and Advanced Individual Training (AIT) for 2 weeks due to holiday exodus. Holiday exodus allows Soldiers to go home for the holidays for 2 weeks if they choose to. This is a privilege that is simply granted by circumstances, the timing of your basic training cycle. If you happen to be in training during the winter months, you get to go home for the holidays. I know that there are a lot of people out there that may not think that is fair to the rest of the Soldiers who attend basic training during the rest of the year, but as the saying goes; it is what it is. Last I checked Christmas and New Year's happen in December and January, not June and July. Either way, I had left home November 6th and so by December 15th I had been away from home for over a month, and quite frankly I was homesick. I missed my family, my friends, and believe it or not, my gym. Not only that, growing up in my house we put a heavy emphasis on Christmas. Christmas is the most important holiday in our house. My dad raised us on the belief that Christmas is about giving to others, not receiving, and more importantly spending time with family. The chance to leave a place like Fort Jackson and return home was way too good to pass up. So when the time came I bought my plane ticket (that was the catch, you had to purchase your own ticket) and got ready to head to the Columbia airport and fly home. There were certain rules and policies in place however. For one, we were required to travel in our Class A dress uniform. We were not allowed to change into our civilian attire until we got home to our final destination. A lot of Soldiers balked at this, but I didn't. I preferred to travel in uniform at that time. For one, wearing a uniform was still new to me, and I hadn't grown "tired" of it yet. Also, I was proud of what I was doing with my life. I was proud of everything that I had accomplished so far in basic training, and I was proud to represent America. I was also anxious to see the look on my father's face the first time he saw his oldest son in uniform. This was a very special moment for me. I was so excited to get home. Finally after a long flight I landed in Albany during the evening. I can still remember giving my dad a hug in that airport, for the first time as a Soldier. He was very proud of me, and for me it was really good to see him. We got on the road after claiming my little bit of baggage and took the 45 minute ride home from Albany international Airport to Saint Johnsville. When I got home, my younger brother Jason was still up waiting for me to get home, but it was so late that after I got home and he welcomed me back, he went to bed. My dad also went to bed. I couldn't blame them though, it was late, and I had 2 weeks to spend with my family and friends so everything was ok.

Even though they were tired and wanted to go to bed, I did not. Even though I was tired and jetlagged, I was extremely anxious to go out, walk around, do something, or even just see the town I missed so much. Yeah, it was a small town but it was my town and I missed it. Can you blame me? I was still in my Class A uniform. I didn't change. I just left the house and took a walk. I felt proud to walk the streets of Saint Johnsville in my new uniform. I was a Soldier now and I was very proud of that. I decided to make my first destination my Gym. After all, it was my Gym, my place of business and I was interested to see for myself exactly why we hadn't turned a profit since I left. Since I had been in basic training I had to send some money home to my father to cover some of the bills that the gym had occurred since I had been away. A gym has a lot of bills to cover; in addition to covering the annual taxes I had to pay since I owned the building, I also had the electric bill, heat, water, and insurance to cover. Mentally it was a lot to have to think about, especially when you're in basic training getting yelled at by drill sergeants all day. For the record, I was the only one in my basic training who owned a business, (even though I was 18 years old) but more on that later. On my way to the gym, the first thing I realized is that the streets and the town itself somehow felt smaller to me. It was a weird feeling. I guess it was because I had finally left my safe haven of Saint Johnsville. Or maybe it was because during basic training you aren't just physically transformed, but mentally as well. Either way, I felt like I could hold Saint Johnsville in the palm of my hand. It was weird. I got to the gym, unlocked the door and turned the lights on. It felt special to be standing in my gym again, but there was something else I felt at that moment. The gym felt dead. Literally, it felt like it died. I didn't like this feeling. I had every reason to believe that my friends that I left in charge hadn't done a good job running the business when I was away; in fact they weren't running it at all. The only thing they were doing was going in there and working out for themselves, and not treating it as a money making venture. I learned then that I should have listened to my father. He wanted to run the business for me when I left, but I was too young and stupid for that. To this day I will always recognize that the biggest mistake I made with that gym was allowing my friends to run it when clearly my dad would have done a much better job.

There were a whole bunch of unread newspapers piled up in the corner by the door. I had a subscription to the local paper, obviously for the purpose of reading. Instead of reading them my friends threw them in the corner and let them pile up, thus making a mess. The floors needed to be swept. All of my CDs were sprawled all over the place in the sound room where I kept the stereo instead of being put in their respective cases. I was disgusted that this was how my place was being treated. As I said earlier, it was my mistake but my friends still could have done better than this. I intended on cleaning this mess up, but not right this very moment. After all, I was dressed in my Class A uniform. I stood there for a second and looked at myself in the full length mirrors that covered the walls of my gym. That brief moment, seeing myself dressed in uniform in my gym made me feel good enough to forget how upset I was about the gym being treated as it was. Out of the blue I decided to go and punch the punching bag for a few minutes. I don't know why I did that, but it felt good. I didn't attempt to work up a sweat or anything, but it was just nice to hit my heavy bag again. Of course, I was also taking the time to glance at myself from time to time as I was doing it. What can I say, it felt good. After a while I realized that it was after 11pm (or after 2300 hours military time), so I decided to lock the place up and continue with my little walk. By this point I had a lot of mixed emotions: Saint Johnsville feels small now. My gym is a wreck and feels dead. God I look good in my uniform. It was a weird night for me. I decided the next place to walk was Cumberland Farms. For those of you reading this that are not from upstate New York, Cumberland Farms is a gas station/convenience store. It is also where I worked just prior to joining the Army. Just because I owned a business, doesn't mean I didn't want to hold a normal job as well. As a matter of fact my business was barely paying for itself and putting a small profit in my pocket, so a simple job like Cumberland farms before I joined the Army was a smart idea. After everything that had changed in my life I wanted to drop in and see my old workplace. I wanted to see what had changed, what was the same, etc. I think there's an emotion in all human beings that always makes people want to not only return home after a long journey (obviously) but also to show the place you left behind how great you are doing now, to show everything that you have accomplished. I know that sounds like a form of "rubbing it in" so to speak, but it really isn't if you think about it. When kids start off in school they always want to rush home and tell mom and dad how great they did on their tests. It's really the same thing if you think about it. So at 18 years old, returning home to Saint Johnsville all dressed up in my Class A uniform I was very anxious to show Saint Johnsville everything I had accomplished. I wanted to tell my friends my story. I wanted them to be proud of me. And deep down I knew they were. So I walked down to Cumberland Farms to see that my old friend Joe Carter had started working there, and in fact had taken the shift that I had left behind; 3rd shift, aka graveyard shift. Ahh yes, I can remember all those lonely nights working 11 pm to 7 am, with the occasional drunk person stumbling in to buy more beer and cigarettes. Now Joe Carter had my old job. I had grown up around Joe. We had study hall together when I was in 8th and 9th grade, and we hit it off immediately. He had a lot of the same interests that I did, Professional Wrestling, Super Heroes, and Sports. Joe even wrestled in my backyard when I was a teenager and I hosted a backyard wrestling federation in my yard for a few years. Joe was always the kind of guy who would give you the shirt off of his back. Always trying to help others, he was and still is a genuinely great guy. To this day he is one of my best friends and every time that I ever went home on leave I would hang out with Joe. It was funny to see him working at my old job, and not only that, he had the same problem with the manager that I had. The manager (who was a woman) had an issue with male employees. I guess she had a terrible fallout in her marriage and now she just hated men in general. When I worked there she would yell at me about the smallest things and I know she did not treat my female co-workers the same way. It was funny how joining the army was a relief because I didn't have to deal with her anymore. I stayed there for about an hour and listened to stories Joe had about her. After a while I realized it was time for me to go home and I could catch up with him some more over the next 2 weeks. That first night back home proved to be such an eye opener for me, between the mixed emotions and the town outright feeling smaller to me, I had a lot to sleep on.

As one would guess, the next 2 weeks went by incredibly quick. As anyone I have ever known in the military will tell you, leave never seems to last long enough and this time was no exception. Christmas and New Year's came and gone, and both holidays were great. The feeling of being home with my family for Christmas was amazing. It was also a very awkward holiday as well, for the strangest of reasons. My Aunt Barbara had come to visit from Germany, and she brought with her a young woman who she knew from back home. As it turns out, things in my father's second marriage had begun to go south before I had even left for the Army, I just didn't know about it. Enter my Aunt Barbara, and her young friend; and next thing you know, my father starts hitting it off with the new friend. Now if that doesn't strike you as awkward enough, please allow me to elaborate: my parents divorced when I was young, and since then my mother and father were able to put their differences aside and be friends for the sake of my siblings and I. Because of this, my mother would come up for the holidays and stay for the week. It was great because we could spend Christmas with our mother and our father. We understood that mom and dad were divorced, and that dad was remarried. That was the way things were, and it wasn't changing. To us it was just really cool to have mom home for Christmas. So back to Christmas 2001, when dad was busy hitting it off with his soon to be third wife, while his second wife/soon to be ex-wife was still living there, it should also be noted that my mother/my dad's first wife was also there at the house as well. Talk about an awkward Christmas dinner! Good times. And it also gave me a cool story to tell my fellow Soldiers when I got back to Fort Jackson to finish off basic training. Besides walking the streets in my uniform and seeing my gym again, that Christmas dinner was the most memorable part of my leave. I will never forget it. After the 2 weeks were up, I suited up (as we were required to fly back in uniform) and my dad drove me to the Albany airport. I knew I would be home again in April, which was my anticipated Graduation date from AIT (Advanced Individual Training). I gave my dad a great big hug bye. I knew I would miss him and everyone else in good old Saint Johnsville, but I knew that I would be back.

As I stated earlier the flight back was in early January, and while the flight itself made its way back to Columbia, we couldn't actually get back to Fort Jackson right away because a strange phenomenon had struck South Carolina . . . that strange phenomenon was snow. Now, as a guy from upstate New York snow was no issue for me, but apparently they aren't very equipped for this sort of thing in the South. They didn't have any plows available to clean the roads right away. Therefore, they could not run the bus back to Fort Jackson. There was a Liaison NCO who worked at the Airport who would normally direct Soldiers where to go when they were flying in or out of that Airport for the first time. There were a lot of Soldiers there who were in the same boat as me, just trying to get back to Fort Jackson to get back to Basic Training and finish the course. I'm not sure if the Liaison NCO had received orders from his higher headquarters or if he was just being proactive, but I will never forget what he did. He had yelled for all of the privates to gather around him, and he shouted (like they all do), "OK! THE BUSES ARE NOT RUNNING UNTIL TOMORROW MORNING! GET YOURSELF SOME REAL ESTATE AND GO THE FUCK TO SLEEP!" What he meant by "real estate" was find yourself a spot on the floor or a chair in the airport terminal and go to sleep. They didn't care how you did it, they only really cared that you did not leave the airport. Here I went from being on leave, feeling like a million bucks walking around in my uniform, to feeling like total crap because I have to sleep on the floor in my uniform. To be perfectly honest, I don't even like sitting on the floor, much less sleeping on it. It feels degrading to a certain extent. This was just one of the many times in my career that I realized that the Army can at times make you feel either extremely proud of yourself, or extremely degraded. There really was no choice in the matter and so I ended up sleeping on the floor that night. First thing the next morning, the bus arrived and took us all back to Fort Jackson to get back to training.

I can remember a lot of the other Soldiers having issues getting back into the swing of things. I guess being away for 2 weeks can do that to a person. I did not have that same issue however. Not only was I able to fall right back into the swing of things, but It strangely felt to me like the 2 weeks of leave didn't even happen. They felt like a distant memory, like they didn't just happen, but instead they happened months ago. I guess I just react a little differently to change. Everyone has their own method of dealing with change. At this point in time we had only a few weeks left and I was just excited about graduating. It was certainly an accomplishment and I knew I had come so far already; I was almost there. Even still I knew I wasn't out of the woods yet and there were still a few more challenges in store for me.

One of the events in basic training that I had always looked forward to was the gas chamber. I had always been enamored with the idea that the Army put Soldiers through the chamber as a way to test their confidence in their gas mask. I also knew people in my life who had become police officers, and the way they were certified to carry and use pepper spray was to be sprayed with it themselves (or so I've been told anyway). I viewed the gas chamber as the military equivalent of being sprayed with pepper spray. It was one of those things that you could brag about when you got home. Furthermore, everyone had to do it. It was one of the requirements to graduate. If you didn't complete the task, you weren't going anywhere until you did. Keep in mind that the idea of chemical warfare has always been very real to our military. Case in point, the US believed that Saddam Hussein had weapons of mass destruction and was willing to use them on the rest of the world. The US Army would have been foolish not to train its Soldiers on the dangers of chemical warfare, and even more importantly the importance of the proper wear and use of a gasmask. I totally understood the use of this particular block of training.

The basic premise is that they first teach you how to wear and seal your mask. When the mask is sealed you are then marched into the gas chamber along with a bunch of your fellow Soldiers. Then, you are required to do some minor exercises, such as jumping jacks and push-ups just to see how great your seal is. So far, so good, right? It is at that point where you are required to remove your mask, shout your name, rank, and Social Security Number. Once you have successfully done this, you have to put your mask back on, reseal it, and then you are allowed to leave the chamber. The gas itself is tear gas and it burns the eyes, gets into your system and usually gives you the worst runny nose you have ever had, as well as possibly forcing you to puke. It isn't fatal, but the gas still hurts like hell. Once you feel this gas on your bare face you realize just how much your mask actually works. The drill sergeants train you on exactly how to survive this task: you are instructed to take a deep breath and hold it, and then remove your mask quickly, state your information and put the mask back on. If you don't take that deep breath, it makes things much harder for you, in fact it makes it close to impossible to complete. The funny thing is, I can still remember my gas chamber experience just like it was yesterday. I went into the chamber. I did the exercises. The mask worked great. It was my turn to take off my mask, only I made a fatal mistake. Instead of taking a deep breath and removing the mask as I was trained to, I instead took a breath AS I REMOVED MY MASK. I inhaled a deep breath of the gas, and it was the most painful thing I ever felt. I collapsed to my knees. Forget about shouting my name, rank and social security number. No, I was in deep pain. The drill sergeants circled around me, but I didn't care. I was now focused on one thing and one thing only: the exit door. I saw it, and despite my condition I sprinted for the door, which also hurt. One of the drill sergeants tried to bear-hug me to keep me in the chamber. What a nice guy. He quickly found himself on the floor because after all I am also a nice guy; who is also trained in martial arts. I viewed this one as a life and death situation, because I had never felt anything like this before in my life. It was the worst feeling ever. When I got outside I puked all over the place. I was in so much pain. Despite being in this condition, I knew deep down inside whose fault this was. It was my fault. Instead of taking that deep breath with my mask on like I was taught, I took that deep breath as I removed the mask which resulted in my own painful demise. While I was puking my guts out and contemplating who to leave the gym to in the event I die today, the drill sergeants were all around me shouting that I had to get back in there and redo the chamber. I knew damn well I had to redo the chamber. It was nothing to hide. You needed a "GO" or a "NO-GO" and I had received a "NO-GO." I slowly regained my composure, put the mask on, and sure enough, I went in there and completed it properly. I had learned my lesson, and that lesson had been a painful one. I left the chamber and the other Soldiers were clapping for me which felt good. Let's be honest, it always feels good to receive a standing ovation. For the record, that was not the last time in my career that I had to go through the gas chamber. In fact, most units make you go through it every 6 months. I can state clearly, for the record, that it does not get any better. You do not get used to it, and it always hurts your eyes and face when you go in there. But that's ok, because that's part of being a Soldier in the United States Army.

The final major event in basic training was something called "Victory Forge." Victory Forge was a 3 day field exercise where you would actually suit up, march out to a campsite, dig a fox hole, set up a lean-to tent and camp there for the 3 days. Over the course of the 3 days you would be tested on various tasks you learned during basic training. You would have to prove you remembered the first aid training that you went through earlier in the course. You would encounter a situation where the drill sergeants threw a can of gas into the living area and everyone would have to don their masks. We would also have to pull guard duty throughout the exercise, do combat drills, and survive on minimum sleep. Also, when the exercise was finished we had to road march back to our basic training area. The march was a 12 mile road march. At the end of these three days the only thing left to do was to graduate and move on to AIT. It was late January in Fort Jackson, and the average temperature was around 50 degrees. Normally I would be ok with those kind of temperatures based on where I was from, but since I had spent so much time there 50 degrees felt cold to me. It got slightly colder at night and sleeping in a 2 man lean-to just wasn't cutting it. I tried to compare this experience to when my father would take me camping as a kid. I can assure you that this is nothing like going camping with my dad. First off, he took the time to buy nice tents. He also didn't make us camp in January. Also, he wasn't yelling and screaming for no apparent reason and he sure as hell wasn't throwing gas canisters at me. I guess there were a lot of differences between being in the field as a Soldier and going camping with my dad. The most important difference was that when the camping trip with dad was over with, I was still just a kid from upstate New York. When this field exercise was over, I was a full-fledged Soldier. The 3 days went by and it was time to march back. After the 12 mile road march I had a newfound sense of pride. I knew deep down it was time to graduate basic training and go on to the next phase of my military career.

Graduation day eventually came. The Drill Sergeants marched us onto the parade field in our Class A uniform. We listened to the Battalion Commander give a speech about how proud he was of what we had accomplished. We also had the option of having our family in attendance. My family didn't come, but it isn't anything I would ever hold against them. We are from New York state and quite frankly the idea of having my dad travel to South Carolina for a small ceremony when he could be at work earning money to support the rest of the family is simply ridiculous. I never have, and I never will hold it against my family for not coming. I will say however that when the ceremony is over and you see your fellow Soldiers with their family and you aren't with yours, it tends to get real lonely, real quick. You feel out of place. At the time it was a little hard for me to deal with, but I got over the feeling real quick. After all, I had accomplished so much in these 9 weeks. I had so much to be proud of. In these 9 weeks I learned all of the basic Soldier skills: drill and ceremony, hand to hand combat, physical training, first aid, the gas chamber, marksmanship and so many other skills. My pride in what I had accomplished was at an all-time high. No one can ever take away from me the fact that I did this. I could go home that very day and know that I accomplished something that no one back home ever did. Of course, I wasn't about to go home. Instead I was about to get on a bus and go to the other side of Fort Jackson to start my AIT. I said goodbye to my friends from basic training. Some of them were staying on Fort Jackson for AIT and some were going away to train at another post. I knew that there was a good chance that the people who were going to another post I may never see again. It was sad to say the least, but I recognized that this in itself was part of the Army life. Either way, it was time to get started on the next phase of my Army career, which also happens to be the next chapter of this book.

CHAPTER 2

AIT

So the "9 amazing weeks" of basic training went by, and it was time to start AIT. It was February 2, 2002, and I had just arrived to the AIT barracks. To be perfectly honest, it felt like an entirely different world than basic training. There were still drill sergeants and they were still mean, but they didn't seem as mean. Now, just to clarify for the non-military reader out there, the purpose of AIT (Advanced Individual Training) is to train you on your individual Military Occupation Specialty (MOS), which is essentially your job in the military, while the only function of basic training was to train you how to be a Soldier in general. The environment here felt different, but it was still the Army. You absolutely had to be on your toes. My MOS at the time was 75H: Personnel Services Specialist; basically a paper pusher. Years later the position listing would be changed from 75H to 42A and the position title would be changed from Personnel Service Specialist to something much more flattering: Human Resources Specialist. The title of "Human Resources Specialist" carries with it a certain amount of respect in the corporate world, whereas the title "Personnel Services Specialist" comes off as some punk kid intern who is just there to make coffee. The new title listing it received in the future proved to be far more accurate to the job itself, but for all rights and purposes in AIT I was learning how to be a 75H.

I will remember the first day of AIT forever. Sometimes in your life you meet someone who you are supposed to meet. Regardless in what capacity you were supposed to meet them in, whether it's a friend, a future spouse, a mentor, an enemy or just someone you can learn something from, there are always going to people in your life that you meet for a reason. I don't care who it is, or what their relationship to a person may be. Everyone has someone in their life that they meet for a reason. As you will see by continuing to read this book, there are many people that I met along my journey that fall into this category, but on Feb 2, 2002 I met for the first time one of my best friends in my entire life. We were outside doing a layout of our equipment, and there was this girl standing next to me. She dropped something near my pile and I took the opportunity to introduce myself. "Hey, my name is Ken. Ken Conklin." She introduced herself as Katherine Quiring, Kathy for short. I immediately wanted to get to know her. Kathy, as it turned out, was from the state of New Jersey, which even though that wasn't New York, it was still some form of common ground considering a majority of the other Soldiers I met so far were from the south. I never understood that fact either. Through the years of my career I had always heard various "reasons" speculating why more of the Soldiers I came across were from the south. A lot of them were absolutely stupid reasons that I was told that I just dismissed as a person's opinion. Reasons like, "Oh, people in the South are more patriotic" or my personal favorite: "People in the north usually prefer to send their children to college as opposed to war." As I stated before, I would learn in the later years of my career that these weren't true facts, merely opinions. Either way it was still early in my career and meeting a fellow northerner was certainly a breath of fresh air. Kathy and I hit it off immediately and even though we were in separate classrooms in AIT, we were still in the same unit. We would eat lunch and dinner together most days. Now, in a training environment there is a strict policy against fraternization, you aren't supposed to associate yourself with members of the opposite sex, regardless if it is purely platonic, which in our case it was. The rules in AIT were not as strict as they were in basic training when it pertained to this particular subject. In basic training, you were outright not allowed to associate with the opposite sex. In AIT you were allowed to if you both had a "battle buddy" of your sex with you. So in other words, for me and Kathy to eat breakfast, lunch and dinner together, she had to have another female Soldier with her and I needed to have another male Soldier with me. I always found this funny. Let's be honest, if you want to prevent fraternization during training, what would make the Army think that adding two more people to the mix would prevent it from happening? If you ask me, twice the amount of people equals twice the amount of fraternization. But then again that's just me and my own common sense talking. She had a friend she would bring along, and I would bring along a guy from my barracks named PVT Hultz. Hultz was a friend of mine, and an overall good guy, but he always seemed to be in a bad mood. I think it may have had to do with the fact that he was well into his 30's and he was just starting out in the Army. Even though most Soldiers join straight out of high school, there are still many that wait until later on in their life, for whatever their reason. Hultz was one of those guys. The problem with this was that it sometimes brought a certain amount of negativity to the table. I liked Hultz a lot, he was a fellow Soldier, but I just couldn't stand the negativity. That's one thing in life I do not like, nor do I believe in. I firmly believe that if you always see the negative in something, then you will end up having more bad luck in life than if you try to see the positive all the time. Simply put: if you feel like your life sucks, being negative about it is not going to make it any better. Positivity is always better for yourself, and more importantly the people around you. So while it was good to have Hultz there because it made it "legal" to have dinner for my newfound friend Kathy, sometimes it sucked because Hultz put us all in a bad mood.

Over the course of the next 8 weeks Kathy and I did a lot of bonding. I can remember having KP with her often. KP is kitchen police. That's when once or twice a month your platoon has to go and work in the kitchen for the day, serving food, washing dishes, mopping floors, basic stuff like that. For me it was better than being in class because class got boring. There were times Kathy and I would be on KP and we would get bored, so we would start singing (Bon Jovi, of all bands) at the top of our lungs just to amuse each other and pass the time. For the record, I am not a singer, never have been, never will be. I try never to do it. Either way, we were having a good time, and for me being a guy who missed home an awful lot, I think it was safe to say that Katherine Quiring became my new best friend. I can honestly say that she got me through AIT, because believe me AIT was not nearly as exciting as basic training. You see from a training standpoint, AIT didn't serve the same purpose as Basic Training. In Basic Training I had a blast throwing grenades, firing rifles and making a fool out of myself in the gas chamber. In AIT however, we did an awful lot of sitting down in a classroom and reading power point slides about our soon-to-be profession in the Army. Then, when we were done going through the slide shows, we would be required to login to Mavis Beacon Touch Typing and work on our typing skills. This was one of the most boring experiences in my entire life and I don't just mean boring, I mean B-O-R-I-N-G. The type of boring that would put you to sleep. I often asked myself, "What the hell am I supposed to be learning today? You can't possibly be teaching me how to type again . . . oh wait we're going to work on typing today. Damn." I went through those 8 weeks of AIT feeling like I hadn't learned a thing about my MOS. As it turns out, I wasn't alone. Everyone in the other class felt the same way, so it wasn't just me. Later on in my life when I arrived to other duty stations and I would meet Soldiers who worked in other fields I would come to learn that they also didn't learn anything in AIT. Apparently this is an Army-wide condition. I would come to learn that the only true way to learn your MOS is through experience, actually working on tasks, making mistakes, and learning from those mistakes. Of course at the time I was in AIT I didn't know about any of this so I felt a little cheated at the time. I felt that since I had so much fun in basic training and I was so bored here that I would end up hating my MOS. I was so depressed about this that I really hoped something better would come along, and a couple of weeks into AIT, a better idea did come along.

The Drill Sergeants made an announcement one day that the Army was looking for volunteers to go to Airborne School. If you volunteered to go, whatever assignment you were supposed to have would be deleted and you would be put on orders to go to Fort Bragg, North Carolina after AIT. Fort Bragg was home to the 82nd Airborne Division. I was already on assignment to go to Fort Campbell, Kentucky for my first duty assignment. Fort Campbell was home to the 101st Airborne Division. At that point in my life, I didn't know the difference but later on in my Career I would. If you decided to volunteer for Airborne school you would begin training for it for the remainder of your time in AIT during PT hours. Airborne PT consisted of a lot of running, jumping, and learning the techniques of jumping out of an airplane without actually jumping out of the Airplane yet. This training method obviously makes a lot of sense because after all, why would the Army teach you to jump out of an airplane if you don't know the proper procedures yet? It would be a waste of time and energy to put Soldiers in a parachute and an airplane that hadn't learned the basics first. I was very excited about the prospect of going to airborne school and jumping out of an airplane. I thought long and hard about it, and ultimately it came down to a few factors. For one, no one I knew back home in Saint Johnsville had jumped out of an airplane, at least to my knowledge. It would give me a few stories to tell to my friends when

I went home for leave. Funny how a lot of decisions I made in my career were centered on having bragging rights back home. I know that may sound arrogant but to each their own, right? If that slight arrogance is what it takes to motivate you to do something extraordinary, then so be it. Just do not allow that arrogance to go to your head. Another factor was the idea that it would make my dad even more proud of me. My dad would tell me when I would call home how proud he was of me and how people at work and around town would ask about me and more importantly the things I was doing in the Army. To me, my father has always been the absolute most important person in my life, and making him proud of me made me feel good. Without my dad I wouldn't be here so I wanted to continue to make him proud. Finally, there was one more thing about jumping out of an airplane that enticed me, and that was the fact that it seemed exciting. I love a good rush and I was pretty sure that jumping out of a plane would provide that rush. After carefully taking all of this under consideration, I decided to go ahead and volunteer for Airborne School and start my Airborne PT.

The next couple of weeks really flew by for me. I would report to normal formation for PT and accountability in the morning, (which was ridiculously early) and after formation the drill sergeants would send the Airborne volunteers to another area to do their Airborne PT. There were so many runs, but a lot of them were long, slow runs. I already had the blessing of being a good runner, so these runs weren't an issue to me at all. In fact, just like in basic training I breezed ahead of most of the platoon during runs. It just seemed to be a natural gift that I had. I seriously loved running too. If going to Airborne School meant running a lot more, then so be it. I'll run for a living, and I'll run for fun. It really doesn't matter to me. They also taught us the special way to jump out of a plane during these training sessions. They would teach us to jump with our knees slightly bent (but not too much), and to have our legs together while doing so. This is because if you jump out of a plane with your legs separated and you land like that, your legs will most certainly be broken upon landing. Now who wants a pair of broken legs? I certainly do not, that's for sure. Sometimes after a run we would spend an additional half hour, maybe even 45 minutes, just practicing jumping off to the side with our legs together and slightly bent. It made sense to me, doing it constantly would built up a certain amount of "muscle memory," that way when the big day came that you would actually jump out of a plane you would automatically know what to do. All of this newfound training had me psyched and ready to go. I was so excited to go to Airborne School. I wanted it so bad I could taste it.

Despite all of the awesome training, there was one crucial part of airborne training that was more important than all of the others. This requirement was absolutely necessary, and you could not go to airborne school without passing this particular test with flying colors. This task that I am referring to was an airborne physical. I really didn't think I would have a problem with this part, but apparently I did have a serious problem. According to my physical, I was color blind and because of this I could not be permitted to jump out of an aircraft. Apparently when it's time to jump, there's a light that switches from red to green. Green is obviously your cue to jump and if you cannot tell your reds from your greens you are going to have a serious problem. I can remember back when I went to MEPS to enlist in the first place, I could not pick some numbers out of a "magic eye" type sheet. The numbers were hidden in a big circle and you had to pick the number. Quite Frankly, I couldn't see a number at all so the Army classified me as color blind and limited my choices for my MOS. Fast forward to 2002, and here in AIT the same exact thing happened to me. I had no idea when I first volunteered for Airborne that colorblindness would be a factor. There I was, colorblind (according to the Army anyway), and I had to face the idea of not going to Airborne school. (For the record, I THINK I can see my reds and greens properly.) I was devastated because I had worked so hard and I had gotten very psyched up about going to airborne school. Now I had to call home to my dad and tell him that I wasn't going. Of course he was still proud of me anyway but on a personal level jumping out of a plane was something I really wanted to do. Ultimately it never came to fruition. Needless to say, I was very down about this but it was ok. I had a great friend in Kathy to confide in and to help me feel better about what had happened. Also, I am a firm believer in the old saying, "everything happens for a reason" and maybe I was supposed to go to Fort Campbell and not Fort Bragg. Either way, I had to get over it quickly, as I still had a few more weeks of AIT to get through.

Most of the rest of AIT was uneventful. There was much more typing which by now I was blatantly sick of. We did go to the field, but it was nothing like Victory Forge in basic training. This exercise was much more boring. The drill sergeants seemed to be giving us classes just to pass the time. Deep down inside I felt that I didn't learn anything in the last two weeks of AIT that I didn't learn or go over in the first two weeks. Honestly I felt that they probably could have shortened the class by two weeks and still received the same result. After the field exercise we started rehearsing for graduation, and we also had a couple of off post passes. In AIT an off post pass is a privilege, you get to go and leave Fort Jackson, in civilian clothing, and enjoy real life. Sometimes the passes end at the end of the day and you have to return, and occasionally the passes are overnight passes. The drill sergeants have a way of making an off post pass an incentive. The funny thing is you end up going to your first duty station thinking that an off post pass is a privilege, and it takes you some time to realize that you don't really need permission to leave post at your first duty station. Its part of the transition from the training side of the Army to the regular full time Army, but more on that subject later.

When you take an off post pass you are required to take a "battle buddy" of the same sex, so of course my battle buddy was good old Hultz. Yep, good old "let's put a negative spin on absolutely everything" Hultz. Walking around Columbia, South Carolina (which was a party town) with Hultz was the same as if you were a broke kid walking through a toy store. You want to have a good time, but you know that in the end there is just no way you are going to pull it off. I ended up spending my off post passes doing a multitude of not-so-exciting things in Columbia. We walked around, went to a few coffee shops, went downtown, and did a whole lot of nothing. Granted, I wasn't old enough to drink (and believe it or not drinking didn't even interest me at the time) but really the whole off post pass experience for me in AIT was very pointless. When you're being weighed down by someone who isn't really having a good time, what are you really supposed to do? So I ended up taking a few pictures and marking Columbia, South Carolina down on my list of places I had been. (At this point in my life this was a very short list, but fast forward to 2011 and that list is MUCH longer. More on that later.)

Graduation day was a hard day for me. If there was one thing that separated my basic training experience from my AIT experience, it was the very fact that even though I made a few friends in basic training, I hadn't made a close friend like I did here in AIT. I did not want to say goodbye to Kathy. Goodbyes are very hard for me. I admit that saying goodbye to someone can be a very tear-jerking experience for me. (It doesn't make you any less of a man to cry about saying good bye either.) Just thought I would take a second to state that for all of you doubters out there. To complicate matters, I knew that I was enlisted on Active Duty in the Active Army, and Kathy was enlisted in the New Jersey National Guard. Active Duty Soldiers serve full time on posts all over the US and the rest of the world, whereas National Guard Soldiers normally serve within their states at a part time basis. So, in other words I was headed to Fort Campbell, Kentucky, and Kathy was headed back home to New Jersey. There was a high possibility that I would never ever see Kathy again. This fact absolutely broke my heart because I built such a bond with her in such a short period of time that I didn't really know how to cope with these feelings. Since I didn't really know how to cope with this problem, I made the stupid decision of withdrawing myself. I slowly limited my conversations with her. It wasn't that I had a problem with her; I just knew that I would miss her and saying goodbye wasn't possible for me at the time. I really had no idea how to deal with this. It kept me up at night. They say hindsight is 20/20. Looking back on this, I realize that when it's time to say goodbye, as hard as it is and as much as you don't want to do it, you have to. As a man, as an adult, you have to. In fact, if you don't, it's almost insulting. Personally I've felt insulted times in my life when so-called friends didn't come say goodbye to me. After everything you had gone through with someone, the least you can do is come and pay your respects to them when the ride is over. So looking back, perhaps I may have insulted her by becoming so withdrawn. It was just so hard for me on an emotional level. Graduation day was a very depressing time for me. I still remember the graduation day. I was called to the front of the formation to receive a special award for my performance in PT during AIT. Under normal circumstances if you did as good as I did at PT, you would probably receive a PT patch and a Certificate of Achievement, but since this was a MOS-related school, I received what is known as a regimental award, meaning it can only be awarded to Soldiers in our field (personnel services/human resources) during a school. The Award was called the President Theodore Roosevelt Medal. It came with a certificate and a special coin featuring the face of President Teddy Roosevelt. I still have the certificate and the coin to this day. It was definitely a cool award to receive, especially since I was the only one in my AIT class to receive it, but it still didn't fix my sad mood. There was nothing that could change the fact that I made a new friend and I was going to miss her. Nothing could change it, and there was only one thing in the entire world that could make me feel better about it. That one thing was going home. Luckily for me, it was graduation day and it was just about time to go home. Throughout my whole life, the one safe haven I always had was home with my dad. I had a little bit of a rough childhood with my parents splitting, and even though I loved my mother to death, I always felt safe with my dad. When there's something bothering me, that's the one person I want to be around. To put it in childhood terms: if I could roll Superman, Optimus Prime, and Hulk Hogan into one person, that person would be my dad. Right now, on graduation day from AIT, I was a full-fledged Soldier, I stood tall and walked proud, yet there was one place I wanted to be: home sweet home. And so, on the day of April 4, 2002, I graduated AIT and boarded a coach bus to head home to good old Saint Johnsville.

I could have taken a plane home, but I decided to take a coach bus for two main reasons. First off, it was outright cheaper. A plane ticket would have been a few hundred dollars, and the bus ticket ran me $55. So financially, it was a no-brainer. (For those of you wondering: no, the Army does not always pay your way home; in fact in MOST cases it doesn't pay it at all.) The other reason I decided to take a coach bus was I really needed to reflect on some things, and I felt that a cross-country bus trip was the perfect way to do that. I was sitting on the bus, dressed in my Class A Uniform again, trying to sort out my thoughts as I stared off into the countryside. I had so much to think about. I missed home a lot. I also was already missing Kathy. Also, I had the business matter of my gym to take care of. I was going home for two weeks and I wanted to see as many of my friends as possible. I knew the awkward feeling of Saint Johnsville feeling too small for me was far behind me, so now it was about me trying to have some fun while also taking care of the gym business. There was a lot I had to get accomplished over the course of the next two weeks. I had a plane ticket to fly out of Albany, NY to Nashville, TN dated for April 17, 2002. April 17 was the day I was required to report to Fort Campbell. (For those of you reading this that do not know, Fort Campbell is located on the Kentucky/Tennessee border. The installation is located about 40 minutes from Nashville, TN, making Nashville the closest airport for Soldiers reporting for duty.)

After the long 24 hour bus trip, I finally arrived home. It was great to be there again, to be able to eat some of my dad's home cooking and to be able to just let loose and relax. However, as relaxed as I was getting, there was still the gym. See, as I mentioned in the previous chapter, I had let friends of mine from high school try to run my gym and as a result I ended up losing a lot. It was a dumb decision and I still regret it to this day. As a business major in college today I can clearly recognize the error in leaving a friend in charge of your business, especially when that friend is 18 years old and in high school. But, everyone makes mistakes. Unfortunately, my mistakes cost some money, a few thousand dollars to be exact. While I was away, the business didn't make a dime, yet there were still bills to be covered. It had bills such as an electric bill, fire insurance, injury insurance to cover any weightlifters (providing we actually had customers), among other bills. These bills piled up, and while I was away Al Kirby, the man who I bought the gym from in the first place, was paying them for me. So in essence I owed Al Kirby quite a sum of money. I needed to figure out a way to get Kens All American Gym rocking and rolling again. I had to pay Al what I owed him and get the gym profitable again. Somehow, when I was still living there in Saint Johnsville, the place was alive. I had a vested interest in the gym, it was where I trained when I was growing up, and I felt an emotional attachment to the place. Under no circumstances did I want it to die, so when I was still living there I tried extra hard to keep it alive. Fast forward just a mere 6 months into the future; I was returning after being gone for 6 months and I only had 2 weeks to work with, not to mention limited ideas to work with. I paid a small fraction of the debt off with some of the money I had saved during AIT, and then I decided to go to Sears and buy a treadmill. The gym had never had a treadmill, so I thought maybe that would attract a few new customers. As it turned out, it didn't. In fact the damage that had already been done was so irreversible that there was really no way to save the place. The building was in bad shape and it was the type of situation where you really needed a take charge owner/manager to get on people about paying their dues. I was that take charge owner, but the problem was that I had a bigger commitment, a commitment to America. I was a Soldier now, and being a Soldier was a far bigger priority to me than being the owner of Kens All American Gym. I ended up having to come to an agreement with Al Kirby. Basically Al would forgive my debt to him if I agreed to relinquish the building and the equipment (including the new treadmill) back to him. It was a heartbreaking decision because I loved owning my own business and I looked at it as an underdog finally "making it" and finally winning the "big one". Seven days after graduating high school I was the owner of that place and here I was being forced to relinquish it, to sell it back. It wasn't an easy decision but I had to do what I had to do. I agreed to Al's terms, and on April 16, 2002, just one day before I was required to report to Fort Campbell, Kens All American Gym was closed down for good. It was very heartbreaking for me in so many ways, especially because Al did not keep it as a gym. He closed the place down, moved the equipment out of it, and sold it to the lady next door who owned a pet shop. She then in turn decided to make her pet shop into one big building. For the record, that pet shop ended up closing down too. Nowadays I am not really sure what is done with that building. I've heard that a band practices there but I've never actually had a visual conformation of that. I can tell you this much: I miss Ken's Gym. Every time I go home, I always get someone asking me about it. "Hey man, whens Ken's Gym coming back?" I almost always indulge them, usually with some sort of generic, comedy ridden answer like "well I don't know when version 2.0 is supposed to hit the market, but I'll be sure to let you know when it does." I always get a kick out of making people laugh, and more importantly making myself laugh. Laughter is what I use to rid myself of the sadness that I no longer own the gym. It was a major part of my life and the fact that it ended so quickly just drives me to succeed that much more. Someday I want to own a gym again, and deep down, I know I will. For now however, just know that there will always be a special place in my heart for Ken's All American Gym.

Other than the whole process of dealing with the gym, there was one more important thing that I did do while I was on leave this time around. I went to visit my high school in my Class A uniform. For me it was something I always wanted to do, and going to visit my old high school to see my old teachers and some of my old classmates that hadn't graduated yet, (yes, I just said that) was something that I felt that I owed back to the community. I remember getting up there and everyone was glad to see me. I felt like I was getting the celebrity treatment. Even the janitors treated me like I was royalty. (Please, do not take the extra time to look into that last statement.) Various students were coming up to me asking me about my experiences, and more importantly asking me for advice. Keep in mind that Saint Johnsville is a very small town so if you do something like join the Army the town tends to treat you really well since everyone knows you. Now compare that to living in New York City, where there are millions of people living there. You cannot reach the same status in NYC simply by joining the Army as you would if you lived in a small town like I did. While I did soak in all of the attention, I did try my best to guide a few kids in the right direction. I felt like a leader to them. Leadership has always been one of my better qualities and I have always believed that the best way to be a good leader is by instilling respect; by respecting those around you, thus receiving respect in return. Some leaders prefer to lead based on fear, I feel that fear is incompatible with leadership. Sure, if people fear you they may follow you RIGHT NOW, but what about when the chips are down? If they see you getting beaten down, they will no longer have a reason to fear you, and thus, you are no longer fit to lead them. See, if someone respects you, they will follow you to the bitter end. That is true leadership. And guess what? It all starts with you. You have to show respect to those you intend to lead before you can expect them to respect you. It starts off with humility. On that very day that I showed up to Saint Johnsville high school in my Class A uniform I did indeed feel like a leader, but more importantly I felt the respect. I will never forget that.

After two weeks of reflecting, having fun, and making some hard decisions, it was time to go. My father took me to the Albany International Airport and we bid farewell. Like all the other times I had to say bye, it was hard, but it was hard in a different way this time. When I left for basic training, I knew when training would be over and I knew when I would be back. I wasn't 100% sure about Christmas exodus when I left for basic training but I had a slight idea of it from my recruiter. After I was done with my Christmas vacation and had to go back, I once again knew when I would be back: at the end of AIT. This time around, I had absolutely no idea. Fort Campbell was a real duty station; it was not training, it was work. That meant there was no definite end to my time there. Because of this fact I honestly had no idea when I would go back home to see my family, and that had a profound effect on me. With that, I bid farewell to my dad and boarded the plane for Nashville, TN. I didn't know exactly what adventures awaited me, but I did know that there would be some adventures nonetheless.

CHAPTER 3

FORT CAMPBELL, KY HOME OF THE 101ST AIRBORNE DIVISION

I arrived to Nashville about midday on April 17, 2002. I had no idea exactly what I was supposed to do upon landing at the airport. I knew that I had to report to Fort Campbell and I knew that I had orders in my possession to do so. I also knew that as a Soldier I was supposed to have some sort of assistance while traveling across the country. Despite knowing all of these facts everything still seemed disorganized to me. I stood in the airport not really knowing very much at all. I felt as if my drill sergeants should have filled me in on a little more. This wasn't the first time something like this happened to me throughout my career, and it wasn't the last. At the time I was still young and relatively naïve, but I was soon to learn over the years that the Army was extremely disorganized when it came to certain things, and overly organized when it came to other things. Unfortunately for me, I learned throughout my years that one of the things that it was disorganized at was communication and keeping people informed on what was going on. Luckily for me, I was raised by someone who had some common sense (my dad), and thus he passed some of that common sense on to me. So I found my way around that airport and was eventually able to find out where transitioning Soldiers like me were supposed to go: over to the guy with the sign that said, "FORT CAMPBELL SOLDIERS REPORT HERE." Now I have to tell you, if walking over to that guy didn't take common sense, I don't know what did. Anyway, after consulting with the gentleman I found out that there were only two other Soldiers going from Nashville to Fort Campbell that day. What exactly did that mean for me you ask? Well, usually there would be a busload of Soldiers who would take the trip to Fort Campbell. But today, since there were only a total of three Soldiers going, we wouldn't need a bus. We also couldn't get a rental car, so the liaison set us up with something I had never experienced before: a limo ride. I don't exactly know how it worked out, but somehow, some way, a limo was cheaper than a tour bus or a rental car. The three of us rode in style to Fort Campbell, complete with all of the luxuries you would expect out of a limo: full leather interior, sunroof, a refrigerator fully stocked with liquor. To me this was a great experience; I didn't go to my high school prom in a limo like I wanted to so for me to finally get the chance to ride in a limo was pretty cool. Now I know that not all Soldiers have been able to enjoy this particular luxury and some may take exception to this, but in my own defense, it wasn't my fault. I did not plan this. The limo ride was given to me. So for all you angry Soldiers who are cursing this book for not getting their limo ride, I apologize. Don't worry though, the rest of this book is worth reading and the rest of my journey doesn't happen in a limo. And I hope that one day all of you can get your limo ride too. I just happened to get lucky this time.

After my 45 minute limo ride I finally arrived at my very first duty station, Fort Campbell, Kentucky. Fort Campbell is the home of the 101st Airborne Division (Air Assault) and has a storied history. Soldiers from Fort Campbell/101st fought in various wars to include Vietnam, World War II and modern day wars such as Operation Enduring Freedom in Afghanistan and Operation Iraqi Freedom in Iraq. Needless to say the 101st has a truly honored history and I was extremely proud to be a part of that division. That was one thing that truly stuck with me when I first arrived to Fort Campbell, the fact that other Soldiers were actually proud to be there. You could literally feel the pride in the air. To this day, I still haven't been to a military installation that had this level of pride; from the leaders at the top all the way to the troops at the bottom. It felt so good to be there. When you first enter the gate, you are surrounded on both sides by two walls (each being 3 feet tall in height) that have all of the different unit insignias on them, along with the words: "Home of the 101st Airborne Division (AASLT.)" Right from your very first time entering the post, you were greeted by this. It was a little overwhelming and I can say that being there really did mean a lot to me. I no longer cared about the fact that I was a support Soldier that couldn't make it to Airborne School because I was color blind. That didn't matter anymore. I was a screaming eagle now.

The first thing you do in the active Army when arriving to a new duty station is report to the replacement battalion. Now, replacement is a lot like reception in basic training, but at the same time it is a lot different. Yes, you are still a private, which means you are still at the bottom of the Army's food chain. However, you are no longer on the training side of the Army, so you are treated slightly more like an adult. The function of replacement is to in-process you, get you accustomed to the new post you are at, as well as issue you your TA-50. (TA-50 is army terminology for your equipment.) Once you spend two weeks there and all of the important tasks are covered, you move on to your unit. In all honestly, replacement is to the real army what reception is to basic training. Except in replacement you don't have to wait in as many lines and you're getting treated slightly better. Even though replacement at Fort Campbell was short, I do still have a few memories from there that are worth noting.

First and foremost at replacement I had a roommate in the barracks there that would end up going to become one of my best friends over the duration of my career. Jason Mays, a fellow support Soldier, although not a Human Resources Soldier like me. We had the common bond that we were not Infantrymen. See, it is an unspoken rule in the Army that many of the infantry Soldiers don't actually like Support Soldiers. I am not speaking on behalf of all infantrymen in this instance, but let's just say that many of the individuals in the infantry world do not feel that Support Soldiers pull their weight in the Army. (Of course, they certainly do, but that is a story for another time.) So obviously, since many of the infantry Soldiers don't hang out with Support Soldiers, usually the Support Soldiers will stick together also. It's perfectly natural. Hell, I was glad to have a roommate there at Campbell who didn't outright disrespect me for the simple fact of what my MOS was. The other thing that Jason and I shared in common was the fact that we were both professional wrestling fans. Now, after reading that you are probably thinking one of two things: 1-wrestling sucks and its fake or 2-wrestling is very entertaining and a lot of fun to watch. Yes, I know there are other things out there. Yes, I do watch boxing and I do watch UFC; however there is nothing like watching wrestling for me. I grew up on it. My entire life I watched it. I've always loved it, and I always will. That's all there is to it. Almost directly across the street from the replacement battalion there is a Recreation Center for Soldiers on post to go to. At the time, the recreation center had TVs, pool tables, game rooms, etc. Well, on Monday nights the recreation center would have a certain room with a big screen TV set aside just for those Soldiers who wanted to come in and watch wrestling. So on Monday nights Jason and I would go to the recreation center and watch it. We continued this tradition over the entire time we were at Fort Campbell and as a result we would meet a lot of other people there during the week. The recreation center itself also evolved a lot over my time there at Fort Campbell; we went from watching RAW on a big screen TV in what looked like an old bar area, to watching it on from a projector on an even bigger screen in a theater-like atmosphere. That place used to fill up quick for RAW and it was nice to see that the recreation center would do something like this for the Soldiers. When you are far away from home and the people that you love, it is always nice to somehow get a taste of home, and I feel that the recreation center truly provided that. Also at the rec. center we ended up meeting another guy by the name of AJ Tiede. AJ was also a fan, but unlike us he didn't seem to have a lot of friends. So we brought him along with us and whenever we would go hang out in other places (as I'll describe later on in this book), AJ would be there too. So all in all, Jason, AJ and I formed somewhat of a trio and really stuck together during our time there. It worked out great for us because we all ended up in different units at Fort Campbell, and the last thing you want to do is ALWAYS hang out with the people in your own unit, because after all, you work with them all day and that could tend to get old. It's always good to have a few allies outside of your own unit. It helps you to vent, and you know that they wouldn't be ones to potentially stab you in the back for personal gain, because after all they aren't even in your unit. There would be nothing to gain for them to stab you in the back. Without the two of them my time at Fort Campbell would have been a lot worse than it ended off being.

Another memory I have from my time at replacement was buying my first car as a Soldier. I was 18 years old and away from home and I knew that I was going to need a car to get around. Of course, I ended up making a huge mistake with this car in particular, but we all make mistakes in life don't we? There is a strip of highway just outside of the main gate of Fort Campbell called 41A. 41A is rated as one of the most dangerous highways in America due to all of the reckless driving. 41A is also home to some of the biggest rip-offs in America. Now, that may not be officially stated anywhere, so I am stating it now: for all of you young, brand new Fort Campbell Soldiers that are reading this, 41A is a rip-off. Do not buy a car there. In fact, don't buy anything there. You can get anything on

41A; used cars, rims, and stereo equipment for your car and even for your home. All of this of course is going to be financed at the highest possible interest rate. They rely on the customer (the young Soldier) being naive and suckered into buying something there. Unfortunately, I did not have anyone giving me the advice not to buy something. So I ended up at a place on 41A called Terry Harris Motor Company. The guy who owned the place was this 450 pound guy named Terry Harris who probably couldn't get out of his chair without help. He would buy used cars at auctions (all of which had problems) and sell them to troops at an extremely high markup. He had an assistant who was a retired Sergeant First Class. He would use him to convince the Soldiers it was a good deal, because after all, a Non-Commissioned Officer would never rip off a junior Soldier, right? Yeah, right. It was a major rip off and it's a shame I didn't see that at the time. I ended up getting a black 1996 Chevy berretta, for a price of $12,000 with an APR of 18%. If that isn't a rip off, then I don't know what is. I can remember the retired Sergeant First Class telling me "how great of a deal I got" and I can also remember Terry Harris himself telling me, "Ya know kid, a lot of guys your age aren't as lucky as you!" That was the biggest load of bull I ever heard. I will never ever forget this important lesson; even if it is a good car, always read the contract. Take someone with you. Get a second opinion. Why couldn't I see at the time that I was being ripped off? Truthfully to this day I do not know why I didn't see that. But I guess we all live and learn. I will never make that mistake again. Not only was it a bad deal but the berretta itself is an overall crappy car in general. I remember getting back to replacement trying to convince my friends how great of a car it was. No one was buying into it. I even put Silver trim on all of the doors, thinking that was going to help the image. Jason kept on asking me when I was going to remove the trim, and I didn't understand why. At 18 years old you don't necessarily see that Silver trim on a crappy car doesn't increase the value or the image of the car in question. I didn't realize it at the time, but I was ripped off. I was stuck with this stupid car I was just in denial at first as to how bad it was. Also, every car that Terry Harris sold came with an exclusive, "30 days as-is" warranty. What exactly does that mean? That means that every car that Terry sells you has a 30 day warranty, and after those 30 days you are on your own. I should have known that was a bad sign, if you go to a car dealer and buy a car, usually a 5 to 7 year warranty is considered ideal. 30 days however, is not ideal. Also, when I left the dealership, Terry Harris and his partner in crime told me that if I had anyone to bring to them as a referral to buy a car they would pay me $100 cash if that person actually ended up buying the car. So therefore, I should go back to Fort Campbell and try to work really hard to get Soldiers the same type of "great deal" that I just got. For the record, Terry Harris is no longer in business. His shop was one of the biggest rip-offs I have ever seen in my entire life and there is no telling how many young Soldiers he ripped off in his time, but I am glad that he is out of business. Now the best I can hope for is all of the car dealers on 41A to go out of business. So one more time, for all you young Soldiers out there, do not waste your time, effort, or money on 41A. You will be doing yourself a huge favor if you stay away from there.

So after spending my two weeks at replacement, I ended up finally getting to my first real unit, the 101st Soldier Support Battalion (SSB). A Soldier Support Battalion consisted of a Headquarters element, a Human Resources element, and a Finance Element. The purpose of a SSB is to provide Human Resources and Finance Support at the division level to the entire post they are assigned at, in which most cases that could end up being a number of 30,000 or more Soldiers. The SSB serves as a final stop for HR issues prior to submission to Department of the Army. Today SSB's no longer exist since a lot of these functions are now performed at the unit level, but I will never forget the "Glory days" of working in an SSB. In an SSB you have the ability to work in one specialized section, which provided you the ability to master one specific skill. Of course there was a negative side to this, that being the fact that you were learning only that one skill, so you ended up being uneducated in all of the other HR functions, unless of course you moved to a new Section. On my first day my Company Commander, (affectionately known as Captain Z) held a formation and brought me to the front and introduced me to the company. Before the formation he took me aside and asked me for some quick background info on myself, which he would use in his speech. I remember him saying, "This is Private Conklin, he just came from AIT, he scored a 300 on his PT test and he's from New York. Other than that I can't remember anything else about him, so be sure to welcome him into the fold." At least he was being honest about not remembering much about me. I found it funny that he felt the need to mention my PT score. Was it that important to tell the entire formation that? Apparently it was. So now I walked around with a chip on my Shoulder because the Commander wanted to brag about me. It's ok though, I'm sure if he didn't brag about me I would have found my own way to brag about myself. That's just my nature.

After my quick introduction I fell back into formation and they called another Soldier to the front for a promotion. He was getting promoted from Private First Class (E-3) to Specialist (E-4). I quickly learned that this unit had a tradition for their promotion ceremonies. When you were getting promoted you had to drop down and do ten push-ups for every grade. If you were getting promoted to E-3 you would do thirty push-ups, E-4 would do forty push-ups, and so on. When you were down there doing your push-ups, two other Soldiers would come out of nowhere and dump two buckets of water on you. It was the tradition of the unit and it was a fun tradition. Upon observing this I realized one thing about this place: the morale was high. People genuinely liked being a part of this unit. It was a fun place to work and a fun place to be. And why shouldn't it be? Why does the Army have to be a place that no one enjoys? It doesn't have to be that way. We also had a great First Sergeant (1SG) in that Company by the name of First Sergeant Guffy. 1SG Guffy was probably the coolest leader I ever met while serving at Ft Campbell. In any company in the Army, a First Sergeant is the top enlisted Soldier. He serves as a mentor to the NCO's that serve under him, as well as an advisor to the Company Commander. A Company Commander should never take any action regarding his or her Soldiers without consulting the Company First Sergeant first. The First Sergeant is ultimately responsible for the actions of all of the enlisted personnel underneath him. Also, the First Sergeant serves as a role model to the junior NCOs and more importantly the junior Soldiers. 1SG Guffy was everything you wanted in a leader, he was approachable, yet stern. He commanded respect, yet he also gave respect to subordinates, which is a character trait that you don't find in a lot of leaders. 1SG Guffy was also a bit of a comedian, he would stand in front of the company for formation and occasionally crack a few jokes for our amusement. Yet when it came time to be serious, 1SG Guffy was as serious as they come. At the weapons ranges he wouldn't act like he was too good to fire a rifle because of his rank. He would get right down in the foxhole with the Soldiers and shoot. And when we went to the field, he would be the last guy you would ever hear complain about the heat. He would also be the first guy to tell his Soldiers to drink some water to stay hydrated. If he felt the Company Commander was doing something wrong or acting like an asshole, 1SG Guffy would go into the commander's office and tell him. Many times I would walk by and overhear him saying, "Sir, you can't do that, that's fucked up." Any leader willing to stand up to those senior to them when they are wrong is a good leader in my book. To top it all off, for some reason he resembled Hulk Hogan. So who better to represent us and be the leader of our company? Who better to be the standard bearer? 1SG Guffy to me embodied everything great about the United States Army and we were truly blessed to have him as our First Sergeant. I learned over the many years of my career that if you go to a place and the leadership is bad, then the unit will most likely be lackluster. If you encounter a good unit with great leaders, then the Soldiers are going to be expected to (and more importantly willing to) mirror that feeling. You can fear your leaders, but it is always more important to respect your leaders. 1SG Guffy was a man I respected.

Another thing about the SSB that boosted the morale was the barracks. Most units on Fort Campbell lived in one of two different types of barracks. One type was the old wooden World War II style barracks, and one was the newer barracks that resembled old hospital rooms. I didn't like either one. Luckily for me, the SSB didn't have to live in either version. The SSB barracks were an old guest house/hotel that had been closed down because a new guest house was built on post. These were the nicest barracks I had seen in my entire life. Every room had wall to wall carpeting, air conditioning that actually worked, and even a bathtub. That's right, a bathtub. Some barracks on that post had community bathrooms where you didn't even get your own bathroom, while we had a bathtub. Some barracks had nasty floors with stains that had been there for thirty years or more and no amount of scrubbing would clean them off. If we wanted to clean our floors, it was a matter of vacuuming the carpet. I know it sounds like we had it easy, and that's because we did have it easy. I was extremely lucky to have this luxury, especially at this stage of my career. Usually privates are put on details to strip and wax the hallway floor . . . we didn't have a floor to wax in the hallway. We had carpeted hallways. The only way it could have been any easier for us would have been if we had our own apartments. I did find it slightly comical though, after all if you were an infantryman spending most of his time in the field, I guess you really would have every excuse in the world to hate us. We really had it good. I am sure that without those barracks the morale in that unit still would have been relatively high, but not as high. Also, most barracks buildings in the Army are located within a close proximity of a dining facility (DFAC).

In most units the junior enlisted Soldiers are given meal cards and end up having to eat at those facilities instead of being able to buy food on the economy and cook it in their rooms. Usually the only exception to this rule for the junior enlisted is if you happen to be married. If you are married you most likely do not live in the barracks to begin with and you wouldn't have to eat at the DFAC. Either way, the food at the DFAC isn't always that good so Soldiers usually end up wasting their paychecks on fast food, which isn't the healthiest way to live. Since we didn't live near a dining facility, we were authorized to eat our meals at the nearby hospital, which was right down the street. The hospital food was actually much better than any DFAC I had ever eaten at. There was a Belgian waffle press set up in the mornings for breakfast, and some of the best chowders I had ever tasted were served every day at lunch and dinner. This was the cafeteria that the hospital faculty ate at, so it had to be top notch. Making that cafeteria the "official" place where Soldiers of the 101st SSB were authorized to eat made things that much better for us. For a first duty station, I would say I hit the jackpot. I lived in the best barracks on post, ate at the best place on post, and the morale in the unit seemed like it couldn't get any better. Needless to say with all of these perks I was ready for my first day of work to get underway. I felt that I needed to start earning all of these perks so to speak.

My first actual day of work came along before I knew it. Here I was fresh out of AIT and about to start working my actual job. After a morning of rigorous PT I showered, went to breakfast and headed to the office. We worked in a big white building directly across the street from the former guest house that we called home. It was convenient for us that we worked across the street from where we lived. We didn't have to waste our gas driving to work. It was just another luxury that we had in the SSB. I was initially assigned to work in the Enlisted Records section of the SSB, affectionately just referred to as "records." Records seemed like an incredibly disorganized area in that building. There were a lot of Soldiers that seemed to just sit around all day without any direction at all. There were stacks and boxes of old paper in the corners just waiting to be shredded, and even Soldiers showing up late. There seemed to be a very low amount of discipline and military bearing in this place. As far as the actual purpose of the enlisted records section; Soldiers assigned to this section were supposed to take customers on a first come, first serve basis. The customers would bring documents that they needed updated onto their file and then get filed away. I know this sounds easy enough, but even the easiest of tasks can be hard if the people performing the said task don't even try. Sometimes Soldiers were stuck in the records section when the unit didn't really have anything else for them and due to that fact the section seemed crowded and overpopulated. I ended up being assigned to work for a guy named Cursey. Cursey was a big dude, about 6 ft. 5 in tall and he seemed to have a chip on his shoulder. At first meeting, I didn't seem to know what was wrong with him. He was really good at putting a bad taste in your mouth. My first day he talked a lot of trash, and of course I tried my best to give it right back to him. I didn't really know what his problem was, most notably what the hell his problem was with me. I didn't do anything to him but he seemed to have a problem. As it turned out, I wasn't the only one who had an issue with Cursey in this unit; he seemed to rub a lot of people the wrong way. Cursey wasn't even an NCO, he was just a Private First Class (E-3) and here I was, just a Private (E-1). So it was obvious that Cursey did outrank me and if I was assigned to work for him then I guess I had no choice but to deal with his crap. The weirdest part about my first day with Cursey is that later on that evening he came by my room and wanted to take me out to dinner with some of the others from the unit. I found that weird, that after being a total asshole all day at work he was going to offer me an olive branch outside of the office. I was very reluctant about him and I figured it was a prank, so I turned him down. When I turned him down he immediately resorted to trash-talking, claiming that I was anti-social and didn't want to try to mesh with the rest of the group. It wasn't that at all; it was the fact that all day long at work he acted like we were enemies. This could be a prank for all I knew.

As the weeks went by working with Cursey, he started to grow on me. He wouldn't always act like an ass towards me and we did end up hanging out a few times. Times we would go to the field or the rifle range Cursey would take me aside and give me a few pointers. He would do this often, and depending on his mood and my mood on that particular day, I would either heed to what he was trying to teach me or just ignore him completely. It turned out Cursey actually did have a lot of what he liked to call "BMK" (basic military knowledge). He didn't actually know a lot about our MOS; in fact he didn't even like our MOS. He hated doing paperwork, (which is exactly what our MOS was) but he did know a lot about the Army in general. He knew a ton about weapons maintenance and other Soldier skills. Of course, me being fresh out of AIT I didn't really know much more that what I had learned in training, in either area of MOS skills or basic Soldiering. So the love/hate relationship that Cursey and I had throughout my time at Ft Campbell looks a lot different to me now when I reflect back on those memories. Yes it is true that sometimes he would get a little over the top. He would run his mouth, firing off insults, often having an attitude for no good reason. I can still see today why I (and some others as well) didn't like him. He had that type of personality. But when I look back on those days now, it has become apparent to me that Cursey was at best just trying to be a "big brother" to me at times. Now, I would be lying if I said he wasn't wrong for some of the trash talking he would produce, but at the same time I wasn't exactly 100% correct in my actions either. I knew that he was older than a lot of the other Soldiers in the unit, and in fact he had given college a try and then decided to give the Army a try. So sometimes in retaliation I would bring that to light. I would rub in the fact that he was a failure at college and how this was a last resort for him. I admit saying that was rude, but then again he started it. And those were the type of love/hate exchanges that we would have. I knew if we were at the range Cursey would look out for me. Hell, I knew at the unit if someone else had something to say to me that wasn't in our platoon Cursey would even take up for me there. It was weird. But, as I stated earlier, hindsight is 20/20. I know now that his intentions weren't bad, it was just his methods that were a little off.

Another person that I met in my time at Ft Campbell was a guy by the name of Jonathan Jones. PT was extremely rigorous at Ft Campbell and usually I would outrun everyone in the unit . . . well almost everyone. There was this one guy that would always be way ahead of me, and that guy was Jones. If I ran a 13 minute 2 mile run that day, Jones would run that same 2 miles in 10 minutes. Jones was from Arkansas, and he was about 135 pounds soaking wet. He was hands down the fastest person I ever met. He was also cool to hang out with. We hit it off immediately. Like me he was a wrestling fan, he just wasn't a die-hard wrestling fan like I was. Also, Jones didn't seem to have the personality defect that Cursey had. I also found it strange that Cursey liked Jones and never had anything bad to say about him. What was it about me that set Cursey off? Sometimes Cursey, Jones, and I would all head to the hospital cafeteria together for dinner after work. As long as I had another person there as a buffer, Cursey really didn't seem bad, in fact he seemed likeable. Jones was that buffer that I needed. Jones also liked fast cars. At one point he bought a Silver Pontiac GTO and drove the hell out of it. He loved that car. He used to dog me about how a lot of the cars I had during my time at Campbell (to include the black berretta with the silver trim) were garbage cars. Jones knew his cars, he knew his engines. He was quick to tell you if what you drove was a piece of crap. He didn't care about your feelings when it came to that. Also, he was quick to compare his car to yours, quick to show you just how great his car was. What he didn't realize is that if I hadn't have gotten myself locked into that stupid contract with Terry Harris for the berretta, than I too could have gotten a nice Pontiac GTO like Jones. I made a mistake, and a terrible one at that. Therefore, I had to pay for my mistake by driving that berretta around until it either died or was paid off. Jones just turned out to be a little smarter than me when it came to shopping for a car back then. Over time Jones ended up falling head over heels for a girl named Emily, but more on that later.

I also made another good friend at the unit by the name of William Reynolds. Like me, Reynolds was a wrestling fan, but he was more of a "die-hard" fan like I was. It was good to have another "die-hard" fan around the unit because Jones (who only moderately liked wrestling) didn't always know exactly what I was talking about. Reynolds on the other hand watched it just as much as I did, every single week. There were even a few times that he came out to the recreation center and watched it, which was rare for the SSB. Usually I was the only Soldier from the SSB that would go there. Reynolds was also good for comedy relief too; he knew how much I loved Hulk Hogan so whenever I walked into the Company area he would yell at me, "Hogan!" and start flexing. Eventually I started doing the same thing to him, only instead of yelling "Hogan!" I would yell "Booker T!" He would then go ahead and do Booker T's pose (which consists of looking at your own open hand and shaking your head all over the place). When we would do this at the unit people would look at us like we were idiots, but we didn't care because it was all in good fun. It got to the point where almost every time we saw each other you heard the words "Hogan" and "Booker T." Our new tradition would end up continuing for a few years.

Things at Ft Campbell up until this point hadn't been that bad. The unit was ok, and I had a few friends there, not to mention I still met up with Jason and AJ at the recreation center every Monday night for wrestling. Even though things were going ok so far there was still a part of me that missed home. I thought about home all the time. I had friends there and I missed my family an awful lot too. I knew that the unit would only allow me to take leave ever so often, since you earn leave at the rate of two and a half days per month (which adds up to 30 days of paid leave every year). We did have weekends off, which of course are not chargeable as leave, they are merely days off. Also, when you're in the Army you get a 4-day weekend off for every federal holiday. Christmas, Thanksgiving, New Year's Day, Columbus Day, Veterans day, Memorial day, Martin Luther King day, and many others. Usually you end up getting a 4-day weekend 10 out of 12 months per year, which is a great deal considering most people that work in the private sector don't always see that kind of time off in addition to 30 days of paid vacation every year. I took the opportunity to drive home to New York during these 4-day weekends. Now, in the Army, there is a thing called a "Mileage Pass." You are under normal circumstances allowed to travel within 250 miles of your Army post during a normal weekend or 4-day weekend without having to put in paperwork for a "Mileage Pass." This is actually covered in Army regulations. If you desire to travel outside of the 250 mile radius you must put in paperwork for a Mileage Pass and wait for it to be approved by your Commander. Of course, it is your Commander's option to approve the pass or not. He doesn't necessarily have to approve the pass. So in essence, it's a hit or miss when it comes to mileage passes. As you can probably imagine, Saint Johnsville, New York is more than 250 miles away from Ft Campbell, Kentucky. So you would think that I would have to put in a mileage pass every time I drove home for a 4-day weekend. As it turns out, the unit didn't even care. I have no idea why to this day, but when it came to mileage passes, there was zero discipline. I was allowed to drive anywhere I wanted during my off time, as long as I was back in time for morning PT formation on the next duty day after the 4-day weekend. This really came in handy because I would hit the road immediately after work on Thursday, and be home by mid-afternoon Friday. I would spend these 4-day weekends home until Monday morning. Monday morning I would get on the road and drive the entire 15 hours back to Ft Campbell. The drive used to take it out of me, it would really drain me and for that week after the trip I would do a lot of sleeping. I would technically only get about 2 1/2 days at home before having to get back on the road, but it was well worth it. I was 19 years old and I missed home dearly. It took me a while to get over it and stop missing home. I carried on driving back home for these 4-weekends for almost a year before it got to be too much. Was it worth it? Sure it was. Not only was I getting to go home without wasting my leave days, but I was also getting to see more of the countryside. The trip would take me north up through the state of Kentucky, through Louisville and eventually into the state of Ohio. Once I hit Ohio I would be driving on I-71 and I would hit the three major cities in Ohio; Cincinnati, Columbus, and Cleveland. It was cool for me to be able to drive through these 3 major cities, and I would make sure to stop in all three of them for either gas or something to eat just so I would have the bragging rights of saying I was there. Once I hit Cleveland I would head north, hit I-90 and end up in Buffalo, NY. Once in Buffalo I would head east for almost 4 hours and I would be home in good old Saint Johnsville. All in all, the trip would take 15 hours, and I find it funny that nowadays I can remember that whole route. I haven't traveled that route in years, but I would bet any amount of money if I needed to drive to Fort Campbell today I could probably still do it without looking up directions.

So I had worked in enlisted records section under Cursey with no real direction for about two months. I really had no idea where my career was going, and to a certain extent I understood that I was a private and I was to do as I was told, but at the same time I still felt like my career was floundering. Updating enlisted records for a living isn't really that hard to do and I felt like I could accomplish so much more. Then one day, it finally happened. I was told that I was to be moved to a new section, a change that would change my career and even my life forever. I was being moved to a section called the NCOER section. NCOER stands for Non-Commissioned Officer Evaluation Report. Basically, an NCOER is a "report card" for an NCO. These reports are written up either annually or when an NCO changes jobs or leaves to go to a new unit. The reports are written by the NCO's supervisor and signed off by their supervisor. A supervisor is actually called a "rater" on an NCOER. Once finished, these reports are signed off by the rater and the rated NCO and forwarded to Department of the Army where they will become a permanent part of that NCO's record. These reports are reviewed years later when that same NCO is being considered for promotions, special positions, and special assignments. As you can probably imagine, an NCO and their rater takes these reports very seriously. The 101st SSB NCOER section was the final stop for any Ft Campbell NCOERs prior to the report being submitted to the Department of the Army. So being chosen to work in this section was very important. Also, as a Soldier working in this section, you're working under a ton of pressure. Just knowing that someone else's career is in your hands gives you a certain type of feeling. You know that you can't make any mistakes. Processing these reports and sending them to Department of the Army is an extremely important responsibility, and messing up just isn't an option. I really had no idea why I was chosen to work that section, considering I knew absolutely nothing about my MOS and had been working for Cursey for the past two months. To this day when I think about moving to that section, I choke it up to fate.

Upon starting upstairs in the NCOER section, I immediately noticed the difference between working there and working downstairs in enlisted records. For one, the office was extremely organized, on many levels. Gone were the massive stacks of boxes of paper in the corner that required filing. Also, all of the Soldiers in this section had a sense of purpose. They knew exactly what they had to accomplish, when they needed to accomplish it, and more importantly; who they reported to. There was a highly knowledgeable NCO who ran this section. His name was Sergeant Michael Ramos. To this day, I hold true to the fact that he was one of the smartest NCOs I ever met. (In fact, there were only two other people in Human Resources that I met in my entire career who knew more than SGT Ramos, and one person happened to be a Warrant Officer and the other a Staff Sergeant but more on them later . . .) SGT Ramos was certainly a better teacher than Cursey, and he taught me my job. He taught me everything I needed to know about NCOERs; he was basically a walking encyclopedia. There wasn't a single thing about our MOS that I couldn't ask him that he didn't know. What was more important was half the time he knew the answers without having to look them up. I wanted to be just like him. I wanted to be that guy; the guy you could ask questions who would ALWAYS know the answer. I used to think that SGT Ramos was smarter than the books themselves. I know that doesn't even make sense, but I guess you would have to meet the man to know what I was talking about. As knowledgeable as SGT Ramos was, he was also a bit of an asshole. He wanted me to learn my job no matter what, and he was willing to use whatever tactics he had to in order to ensure that was carried out. He gave me a class on what stuff to look for on an NCOER. There were so many different parts of the report and so much attention to detail was required. He stressed this to me over and over again. I thought I knew what I was doing, so he put me out there to do NCOER customer service.

I would review reports that unit S1s (HR managers) would submit. After I thought they were ok, I would log them in, make any changes I felt were necessary, and then I would sign off on them and turn them in to SGT Ramos for review. Once SGT Ramos said they were ready, they would go to Department of the Army. So far, so good right? I would review and sign a stack of 20 reports and drop them off on SGT Ramos' desk. Then a couple of the other clerks would do the same, and while that was going on I would submit 2 or 3 more stacks of these reports to SGT Ramos' desk. The pile of reports he had was starting to get high. I was starting to build up some confidence that I was doing such a good job. He would walk a stack back over to one of the other clerks; show them the 1 or 2 mistakes they made then move on. I assume the clerk was correcting the mistakes. SGT Ramos hadn't come over to my desk yet to point out errors, so I assumed my work was perfect. I was a little nervous so I was watching him out of the corner of my eye and I would notice that every so often he would look over at me. I kept telling myself that he was looking over at me over and over again because he was so impressed with what I was doing. Yeah, right. Right as my confidence had hit an all-time high, he strutted over with an entire stack of NCOERS. I figured he was going to point out one, maybe two errors, and then wait for me to correct them. Instead, he looked me right in the eye and raised the entire stack of NCOERS in the air, and threw them on the ground. He started yelling at me, telling me that this was the worst display he had ever seen. Apparently, he was pissed off that he had spent time giving me a class on how to do this and here I was making mistakes. Not only was I making mistakes, but I was making a lot of mistakes. I was extremely embarrassed because he was doing this in front of all of the other Soldiers, as well as the civilian clerks that worked in the section. Then he told me I was to work late until I had all the reports correct. I went over and picked them all up off the floor feeling humbled. I wanted to walk over and punch SGT Ramos right in his mouth, but I knew that was the wrong option. I would have gotten unlimited satisfaction out of that, but I also would have gotten unlimited punishment as well. So I picked up the NCOERS, kept my tail between my legs, and did my job. This had literally been the first time that anyone (besides Cursey) had told me that I sucked. I remember hanging out with Jones after work and he would tell me that he had "heard stories about SGT Ramos" and that "SGT Ramos was way too hard of an NCO." I didn't need to hear any stories, I had to experience SGT Ramos first hand,

and so far it wasn't exactly fun. But I will say this much: SGT Ramos knew his job. He knew his MOS. He knew about NCOERS. With that said, over the next couple of years I worked directly for him processing NCOERS. Indeed, he was hard on me, harder on me than the other clerks in the section; but without him I may not have ended up being as good at my job as I am today. He stressed attention to detail to a high degree. He understood the importance of an NCOER because after all he was an NCO and someday his own NCOER would come through that section. As I continued to work in his section I would learn my job that much more. His eye seemed to catch the slightest of mistakes and believe me, I paid for it. He would make me do push-ups in front of the rest of the office or he would just outright yell at me. In retrospect I guess it was because I was the youngest private in the office. Some of the other Soldiers had been stationed elsewhere, and here I was a 19 year old kid working there. Eventually I started to catch on and my stats were getting better. Soon enough, I was doing better than the other Soldiers in the section and SGT Ramos wasn't coming down on me anymore. I understood the importance of my MOS, and more importantly the importance of an NCOER in relation to an NCOs career. Today, I understand that he had a method to the madness. There was a reason for him to act the way he did; these reports were crucial and as far as he was concerned I walked in there as a young, arrogant kid who didn't care about anything. Later on in my career it ended up being my knowledge of my MOS that enabled me to rise to prominence, and I owe great thanks to SGT Ramos. Without him and his training style I may not have mastered my job the way I did. Granted, I didn't train my Soldiers the way he trained me, but either way his methods worked for me. Michael Ramos, if you are reading this, thank you for being such a good teacher.

Earlier in this chapter I touched on the fact that I had obtained (through the persuasion of Mr. Terry Harris, of Terry Harris motor company), a black 1996 Chevy Berretta with silver trim. I had been driving this car around the greater Ft Campbell area, to include taking it home to Saint Johnsville on a few four day weekends. Next thing you know, my transmission started skipping and I needed the transmission to be rebuilt. This totally sucked for me. As bad as that berretta was, it was my only method of transportation. I took it to Terry Harris and he kindly informed me that I had exhausted my "30 day, as-is warranty." (I know I stated this earlier, but for any young Ft Campbell Soldiers that may be reading this: do not buy a car on 41A!) I had absolutely no choice but to get the transmission rebuilt on my own wallet, which ended up forcing me to take out a loan. By now I had been promoted and I was an E-2, but I didn't just have the kind of money to throw down to rebuild my transmission. It definitely caused a hardship for me, and it also reminded me of how bad of an idea it was to buy a car from a bad dealer like Terry Harris. Either way I was doomed to live with my mistakes, thus the berretta got put in the shop for its new transmission. When I got it back I was glad to see my car, silver trim and all. Knowing that it had a completely rebuilt transmission made me feel like I had a brand new car. Well, at least a brand new berretta anyway. I had so much confidence in that car now. It was like the greatest thing in the world. I had taken a terrible situation and breathed new life into it. I took it to a car wash and washed it, waxed it up real nice. I don't know why, but I felt like showing it off. (As if anyone wanted to see a berretta.) I took my shiny black berretta for a cruise down 41A. I'll never forget this day, I had Hulk Hogan's old WWF theme song "I am a real American" playing on the CD player. God, that was one of my favorite songs. To this day it still is. (I believe the song was written and performed by Rick Derringer.) I sat in traffic at a red light with that glorious song blasting and I looked to my left and to my right to look at the other cars. Yeah, they heard my music. That's what made it that much more fun. When the light turned green I punched it because after all, a berretta is a fast car, isn't it? (It's not, but I thought it was at the time.) As I sped ahead, something terrible happened. I was driving straight ahead and suddenly a car attempted to cross 41A. That car (which happened to be a Honda Civic) didn't cross the highway fast enough because I ended up crashing into it head on at full speed. This type of crash is typically called a T-Bird crash, when one car is trying to cross the highway and another car crashes into its side. As my car hit the other one, my airbag deployed and hit me dead in the face. It was an extremely hard blow, and for any of you that may have been hit with an airbag in your life, you know exactly what I am talking about. It felt like I was punched right in the nose. It hit me so hard that I got angry. To make matters worse, I couldn't get out of the car because the other car had slid from the front of my car all the way down the side and pinned my door shut. The other car most likely slid as far as it did due to my own speed being so high. I crawled out of the passenger side door, trying to dodge the glass that was all over the seat. (Also please note that the radio was somehow still blasting. This got a little awkward later on when the cops came, especially because I had the CD on repeat, so "I am a Real American" kept playing over and over again.) I got out of the car thanking god that I was unharmed. I walked over to the other car and yelled, "Is everyone ok!?" They slowly started getting out of the car, and no one said a word to me. I asked again, "Is everyone ok?" Finally, one of the men looked at me and started speaking, in Spanish. Then they all started speaking Spanish. "Damn." I thought to myself, "I don't know Spanish." Luckily for me by now some people who had witnessed the accident had called 911 and the cops and ambulance were on the way. Granted, I was glad that everyone was alive, but at the same time I was angry. They caused the accident, not me. I had no idea at the time how I was going to get a new car. As we were waiting on the police to show up and take our statements, Terry Harris of all people pulled over and got out. He immediately went on his sales pitch. "Oh, good to see you're ok. Sorry to see you had this accident . . . tell ya what kid, come on down to the dealership today, and I'll put you in a '92 Dodge Grand Caravan tonight!" Wow, this guy was trying to make a new sale right here at the scene of my accident. That pissed me off. Furthermore, what the hell made him think that I wanted a '92 Dodge Grand Caravan? Terry Harris was out of his mind. I looked him dead in the eye and said, "Get the fuck out of here." He just stared at me blankly for a second and said, "Ok. But if you change your mind, these Caravans just came in." He drove off and I couldn't believe his audacity. I really couldn't. Finally the police did arrive, they took down my statement and one of the Police Officers was able to translate the statement of the driver of the car that I had hit. Clearly I wasn't at fault for the accident since I did have the right away. An ambulance took me to the hospital to check to see if I had whiplash. By the grace of God I ended up being perfectly fine after this accident. Over the next few weeks I was constantly in touch with my insurance company to get the other driver's insurance company to pay for the damages to my car. Since my car was totaled, they would be required to pay off the car along with an additional amount for damages. It also took a longer amount of time than normal to receive payment for this accident because it turned out that the driver of the car was not the owner of the car. The owner of the car was the passenger. Everyone in the car except the owner were illegal immigrants, and the drivers' license of the driver turned out to be an expired license from Mexico. So now there was the immigration issue to deal with. I was sorry to hear about their bad luck, but at this point I just needed to get driving again. I needed a method of transportation. Everyone at the unit was happy to see that I survived the accident so I ended up getting a few days off to decompress from it. That was nice of them considering they didn't actually have to do that for me.

Finally after about a month I received word from my insurance company that the check from the other insurance company had finally come in. It wasn't enough to buy a new car outright, because a portion of it had to pay off the old car. It was however enough to get a new car on what is called a "substitution of collateral." The insurance company explained to me what a substitution of collateral was. That's where you can take your contract and the check to a dealer and get a car for equal to or lesser value than the car you had totaled. I had never heard of this before. I suppose I could have just taken the remainder cash and used it as a down payment on a new car, but I didn't have any real credit at the time so the likely hood of being approved for a loan on a brand new car was slim to none. Either way, I wanted to give it a try anyway, so I started to call dealers in downtown Clarksville and Nashville as well. Every dealer told me the same thing that I had already assumed, that there was just no way that I could get financed with the credit that I had. I was determined to own a better car than the Beretta. Never again would I suffer that embarrassment. As it turned out the substitution of collateral only qualified me for a small number of vehicle contracts. I ended up resorting to searching 41A again, but this time not out of blind choice, but instead out of forced circumstances. I outright refused to do business with Terry Harris again, even though he kept leaving me voicemails about his freshly arrived 1992 Dodge Grand Caravans. I'm not sure if Terry knew this was 2002 or not. I'm also not sure if Terry knew that I didn't have kids so there was no reason for me to have a family vehicle. Either way, I wasn't interested in Terry Harris. I ended up going to another dealer on 41A named ASAC. To this day I really do not know what ASAC stands for. In ASAC's lot there were only two cars that I qualified for given the circumstances. One of the cars was a red Plymouth Neon, and the other car was a white Plymouth Neon. Wow, what a set of choices. I ended up going with the red Neon because I just didn't like white on a car at the time. I wasn't exactly happy with the car, it wasn't the toughest looking car to say the least but then again, it was a car. It was something to get me from point A to point B. It was definitely a better car than the berretta, but that wasn't saying much. I signed the contract, left with the car, and prayed that my fate wasn't to drive a red Plymouth Neon for the rest of my life. It wasn't even a Dodge Neon. It was a Plymouth. I know they both had the same parent company, but the word "Dodge" just sounded a little tougher than the word "Plymouth." It just didn't seem like a very good car, and as I was soon to learn, it wasn't.

Of course, just like any car on 41A, the Neon also came with the typical 30 day, as-is warranty. By now I was accustomed to this. After having the car for about 6 months, it seemed like it started to have every problem imaginable. Out of the blue one day my driver's side tire burst while I was driving home to Saint Johnsville for a 4 day weekend. I ended up having to change the tire and put the doughnut spare tire on. The problem with this was that I was low on money at the time, so I ended up having to drive around with a doughnut tire for a little over a month. That's embarrassing by the way. There was also a problem with the wiring of the Stereo system. When I signed for the car, ASAC installed an aftermarket CD player in it for me free of charge so I could have the comfort of listening to CDs. They called it a "free gift." It was an aftermarket brand stereo that I had never heard of and thus I can't remember the brand. All I do remember about the brand name was it seemed like something you would buy at a dollar store. Anyway, whoever installed it must have messed up on the wiring because there was absolutely no bass, and the music always sounded like the treble was turned all the way up. This not only got very annoying, but very painful as well. After a while the high pitch was too much for the speakers to handle and every so often they would let out an even higher pitched scream which would not only hurt my ears but distract me while I was driving. Everyone I knew made fun of me for having that stereo in the car. Of course, ASAC refused to replace it. After all, I was outside of my 30 day warranty. Eventually, the high pitch music and the high pitch screaming became too much for the speakers and one of them just blew. Trying to listen to music in stereo when one speaker is blown is very hard to do. Also, the Neon was made of 95% plastic and fiberglass; unlike the Beretta which at least had some steel to protect me. I knew if I did get into an accident with the Neon, that plastic wasn't protecting me. The car also didn't have much horsepower, which made the long trips home much harder. I felt like the Neon didn't want to go past 50 MPH. Hands down, I hated this car. It turned out that ASAC wasn't really much of an improvement over Terry Harris, but at least ASAC didn't try to sell me a '92 Dodge Grand Caravan at the scene of my accident.

There was one particular incident regarding the Neon that I will never forget. I was riding around with Jones and Jason. We were most likely on our way to go watch wrestling or something, and suddenly the car stalls. I tried to restart it, and nothing. The electronics in the car didn't work either, so I figured it had to be either the battery, or even worse, the alternator. I ended up flagging someone down to give me a jump. The car started so we took a quick ride to Auto Zone to get the battery tested. The battery was dead. The guy at Auto Zone couldn't tell if the alternator was bad, but he could sell me a new battery. Before buying the new battery, we danced around the idea of getting the old one recharged (which wasn't actually possible). Before I knew it, not only Jason and Jones were cracking jokes about how bad the car was, but the Auto Zone employee was too! Here you had these three guys just laughing it up about how terrible my car was. The new battery would only cost me $40, and the Auto Zone guy made sure to mention that in front of the whole group. So of course, Jason and Jones started cracking even more jokes now; this time about how at this very second in time, my Plymouth Neon was worth no more than $40, the cost of that battery. Thank god it was just the battery that needed replacing, because I have no idea what a plastic alternator for a plastic car would cost. I knew there was one thing that wasn't made of plastic. That thing was my pride. On that day my pride told me to do whatever I could to get out of that terrible car. Unfortunately, that was easier said than done.

Back at the unit, things were starting to change. 1SG Guffy's time on Fort Campbell was up and he was set to leave. His replacement came in and they transferred authority for the company. The day that 1SG Guffy left the 101st SSB had to be the saddest day in the history of that unit. He was a true leader that was loved and respected by everyone. Soldiers adored him, looked up to him, and followed his commands. If that isn't respect, I don't know what is. 1SG Guffy was a hard charger and as I stated earlier, he was like our Hulk Hogan. Unfortunately, nothing lasts forever and it was indeed his time to go. I remember when his replacement came on things changed. He wasn't nearly as nice as 1SG Guffy and he also seemed a lot lazier. Also, the new First Sergeant didn't seem to be the type of guy that would fight for his Soldiers if need be, whether it was on the battlefield or if it was behind closed doors against senior officers. No one really seemed to like him, or even respect him, and as a result the morale in that unit started to take a devastating fall. I could see around me that other Soldiers were slowly starting to not care about their job performance anymore. They also started to lose discipline and a lot of the Soldiers there started getting in trouble and receiving Article 15's. The unit became extremely undisciplined under this new leadership, and I was astounded that one man ended up being the glue that kept that unit together. It was sad to tell you the truth. This was the first time in my career that I had witnessed such circumstances. Unfortunately, it wasn't my last. At this point in my life I learned that sometimes all it took was a change in leadership for a unit to begin to fail. As much as you can possibly hope that this fact isn't true, it is, and as 2002 slowly started to come to a close the 101st SSB was stuck with a less than desirable First Sergeant. Not only did a lot of the unit's discipline begin to falter, but much of my own began to as well. I slowly started to put on weight, caring less about what I ate outside of work. At first I didn't care, until I got onto a scale and realized that I had put on roughly 25 pounds since AIT. Since Christmas and New Years were coming up, I just put off getting the weight off until after the holiday. It's truly amazing how easy it is to put something like losing weight off. You keep putting it off and telling yourself, "Oh ill start next week" or "I'm gonna lose this weight after the holiday." Often times, it doesn't work out that way, as I was soon to find out.

Christmas 2002 came along, and I took the long trip from Fort Campbell to Saint Johnsville in that Plymouth Neon. (This would prove to be one of the final times I would take that trip with that car, thank God!) Things were slowly starting to heat up in the middle-east, and all of us back at the unit could see the writing on the wall. It was only a matter of time before Soldiers from the 101st Airborne Division would be deployed somewhere in the middle-east. Wherever the infantry and aviation units of the 101st went, our PSB had to follow up with Support. At times in the past when only a few units would deploy, the SSB would send a few Personnel and Finance Soldiers to set up a small shop and support them throughout their deployment. Even though they were doing paperwork, those SSB Soldiers were in danger too and would come back home with stories of being attacked on convoys or stories of times that rockets would come flying into their camp. As the idea of deployment started to look like a possible reality, the idea of being attacked also became a reality. When we all went home for Christmas in 2002 there was an unspoken feeling in the unit that this may be the last time a lot of us see our family for a very long time. There was no official word, no deployment orders or anything else of the sort; it just FELT LIKE something was going to happen. I guess when you're stationed at a combat post such as the 101st and you see stuff on the news everyday about the war you start to develop your own reservations about the situation. President George W. Bush had given his famous "Axis of Evil" speech earlier in the beginning of 2002 during his State of the Union Address. He talked about Iraq, North Korea, and Iran being the "Axis of Evil" and labeled them as countries that supported terrorism. Between all of the coverage of 9-11 in 2001 and all the commentary on President Bush's speech, you start to imagine what will happen if you do have to become personally involved, because in all reality it is in your duty description as a United States Soldier to get involved. It just seemed to be only a matter of time.

I tried to have the best time I could at home for my Christmas leave. I like to think I had a good time too. I spent a lot of time with my family, and of course took the time to go hang out with as many of my friends as possible too. Other than the idea of not going home for a while, there was one other eventful thing that took place during that particular vacation. We had just recently had a major snowstorm (after all that is what winter in upstate NY is like) and I was outside the following morning trying to help my dad shovel all of the snow. My Neon was parked alongside the side of the house, and next thing you know, a massive snowdrift falls off of the roof, right onto the Neon, crushing the roof. I stood there and watched this happen. So now I had a Neon that didn't want to start all the time, had a major treble/screaming problem with the stereo, with no horsepower, and now the roof was caved in. Honestly that car was so bad that the snow may have increased the value of that car. The car wasn't totaled however, my dad got the driver's side door opened and managed to gorilla press the roof back up into place. Of course, it wasn't a perfect job, there were lumps all over the roof, but at least I could drive the car. So now to add to the overall embarrassment of being a guy who owns this crappy neon, the neon now has a lumpy roof. Great.

The two weeks of leave flew by relatively quickly, as they always do. I took my final walk around Saint Johnsville, said my byes and got on the road, lumpy roofed Neon and all. I pulled off the 15 hour trip with ease, by now I had been up and down this particular route at least 5 times, so I knew my way perfectly. We also recently brought in a new addition to the NCOER section, a guy by the name of Chad Defrates. Chad was an ex-marine who was formerly a Corporal in the Marine Corps. He took exception to the fact that in the Army the ranks of Private through-Specialist (E-1 through E-4) are automatic based on time in service, while in the Marines the rank of Corporal (E-4) is not automatic, it is something that is earned. He also took great exception to the fact that there was zero discipline in the unit. The Marine Corps was all about discipline. Not only was Chad no longer a Marine, but he was working in an office, which is considered some of the easiest work the Army has to offer (at least through the eyes of a Marine or an Infantryman anyway.) I wished he was here when 1SG Guffy was still around, because the unit was genuinely a better place when he was around. Maybe Chad would have liked the place a lot better. Either way, you could just tell that Chad couldn't stand being there. He was still a model Soldier, and I did look up to him to a certain degree. Here he was one of the most proficient Soldiers we had on a tactical level. He was older than us and already had some life experience. Why wouldn't anyone look up to him? I understood his frustration, he was a leader in a disciplined environment in the past and now he was a junior troop again, here in the SSB. I got along with him really well, even though we would have words at times because he just didn't feel I was disciplined enough. But then he would remind me that it was nothing personal, he felt that way about the whole company. It was nice in an odd way however that he didn't take the job seriously, because that made my performance look that much better. That may sound harsh, but it's true. Put a good worker next to an average worker and the good worker appears to be a great worker. As I said before Chad was a great Soldier on a tactical level but he hated paperwork. Overall, he was a good guy and I am glad to say that when I eventually left Fort Campbell years later that we were friends. One other cool thing that I remembered about Chad was that he used to brew beer in his basement. I was amazed by this. By this time in my life, I occasionally had a drink, by no means was I a drunk but I still thought it was cool that there was someone I knew that brewed beer in his basement. That's not something you see every day.

Remember earlier when I mentioned that there was a "feeling" within the unit that at some point we were going to deploy somewhere to the middle-east? Well as the 2003 got underway, we received our Warning Order to deploy. We weren't 100% sure yet where we were going, but we all thought it was going to be Iraq. At this point there was just too much coverage on the news about Saddam Hussein being a threat to humanity. Constant talk about Saddam having "Weapons of Mass Destruction" was the norm. We now had to start to get our equipment ready for this deployment, as well as get ourselves ready. We spent long days in our motor pool in the cold rain, and sometimes even snow, getting our equipment ready for deployment. We were taking everything; our Humvees, tents, camouflage nets, Generators, First Aid Kits, you name it. As the old saying goes, we were taking everything except the kitchen sink. The idea that we were bringing our own tents also further cemented the idea that we were going to Iraq. Iraq meant a full scale invasion of a new country, as opposed to settling in on established sites in Afghanistan. An established site would have its own tents. Here we were bringing ours. So even though the word wasn't "official" that we were going to Iraq, common sense just pointed in that direction. Also during this time we started doing a lot of Chemical Training. We would spend hours in our chemical suits and masks "just to get acclimated." I found it very hard to sit at my desk in the NCOER section with a mask on and do my job. It felt claustrophobic. But I pushed on, just like everyone else. The idea of leaving the United States for the first time in my life actually excited me. I always heard how the best gift the Army can give you is free travel, and up until now all of that travel was restricted to various states. I was ready to get on a plane and go to another country. That would be a real trip. As time dragged by and we continued to train and pack, we finally received our official deployment orders. The orders were for Iraq but they would not limit our service to there, as the orders covered other countries such as Kuwait, Qatar, and Jordan as well. Later on I would learn exactly what this had meant. At the time it didn't matter, we all knew where we were going, and that was Iraq. The date on our deployment orders read: "O/A 01 MARCH 2003". That stood for: on or about the date of March 1, 2003. This was as real as it got, especially considering we were in early February. It quickly settled in that I wasn't going to get another chance to go home and see everyone before the deployment. I called my dad later that evening to give him the news. Of course I would get the chance to talk to him many more times before March 1 since we still had a few weeks left, but he still told me to be careful over there anyway. Everything on the news made the threat seem very real, and he didn't want to lose his son. I understood the threat of going into a place like that, but I was still very excited to go regardless. Travel was travel as far as I was concerned, and not only that, I did have a duty to fulfill as a Soldier. Had I seen all of the coverage on the news and I didn't end up deploying I would have felt empty inside. I would have felt like I didn't contribute. So I guess deep down, I needed something like this.

One final task that our unit had to complete prior to deployment was the rail load. The rail load is where they would load all of our equipment that we had previously packed up onto a train. This would include driving our Humvees onto rail carts as well, which is much harder than one would think. Once our equipment was on the train, it would be taken to a seaport. There, everything we loaded would be put on a ship and sent to Kuwait, which would take about 3 to 4 weeks to arrive. Essentially, the rail load was the last time we would see our equipment before we arrived to Kuwait. Loading your vehicles and trailers onto the rail is an extremely lengthy process. You end up waiting in line behind hundreds of other vehicles just waiting to slowly drive up a ramp and park the Humvee and chain it down. The reason there were hundreds of vehicles in line was because they were all somehow scheduled for the same day. I guess whoever planned this out was considering the idea of "rapid deployment," but the execution didn't end up being such. Instead you had many units, with hundreds of vehicles waiting in line, sitting completely still in the freezing cold. This boils down to the basic idea I stated earlier in this book of how not everything in the Army makes sense. This was one of those times; for the welfare of the freezing Soldiers they could have organized this better so only a couple of units passed through per day. Also, for your vehicles to travel overseas they had to have the canvas tops removed from them, so we had no cover to protect us from the elements. The strange thing about this was that it happened to be one of those days that it was actually snowing on Fort Campbell. It really sucked; we were sitting their freezing our asses off with absolutely no idea how long this would take. I was the driver of my Humvee, and Jones was my passenger. To pass the time we made jokes about how there was a "Fort Campbell weather machine" that intentionally made the weather bad when Soldiers had to be outside. If this sounds anything like the "weather dominator" from the cartoon GI Joe, that's good, because it should. After all, that's where Jones and I got the idea. Such tom foolery and dumb jokes had become commonplace in my unit, between myself, Jones, and even Cursey. The thing is, sometimes in the Army when you are faced with one of these endlessly crappy situations, dumb humor can serve as an effective tool to get yourself through it. You crack stupid jokes with your fellow comrades about the dumbest of things in an effort to lighten the mood and get through this. It is just another way how Soldiers look out for each other. We all knew we had a crappy task that we had to get through, and the best way was through the use of humor.

The most memorable part of that rail load wasn't the extreme cold, the disorganization, or even the bad jokes. Instead, the most memorable part of this night came in the form of a man walking all the way down the entire line of Humvees, taking the time to shake the hands of the driver and passenger of each vehicle. This wasn't just any man, however. This man was Major General David Petraeus, who was then the Division Commander of the 101st Airborne Division. Years Later General Petraeus would end up earning his third and fourth star and end up taking even higher positions of command, but for now General Petraeus was our Division Commander. He had been credited as the inspiration for why PT in the 101st was so challenging, since he was an excellent athlete in his own right. Tonight General Petraeus didn't care about the cold or anything else, his Soldiers were out there in the freezing cold and by god he was going to make sure that he shook the hands of each and every one of his troops, even though there were thousands of troops out there. I had a lot of respect for him up until now, and his actions on this night gave me even more reason to respect him. As a General, he most certainly did not have to be out there, but he was. That is a true sign of a good leader; the acts of getting out there in the tough situations where your troops are, letting them realize that you too are still a Soldier. 1SG Guffy did the same thing when he would get down in the trenches with his Soldiers at the M16 range, and General Petraeus was doing the same thing now. He was about to take his entire division on a deployment to Iraq, with all sorts of dangers and surprises ahead. We were the troops in that very division. The same surprises and dangers that he was facing, we were also facing, only as a leader it is far more different because you have the idea of not bringing Soldiers home on your conscience. A leader never wants to leave one of his Soldiers behind, no matter how high up in the rank structure a leader goes, a real leader will always hold this true. Years later when I would turn on CNN and see General Petraeus on talking about the situations in Iraq and Afghanistan, I would feel a little bit of pride deep down inside of me, not just because I was seeing someone that I met in the past on TV, but also because that was a true leader that I had the honor of serving under.

In the days following the completion of the rail load, we spent our last remaining time finalizing our preparations for the deployment. We all packed our bags up, bought last minute hygiene items and bags of beef jerky from the local Wal-Mart. The unit was briefed on the fact that the country that we were going to invade was mostly a dessert wasteland aside from the major cities. We knew there were next to no amenities there and we would be surviving off of whatever we took with us. Even though I was excited to go, I knew deep down that this would probably be the most challenging events of my life. As a unit there were a lot of "cliques" which were more or less small groups of Soldiers that stuck together. I knew who my friends were: Cursey, Jones, Defrates, Reynolds and a few others. We were going over there with some good NCOs, but the First Sergeant was messed up. The days of 1SG Guffy were long gone, but we knew that we could still pull it together and make it through this deployment. The night before we were supposed to fly we were all required to be on lockdown status at the unit area and await our bus from the flight line. Many units will fly through civilian airports when traveling overseas but for this deployment we were going to fly out of the airfield on Fort Campbell. There were so many emotions in the air: excitement, nervousness, and even sadness for those Soldiers who were leaving behind family. I took the time to call home to Dad one last time before I went home. I wasn't sure when the next time I would talk to him would be. We were all briefed that there weren't working phones everywhere, and internet was also just as scarce. Therefore, we would be restricted to the use of regular letter mail, affectionately referred to as "snail mail." My dad told me to be careful, and that he couldn't wait for me to come back. He also told me he was extremely proud of me. This made me get a little choked up, but I got it together. For now we all had a mission to deploy to Iraq on what would prove to make history. The journey that we were all about to embark upon would later end up being taught in History Classes to kids in school, right alongside both World Wars, Vietnam, the Gulf War, and so many others. Finally the bus came. It was time to go. We rode to the flight line and took a look at the 747 that we were about to board. As we got on that plane, none of us really knew when we would be home since the orders were open-ended and this was the first deployment to Iraq during this invasion. The only thing we knew was that despite the type of work that we did for a living, we still had something to contribute, a mission to accomplish. Now, we would go and accomplish that mission.

CHAPTER 4

THE INVASION OF IRAQ-2003

The date was March 1, 2003. The media was buzzing with all of the talk of the "War on Terror." Constant coverage was being given not only to the fact that the United States had troops in Afghanistan, but also to the fact that the Bush Administration was set on removing Saddam Hussein from office in Iraq. Saddam Hussein was an evil dictator who had ruled over the people of Iraq with an evil, oppressive fist for decades. Those who crossed Saddam were punished through various ways, not just by going to jail, but also through torture and even through death. Saddam would hold grudges against people who crossed him even after he killed them, so often he would kill that individual's family. Saddam once plotted to have former President George H.W. Bush assassinated. Saddam was also guilty of using Weapons of Mass destruction against the Kurdish who lived in Northern Iraq. The US was concerned that Saddam could potentially use the same weapons against his neighbors in the middle-east and also against the US. The time had finally come for someone to take action, and that "someone" was the United States of America. I need to stress that the events that I am about to write about in this chapter are among some of the proudest moments of my entire life. My deployment to Iraq in 2003 will be one of those things that I tell stories about forever. I will never forget what happened there and there really isn't much to compare to it (aside from other deployments that would come in the future.) Also, regardless of what some other Soldiers felt about this war, I did indeed agree with everything that I had heard on TV, that Saddam Hussein was evil and did need to be removed from office. Since he wasn't willing to step down willingly he needed to be removed the hard way. Usually that is how it goes when it comes to dictators. Hitler didn't step down, he committed suicide. Saddam didn't step down either. Instead, he waited for the US to invade his nation, which he had ruled for so long under his oppressive fist of tyranny.

After the long 15 hour flight we finally arrived to Kuwait. Over the course of the flight we had 3 layovers, (in Newfoundland, Ireland, and Cyprus) all of which were at least 6 hours in length, so in all actuality we were traveling for over 30 hours. I thought it was pretty cool that on the way over to Iraq we stopped in so many places. We were able to get out of the plane, go into the terminal and stretch out, buy a few souvenirs, maybe even call home. So far it was a matter of sightseeing and what not, but now that we had finally touched down into Kuwait things started to get real. We settled into a place called Camp Udarri for the next few weeks. Camp Udarri was a transient camp used for Soldiers who were in transit into Iraq, waiting for their vehicles and equipment to come into the port. (Remember, the rail load). It was basically a stretch of land in the middle of the dessert with a bunch of circus tents set up for Soldiers to sleep in. I remember it being so hot there, often getting as hot as 120 degrees. It also got windy often, so you not only had to deal with the hot wind in your face which was painful enough but also the sandstorms from all the sand that would come up off the ground. The sandstorms would get so bad that everyone would have to relocate into their respective tents and wait out the storms. I guess you could compare it to trying to hold a picnic back home in the US, but then it downpours and everyone has to rush into the house. Of course, there are a few major differences, one being you don't have a house, you have a circus tent, and also it wasn't raining, it was dry sand. It would get so dry in Udarri that my hands would dry out and I ended up coming down with a case of eczema for a little while.

Conditions in Udarri were harsh not just from a weather standpoint, but also from a logistics standpoint. There were many troops there, not just from the 101st but also from other divisions such as the 3rd Infantry Division (based out of Ft Stewart, GA) as well as some Marines. Camp Udarri was well over its capacity and as a result Soldiers were not allowed to take showers every single day. The water trucks would only come in twice a week, so it worked out that we could only shower 3 times a week. There were so many Soldiers there and the water would constantly run out, so there was no other choice. The problem with this was that it was so hot that we were always sweating, and there was almost always a sandstorm so we were dirty most of the time as well. When you would go and take your allocated shower, it really didn't matter much because within 30 seconds of leaving the shower trailer you were covered in sand. Obviously this didn't stop me or any of the other Soldiers from taking their showers when the time came. At this point in our lives a Shower was so much more than a privilege. It was something to look forward to. It's amazing how you miss the little things. Laundry also became an issue because of the water problem. When it came to getting our laundry cleaned, we had 2 options: turn it into the Kuwaiti laundry service that came by twice a week, or to wash it on our own by hand with water bottles. First I tried option 1 but my laundry came back to me stinking of kerosene. In case you have never tried wearing clothes that smell as if they were drenched in kerosene, I'll just tell you now, they stink. Do not try this. Of course I didn't know they would come back this bad so I was restricted to option number two, washing my own clothes by hand. I had bottled water at my disposal, and there was a small exchange shopette on the camp that you could buy very basic amenities. They didn't have laundry soap, but they did have vanilla scented shampoo. Since the shampoo was my last resort, I picked up a few bottles and got to work. I must say that sitting outside in the hot Kuwaiti sun and washing your own clothes with vanilla shampoo is possibly one of the most humbling experiences I ever had to go through, and believe me that is saying a lot. As much as it sucked, I just told myself that this was part of the job. Things aren't always going to be perfect. Sometimes you are going to have to be stuck with crappy circumstances, and this was one of those times.

In addition to the water problem at Camp Udarri, there was also a food problem. Camp Udarri had a decent DFAC that served pretty good food given the circumstances. The problem with this DFAC was that it was burned down 2 days before we arrived to Udarri. Therefore, we were stuck eating MREs (meals ready to eat). An MRE can either be really good or really bad depending on which one you get. The problem was even if you get the very best MRE, (which in my opinion was Beef Ravioli) you still didn't want to eat them 3 times a day. Luckily a Kitchen tent ended up getting set up on Udarri, however it only served breakfast. What made this even more "comical" was that every day breakfast consisted of 2 hard-boiled eggs, 1 hot dog, and a scoop of white rice. This was probably the worst breakfast I have ever had, but it was still a lot better than an MRE. Over the next few weeks we all just got used to our breakfast and were thankful that we were at least getting some sort of hot food every day.

As it turned out our biggest concern of all at Camp Udarri wasn't the water issue or the food issue. Instead, our biggest problem there was the whole reason we were sent here in the first place: Saddam. US troops were in Kuwait awaiting orders to move in and cross the border into Iraq. Obviously Saddam took exception to this, so he started to fire Scud missiles at Kuwaiti camps. I guess he figured he could at least slow us down by firing Scuds at us. They were fired off almost daily. Most times US Patriot missiles would intercept them and destroy them in the air. Only a few actually hit Kuwaiti soil and there were never any reported casualties, at least in my unit there wasn't. The problem with these Scuds wasn't just the fact that they were being fired as missiles. There was also the WMD threat. No one knew if the Scud missiles themselves were loaded with gas or not, so every time one was fired at us we would have to don our Gasmasks and chemical suits. We would sit there in our masks and suits sometimes for hours waiting for the "all clear" signal. This became a huge problem for us because we would end up sweating our asses off in our chemical gear in the 120 degree weather. Just the idea of having to do this once is a horrible idea, but having to do it every single day in the heat is just outright inhumane. I guess that's one of the many sacrifices you have to make in war.

SPECIAL NOTE: Today when I hear the media and politicians talk about the war in Iraq, I often hear a lot of negativity. Most of this negativity refers to President Bush invading Iraq on bad intelligence because there were never any WMDs found in Iraq. I take great exception to this because I was part of the initial invasion, and I lived through the above mentioned Scud Missile attacks. My reasoning for taking this personally is a matter of personal theory, which I will gladly share with you now. I stated above that most of the Scud missiles were destroyed by US Patriot missiles. I still hold true to my heart that there is no way of knowing if those missiles possessed poisonous gas because of the fact that they were destroyed before they got anywhere near us. I do understand that no WMDs were found in Iraq (at least that's what the media claims) but I will never, ever dismiss the notion that those missiles may have been more than just average missiles. It is purely speculation, my own opinion if you will, and I am indeed entitled to my own opinion. The main thing to take under consideration is that we will never know what those missiles possessed. What I do know is that I did live through the days of having to sit in 120 degrees under the Kuwaiti sun in full chemical gear. I know how much I hated doing that, and I know how much I hate the media consistently burying the Bush Administration for something that can't truly be confirmed in my opinion. And remember the word: OPNION.

For the most part in Kuwait we killed time working out at the small weight tent and playing cards with my fellow Soldiers in the giant circus tents that we had to live in. I had set out to lose the weight that I had gained recently at Campbell so I was spending as much time in the weight tent as possible. I figured between working out in the heat and sitting in the heat wearing my chemical gear I could lose the weight. This was pretty much all we did while we waited for our vehicles and equipment to arrive at the port. I can remember the day they finally came in and we had to go and retrieve them. We took a bus down to the port, which was a nice break from sitting on Udarri. We all hated Udarri and any excuse to get off of that camp was gladly welcomed. It was so boring there and the place was an utter toilet. When we arrived at the port it was strangely refreshing to see our vehicles and equipment, in an odd way. Obviously what we were looking at was just equipment, but it was OUR equipment that we prepared at home in Fort Campbell and sent overseas. I wouldn't say that it was a taste of home, but it was certainly a reminder of home. For many of us on that deployment (myself included) it was our first time deployed. This didn't just pertain to the younger Soldiers such as me; many of our leaders in the SSB had never seen a deployment in their entire career up until now.

The trip back to Udarri was quite an adventure in itself. We convoyed back as a unit however this was the first time most of us had been on a real life convoy outside of any sort of convoy training. On an organizational basis, there was a ton of disorder on this convoy due to this fact alone. In our brief we were told to keep the convoy together, to try not to go so fast that the vehicle behind you loses you. Well, it seemed like those rules went out the window. People were driving like madmen, speeding, passing each other, sometimes even driving alongside the convoy instead of directly in line with the rest of the convoy. I was driving my vehicle, and my TC was my good old buddy Jones. I can say that throughout much of my journey in the 101st Airborne Division Jones was probably one of the Soldiers I could rely on the most. We stuck together, on this night included. There were a ton of potholes on the trip also and we kept hitting them. Keep in mind; we were hitting these potholes at full speed. It wasn't like we were slowing down to 10 or 15 MPH to go over these potholes. No, we were taking these potholes at 45 or 50 MPH. As you can probably imagine this wasn't the most pleasant feeling in the world. We also had no roof or doors on these Humvees, since we were required to remove all of them for the rail load back at Campbell. Of course, without our roof and doors a lot of our gear flew out of the vehicle, never to be seen or heard from again. In addition, sand was a major problem on this convoy also. Most of the route took place over dessert roads, thus we were driving through a lot of sand. Without our roof and doors the sand got to us. We were wearing safety goggles, but there is only so much they can do to keep the sand out of your eyes, not to mention the crazy amount of sand that would get in our mouths. Hands down this was the craziest thing I had done at this point in my army career. The entire time we were struggling to keep up, hitting potholes and yelling each other's names to make sure we were ok. I remember shouting, "JONES!" and in return I would hear, "CONKLIN!" That is how I knew that Jones was still alive, the fact that he was able to yell "CONKLIN!" back to me.

Despite all of the adversity that I just mentioned, there was still one particular incident of the convoy that sticks out above all of the others: a SCUD attack. I had thought and hoped that maybe we could just get through this mission without one of those attacks, but that definitely wasn't the case. Up in the sky we saw a huge explosion and then we heard the Convoy Commander come over the radio and shout the gas attack signal, "GAS! GAS! GAS!" In front of us we saw all of the other Humvees come to a screeching halt so everyone could don their protective masks. The positive was that I didn't have to worry about any more sand getting in my eyes or mouth. The negative was that now I had to drive with a gas mask on, which isn't very easy to do. It ended up being very hard to drive with the mask on, since wearing a mask seriously limits your peripheral vision. I did notice however that the convoy speed slowed down significantly when everyone was masked, which for safety purposes was a good sign. Before long, we heard the "ALL CLEAR" signal over the radio and we were able to remove our masks. It was such a relief to take the mask off and feel the fresh air on my face. The funny thing that I realized that night was how much everyone calmed down after the attack. Here you had a unit driving across the Kuwaiti desert like a bunch of madmen, and all it took was one SCUD missile attack to restore some order. The rest of the convoy went by smoothly, and we safely returned to Camp Udarri. It was late at night and we all needed some sleep, but before we had the opportunity to go to bed our First Sergeant made sure to take the time to yell at the whole unit for performing so horribly during the convoy. Granted, there were a lot of mistakes made that night, but I am a firm believer in the phrase, "lead from the front." I can honestly say on this night that his driver in his vehicle didn't perform that well either. The onus may have been on all of us, but it was on him as well.

Once we had our vehicles and equipment at Udarri with us, there wasn't really much left to do in Kuwait except wait for orders to advance into Iraq. At the time no one knew exactly when that would take place, so in an effort to kill time we set up a work tent to attempt to provide personnel service functions to the Soldiers who were on Udarri. I'm not going to say this was a bad idea, but I will say this much: even with the tent set up and established "open" hours of business, we were still almost as bored as we were without the work tent. We had maybe three customers come in every day, and it wasn't because there wasn't anyone there, in fact there were too many Soldiers on Udarri. The reason we didn't have a lot of business in our makeshift personnel services tent is because the other units on Udarri weren't exactly worried about turning in their paperwork to the local personnel office. Instead, they were more worried about getting ready for their upcoming missions, and rightfully so. We, the SSB were clearly ready for our mission since our mission as a unit was to provide personnel support. Some of those days in that tent got so boring. The internet there was close to non-existent; it would sometimes work and sometimes not work. The phones were the same, and to get on a working phone and call home required waiting in an extremely long line. Also, waiting in that extremely long phone line meant waiting in the heat which wasn't always a sacrifice we were willing to make. Of course it was just as hot in the tent, but we didn't have to stand in the tent. Some days out there it would get to 115 degrees, and that was just in March. In the summer it is so much worse. Sometimes when I reflect back on those days I still do not know how we all made it through. I guess we made it based on necessity, the fact that we didn't have any other choice but to survive.

After sitting in Kuwait for a little over 2 weeks, there was finally some major news. On March 17, 2003 President George W. Bush gave another speech. In this speech, he gave Saddam an ultimatum to step down from power within 48 hours or the United States would finally invade Iraq and forcefully remove him from power. Saddam was a ruthless dictator who ruled Iraq with an iron fist. It was time for him to go. The 48 hours went by, and Saddam hadn't surrendered, so it was time for the US to invade. We had been sitting there in Udarri for weeks so we were anxious to move on and get things started. There's only so much sitting around a Soldier could take. The combat units rolled across the border first, and a few days later the SSB was given clearance to cross the border. The unit was going to cross on its own, as a battalion. Nowadays in the Army, this is rarely done. Usually if a support unit needs to convoy somewhere they will travel with an Infantry Unit or a Military Police unit. This time however, was different. Our Commander had no idea how long we were going to be in Iraq for. No one seemed to know, so we all viewed this as a short term mission. The Commander had gotten wind that there was going to be one or two units that would stay on Camp Udarri for the next few weeks or months (however long this mission took) so he decided to leave a five Soldier team behind to run personnel functions on Udarri while the rest of the battalion crossed the border into Iraq. I ended up being one of those five Soldiers. It was very heartbreaking to see the rest of the unit leave without us. I felt like we had gotten ready for something for so long, and then we ended up being deprived of that very thing we had been preparing for. It was disappointing to say the least. Sure, life on Udarri was sure to be much easier than in Iraq, but that wasn't what I wanted. I wanted to be there with my brothers in arms. I wanted to be there in the harsh conditions right alongside SGT Ramos, Jones, Cursey, Defrates, and everyone else. I didn't want to be stuck in boring Udarri while my friends were going on this big adventure. So the unit ended up leaving, and the five of us sat and twiddled our thumbs for about a week. It was so boring. We had no customers, even from the few small units that stayed behind. We were supposed to be there to support those units but they had nothing to offer us. I began to contemplate just how bad this deployment would be if I had to sit on Udarri for the entire tour. The only story I would have for my family was the convoy back from the port. Granted, that was exciting but one story tends to get old after a while, especially if that story didn't even take place where the war actually was, which was in Iraq. During one of the times that we had a working internet connection I decided to start searching the Army Knowledge Online (AKO) database for old friends that I had lost touch with. I immediately searched for Kathy. I hadn't seen her since the end of AIT, which by now was close to a year and I definitely missed her a lot. I knew deep down that I was wrong for not saying goodbye the proper way when we had finished AIT, and I definitely knew that I wanted to get back into contact with her. I was very interested to know how the NJ National Guard was treating her. Luckily for me, she ended up getting my message and immediately emailed me back. It was great to hear from her and we caught up over the course of the rest of the deployment. It was my mistake for not trying to reach her sooner, and I guess that my loneliness at Camp Udarri caused me to do some soul searching and realize the mistake I made in the past. That's the thing about mistakes: if we are lucky, we learn from them. This experience definitely caused me to learn, that's for sure. Even though I was deployed, I made it a personal mission to visit Kathy someday.

One day, I awoke to see that the other units on Udarri were getting ready to leave. Where were they going? Well, they were going into Iraq of course. They had all received word from their higher headquarters to pack up and head to Iraq. This was great news for me because it signaled to me that there was a chance we would get to leave too. Before long, we got that chance. There was just one problem however: we didn't have any Humvees. The rest of the unit took them all with them. As a 19 year old Private First Class I had no idea how we would get across the border. The solution that was soon revealed to us by our Officer in Charge (OIC) was that we would be flying in on a CH-47 Chinook helicopter. This really excited me, since it was the first time in my entire life that I would fly on a helicopter. (Thankfully, it certainly did not end up being my last.)

The five of us ventured to the flight line to take the flight into Iraq. I was so excited to know that I was finally going to get my chance to go into Iraq. I was so sick of Udarri, and I had too much pride to go home and tell my family that I stayed in Kuwait for the whole tour. Of course, in typical Army fashion, our flight wasn't on time. In fact, our flight was so late that it ended up taking place the following morning. To this day I am still not sure if it was because the pilot needed rest or if the helicopter needed maintenance, but either way we were stuck. Since we had already traveled all the way to the flight line we weren't about to head back. We ended up staying the night at the flight line and slept under the stars. This was a bit of an odd experience for me, especially because I ended up experiencing the nighttime temperature drop for the first time out in the open. Granted the convoy back from the port took place at night, but there was so much adrenaline flowing the night of the convoy that I could hardly notice that it was chilly at night. This night however was different. The temperature dropped at least 30 degrees, which is quite a drop when you're used to consistent heat. I laid there on the pavement of the flight line in my sleeping bag trying my best to sleep. I wasn't just dealing with the chilly temperature, but also with the sheer excitement of knowing that tomorrow morning I would be leaving the country of Kuwait and flying into the country of Iraq. Needless to say I had a lot to sleep on.

After getting a few hours of sleep, we all woke up ready to go. I found myself a piece of ground just off of the flight line to knock out my shaving. Contrary to popular belief, standards are standards in the Army, and you still have to shave when you're deployed. I didn't want to get to Iraq and have SGT Ramos catch me for not shaving. He was strict on things like that. After hanging out and enjoying an MRE for breakfast, we boarded the helicopter. Right before boarding I had a fellow Soldier take a picture of me on the side of the Chinook doing the classic Hulk Hogan "bow and arrow" pose. I like to do this pose whenever I go to a new place; it's like my way of putting a personal stamp on whatever place I am visiting at the moment. Granted, I stole the pose from the Hulkster himself, but I am sure he won't mind. Up until that part in my career the only major places I had taken a picture with the pose was in front of my gym, (before it closed of course) the University of South Carolina when I was in Fort Jackson, the Fort Campbell Gate, and in the seat of a Humvee the night of the convoy back from the port. Therefore there was just no way that I was going to pass up the opportunity to break out the legendary pose just before riding in a helicopter for the first time in my life.

When we boarded the Chinook, the pilot told us that there was a third seat in the cockpit for a Soldier to sit in if they wanted to have a better view. They asked for volunteers, but no one in the crowd volunteered. I thought to myself, "you only live once" and I decided to take the pilot up on his offer. I saddled up in the middle seat of the cockpit and watched everything. I had a portable CD player that I could use to listen to during the flight and I sat back and enjoyed not only the ride, but also the view. This was such an amazing experience. I was gazing off into the Iraqi countryside from the cockpit of a CH-47 Chinook helicopter. Obviously the Iraqi countryside is nothing like the American countryside. Unlike the American countryside, there were no forests, lakes, or trees. Instead, there was nothing but baron dessert; a wasteland if you will. Occasionally I would see a small settlement of Iraqi people living in tents in the middle of nowhere. I wondered to myself how the hell they could possibly survive, without a nearby body of water to drink, in addition to the fact that I just couldn't see how there was any wildlife for them to hunt to eat for survival. The image not only puzzled me, but amazed me. This was truly a third world country. I felt bad for the people, but at the same time, there was always the chance that this was considered the "good life" in this country. I didn't know too much about Iraqi culture, but I did know that Saddam had kept the riches in that country for himself. Since the only rich people were the people that owned the oil or the people that worked for Saddam, I asked myself "what exactly is considered poor in this country?" Were the nomads that I was looking down at from the helicopter considered poor? Or were they considered "lucky" that they were so far from Saddam's evil grasp? It was at this point that I realized that there is so much more in this world than just American culture. The world isn't just what you see in the US. There are so many more countries with different cultures, customs, and political climates. It's possible that here in Iraq those people weren't really considered to be doing that bad compared to others. Of course, in the US those people are considered homeless, poor, etc., but once again we were no longer in the US. Over the course of this deployment I would learn the painful fact that this country did not have a middle class, only the super-rich and the extremely poor. By seeing this contrast I realized just how important the middle class was to our own country, the US. Iraq was such a different world, and although I was glad that I could contribute to liberating Iraq in some way, I am truly proud to say that my country doesn't live that way. Today when I hear the phrase, "god bless the USA" I always think back to that day in the helicopter when I saw those families living out in the middle of nowhere, just trying to survive.

After a quick flight we finally arrived to our destination, which was a camp called Iskandaria. It was located near a village called "Iskan," thus the name "Iskandaria." I guess we shouldn't really credit the US for being very original, after all my camp in Kuwait (Udarri) was the only one with a name that even sounded Kuwaiti. The other camps in Kuwait were named Camp New York, Camp New Jersey, Camp Virginia, and Camp Pennsylvania. How original; I wonder where they got those names from? Iskandaria was yet another wasteland similar to Udarri, with only a few minor differences. For one, there were a lot of wild dogs walking around the camp that would start howling early in the morning, sometimes when we were still sleeping. If for some reason the dog howling didn't awaken us, there was no reason to worry, because we were also getting woken up from the Muslim prayers that would be broadcast over the loudspeaker in the nearby village of Iskan. It became like clockwork, every single morning promptly at 5 am we would hear the prayer. After a while we all got used to hearing it and started to get to the point where we no longer noticed it. This scared me a little because I wasn't sure if I would end up missing hearing the prayers every morning when I returned to the US. Another major difference at Iskandaria was the difference in the sand. The sand here was finer sand than what was found in Udarri, and by just walking around the camp we would kick a lot of it up without realizing it. The sand would almost always get in my mouth, which can be quite tedious when you are trying to go out for a morning run, or when you are sitting under the sun enjoying your lunch.

When I arrived everyone in the unit was glad to see me. Jones and Cursey had all kinds of wild stories about how the convoy went. It seemed like they had a little bit of an adventure on the convoy and I was envious that I had to miss out. Then again I did get the privilege of flying in the cockpit of the Chinook, but that still wouldn't have been as cool as if I rode alongside my fellow Soldiers on that convoy. I was part of this team and I didn't appreciate being put in a position where I wasn't alongside the team. There was also a legitimate work tent set up at Iskandaria and there were enough units there that we actually ended up having steady work to do. This made me happy because getting to do my job again returned a sense of normalcy to the deployment. There weren't any working phones on Iskandaria, but there was dedicated internet in our work tent. The internet was an even bigger bonus because I could stop relying on the "snail mail" and just email back home to my family and friends. When you are thousands of miles away in a warring country it really does help to have a direct line to home.

Another thing that I noticed about Iskandaria was the SCUD missile attacks were now non-existent. This had to do with the fact that Saddam had went into hiding as soon as we started to cross the border. Most of the Iraqi Army had surrendered since they were only serving because they were forced into it to begin with. That is the one major difference that the US Army has in comparison to the rest of the world; the fact that we have an all-volunteer Army. Many other countries aren't like that, to include Iraq under Saddam's rule. The next couple of weeks ended up being quiet, normal routine. We would get up in the morning, do some PT, and then go to the work tent. Granted, we didn't have any real amenities, we were taking "showers" with bottled water and eating MREs for 2 out of our 3 meals each day, but other than that everything was feeling ok. It almost felt too good to be in a war zone. We all started to speculate when we would be heading back home to the US. No one really knew, all we knew was that Saddam had to be removed from office, and that was taken care of when he went into hiding. Throughout all of our speculation as to when we were going to go home various rumors started to sprout up. Some rumors were spread that we would be going home by July 4th because General Petraeus wanted us back at Fort Campbell to march in a parade. Other rumors that were spread saying that we were going to be home by Christmas 2003. The idea of being home for Christmas is an idea that would make almost any Soldier happy, providing they celebrate Christmas that is. The one fact that stood out amongst all of the rumors however was the fact that no one really knew when we were going home. It was all just speculation. Sure, we were all together on the same camp, laughing it up and trying to keep each other's spirits high, but all in all we all missed our families and we all resented the fact that this deployment had open-ended orders. As the month of May 2003 began, we painfully realized that despite everything that we had been through, we were in reality only there for about 2 months and there was no telling what else was in store for us. Slowly but surely, the routine on Iskandaria slowly got boring, just as it had on Udarri. Luckily for me, there was some adventure right around the corner.

A tasking came down to our battalion to provide a small team of Soldiers to go up to Mosul Airfield and provide personnel support for a small group of Soldiers who were going to be convoying up there. The Mosul Airport terminal had recently been cleared out and was going to be set up as some sort of base for US troops. No one really knew exactly what the purpose of the base would be. All we really knew was that we now had a mission to provide support. The tasking only required about 7 Soldiers, which included an Officer and an NCO, along with a few junior Soldiers. Those who were chosen would ride up to Mosul on a convoy and assist in setting up operations up there. When choosing which Soldiers to send up there, the SSB had to be careful to send a variety of expertise, which meant one Soldier from each of the main sections: ID Cards, Actions, Evaluations, and Promotions. Out of the Evaluations section, SGT Ramos chose me to go on the mission. I was honored to go, not only because it finally was going to give me some convoy experience in Iraq, but also because being chosen by SGT Ramos was a sign of trust. There was no one else going that knew NCO evaluations, meaning that I would be working on my own. He chose me because he knew I was up to the task. He knew that I had enough knowledge to survive on my own while the other Soldiers in the evaluations section needed more monitoring. I think deep down he knew that he trained me well and all those times at Campbell when he would flip out on me and throw stacks of my reports on the floor actually paid off.

We left Iskandaria early one morning on a convoy that consisted of a few different elements. There were infantry Soldiers with us along with civilian contractors. When the invasion kicked off there were various corporations that sent contractors to different parts of the country for all sorts of reasons. Mosul was no different; there would be contractors there too. I was under the impression that I was going to have to drive, but as it turned out another Soldier was assigned the task so I ended up provide security on the trip. Much of the areas that we passed through were deserted so I managed to snap a few pictures. I was unsure of the idea of taking pictures, but when I looked in the front seat and saw our officer in charge taking all kinds of pictures I figured it was ok. Today I have a huge envelope of pictures from that deployment, and from time to time I take them out to reminisce on the good old days. So much time has passed since then.

Not every part of the country that we passed through was empty wastelands and deserted towns. We also had to pass through a fair amount of population just to get to Mosul and when we got to Mosul we had to drive through the city just to make it to the airport terminal where we would be stationed. Moving through the city was much slower than moving through the dessert. We had to be careful not to run anyone over. As we passed through, hundreds of Iraqis would flock to us, giving us the thumbs up and saying, "Thank you Amrika, Bush Good!" The word "Amrika" was their way of saying "America" and saying "Bush Good!" was their way of saying they approved of President Bush's decision to take Saddam out of power. It was a good feeling and it made my chest swell up with pride. Back home in the US everyone supported the troops, but not everyone supported the idea of the war. To me, I was on board with the idea of knocking Saddam out of power, so it made me feel really good inside that I was part of this. This was a huge deal for America, and an even bigger deal for Iraq.

When we got to Mosul Airfield, the place was completely empty, with nothing but a wire fence surrounding the outside of the camp. We pulled in, lined up our vehicles and immediately began to set up shop. It was then that I realized that I was indeed one of first 100 Soldiers on this camp. It was also then that I realized that this deployment was now the biggest adventure of my life. Since there were so few of us, we didn't even bother to set up tents outside of the terminal, we just slept in the terminal instead. Our OIC thought it would be a great idea to set up a small tent on the roof of the terminal for him to sleep in. All of us junior Soldiers ended up having to give him a hand setting it up. The tent was too small to fit us all in it, so the rest of us got to sleep inside the terminal. I decided instead to sleep on the roof of the terminal, under the stars. It gave me a feeling of peace and tranquility to sleep up there. I would wake up with bug bites from all of the mosquitoes but I really didn't care. In addition to the impeccable sleeping arrangements, the terminal had a few other priceless amenities: there was a working phone, and there was also a small working shower inside the terminal. Since there were so few of us there it was very possible for everyone on the camp to take a real shower every day. A real shower was such a breath of fresh air after having to take the bottled water showers in Iskandaria and the once every 3 days showers in Udarri. As far as our office for work, we had an actual ticket counter in the terminal. The funny thing about this was we had a similar workflow to Udarri, which was next to nothing. I didn't care though since this was all part of the adventure. Being chosen to go to a new camp before everyone else doesn't feel the same as being left behind in Kuwait. It was definitely a much better feeling to be there in Mosul.

There was a day that came along when I finally had the time to get in the phone line to call home. I hadn't called home in a while, and while standing in line I started to psych myself up about the idea of hearing my father's voice and hearing about what was new at home. I had waited in the phone line for about an hour, and suddenly there was some commotion at the front of the line. Apparently the connection was lost. There was nothing on the other line, no dial tone, no sound, no nothing. In other words, the phone had gone dead. Everyone in line, including myself got real disappointed. Here I had actually taken the time to get in line and get psyched up to call home, and it didn't pay off for me. For the rest of day I was really down about this happening and was dying to reach home. Luckily for me, the chaplain that came with us just happened to have a satellite phone that could work anywhere in the world. I went to him and pled my case to use the phone (which I assumed was just meant for emergencies) and he let me use it. He told me I had to bring it back to him in 20 minutes or less, which was fine for me, I would have been ok with 5 minutes just as long as I got to hear my dad's voice. I took the phone to the roof of the terminal and called home. I stood there on the roof and looked off into the Mosul skyline and just talked to my dad. I filled him in on everything that had happened so far, to include the circumstances of this very phone call. I told him where I was standing, and what I was looking at. For some reason, this particular phone call stands out in my mind today. Maybe it's because it was the first time I ever used a satellite phone, or maybe it's because I was looking off into the Mosul skyline. While I am not exactly sure the reasons why I will never forget this call, I do know that there is a chance that I may never experience anything like this again. A special thanks to that Chaplain who afforded me that opportunity.

We sat on Mosul airfield for a couple weeks anticipating orders to pack up and head back to Iskandaria to meet up with the rest of the battalion. There wasn't really much going on up there, so we just assumed we would be packing up and leaving soon. Instead of getting the orders to head back, we instead received word that the whole battalion was coming up along with a good portion of the division. It had been decided that the 101st Airborne Division was going to run operations out of the city of Mosul and the airfield was going to be where a good portion of the division would be stationed at for the deployment. By late may the entire unit arrived and everything changed on the airfield. No longer were we allowed to use the shower in the building. There was only one shower in the terminal and thousands of troops, so it was now "off limits." I am sure that the post commander still used the shower, but it wasn't open to average junior Soldiers such as me. Also, we had to move out of the terminal. We had brought our own tents from Fort Campbell, and by god we were going to use them. We ended up setting the tents up in the middle of the airfield. For a floor we obtained some sheets of plywood from the local Iraqi economy and laid them on the ground so we had a hard surface in our tent. We also had to spend long hours in the sun filling hundreds of sandbags to line up on the side of the tent. The purpose of this wasn't just to keep out any water if it were to rain, but also to provide us a minor bit of protection in case there was any nearby explosions. Maybe the filled sandbags could slow down flying pieces of shrapnel. We also didn't have any way to take a shower, so we literally built our own shower out of plywood, a giant blue plastic barrel, and a rubber hose that we stole from the motor pool. The blue barrel sat on top of the wooden shower box that we built, and the rubber hose had a valve at the end that would control the flow of water. All we had to do was make sure to put a container of water in the barrel right before we showered. We had to be real careful not to fill up the water and leave it there, because the water would heat up quickly, thus leaving an extremely hot shower for whoever showered after you. I must say in this experience we took a lot of pride in setting this place up for us to live there. We set up a tent that we would live in and a shower to use all on our own. If that doesn't show the true American spirit then I don't know what does.

Having the rest of the battalion there ended up being a good thing actually. We had a big tent set up with all of us living there, and our gang had its own little corner in the tent. My cot was alongside the "wall" of the tent, and directly across from me was Defrates. Next to him was Jones, and across from me and Defrates were Cursey and another guy in our unit named Jeremy Mehring. Mehring worked in the evaluations section with me, only he worked on the Officer evaluations most of the time, while I worked on the NCO evaluations. Either way, he was definitely part of the team and while many people in the unit broke off into "cliques" and did their own thing it turned out that we already had our own clique. The only difference between our clique and the other cliques was that we were the smart ones. Other Soldiers on the deployment would get busted drinking alcohol. When this would happen, they would end up ratting out their friends. Our clique on the other hand wasn't anything like that. We weren't getting busted for anything stupid like that, and if we did we wouldn't rat each other out. We all had each other's back. Earlier in this book I mentioned times that Cursey and I bumped heads. I can assure you that on this deployment, while there were some rocky times we still had each other's back. That's one thing the other cliques on that deployment were lacking, was loyalty. We had it, the others did not. We all left that deployment alive, with our rank and our records intact. That, my friends is what loyalty can do for you.

During this deployment there was also a slight transition amongst the officer ranks in the unit. We ended up having a company change of command since our current company commander; CPT Z had to return to the US for career progression and was subsequently replaced by another Captain. We also had a new Lieutenant arrive to our company. Her name was Allison Pfundtner. Even though she was an officer, I took an immediate liking to Allison. She was down to earth and didn't let rank be an excuse not to get to know you. There is a rule in the military, (in fact it is regulation) that officers are not supposed to befriend enlisted Soldiers. This is referred to as "fraternization." Allison wasn't the type to be stuck up because of this stupid rule. I am a firm believer that as long as you can get the job done, then it doesn't matter if you are friends with those who work under or above you. You just have to know when to separate your personal and professional life when the time comes. Over the course of the deployment I ended up befriending Allison. There were times that I had issues with a lot of the NCOs above me (occasionally even SGT Ramos included) and Allison would be there for me to vent to. She would offer me her advice, not as an officer, but instead as a friend. I am happy to say that today Allison and I are still friends. We are still in touch and we still talk to this day. Over the course of my time in Iraq and at Fort Campbell after the deployment Allison would always serve as a true friend who would always listen to my problems and offer true, sound advice. That's all you can really ask for in a friend, regardless of their rank.

Even though we were forced to vacate the airport terminal for our living arrangements, we were required to stay at the terminal to perform our mission. We ended up taking over the entire ticketing area and opening up shop there. Also, it was unlike performing our mission at Udarri and Iskandaria. On those camps we didn't have a lot of work, we would have a few customers a day and then that would be it. Here on Mosul airfield however there were thousands of Soldiers stationed there, thus there were a ton of customers needing support. We had to work every single day, 7 days a week taking care of the personnel actions of all of these Soldiers. I didn't mind however, for 2 main reasons: 1-there were Soldiers in combat in the city that were making much deeper sacrifices than we were making, and 2-I had been so bored previously in the deployment that I actually welcomed the idea of having something to do. During this time I also ended up learning a little bit more about the 42A MOS. I learned how to make temporary ID Cards for Soldiers, and I learned how to process a Soldier for emergency leave. I found it amazing how many Soldiers had emergencies at home while on this deployment. I felt bad for every single one of them. At the time, I couldn't imagine what it would be like to be deployed there in Iraq and have a family emergency at home to worry about. That could be such a strain on a Soldier. Sometimes in the Army you get crooked, unfair, asshole NCOs who will actually try to badmouth these Soldiers who had emergencies at home. I witnessed this take place my entire career and I always took exception to it. As far as I am concerned, if you have a family emergency you should be allowed to fly home to take care of it without any fear of reprisal or discrimination. It's just too bad that many leaders in the Army do not feel the same way that I do on this particular subject.

Another thing that changed as more Soldiers arrived to Mosul Airfield was the DFAC conditions. The US Government signed a contract with KBR (Kellogg, Brown and Root, Inc.) that allowed them to exclusively set up various dining facilities on camps throughout the entire country. Although it was clearly a corporate gain on behalf of KBR, it still ended up working out for all of us Soldiers. The food was top-notch, American quality food. They served three meals a day, and while it wasn't as good as "home cooking" it was still 100% better than eating an MRE. There was always a lot of speculation that the US was severely profiting from this war. This speculation came from the fact that Vice President Dick Cheney was the former CEO of Halliburton, the parent company of KBR. I still don't know if any of this speculation was true, or if it ended up being pure rumor. Either way, it didn't matter. The presence of these DFACs definitely did help boost the morale of deployed Soldiers. KBR ended up setting up DFACs on various military installations across not only Iraq but Afghanistan as well, and while I do not know exactly how much they profit, I do know that their employees are highly paid for having to work unarmed in dangerous war zones. The food is good, and I can honestly say that without them our deployment may have been a lot worse. Therefore, KBR is good in my book.

It wasn't long before the SSB started getting tasked for various types of missions. We were going to have to get past the idea of our mission being solely sitting on Mosul Airfield and providing personnel support. There was so much more going on in Iraq outside of the airfield. There were infantry units deployed to various outposts all over the county. Those Soldiers still needed our support, but they couldn't make it to our airfield due to their own mission requirements. I guess at this point I need to re-iterate some facts. All Soldiers have a chance at being promoted. Someone has to process those promotion packets. All Soldiers run a risk of going home on emergency leave. Someone has to process that leave packet. All leaders receive an evaluation report. Someone has to process and forward those evaluations to the Department of the Army headquarters. In each one of those mentioned examples, we, the SSB were that "someone." So when the time came that we had to start sending small personnel teams to the more desolate infantry camps, we all understood why. The infantry units were often too busy carrying out their missions in the city to run a quick convoy to our airfield to take care of their issues, regardless of the fact that these issues had to be taken care of. I volunteered to go on as many of these convoy missions as possible, for so many reasons. For one, going on a mission every so often would break the constant monotony of sitting on the Airfield all the time. There was also a certain amount of adventure that came with these missions. In most cases we would convoy there on our own, without an escort from another unit. I carried the M249 SAW (Squad Automatic Weapon) for most of these convoys, so if something did happen I would be the first one to provide security since I was sticking out of the top of the vehicle. Of course, this also made me a very big target as well, but as a Soldier that comes with the territory. The funny thing is that even though you are the first target, that's not really what is on your mind during these convoys. Instead you're thinking about providing backup and protection to your fellow Soldiers. I would find myself more concerned about the safety of those Soldiers that were inside the vehicle as opposed to my own. That feeling is called Selfless Service. It is one of the seven Army values that are taught to you right from the beginning in basic training. On a deployment like this, you learn the true, real life meaning of this, as opposed to the "textbook" definition you learn in training.

Another thing that made these missions rewarding was the feeling that you were actually contributing something to the overall war effort. Of course during the long work days at Mosul Airfield you would feel this, especially when you had a line of customers about 400 deep, but it wasn't the same as traveling to an outpost out in the middle of nowhere. I remember I was on a mission to a camp called Sinjar. Sinjar was close to the mountains by the Turkish border, making it one of the farther out of reach camps. There were some infantry and support troops at Sinjar whose main mission wasn't in the city of Mosul, but instead out here in the middle of nowhere. I felt bad because it seemed like they were disconnected from everyone. There were only a handful of Soldiers to provide support to, and for the week that we were there we didn't have much work to do. As a result of the low population the rules there were a little more relaxed, which made things more enjoyable, but since the place was so far out of the way, the automation there didn't always work, so the Soldiers there didn't always have the ability to call or email their loved ones. Once again, I felt bad for the Soldiers there. Being there to at least provide them with some sort of support gave me a feeling of self-fulfillment, that I was really contributing something. It also showed me that things were not always going to be as glamorous as they were on the airfield. Many Soldiers had it much harder than I did, and I should be thankful that I lived on that airfield. Don't get me wrong, we were still making a ton of sacrifices on our deployment, but going to Sinjar did help bring me down to earth.

The other thing about Sinjar was that the living accommodations were limited. When we left the airfield we were told not to bring a tent or anything, that there would be a place for us to stay. All we had to bring was our own cots. When we got there, we found out that we were given some misinformation. They had no place for us to stay, so we had to sleep under the stars. I actually didn't mind, we were further up north so it wasn't as hot at Sinjar as it was at the airfield. Also, since the camp was just outside of the mountains we had a nice view. I would lie in my cot and just look up at the stars and the mountains, thinking about home, thinking about my family, my friends, and my town. It was times like this, these little moments looking up at the stars in a foreign country that made this deployment experience priceless. There is absolutely nothing like traveling the world. To this day I still tell people that the greatest gift the Army ever gave me was travel. And I also tell people that you can put a price tag on a plane ticket, but you simply cannot put a price on the experience. It just isn't possible.

Sinjar wasn't the only cool mission I went on during this deployment. There were many others. One thing that my unit got wrapped up in was humanitarian efforts in the city. There was some sort of agreement that certain units would go to local Iraqi schools and do some work for the School. This work usually included painting hallways and working on plumbing. This seemed an awful lot like custodial work to me, but who was I to open my mouth, right? At this point any day off of Mosul Airfield was a good day. Now, I need to stress that this was before things really started to heat up in Mosul. And by "heat up" I am not referring to the temperature, I am referring to the frequency of the attacks. During the time that we were working on the school we rarely got attacked. Things during this time were very peaceful. Of course, Saddam Hussein hadn't even been found yet, and believe me things were going to change, but for now we enjoyed the idea that we weren't getting attacked very often. During these humanitarian efforts I was never actually chosen to do some of the work, but instead I would go on the convoys and provide security. Someone had to do it, right? The nice thing about providing security is that we didn't just have to do that on the convoy. Sometimes, our Battalion Commander and Sergeant Major would go to meetings with the principals of these schools and I would get to come along as security. This definitely offered a nice change from doing Human Resources work in the terminal all day long. The other nice thing about going to these meetings to provide security for the command team was that the school staff would prepare a massive spread of Iraqi food for all of us to feast upon as a gesture of gratitude. It was during these times that I had my first taste of Iraqi food, and to tell you the truth it wasn't bad. It was certainly a nice change from the MREs and T-Rations that we had to eat for most of this deployment (before real DFACs were finally set up that is). I especially liked the pita bread that the Iraqis would serve us. The bread had a great flavor and actually became quite addicting over time. Over time I was able to develop a nice balance between time spent on the airfield and time spent off of the airfield, thus making little adventures like this one more enjoyable as opposed to more of a routine.

Not all of these security missions featured humanitarian efforts and a delicious feast however. Sometimes we had to go on convoys into the city for other purposes. Sometimes it would involve an officer in our unit having to meet with a contractor about an on base project. Sometimes, it would just be another Personnel Services mission. Either way, security was always necessary. On a lot of these missions I would have to stay outside with a few of my fellow Soldiers and pull security on the vehicles to ensure that no one tried to attack us or blow up our vehicles. Things had been somewhat friendly at times, but there were still reports of some violence throughout parts of the city. Just because we had good luck on our convoys thus far did not mean that Iraq was the safest place in the world. We were occasionally getting rocket attacks that would hit the airfield, so we knew the threat was very real. Many times when standing outside with the vehicles Iraqis would come up to us and strike up a conversation with us. We knew that we had to be careful, but there was also a message (at least in the media) that we were supposed to win the "hearts and minds" of the Iraqi people. So if an Iraqi came up and spoke to us, we wouldn't just shoe him away. (Providing he wasn't a threat to us in any way, shape or form.) These Iraqis would talk to us about all sorts of things. They would tell us how bad it was when Saddam ruled Iraq, and they would thank us for coming. They didn't see the difference between an Infantry Soldier and a Support Soldier. All they see is a US Soldier. They see an American, and they see a uniform. They would say things like "Bush Good" as a sign of respect for President Bush. Sometimes the Iraqis we would encounter would have much better English skills, and sometimes they wouldn't. The ones with better English would have more graphic stories to tell. A lot of these stories would prove to be very heartbreaking, and would further cement my own belief that the United States coming to Iraq wasn't 100% a bad idea. The people of Iraq did need help; there was no doubt about that.

I was once told a story from an old Iraqi man who was a former police officer. He told me that Saddam wanted him to interrogate a member of his own family for a crime that he knew as a fact he didn't commit. When he refused to interrogate him, Saddam had his ear chopped off and he fired him. He showed me the scar from where most of his ear used to be. It was a very sad display and I felt very bad for him. I could see the tears in his eyes when he told me this. He told me how he considered himself lucky that Saddam didn't just outright kill him. This was just one example. There were many more stories similar to this. There were also a lot of children in the streets, most of them barefoot, which was also very sad. They would come up to us and try to touch our uniform, our equipment, everything. The kids were so amazed by our presence there. Sometimes they would try to sell us things. They were such great young entrepreneurs. They would not only try to sell us things that were looted from many of Saddam's palaces, but also things like cases of Pepsi and cartons of cigarettes. I found it funny that some of these kids who were maybe seven years old were trying to push a carton of cigarettes onto a US Soldier. Obviously the cigarettes and Pepsi were also looted, but those kids didn't care. Some of my fellow Soldiers would buy them too. The most memorable child salesman that I ever encountered came to me one day with a big coffee can. He said, "Mister, mister, you buy? You buy this?" I thought maybe there was coffee in the can. After all, it was a big coffee can. He opened the lid of the can and I looked down into it to see two beautiful white doves. These were the nicest birds I had ever seen and they were clearly looted from one of Saddam's palaces also. Unfortunately we couldn't have pets, so I had to tell the young boy that I wasn't going to buy his birds. I was simply astonished that a kid would walk the streets trying to sell some birds out of a coffee can. This further displayed to me the condition of the country. During all of these times I found myself being thankful that I grew up in the US. Sometimes it takes an eye opening experience like this to really show you just how good you have had it in your life. I really hope that one day life can improve for people who live in third world countries like Iraq. It is sad and unfortunate that there are children in our world that have to grow up this way.

One time on a mission into the city I found myself in a particularly odd position. I was on a security mission with some of the officers of the unit as one of the SAW gunners for the convoy. They had me and the other SAW gunner stay outside and pull security on the vehicles while they went inside and conducted their business. The other SAW gunner was another buddy of mine named Pendleton, who had been in the Army a little longer than me. I remember we were just out there just shooting the breeze, trying to make the time pass. We were each standing on the back of a cargo Humvee with our weapons. This was because our SAWs were mounted to the vehicle, so we really had no choice. You never leave a weapon unsecured. My vehicle had some spare water bottles and MRES, which we didn't really need at the time. There was the occasional Iraqi kid who would walk up and strike up a conversation with us, and as long as they were peaceful I would allow it. After all, we are here to "win the hearts and minds" of the people of Iraq, right? After a while, some of these kids would ask if they could have a bottle of water. Since we had so much, I obliged and handed one to one of them. Sooner than later, it turned to asking for some of the MREs. Apparently they interacted with US Soldiers in the past because they definitely knew what MREs were. Still, I didn't see the problem with handing out a few pieces of food to these kids, because like I said before they were peaceful. After a while, there were tons of kids coming out of the woodwork. I had no idea where they were coming from, but before I knew it there were at least 50 kids around my Humvee, and by now I was well out of food. Pendleton looked over at me at me and said, "Looks like you've got a following!" Realizing that these kids were suddenly hanging on my actions, I decided to test them. I looked at them, and in a playful manner I shouted "YAY!!!!" and started clapping my hands. This made the kids start cheering. I looked over at Pendleton, who my now was laughing his ass off. Of course, the whole time I was still scanning the area for any signs of an attack, and so far there was none. It was also comforting to know that Pendleton had my back in case something did happen. After a few minutes of allowing the kids to cheer, I motioned my hands down to signal silence. THE KIDS ACTUALLY GOT QUIET! They waited for my next words. Feeling like a celebrity, I decided to play with them again. Once again I shouted "YAY!" and clapped, and once again the kids started cheering like maniacs. I did this two more times, and each time Pendleton was laughing at the whole time. Finally on the fifth time, I decided to change it up a little. I motioned the kids to silence, and they did. I then looked around the crowd and shouted the following words at the top of my lungs: "MICHAEL JACKSON!!!" I had learned earlier in the deployment that Michael Jackson was very popular in this part of the world. Many of the Iraqi contactors I had worked with were big fans of his. This time was no different. The kids started going nuts, yelling and screaming, grabbing each other, shouting, clapping, everything. I just wanted to know if they liked Michael Jackson. Obviously they did. I motioned for silence like the previous times, but it didn't work. They got crazier. I tried multiple times to silence them, but they just wouldn't give this time. They kept going nuts. After a while they realized that I just wasn't going to produce Michael Jackson. I think they thought by shouting "Michael Jackson" that I had Michael Jackson in the back ready to come out and perform for these kids. I obviously didn't. I will admit, I didn't think my actions all the way through on this particular day. Once the kids finally realized that Michael Jackson wasn't here they started to get angry with me. They started off by yelling at me, but that just wasn't enough . . . they started to throw rocks at me. And even though I was wearing my Kevlar helmet and my body armor, a lot of those rocks still hit my arms and legs, and they hurt. These kids were mad that someone (me) promised them that their hero Michael Jackson would be here, and he wasn't. Pendleton was laughing the whole time. He thought the whole thing was hilarious. Kids were throwing rocks at me because I told them Michael Jackson would be there, at least according to them anyway. Eventually the officers came out from their meeting, and we got out of there. As we drove away, the kids were yelling stuff in their language at us and I'm pretty sure they were angry. Yeah, I guess looking back it was a funny experience, but I should have thought that one through a little more. Oh and for the record, I love Thriller.

The most enjoyable mission I ever went on was a two week long mission to the Main Divisional Headquarters operations area in the heart of the city. The Division had two main areas for the headquarters, one was located at one of Saddam's former palaces in the middle of the city, and the other was an area referred to as the "CMOC" located inside an old pyramid shaped hotel right along the Tigris River. Now, while I cannot remember what the acronym "CMOC" stands for no matter how hard I try, I can remember the exact details of that trip. The purpose of the trip was to make ID Cards for Iraqi contractors who worked in the hotel. There were some rules however. We could only make them an ID card if they had successfully completed a screening and an interview from the MI (Military Intelligence) unit that was deployed at the CMOC. Once the MI unit gave us the signal that they were able to work there, we would cut them an ID card. Also, the MI unit had a policy that they only completed six interviews a day, which means we were only going to complete six ID cards a day. In other words, a two week mission to the CMOC meant you were on two weeks of the lightest possible duty. Not bad, huh? The SSB had been tasked with this CMOC ID card mission, and thus they treated it as a way to rotate their Soldiers out of the airfield where we were working long 12 hour days. It was almost like getting a small vacation, only we still had a small mission.

The amenities at the CMOC were the very best on the entire deployment. We lived in a nice hotel room with air conditioning. The hotel rooms had balconies with a terrific view. My room had a view of the Tigris River, as well as the highway next to the hotel and the hotel's courtyard. There were also stories about these hotel rooms that the Iraqi workers would tell us. They told us stories about how Saddam issued an order that the richer and preferred customers would have a room with a balcony that faced his palace, and the poorer, not-so-preferred customers would have a room facing the river. Apparently Saddam was so vain that he believed that it was a greater privilege to look out at his palace than it was to look at the beautiful river. Personally I preferred the river. There are a lot of things that can be said about Saddam Hussein, but you cannot ever say that he was modest. Hearing these stories further cemented my low opinion of the evil dictator.

The CMOC also had an amazing courtyard, complete with a swimming pool, an area for the Division Band to come and play, and a small restaurant set up that served chicken and beef kabobs as well as many other things. Many times when we got off our relaxed shift of making ID cards we would go out to the courtyard and unwind even more. We were allowed to swim in the pool if we wanted and we certainly enjoyed the quality food that was served there. Sometimes the Division Band would come and play. Some nights when the band was playing I would sit on my balcony and enjoy a Cuban cigar while I looked off into the Tigris River and enjoy the music. It was such a peaceful feeling and it was indescribable. As I stated earlier, you can buy a plane ticket, but you cannot put a price tag on experience. This was one of those experiences.

The CMOC also had a coffee shop in the hotel lobby near the counter that we worked at. Every morning I would stop there on my way to work and the best part about it was that the coffees, cappuccinos and lattes that were made there were given to Soldiers for free. There's nothing like a free coffee first thing in the morning to really get the day started. I've been a coffee aficionado my entire life and I can tell you that by no means was it the best coffee that I ever had, but it was free. Free usually trumps all in most people's books. There was one thing the coffee shop did sell however; Cuban cigars. Throughout my years in the Army I took a liking to cigars and would enjoy them from time to time, especially when I was deployed. Prior to this deployment however, smoking cigars wasn't really my thing. It was during this time at the CMOC that cigar smoking really started to grow on me. After all, these were real Cuban cigars that were being sold at a reduced price. They were all looted from Saddam's palaces by the locals and then Sold back to us as well as other Iraqis on the street. Cuba and Iraq didn't have a trade embargo like the US and Cuba does, so getting the opportunity to have a real Cuban cigar is one of those pleasures that you probably won't get to enjoy if you've never left the US. I ended up smoking one a day for the entire 2 weeks that I was at the CMOC, and then when I returned to Mosul Airfield at the end of the 2 weeks I brought a few of them back with me to enjoy on the rest of the deployment. As it turned out, this opportunity didn't end up being my last chance to enjoy a Cuban cigar. Slowly they started surfacing at the little Iraqi shops at the airfield as well as at other camps across Iraq. Either way, I enjoyed it so it worked out for me.

After my 2 weeks of luxury at the CMOC were up it was time to head back to the Airfield and go back to work. It turned out that my rotation there ended up being the last rotation that the SSB would support, which the rest of the Soldiers didn't like because they hadn't yet gotten the chance to experience going there. As of that moment I had received my fair share of time off of the Airfield between the convoy missions and my time at the CMOC. It became an unofficial way for us to gauge how much we had accomplished on that deployment. The consensus amongst our little circle was that if you had spent the entire deployment on the airfield so far, then you probably didn't do as much as those who did go off the airfield. I know that sounds wrong, but trust me there was so much more adventure to going on a convoy (even if there wasn't any attacks on the route) than just simply sitting there doing paperwork all day, every day. I was very thankful to get to be one of the ones who left from time to time.

Just because some Soldiers sat on the Airfield all the time did not necessarily mean they were safe all the time. This is a popular misconception that I think people who have never served seem to believe. Every single part of a country like that is considered dangerous when you are deployed. Granted, the degrees of that danger may vary. Over the summer of 2003 the amount of rocket attacks that we would get on the airfield would begin to increase, and by fall and winter it was almost like we were getting attacked every other day. The only time that the attacks started to calm down was during Ramadan. During Ramadan we still got attacked, it just wasn't as often. The thing to realize about these rocket attacks was that they were being fired off by random groups of Iraqis, from random locations. Sometimes we would get reports of a group of guys in a pickup truck out in the middle of nowhere firing these things off into the vicinity of an American camp. Quite often they didn't care who or what they hit, as long as it was American. Then sometimes you would hear about the more organized ones. These groups would pay off an Iraqi contractor worker to come onto the airfield and mark down locations or take a pace count of distances to certain locations on the camp. Usually these locations would include highly populated areas such as DFAC tents and living areas. These attacks definitely kept us on our toes. Often times we would get hit in the middle of the night and everyone would have to rush to the makeshift bunker that we had dug into the ground ourselves. It was certainly a crazy time for every one of us there, and that is why it pains me when I hear people say that there isn't any real danger on the airfield. That statement simply isn't true. Could a rocket attack potentially injure or kill a Soldier? Certainly. Do the Soldiers on the airfield receive the same amount of hazardous duty pay as the Soldiers in the streets? Of course they do. The rocket attacks that we sustained over the course of that deployment were all too real. There was also a time closer to the end of the deployment when a DFAC on the other side of the airfield was bombed. A lot of Soldiers were hurt that day, luckily none from our unit. That was the thing about being on the airfield; life could seem perfectly normal one minute, then the next minute everyone is going nuts because there was some sort of an attack. This was how it was on the airfield. Sometimes we would get a rocket attack every day for an entire week, and then suddenly everything would be quiet for days or even weeks at a time. It seemed as if the people who were attacking us didn't have much of a strategy. Sure, there would be the occasional Iraqi worker that was caught on the airfield walking a pace count, but other than that there wasn't any real strategy. That was one of the things that made this war different. In previous wars the US would be engaged in conflict against the Soldiers of another country. In this war however, the Iraqi Army had surrendered almost immediately. At this point there was no Army, just fanatic attackers who were either just terrorists, followers of Saddam, or average citizens that weren't pleased with the American occupation of their country. It made things much different for the Soldiers of this generation. There were times I was on convoys in the city and I had no idea who would attack me if an attack would happen. There wasn't any uniform for them, they all just wore normal clothes the same way the peaceful Iraqis did. I am sure that this made the mission of the average infantry Soldier much harder as well.

There was also another extremely dangerous day at the airfield that didn't involve an attack at all, but still a ton of gunfire and explosions. Directly across the street from the air terminal where we all worked was an old building that the division used as an ammunition supply point (ASP). On this particular day it was so hot that the ammo in the building literally started to "cook off." It started with just a few minor explosions. Then, some grenades and rockets that were being stored started blowing up, which created enough of a rumbling to make all of the big glass windows on the terminal shatter. We all thought we were being attacked. Suddenly out of the blue someone shouted "EVACUATE THE BUILDING! EVERYONE HEAD TO THE DIRT MOUND!" We all ran for our lives to the other side of the mound which sat around our living area to take cover. No one fully understood the things that were happening right now. Soon enough, we realized that this wasn't an attack at all, just the result of the temperature causing the ammo to explode. As we took cover on the mound, we could hear constant explosions and what sounded like gunfire. This went on for hours. The worst part was that there was nothing that anyone could do about it since it was uncontrollable. The only thing that could possibly be done was to sit and take cover and wait until every last piece of ammo was expended. To say that this presented a dangerous situation would be an understatement. But, like everything else that came our way thus far, we got through it. As far as the terminal where we worked, all of the glass was shattered and it took a few weeks to replace all of the windows. Once it was all over, it became something that we all looked back on and laughed at. In the time that it took to replace the windows and clean the glass off of the floor, we would come in to work and see the glass everywhere and just laugh about it. After all it was in the past, so why not?

Another issue we had to deal with at Mosul was the electricity. Although we brought some small 5K and 10K generators with us from Fort Campbell, we still had to rely on other sources for most of our power, both in the airport terminal where we worked and the tents in which we lived. As far as the tents were concerned, we had heating units installed in the fall. Since we were in the northern part of Iraq we knew that it was going to get cold sooner or later. The thing was; these heaters weren't connected to the generators that we brought with us from Fort Campbell. Instead, they were connected to a local power grid that was linked to the city of Mosul. This wasn't the most reliable of power grids either. Often the power grids would go out for weeks at a time. Unfortunately for us, there was a time during Mid-November that the power went out for roughly two weeks. At first this was a problem because the temperature in Mosul would drop to around 40 degrees at night in the fall and winter. It got much worse when I realized that the heaters in our tent were connected to the same power grid that was connected to the recently built shower tents, meaning the hot water heaters would no longer work in the showers either. Then, when I thought things couldn't get any worse I went to work one day at the terminal. I walked in and felt the temperature. It was freezing in there. I asked the Soldiers at the finance counter about what happened to the heat and they told me the same thing that I had heard about the tent earlier, that the heat in the terminal was cut off because it was connected to the cities' power grid. This was some horrible news. Just to recap, in an effort to put things into perspective for you: there was no heat in the tent, therefore we had to sleep in we tent that was roughly 40 degrees. There was no heat at the terminal, so we had to work in cold temperatures, and to top it all off there was no hot water, so we had to take COLD showers through all of this. This went on for about two weeks. I have to be absolutely honest about those two weeks; they were probably the hardest two weeks of the deployment to get through. Granted, there were other times during the deployment that things were bad because of the heat or because of the attacks, but this time was totally different. Setting aside the simple mind-fuck that we were all cold in Iraq, there was also the issue that everyone around us was simply miserable. It didn't matter if you were normally a cool, mellowed out guy. If you have to resort to taking a cold shower every single day for two weeks you are likely to be pissed off. I can remember this particular part of the deployment being one of the more miserable times for our unit. No one was happy at any time. Not even me. The funny thing is I can remember the day the heat turned on just as clearly as I can remember the day that the heat turned off. When it turned back on, everyone just got silent for a second and stared at the heater like it was a god . . . the heater was on, and it was blowing hot air. This very moment rescued us from one of the harder times we had to endure over this deployment. The mental damage of having to deal with the constant cold, as well as everyone else's constant anger is something that I just cannot describe. Believe it or not it was one of the harder times to get through during that deployment and believe me, I thanked god that it was over.

In addition to the frequent yet random attacks and the lack of amenities on the airfield, there were some other problems on the deployment. One thing that slowly became a problem over time was dealing with each other. You're stuck on a long deployment with the same people. At first things are ok because the deployment feeling is still new and exciting. Then people start to grow on each other's nerves. It's perfectly natural and it happens in any work environment, not just on Army deployments. The main difference with an Army deployment however is that you're not just working together all day, but also that everyone lives together at night. Everyone is forced to see each other 24/7. In a normal work environment everyone would go home to their families every night. We were going home to each other. Earlier I alluded to the fact that our "clique" had loyalty; we had each other's backs. That wasn't the case with the other "cliques" all the time. Sometimes a Soldier would get caught drinking, and would immediately rat out whoever hooked them up with the alcohol.

Now, I know it is perfectly illegal to drink in a deployed environment, and I do not condone it by any means. I also do not condone ratting out your "battle buddies". If you got caught with the booze, then just be man enough and take the wrap for it. It's that simple. We didn't have that problem in our group. If Cursey or Defrates were to get caught doing something, they weren't going to sit there and bring Jones or myself down. That's how it went. That's what loyalty is. (Of course none of us would get caught doing anything because we didn't do things wrong, ever. And, if you can't sense the sarcasm in that last statement, then I don't know what to tell you. And I'll leave it at that.)

Speaking of having loyalty to each other, I mentioned in the last chapter that right before this deployment Jones fell in love with a girl named Emily. Emily was a new Soldier that came to our unit from AIT shortly before out deployment. Jones took an immediate liking to her and they began to spend a lot of time with each other. As a close friend of Jones, I was privy to all of this information. Unfortunately, Jones was soon facing a severe dilemma. Jones feelings for Emily were sadly in vain because Emily ended up falling for someone else just before we were going to deploy. We weren't really sure if Emily did this because Jones was deploying and she didn't want to wait for him, or if she did this because the feelings weren't really mutual. Either way it took a toll on Jones, and this ended up being one of the things that we all tried to help Jones through over the course of the deployment. Jones stayed in touch with her constantly. Emily would send Jones care packages and email him often giving him updates on what was going on in the Rear Detachment at Fort Campbell. If anything, Emily was at least proving herself to be a good friend of Jones.

It wasn't long before we got word from Jones that Emily had gotten married. Obviously Jones wasn't happy about this and quite frankly as a friend I wasn't either. I took exception to seeing one of my best friends go through something as painful as this, especially on a deployment so many miles from home. Even though Emily and Jones stayed friends, I could tell just by talking to Jones that things would never be the same again.

One day on our deployment some new Soldiers had arrived from Fort Campbell. The unit had requested that the Rear Detachment send a few Soldiers out to help pull the workload of some new missions. Usually when this takes place the term used to describe them is "late deployers". Jones had received an email weeks earlier about these late deployers so we were all expecting them. Out of all of the new Soldiers that arrived, one of them was none other than Emily's husband. None of us was really happy about him coming out there, since we were all obviously on Jones' side in all of this. I remember the day they arrived to the air terminal, where we had our personnel services counter set up. I spotted Emily's husband from the counter, and Jones was standing there. We had already talked about what would happen if Jones had to encounter him, and in all reality Jones wanted to avoid trouble. He hated the guy, but at the same time he didn't want to destroy his friendship with Emily so he took no action. I on the other hand had nothing to worry about, so I got up from the counter and met him halfway in the air terminal. (I do wish to state now that I regret the actions I am about to tell you about, but in the in interest of full disclosure I will still share the details with you.)

I met him halfway in the middle of the terminal and he said to me, "Oh Conklin I remember you. How are you?" as he offered his hand for a handshake. I refused to shake his hand and I said to him, "You're new here, so let's get this straight. I'll kick your ass. Don't step over the line here. You don't say anything out of line to Jones because as long as I am here, I'll kick your ass. Do you understand me?" He immediately responded with, "Oh no man, I don't want any trouble" as he once again offered his hand. This time around I shook his hand and got on with my day. I went back to our personnel services counter, where Jones was watching from and I could tell that Jones felt like a million bucks. To him what I had just done was the greatest thing in the world. I felt the same way. Hours later when I got back to the tent, Cursey started to come down on me for what I had done. He understood that I was really just looking out for Jones, but Cursey explained to me how stupid my actions were. After all, we are in the middle of Iraq on a deployment and I am over there threatening another Soldier because he was married to a woman that my friend Jones was in love with. I really didn't see the problem at the time, but then again I was young too. For the rest of the deployment things were smooth between Jones and Emily's husband. All it really took was for the two of them to just stay clear of each other. There was never a problem, aside from the day that I got in the guy's face.

Today, with hindsight being 20/20, I do realize that my actions were the wrong ones. I guess if they were in a fist fight and maybe Jones needed some help that would have been one thing, but given the circumstances that actually did take place I firmly do admit that I was wrong. The whole thing was stupid, and granted I was really just taking up for a friend, but it was still stupid. You would never hear me say the following statement very often when I was still at Fort Campbell but all in all, Cursey was right. That was a dumb move on my part. I really don't know Jones' take on the whole thing nowadays. I think on this one it is best to just leave the past exactly where it is; in the past.

Around October the Army started letting Soldiers go on R and R leave or Pass. Our unit had been there since March and after nearly 8 months of working hard, getting attacked, and going on Convoys a lot of the Soldiers were ready to get in a break. On this particular deployment we had the option of either taking two weeks of leave to the US, or taking a 4 day pass to a small middle-eastern country known as Qatar. There were a few stipulations however. We could only go back to the US if we actually had the leave built up to do so. Also, the unit was only allowed to send so many people home to the US at a time. By now we all knew that the deployment was going to be a 12 month long deployment, so we were faced with the choice of taking leave or just saving our leave days up until we all returned to the US at the end of the deployment. If we chose that we wanted to go home to the US, we would tell our leadership and they would put us on a list. Then they would decide out of that list who would be able to go, based on the unit only being allowed to let a limited number of Soldiers go home at a time. Ideally, a unit would allow the most Junior Soldiers to go home first, but in this case that isn't what happened at all. Some juniors went home, and some seniors did as well. I personally believe that you should always put the needs of your junior Soldiers above your own when you are a leader. That is actually taught to leaders in the Military, but believe me it isn't always practiced. This was one of those times.

Those of us who chose not to go home were given the opportunity to take the 4 day pass to Qatar. That was the choice that I went with. Qatar to me seemed like much more of an adventure. It's always a great experience to see another county. So far on this deployment I had gotten to see Kuwait and Iraq so why not add another country to my resume? Qatar was a great R and R spot. You could wear regular civilian clothes as opposed to having to be in uniform all day. There was also various off post trips that were ran regularly throughout the 4 days that you were there. These trips consisted of trips to the beach, local markets called Souqs and trips to the mall. It was definitely a nice change of pace from the day to day life in Iraq. My trip to Qatar was also great because I went with a friend. Going on a trip like that isn't as cool if you have to go it alone. That could get lonely. The unit ended up sending me with Allison, which I was cool with because we had become friends earlier in the deployment.

The experience that we had in Qatar was a good one. In Qatar they actually serve alcohol to the Soldiers, but you have to be 21 years old and there is a 3 beer limit. Even though it is an R and R location you are still technically deployed and they do not want Soldiers getting really drunk. From a readiness standpoint I do understand it. At the time, I was still 20 years old, and I wasn't even a drinker at the time so it didn't really matter to me. There was also a coffee shop called Greed Beans Coffee on the base in Qatar which I spent a lot of time at. Green Beans Coffee is the official coffee shop for US Military installations worldwide. I remember the first time during that trip that we went over there and they had Iced Chai Latte, which I had never had up until that point. Allison and I grabbed one and they gave us this card that they would stamp off. If you bought something like 12 lattes you would get one for free. We decided to make it our mission over the 4 day pass to get that free latte. I couldn't legally drink 3 beers, but dammit I could buy 12 Lattes! When we weren't on a trip we continuously went to the Green Beans coffee shop to load up on Chai. And on our final day there, I got my free latte. Sometimes it's the little things in life that bring a smile to your face.

Allison knew some people who were actually stationed in Qatar who were gracious enough to pick us up and take us out to dinner one night. That was another rule in Qatar; you could also go off post on a non-sponsored trip if you had a Sponsor there who was of the rank of E-5 or above. It didn't matter that Allison was an O-2; the rule was simple. Your sponsor had to be an E-5. They ended up taking us to a seafood restaurant on the Ocean. The food was not only great, but they also brought us out some hookahs to smoke flavored tobacco from while we enjoyed the view. This experience in itself was enough to further cement my love for traveling. I realized then that if this country here in the middle-east (that I had never heard of before the deployment) could be this beautiful, then there must be so much more to see around the world. I will never forget the experience that night of sitting by the ocean and looking off into the water while I enjoyed a hookah with some friends, all taking place in another country. Even though the trip to Qatar was over in a mere four days; it was perfectly fine with me. I relaxed enough and saw enough in those four days to be fully refreshed and ready to go back to work. I had a great time and made a lifelong friend in the process, and even though it was the first time I ever traveled to Qatar in my career, it didn't end up being the last.

Around November I slowly found myself doing a new job within the unit. I was taken away from the Personnel Services counter and put into the supply room. The real reason this happened was because the unit started letting Soldiers who fell victim to the stop loss to go home and get out of the Army when the stop loss was temporarily lifted. One of the Soldiers that fell into this category was the Supply specialist and thus they needed someone to fill in do the supply work. I ended being the one chosen to do the work, which I was ok with. I ended up working for a great (yet very strict) supply NCO, and a junior officer, who turned out to be Allison. This worked out well for me because I had already made friends with Allison earlier in the deployment and on the Qatar trip. The work itself was a change of pace also. Instead of sitting in the office doing paperwork all day, I was now doing things like taking accountability of unit equipment, minor maintenance issues, and making runs to pick up and drop off supplies from various parts of the airfield. The work amounted to longer days for me, considering the fact that doing supply work was more physically demanding than just sitting around all day. There was a lot of moving of boxes and equipment involved. Even still, I was perfectly ok with that. It still boiled down to the basic question of: How much can I accomplish on this deployment? Would I end up being a Soldier that just did the office work for a year, or would I have the privilege of contributing more? Working in supply for this short period was very rewarding for me because doing it made me feel like I was contributing something more. I've always taken great pride in contributing to the overall team effort.

Our unit also had an Iraqi worker that worked for us for the duration of the deployment who I was now responsible for. The man's name was Youssef, and like most Iraqis he didn't know very much English. Every morning I would have to go to the security checkpoint at the front gate where Youssef had to pass through security every day. Once he was patted down by the gate guards and checked in at the front office I took him to the unit and he would help me with whatever tasks we had at hand for the day. He worked alongside me and other Soldiers in the unit for so long that we eventually started to treat him like one of us. He was such a loyal worker and never did any of us wrong. He also started to learn a few English words as well as teach us some Iraqi words. Most Soldiers would want him to teach them swear words in Iraqi, which a lot of us found funny. I really don't know what it is inside of an American's mind that causes them to want to learn the swear words of another language as quickly as possible when in another country. I admit that I shared the same desire to learn the "forbidden" words. Youssef didn't care though. He found it funny as well, which slowly strengthened the bond that we had between us.

Youssef's connection with us started to grow so strong that he would sometimes bring Iraqi food back with him from the city. He would bring us kabobs and bread, as well as many other different types of Iraqi food. This was much different than earlier in the deployment when I was on a security mission that ended up stopping near a chicken stand. Even though we were told that we probably shouldn't eat the food from the stand, I bought a chicken anyway and brought it back to the airfield with me. Eating that chicken ended up giving me food poisoning, which resulted in me going to the TMC for medical help three days in a row. At times the pain was so bad that I felt like I had a knife in my stomach. I never want to live through an experience like that again, and we were all very thankful that the food that Youssef would bring us didn't give anyone the same type of illness that I had suffered. Youssef was always so loyal to us and he always had our best interests at heart. He wouldn't hesitate to help us out with things that weren't even in his scope of duties. He tried his very best to be part of the team, even though in all reality he was just an Iraqi contractor that we would probably never see again after this deployment. At that time however, none of that mattered to him.

About a month before the end of the deployment, we had to part ways with Yousef. For obvious security reasons we couldn't have him hanging around the unit while we were planning our trip back to Kuwait. Even though he was a friend to the unit, he was still an Iraqi citizen and for that reason alone we couldn't let him near any secrets. If we had kept him around until our final days, there is always the possibility that would have put our lives in danger. Even still, Youssef had been good to us and we decided it was a good idea to pay him back for everything. Like most Iraqis, Youssef was incredibly poor and had to support a family off of the little pay that he received from whatever contracting company he was working for. Our unit didn't pay him directly; he was technically being outsourced to the SSB. So as a way to pay him back for all of his service, we decided to give him most of the things that we had acquired over the deployment that we bought to make our lives easier. We gave him the Xboxes and TV sets that we had bought over the deployment to pass the time. We gave him some of the air conditioning units that we bought on the local economy. We all figured that since these air conditioners made our lives a lot easier that maybe they could make Youssef's life easier too. I know that it may sound like a cheap move to give him a bunch of used stuff that we couldn't take back to the US anyway, but believe me it wasn't a cheap move. Yousef was very thankful for all of this. Granted it may have been used; but this is all stuff that he didn't have to begin with, so it was still an improvement to the overall quality of his life.

Even after giving Youssef all the stuff that we could possibly give him we still didn't think this was enough. We all knew we would genuinely miss him, so we wanted to do something really special for him. Our First Sergeant came up with the idea that we should all collect donations from all of the Soldiers in the unit and present it to Youssef sometime during his last week at the unit. Considering he was earning roughly five dollars a day, collecting up even the smallest bit of money would be a nice gift for him. Everyone donated something, whether it was just a few dollars or more. Some of us donated as much as twenty dollars, and despite the fact that twenty dollars isn't very much to the average American, it was equivalent to four days of Youssef's pay. When we were finished collecting up all of the money we had a little over $450. This was probably more money than Youssef ever had in his entire life. We all knew that this amount of money would help him out tremendously. The unit held a formation for Youssef during his final week with us. The First Sergeant called him to the front of the formation and said some great things about him. He then looked Yousef in the eye and thanked him for everything as he handed him the envelope. Youssef looked into the envelope and got quiet for a second. He then began to shed a tear and barely managed to say the words, "Thank you." Then everyone fell out of formation and took turns shaking his hand and hugging him. It was such a moving display; most of these Soldiers probably wouldn't see him again. I still had a couple of days left with him because I worked with him. It was a great thing that we could all come together in the interest of giving to another person. I am willing to believe that our gift to Youssef probably helped him out so much, and hopefully he will never forget us.

There was a surprise on my final day with Youssef. On my way to take him to the gate at the end of the work day, he pulled a case out of his jacket and handed it to me. I opened it up, and there was a brand new silver watch. I don't remember the brand name of the watch but it resembled a watch that I saw for sale at the CMOC and in other parts of the city during my travels. It probably cost around $20 out on the Iraqi economy, but that didn't matter. It's the thought that counts. Youssef looked me in the eye and said, "For you, Conklin." I thanked him and gave him a big hug. He was a good man and even on his way out he still wanted to give. I watched Youssef walk out of the gate, and I knew that I would never see him again. And even though I will never see him again, there will always be a special place in my heart for Youssef. I still have the watch. Granted, it no longer works, but I will never throw it away. It was a gift, and I will keep it forever.

There is a lesson to be learned in all of this. Many people that have never served in the military or never traveled to the middle-east have a negative conception of people that are from that part of the world. I am here to tell you that you should NEVER judge a book by its cover. Do not just judge someone based on where they are from or where they grew up. There is so much more to people than what you see on the outside. Youssef was a man who was from Iraq. Iraq is indeed a third world country and there are a lot of bad people there that do not like Americans. But would that fact alone give us the right to judge Youssef? No. If you are going to judge someone, at least judge them by their actions, not by where they are from. There are bad people in all parts of the world, including the US. While working alongside Youssef I learned first-hand that he was a man who had goodness in his heart. So with that said, I will say again: do not judge a book by its cover.

Among all of my memories from this deployment, the most memorable for me took place on December 13, 2003. It was on this day that Saddam Hussein was finally captured. He was found in an underground bunker in a town just outside of Tikrit by US Soldiers. Even though he wasn't found in Mosul where we were stationed, the effects of his capture still rippled all the way through the entire country. The news spread like wildfire, not just to the US camps but also to the local Iraqis as well. We all felt a sense of accomplishment when we found out the news of Saddam's capture. For that moment, it started to feel like the war truly had a purpose, and now that purpose had finally been fulfilled. Personally I was extremely excited because I knew that the events of this deployment would go down in history. Knowing that I was living this history was amazing. President

Bush was set to give a speech that evening that would be broadcast all over the US and since we had AFN cable by now I intended to stay up late and watch the speech. I was interested to see what our president had to say about Saddam's capture. To be honest, I felt that it was my duty as a Soldier to watch the speech. Most of the other Soldiers in the company didn't feel this way, but that is their prerogative, right? To each their own. Given the time zone difference of Iraq I ended up figuring out that President Bush's speech would air roughly 2 am, Iraqi time. I set my alarm for 1:45 hoping to get a few hours of sleep, catch the speech, and then get a few more hours of sleep before morning PT formation. Unfortunately for me, this plan didn't exactly pan out as I had planned.

Halfway through the night, our camp suddenly came under a rocket attack. We all ended up rushing to the bunkers for protection and waited for the "ALL CLEAR" signal to come across the radios. Obviously, the signal did end up coming across. I went back to the tent, hoping to catch a little more sleep and still watch the speech. Next thing you know, were getting another rocket attack. We all rushed to the bunkers yet again. This ended up continuing all night long. It was very clear that this was a retaliation for Saddam getting captured, since the next day there were reports that it happened all over the country. Thankfully, none of us got hurt from the attacks. Even though the Iraqi army had surrendered when the US first invaded in March, there were still a handful of Saddam loyalists that apparently had been in hiding. I could never understand how so many people could be so loyal to such an evil dictator. To me that was crazy. Over the next few weeks, the attacks continued to pick up all over the country. The days of going weeks without an attack were long behind us. And for the record, I never did get to see President Bush's speech on that fateful night. I was too busy being awoken by rockets and rushing to the bunkers with my fellow Soldiers.

The holiday season during this deployment was also interesting. The first major event that I noticed was that the USO still does tours of combat posts. Usually the USO will contact a few celebrities and ask them if they would be willing to visit with the troops just before Christmas or Thanksgiving. A lot of times the USO would get a combination of different types of celebrities to come over, ranging from comedians, actors and actresses, models, singers, and professional athletes. Bob Hope was famous for doing this for years. He took a lot of pride in going over and entertaining the troops who had to spend the holidays without their families. Even though the legendary Bob Hope has long since passed away, the USO has kept the tradition going. This year was special for me however. The USO sent over comedian Robin Williams, and one of my favorite wrestlers of all time: Olympic Gold Medalist Kurt Angle. Kurt Angle was an Olympic Gold Medalist who later on went and became a professional wrestler in the WWE. Of course, me being a huge WWE fan I had to go to the event and meet him. WWE was also doing their annual 'Tribute to the Troops' wrestling event, but that event was performed in Baghdad as opposed to Mosul. I was disappointed when I had found that out because I wouldn't be able to see it. When I found out Kurt Angle was coming to Mosul I had to go over and meet him. I had no choice; he was one of my favorite wrestlers. The DFAC that day was absolutely packed. There were probably over 1,000 Soldiers in there, possibly more. He got on stage and gave a small speech where he talked about how proud he was that we were representing America, and how he could relate to that because he too represented America during the Olympics. Kurt really came off as a standup guy. I ended up having to wait in line forever to get a picture taken with him as well as his autograph, but it was well worth it. I chatted with him for a few minutes and got my picture taken with him, which I still have. The person who took the picture must have hit the button at the wrong time, because in the picture you see me from the side while he is looking at the camera. It was certainly a special day for me considering I was such a huge wrestling fan. Up until that point the only other wrestler I had met was the legendary Tony Atlas, who I met at the county fair when I was 14 years old in Fonda, NY. He was there to wrestle in the evening and he won a small stuffed animal from a game while walking around the fair. He ended up giving that stuffed animal to my little sister Jen, which we also still have. It was a cool moment from my childhood, but with all respect to Tony Atlas, meeting Kurt Angle in Iraq trumps it. Sorry, Tony.

That night wasn't all about Kurt Angle however. As I mentioned earlier, Robin Williams was also there. He got on stage and gave us a hilarious comedy routine. This was the first (and only) time that I had ever seen Robin perform live and I was shocked at how vulgar he was. I had always seen him in a lot of family and children's movies, so I guess I didn't expect to see him in this new light. As a vulgar comedian he was great. The entire audience loved it, and at one point he even ripped off his shirt and started flexing like a wrestler. I'm still not sure if that was meant to be a rip on

Kurt Angle or not, but that didn't matter. It was funny. He also made sure to pay tribute to Bob Hope for all of his years of doing this for us, which of course was met with a standing ovation from the troops. After he was done on stage he also did the meet and greet/autograph routine that Kurt Angle had done. I didn't even think to have my picture taken with him, but I was still able to shake his hand and thank him for the performance. I asked him if this was a one-time thing or if he was going to keep coming back for the Soldiers, to which he replied, "Oh, I'll definitely be back."

We also managed to pull off a small company Christmas party out there. I know that must sound crazy, but we did it. We all came together in our morale tent. There was a small PX on the airfield that sold us soda and Christmas candy, and we all bought a little to take there. In all honesty, it wasn't much of a party, but we all made an effort to make the holiday season feel at least somewhat normal. I personally decided to make the party a little more memorable by doing a comedy routine. There was however a major difference between my comedy routine and a normal routine. I had this "bit" that I liked to do where I would impersonate some of the NCOs in the unit. Usually I would pick an NCO that was more of a "character" so to speak. This was so it would be so people knew who I was trying to impersonate when I was doing the act. For instance, earlier in the year I had a really bad work day where SGT Ramos had come down on me big time. I ended up getting sick of his crap so I decided to do an impersonation of SGT Ramos. He had a huge bald spot on his head that we all called a "skin yarmulke." (Pronounced yamakah). Often times some of the Soldiers would pick on him because of it. So I decided to grow my hair out for a few days and then shave a bald spot onto my head, and then go walk around impersonating him. The main goal was to make sure he saw it while there were a lot of people around, in an effort to humiliate him. It ended up working, and I thanked god that SGT Ramos could take a joke. At our Christmas party, I was looking to capitalize on the success of the SGT Ramos incident by impersonation another NCO, one by the name of SSG Tarver.

SSG Tarver was a NCO who was relatively new to the unit. He actually transferred in halfway through the deployment and had a reputation for being too tough on the Soldiers in the unit. There are some cases when it is a good thing for an NCO to be tough on his Soldiers, but he took it too far sometimes. He also for some reason didn't mesh well with the other NCOs. Overall, he didn't seem to get along with anyone very well. He always had a bad attitude. Tarver also had this strange habit where he called anyone he outranked "Big Timer." It ended up getting very annoying for all of the Soldiers. Luckily for me his fascination for the word "Big Timer" gave me all of the material I needed to launch a makeshift comedy routine in the middle of Iraq. So I took a pillow and taped it to my chest (since Tarver was an avid weightlifter). I then took my DCU top and put a piece of duct tape over my name tape. On the duct tape, I wrote the words "BIG TIMER". Then, since Tarver had gold teeth I put aluminum foil on my teeth. (I know, aluminum foil is silver not gold, but give me a break, this is Iraq so the amenities are limited.) Once my costume was complete, I walked over to the Christmas party and did my routine. Luckily, Jones was willing to help me out with the act. Jones played the role of a Soldier that was getting yelled at by big bad SSG Tarver. I was laying into him and throwing out the phrase "Big Timer" at the end of every single sentence. At one point the First Sergeant noticed the foil in my mouth and broke out into hysterical laughter. The entire party was laughing their asses off, except for one man. In case you can't guess who that one man was, it was SSG Tarver. He sat there the whole time quiet, just steaming. Granted, it may have been wrong for me to make a joke out of him, but he had spent quite a lot of time treating the junior Soldiers (including myself) like crap. As far as I was concerned, Tarver had this coming. And to be perfectly honest, it did feel good to bring smiles and laughter to the whole unit during the holiday season, a time when everyone had no choice but to spend that Christmas away from home. I think many people would agree with me that it is better to have your whole unit walking around laughing than it is to have everyone in the unit walk around sad and depressed. All in all, I like to think today that my comedy routine was the highlight of our makeshift Christmas party. Too bad SSG Tarver didn't take it as lightly as SGT Ramos.

A couple of weeks after the USO ran its annual holiday tour and our company Christmas party, Christmas day finally came along. Things were still hard to deal with because I missed my family a lot, and so did all of the other Soldiers. It was just very hard for me (as well as my fellow Soldiers) to miss the holiday. When I was growing up Christmas was always my favorite time of the year. To this day, spending Christmas at home is priceless for me. Christmas 2003 was the first Christmas that I was ever away from home. I did get a bit emotional that day for that very reason. We did have the day off from work that day, which definitely helped make Christmas still feel like a holiday. I made sure to call home and talk to my family that day. I missed them so much. Of course, on Christmas day the phone lines were the longest I had ever seen. Everyone was trying to call home, and thus there was a 15 minute time limit. This was perfectly understandable. Everyone deserves to get a turn to call home on Christmas. I can't imagine how bad I would have felt if I didn't get the opportunity to call home on Christmas day.

The feeling amongst the Soldiers in the unit was much different on Christmas day also. It was different in the respect that everyone seemed to get along. The petty arguments that some of the Soldiers had amongst each other dissolved on Christmas. Even though we couldn't be with our families, we all became like a family to each other out there; especially on this day. Aside from calling home, there were still some things to do on the airfield to stay busy. There were a few Iraqi shops on the airfield that I didn't go to very often, so on Christmas day Jones and I grabbed a Humvee and took a ride over to one of the shops that was on the other side of the airfield. It was something to do. When I got a good look at the shop I was surprised at the selection of things that they had there. They had the typical selection of bootleg electronics like most of the other shops (which didn't actually interest me), as well as a nice selection of cigars. I also noticed that this shop happened to have a nice collection of leather jackets that were made in the local Iraqi markets. These jackets were so nice that you couldn't tell the difference between one of these jackets and one that you would buy in the US. They had a price tag of $80, which made them a steal. I ended up buying one, along with a few Cuban cigars. I don't remember what Jones bought, but what I do remember was that it was refreshing to get out on the airfield and do something besides work or PT. As far as the jacket, it actually held up to the test of time. I still have it now and it some of the seams only just finally ripped in 2011. Even if I decide not to get it fixed, I will never throw it away just because of the sentimental value that the jacket has to me. After all, I bought that jacket on Christmas day in a foreign country. Now that's what I call a conversation piece.

The KBR DFAC also took great care of us on Christmas. The elaborate spread of food that is flown in from the US and Europe for this occasion is simply astounding. For those of you reading this that have been deployed before, you know exactly what I am talking about. And for those of you who have not, I will elaborate. KBR is in charge of providing quality food to the Soldiers during their deployments, which of course boosts the morale of the Soldiers. What better day to try to boost the Soldier's morale than on the biggest holiday of the year? The DFAC staff works extra hard on Christmas day, often extending their work hours to ensure that all the Soldiers on the camp can get in to eat. They don't just serve regular food either. Real turkeys are flown in and carved at various carving stations throughout the DFAC. There's also Shrimp cocktail, ham, mashed potatoes, yams, vegetables, assorted pies and cookies as well. There's also usually a huge cake with the division's insignia on the frosting. They even serve eggnog (non-alcoholic of course). Christmas day is literally the biggest day the DFAC has every year. I've never known a Soldier to be disappointed with the Christmas meal on a deployment. For our unit, we tried to get as many of us together to go at once. We didn't get everyone, but with everyone we did get it did help foster the "family" feeling. On a deployment its days like Christmas that make you realize the most important thing you have when you are out there: each other; your fellow Soldier. Even though I wasn't home with my family for the Christmas 2003, I will always have fond memories of getting a day off from the office, buying a nice leather jacket that lasted for a very long time, and enjoying a great meal with my brothers and sisters in arms.

After being in the dessert for so long, 2004 finally came along. Everyone knew this was a good sign because we knew that we would be heading home in 2004. Despite all of the hardship that we had encountered so far, the morale in the unit slowly started to increase with each passing day. The very idea of going home was enough to improve everyone's spirits. We ended up having a formation one day where we were all told that our convoy back to Kuwait would actually be taking place right then in January. We started packing up all of our equipment as quickly as possible. We all had one thing in mind, and that was going home. Nothing else mattered and there was nothing that was going to hold us back. BASEOPS ended up moving us into brand new Containerized Housing Units (also known as CHUs) so we had a place to stay while we started to take our tents down. This definitely boosted morale because we were finally getting to stay in some sort of housing as opposed to a tent. Trust me, living in a tent for nearly a year can take a toll on you. Let's just say that it gets old after a while.

About a week before the actual convoy we had a briefing/meeting with all of the drivers and TCs for the convoy. When I made the move to the supply section earlier in the deployment I became a driver and had to trade my SAW to another Soldier for an M16. Since I was working in supply, I would be required to be the driver for the supply vehicle, with the OIC of supply (my good buddy Allison) as the TC. It seemed like a perfect fit because we were friends and we got along. If you're going to spend three days on the road with someone it is definitely better if the person you are on the road with is someone you actually like. Aside from an excessively long slide show about safety and our order of march we were also informed during this briefing that we would be stopping in a total of 2 different camps for rest over the course of our trip. The driving and rest cycles were also timed out in a crucial manner. We would be passing through Baghdad at midnight. This was because there was a curfew in place for people to be off the streets at this time, which would minimize the risk of attacks and more importantly the risk casualties. This type of schedule for our convoy made perfect sense. Why not pass through the most populated areas of your route while there is no one allowed on the streets? Personally, I approved of the idea.

The convoy ended up taking place in the middle of January. Allison and I prepared accordingly. We picked up a lot of snacks and soda from the PX to last us through the trip. We wanted to try to avoid eating MREs if we could. When you've been deployed for as long as we had been you tend to not want to eat MREs anymore at almost any cost. I also picked up two Cuban cigars out on the airfield to take with us. The purpose of these cigars was to be a "victory smoke" when we passed the Kuwait border. I also had a CD player boombox that I used for most of the deployment that we brought with us, along with a stock of "D" batteries that we got from the PX. We figured that if we were going to have to spend three days on the road, we may as well make it as livable as possible. Having music on the trip would certainly help pass the time. I had Jones burn a few CDs for me on his computer prior to the convoy. Me being a big '80s buff, I had one particular CD with a lot of that kind of music on there. Allison also had a CD collection with stuff she wanted to hear too which obviously didn't feature '80s rock. The thing was I had this perfect plan in my head that we would roll out of Mosul Airfield for the final time, with one special song blasting on the radio. That song was Europe's one hit wonder, "The Final Countdown." The song seemed to fit the moment perfectly for some reason. I ended up convincing Allison that listening to "The Final Countdown" as the very first song of the trip was the right thing to do. Right before the convoy took off we all had one last, quick brief. I had the CD in the boombox, on pause. All I had to do was hit the play button. Everyone got into their vehicles, and I looked at Allison as she put her Kevlar helmet on. I asked her, "Are you ready?" and she replied "Yes." I think that she may have thought that I was referring to the trip when I asked her if she was ready. No, I was actually referring to the song, as in, "Are you ready to hear the final countdown?" As the convoy began to pull out of the lot to begin its journey, I slowly reached over to the boombox and hit the play button. The song started. And for those of you who don't know the lyrics of this epic tune, I'll give you a quick preview: "We're leaving together, but still its farewell, and maybe we'll come back, to earth, who can tell? I guess there is no one to blame, we're leaving ground, will things ever be the same again? It's the final countdown, the final countdown!" That epic song played as we embarked on our final journey in Iraq, a journey that will never be forgotten.

The convoy itself was a long and tiring one. It will also be something that sticks out in my memory forever. We did indeed pass through Baghdad at around midnight, and there were zero incidents. There was also no one on the street, thanks to the curfew. We took our breaks accordingly, but due to the strict way that everything was planned out, we didn't get much sleep. We arrived to our first rest stop a little later than we had planned, but due to the strict schedule we weren't going to put off leaving by just a little bit. We ended up getting less rest on each of our stops than we had intended. It got to the point where the second we parked at the rest stop we climbed into the back of the vehicle and passed out. It was a long trip. Granted we were very excited about going home, and that kept us awake to a certain degree but even with the adrenaline running we still started to get very tired after a while. It ended up making the last few hours of the trip a lot harder to handle. Even still, we pressed on. We had a goal, and that goal was to get to Kuwait so we could go home. Going home meant so much to all of us. Most of us didn't get to go home on R and R leave. It had been a long deployment. All anyone really wanted at this point was to go home, and this convoy was the last major obstacle that stood in our way.

Eventually we made it to Kuwait. When we passed the border, we immediately had to stop at the first camp to unload all of our ammunition. Kuwait is a safe, non-warring country and thus there was no reason to keep our weapons loaded. I remember being greeted at the camp by Soldiers who worked there. The first thing they said was, "Welcome to Navstar."

Navstar was obviously the name of the camp. We parked all of our vehicles parked in a straight line in the same order as our convoy. So that it now reads as follows: We parked all of our vehicles in a straight line in the same order as our convoy. Our leadership had to briefly get together to make sure everyone was on the same page for our next destination. I took this opportunity to briefly celebrate. I put my hands in the air and did the legendary Hulk Hogan pose that I had done so many other times during this deployment only this time instead of standing there with the pose like normal, I ran up and down the long row of vehicles with the pose in the air. This was a victory for all of us, and what better way to show it. After I was finished posing and unloading my ammo, Allison and I decided to light up our victory cigars. Allison wasn't a cigar smoker like I was so this was a new experience for her. We climbed up onto the hood of the Humvee to take a quick picture with our victory cigars which I still have to this day along with all of my other pictures from this deployment. Overall, the day that we all arrived to Navstar was probably one of the happiest of the whole deployment. Gone were the harsh living conditions, the rocket attacks, and the bad feelings. After our brief check in, we all geared up to convoy down to Camp Arifijan, where we would wash our vehicles of all of the Iraqi sand and mud, and subsequently await our flight back to the US.

Camp Arifijan wasn't a bad ordeal whatsoever. The living conditions were great there. We had modern showers with running water, both hot and cold. We lived in giant garage like bays. Although there was no privacy in these bays, they were at least clean, warm and organized. It was a definite improvement over the tents and the CHUs that we had to live in while we were still in Iraq. Of course, the eating arrangements were better there too. We had a great DFAC that trumped anything that KBR had to offer in Iraq. There was also a food court there that had a Burger King, Pizza place, a Green Beans Coffee shop and a Hole-in-one doughnut shop. Needless to say, Camp Arifijan was a very comfortable place. It almost felt like a resort, especially after everything we had been through. We also didn't have any work to do whatsoever, so we had a lot of free time on our hands. After the long deployment, a little free time on our hands wasn't a bad thing. In retrospect, I think having that time to slightly decompress helped us when we got back to the US. It wasn't like we landed in the US straight out of a war zone; we had some time to "stretch out" a bit in Kuwait. In fact, we had a little over two weeks to "stretch out". That's how long it took to get our flight booked to head back to the US.

One day while we were still there our First Sergeant was able to set the unit up with a bus trip to Camp Doha. Camp Doha is probably the only camp in Kuwait that has better amenities than Camp Arifijan. Today Camp Doha is closed down but back in 2004 it was still alive and well. The cool thing about Camp Doha was that we could wear civilian clothes there, meaning we didn't have to wear uniform if we didn't want to. For many of the Soldiers in the unit, this was their first time wearing civilian clothes in almost a year. I was different however, since I was able to go to Qatar earlier in the deployment I had already experienced this. Even still, Camp Doha was a nice place to visit. They had even better places to eat and shop than Arifijan, including a Starbucks. I made it a point to go to the Starbucks and buy a Kuwait "city mug". I had bought one when I was in Qatar and I thought it would be cool that I bought one there in Kuwait too. This would also cement bragging rights that I got to drink coffee at a Starbucks in Qatar and Kuwait, two foreign countries. In addition to all of this, Camp Doha also had something else that interested me. There was a giant cardboard poster of Saddam Hussein's face with the words, "MISSION ACCOMPLISHED". To me that was the coolest thing that I got to see while I was in Kuwait. I made sure to take a picture with it, after all there's a good chance that I may never see something like that again.

After waiting over two weeks, the big day to fly out of Kuwait finally came. Everyone was truly excited, but there was also a hint of nervousness in the air. I could sense it. I think for some people, when you haven't seen your loved ones in so long there may be a certain feeling of tension and nervousness. That's not the case with me but definitely for others. There's nothing wrong with that however. The flight itself was a long one, about 18 hours with all the same stops in the same countries that we stopped in when we came. Even though there was a feeling of excitement on the flight back, I took this time to reflect on a lot of things. I had a lot to think about. I felt that I had grown a lot as a man over the deployment. I was only one year older, but all of my experiences made me feel much older. I had worked very hard on a lot of things. I had traveled to a few new countries. I got to see many parts of Iraq. I had learned my job and nearly mastered some aspects of it. I had become a better Soldier. I hit the gym extremely hard and lost about 30 pounds. I was promoted to the rank of Specialist. I made a lot of great, lifelong friends. I had experienced so much more than anyone my age that I knew from back home in Saint Johnsville. I had made my family proud. I was very thankful for all of this, but most importantly I was thankful for the memories. I now possessed memories that I would carry with me for the rest of my life. These were lessons that I had learned throughout all of my travels. Overall, this deployment was an adventure, the biggest adventure of my life so far. Yet I knew that this adventure wouldn't be the last adventure of my life. If there was anything that this deployment taught me, it was that there was a big world out there, so much to see and so much to do. The world had a lot more to offer than Saint Johnsville and Fort Campbell and I was ready to embrace just about anything. To be honest, going over there at the young age of 19 was a blessing for me. Granted, it was hard and there were a lot of sacrifices to be made, but in the long run it was well worth it. No matter what happens in life, I will always have my memories.

Before we knew it we had entered United States Airspace. Suddenly the long flight didn't seem so long anymore. We were almost there. Before we knew it, we were descending upon the airstrip on Fort Campbell, preparing for landing. Everyone on the plane turned their attention to the windows. It was as if everyone was glued to the scene, just wanting to see the airplane's tires touch American soil. You could literally feel the anticipation. As the tires touched the ground, the pilot came on the radio and said to the crowd, "Ladies and Gentlemen, welcome home to the United States of America!" The entire plane broke out into the loudest round of applause and cheering that I had ever heard. I felt as if I was going to shed a tear. I have a feeling that I wasn't the only one.

CHAPTER 5

HOMECOMING

Once all of our baggage was unloaded from the plane we were all loaded onto coach buses to ride over to one of the gyms on post for our welcome home ceremony. The Battalion's rear detachment was responsible for not only planning and coordinating the ceremony itself, but also for contacting the families of all of the returning Soldiers. Even though the unit had contacted my dad and informed him that we were on the way back, I had already emailed him previously and informed him that we were leaving Kuwait to fly back to the US. I had also told him not to bother packing the family up to drive all the way down to Fort Campbell since I was going to be leaving Fort Campbell to drive back to Saint Johnsville on leave anyway shortly after our return. On the bus ride to the gym I remember half of the Soldiers being extremely excited about the prospect of seeing their families at the ceremony that we were about to take part in. I on the other hand borrowed a cell phone from one of my fellow Soldiers to call home and tell my dad that I made it home to the US safely. I was glad to be on US soil again, but I was even more anxious to get home as soon as possible. There was also a very safe, positive feeling on the bus as well. We had spent the past year of our life on a dangerous adventure and needless to say we were extremely happy to be on safe ground again. It felt so good to be back in the US. When we stepped off of the bus I can still remember how good the air smelled. It wasn't just cleaner air; it was free, American air. It was the air that you breathe in your home country. This feeling is something that can't be compared to anything else. I often hear people complain about how bad they think things are here in America. Granted, things aren't perfect here, but after you spend a year of your life enduring the hardships that we endured in Iraq, the US now seemed like the most perfect paradise imaginable. On this day, there was absolutely nothing that could bring me down.

The ceremony itself was a quick one. They marched us in to an extremely loud round of cheers and applause and went through all of the formalities. I must say that it was one of the loudest crowds that I had ever heard, and that includes the crowd of Iraqi Children that were convinced that I was going to produce Michael Jackson for them earlier in the deployment. During the course of the ceremony the Army Song as well as the National Anthem was played. Obviously we were required to sing along, but the crowd sung along too. The reaction of the crowd made us feel like heroes. The feeling was unlike anything I had ever experienced before in my entire life. After all of the pageantry, our Battalion Commander gave a quick speech and we were released on a four day pass. For some of us, (who didn't take R and R leave or go on pass to Qatar) this would be the first time that we got four days off in a year's time. Of course, there was the standard safety brief: don't drink and drive, don't beat your wife, don't beat your dog, don't drink and boat, don't get into fights, don't fight and boat, if you feel like committing suicide, call someone immediately. This was very similar to the safety briefs that I had heard before the deployment, but the difference was that now that we had been through some hard times this stuff actually held some substance. It wasn't unheard of for a Soldier to come back from a deployment and get into an altercation with his or her spouse. Alcohol abuse was also running rampant in the Army, and the DUI rate amongst Soldiers returning from deployments had risen sharply since the US started sending Soldiers on deployments to Iraq and Afghanistan. To say that our leadership was worried about incidents would have been an understatement.

For those of us Soldiers that didn't have family there to meet us, we were issued our new barracks room (in the same building as before the deployment), and then released for our four day pass. The unit was also generous and allowed us to choose who our roommate would be. Usually, a unit First Sergeant doesn't have to do this and can actually force us to room with anyone that they choose. I can honestly say that I was thankful to choose who I would stay with because as far as I was concerned there was only person I wanted to stay with. That person was the person that I ended up choosing to be my roommate: Jones. By now, Jones was pretty much my best friend in the unit. We had been through an awful lot together and I trusted him. I was there for him when he had his problems with Emily, and he was there for me when I had problems as well. If there was anyone in the SSB that I knew that I could trust, it was Jones. I also knew for a fact that Jones wouldn't rob me. Even though I knew all the other guys fairly well, I knew Jones that much more. Luckily for me, Jones felt the same way.

Jones and I pretty much hung out for the four day pass. His mom had come to town from Arkansas for the ceremony, and she took us to dinner to Texas Road House one night for dinner. We were offered free dessert or free beer since we went to the restaurant in uniform. Since neither one of us were drinkers (or even 21 for that matter) at the time, we took the free dessert. Even still, it was nice to be offered something for free as a "thank you" for our sacrifices.

Another thing that all of us had to do during this four day pass was to pick up our cars from the post storage lot. Before the deployment started I had left the Neon in the lot, and over the course of the deployment I was lucky enough to forget that I had owned the damn car. Unfortunately, I was quickly reminded upon return that the Neon was still my car. When I picked it up from the storage lot, it was still the same old bad car that I had left behind. It still had the slightly dented roof. It still lacked any real horsepower. It still had an extremely loud screaming type sound that came out of the speakers every time you turned the radio on. Above all else, it was also still the same embarrassment of a car that it was when I had left it behind. I had traveled the world and encountered tons of adversity and upon return I was smacked in the face with the hard reality that I was the proud owner of a 1998 Plymouth Neon with a dented roof. After everything that we had been through Jones still had wise cracks for me about the condition of my car. Of course, I took it all in stride. I had no choice but to take it in stride until I got rid of that god awful car.

After the four day pass was over with we started our redeployment processing. There were all sorts of things that we had to get handled over the next few days. Some of us had to get a few shots, while we all had to do a ton of paperwork and attend a lot of briefings. Some of the briefings were a redo of the safety brief that we had when we first arrived back to the US. There were a lot of anti-DUI briefs and a lot of anti-spousal abuse briefings. Apparently this had become a severe problem throughout the Army, so much so that it had to be re-briefed to us four days after it was initially briefed to us. It was news like this that made me feel bad. I hated hearing that Soldiers were having problems coming out of the battlefield. In a picture-perfect world you would imagine that a Soldier's life would come together in the greatest way after a deployment like this. You would want everything to go well for them and there to be no problems whatsoever. Unfortunately, this wasn't the case. Some Soldiers didn't know how to re-connect with their families or even society upon return. This kind of news being dropped on us was very sad. We had a great unit and we all looked out for each other, these problems didn't affect us directly, but it was still an Army-wide problem.

One good thing was that the redeployment processing only turned out to last about three days. We had planned on it lasting anywhere from one to two weeks, but since the rear detachment element of the SSB ran some elements of the processing we were able to move through the process quickly. Also, every one of us moved through the stations with a sense of urgency. No one wanted to sit on Fort Campbell any more than we had to. Our unit had just spent a year in Iraq, the only thing that anyone really wanted to do was take a break. I remember rushing through a lot of my paperwork myself. As cool as it was to be back on US Soil, I knew deep down that it would be so much better to be back home on Saint Johnsville soil. On the third day of our processing, our First Sergeant held a formation and told us that we would be authorized to take our leave early. We wouldn't have to wait two to three weeks like we had originally thought. To be honest, this was a long time coming anyway. We knew that we were done with our processing, so why would we have to sit there for two extra weeks anyway? We all knew the way the Army worked. It was common knowledge that the Army didn't always make sense, which is why we were all prepared to sit there for two more weeks for no reason whatsoever. I know that must sound crazy, but it's true. Just like any corporation in America, sometimes you have to deal with "red tape." Thankfully, our redeployment from Iraq would not end up being one of those times. After I took care of my leave paperwork I bid my temporary farewell to Jones, (who wasn't taking a full 30 days of leave) and I departed Fort Campbell in my estranged Plymouth Neon. This would prove to be my final trip from Fort Campbell to Saint Johnsville in the Neon.

The drive back in the Neon proved to be uneventful however. I guess I expected it to start stalling out on me again like it had before the deployment, but it didn't happen. The only thing that I had done to it before I left Fort Campbell was an Oil Change. The car still needed much more than an Oil Change however. The car actually needed exactly what I needed: a new car. Unfortunately for me I hadn't saved enough to buy a new car over the course of the deployment, so I was stuck with the Neon for now. I made a personal vow to try to get rid of the Neon when I returned to Campbell, at any cost. If that meant that I would have to take out a new loan to get a new car on a contract then I would do it. I even contemplated the possibility that maybe I would be "lucky enough" to get into another car accident and get a new car that way. Either way, I was sick of the embarrassment of driving the Neon. I did eventually make it home, and after the 15 hour trip I parked the Neon on the side of my dad's house and tried my best not to be seen driving it while I was home. It's amazing how the pride of spending a year in Iraq can be trumped by the embarrassment of driving a bad car.

When I got home, there was a small sense of nervousness when I entered my house. It was weird, I knew that it was my home, yet after spending a year gone I felt a strange feeling deep down inside of me. It's not like I wasn't going to be welcome there at home; because I was. I guess it was a small sense of apprehension towards normalcy as a result of the deployment. This feeling hadn't settled in yet when I was still at Fort Campbell, and I knew why. It was mainly because at Campbell I was still surrounded by the same people that I was with in Iraq. In retrospect, I guess I was slightly nervous about being around people that hadn't been through anything that I had been through. At least at Campbell I knew that Jones and Cursey had experienced the exact same things that I had, so it wasn't a problem. Luckily, when I finally did get home the odd feeling of nervousness dissolved quickly. My dad (as well as the rest of my family) was glad to see me. My baby brother Jeremey had grown a lot since the last time I saw him at Christmas 2002. Considering he was born while I was home for my Thanksgiving break in 2002, seeing him in 2004 was quite a treat. It had only been the third time that I had seen him and I wanted to be a part of his life as much as possible.

While home I was also getting accustomed to having this much free time on my hands. Not only was I used to being in Iraq where we worked almost every day for the entire year, but I was also used to the idea of not being home for long periods of time. The only times that I had been able to come home to Saint Johnsville while I was in the Army I had only been able to go home for either a four day weekend or a two week time period. This was the very first time that I had an entire month off during my career. It was a lot of time to adjust to. Before long, I found myself going out for long runs in the morning to help pass the time. Running in the morning also helped me to maintain a small part of Army mindset. I knew that I would have to go back to Fort Campbell sooner or later, I didn't want to fall into a state of mind where I had forgotten everything I had learned.

Being home was a lot of fun for me. Having the chance to re-connect with all of my friends and family was priceless. With everything that I had been through so far, it was easy to forget that everyone at home had been through a lot too. Just as I had encountered challenges over the past year, they had encountered challenges as well. I would have been arrogant to think that I was the only one that had changed over the course of the year. Still, all of my friends wanted to hear the stories. They wanted to know what Iraq was like, and they wanted to hear the stories of what I had been through. One thing to note is that a lot of people don't fully understand the concept of a support Soldier. Many times in my career I have found myself trying to explain to my non-military friends exactly what my job entailed, and they would still get it confused. Once or twice one of them would finally get it, but often times they wouldn't. And that's the difference between being a Soldier and being a civilian. If a fellow Soldier asks me what my MOS is, they will almost always know exactly what I am talking about when I tell them that I am a 42A. That's not the case with my civilian friends. I think the mainstream media is to blame for that. Movies, TV shows and even the news constantly portray the Army as strictly a bunch of combat killers. Granted, the Army is a proven combat force, but us Support Soldiers are too often forgotten. I stated in the beginning of this book that this fact was one of the main motivating factors in writing this book.

I can tell my friends all day long that I am not Infantry, and yet they will still want to hear all of the stories of me shooting people, kicking in doors, and fighting the "bad guys." Unfortunately for them, I didn't have any of those types of stories. Luckily for me (and for my friends) my deployment still consisted of enough adventure to give me a few good stories to tell, despite my chosen profession. I guess the idea of being part of a full scale invasion of an uncharted, third world country is exciting after all. I told the Stories of the places that I had been, as well as the hardships that I encountered. Those hardships included the rocket attacks as well. Sometimes my dad would mention that to people too. At work he would say, "Just because he isn't Infantry doesn't mean that he isn't in danger." He had a good point there. Over the course of the wars in Iraq and Afghanistan there have been many casualties, Combat Soldiers and Support Soldiers alike. Even government employed civilians and private contractors have found themselves in danger over there. Believe me when I tell you, the enemy does not discriminate. They don't stop attacking because you are a support Soldier. All they see is an American Soldier, who they would like to kill regardless of profession.

The funny thing about me not being an Infantry Soldier is that I would also sometimes use that as an excuse for my family and friends to not worry about me. Even though I knew things were dangerous over there, I would try to put people at ease when I would call or write home. I appreciated the support, but I really didn't want anyone to be overly stressed about me. I used this tactic especially when I would call my mother from Iraq. She would always tell me, "Ken I'm so worried about you. I need you to come home safe." I would just tell her, "Don't worry Mom. That's not my job. I'm in the safe part of Iraq." Some parts of that country are safer than others, but no place is truly 100% safe. That's just how it is.

Aside from hanging out with my friends and catching up, I did manage to do one very important thing while I was home after the deployment which I will never forget. One of my lifelong friends, Hillary Cool asked me if I would be willing to speak at an assembly at the Saint Johnsville Elementary School. Her mother Linda was a teacher there and she asked Hillary if I would be willing to do the speech. Since the war was on the news just about every day, most of the kids knew about it, but almost none of them had ever met a Soldier before. This was the opportunity for the school to not just present a Soldier to them, but also for someone to send a positive message to the kids. Hillary asked me if I would do the speech in uniform and of course I agreed. I felt that given the circumstances the most appropriate uniform to wear would be the Dessert Combat Uniform (DCU) that I had worn in Iraq for the year that I was there. Other times that I visited home in uniform I had worn my Class A uniform, but not this time. I had just returned from Iraq. I would wear the same uniform that I had worn over there. I also felt that the DCU would send a more realistic message to the children. That boils back to the media. The DCU is what the kids saw on TV, so that is exactly what I would give them.

As I was getting ready to go on stage, I remember Hillary saying to me, "Remember Ken, you can't swear." This was the first time that I had been in front of a crowd in a while. I had taken public speaking in high school (I got an A) but that was so long ago. I was a little nervous about giving the speech, and now I had the added pressure of being told I couldn't swear. Of course, I wasn't going to swear to begin with, but I think being told not to do it added a certain level of nervousness because now I had to consciously think about not swearing during the entire speech. The funny thing was, I hadn't formally prepared a speech. Usually when I give speeches that is actually my tactic. I don't actually prepare a written speech or even note cards; I just briefly think about my topic and just "wing it." This probably doesn't sound very effective, but for me it works. It's proven to work for me on many occasions and I've had people come up to me after speeches telling me they thought it was great and it looked like I prepared a lot. Honestly, my preparation tactic for speeches is not preparing at all. To me as long as you have an idea of what you want to talk about, the rest should come from the heart. That is real passion, and that is what captivates people. Put it this way: do you want to spit out a bunch of recorded facts, or do you want to say something that will truly move someone or ignite a fire within them?

I pulled off the speech without a hitch. I touched on a few topics while I was talking to the kids. I talked about patriotism, and what going over there meant to me and more importantly what it meant to the United States of America. I also talked to the kids about self-sacrifice. Sometimes in life you have to do something very hard for the benefit of others. I told them a watered down version of some of the things that I had been through, and how there were kids in Iraq that had it way worse than a lot of the kids here in America. We as Americans had a lot to be thankful for. I gave the most positive speech that I could, and afterwards I stayed to shake hands with as many of them as possible. They all came up to me like I was their hero, and it made me feel very good inside. The school faculty was very happy with the results and they all thanked me as well. All in all, it was a very touching experience for me that I will never forget. After the speech I was also told that the local newspaper The Evening Times was there to cover the event. The next day I was delighted to see that a picture of me on the stage in my DCU uniform with the microphone in my hand was on the front page of the newspaper. I still have the issue of that newspaper to this day, and I'll never throw it out. It wasn't my first time on the front page of the newspaper at home, but it was certainly my proudest time on the cover. I hope that the day is as memorable for the kids and for the faculty as it was for me. And for the record, I did the speech without uttering one swear word.

Before I knew it, my 30 days of leave was up. The time went by quickly (as it always does), but it was time well spent. I spent as much time catching up with friends and family as possible, and I had also had the chance to do something meaningful in my hometown. I was sad about having to leave Saint Johnsville for the 15 hour drive to Fort Campbell, but at least I knew I made the best of my vacation. I bid everyone farewell and I promised I would be back to visit soon. Part of me wanted to cry inside. This was the first time in my entire career that I had a whole month off from the Army. I had grown attached to being home again and I secretly thought about the possibility of getting out at the end of my four year enlistment and moving back home. Luckily for me, these thoughts were just based on emotion, and not logic. The logical thing to do was obviously to stay in the Army. The rest is history. I loved home so much, but the thing about home, is that it will always be home. It will always be there for you no matter where you travel, wherever your life takes you. So I knew it was time to get my life's journey started again.

Of course, the drive itself wasn't the easiest trip to pull off. In case you forgot, I was still the not-so-proud owner of the worst Neon on earth, and I had to pull the long drive off in that thing. At this point in my life I didn't even consider it a car anymore, it was a "thing". Luckily for me, I wasn't going to be driving this "thing" much longer. I'm sure that by now, since you have read this much of the book you are probably wanting to ask me the question, "Why didn't you just put some money into the car to improve it, to make it better?" I'll gladly answer that question now, "No." Now, I know I just answered "no" to a question that wasn't even a "YES or NO" question. That's ok though. I just want to stress that this thing was beyond the idea of saving. It was better to just take it behind the shed and put a bullet in its head, figuratively speaking. Thankfully, my chance was coming soon.

I arrived back to Fort Campbell ready to get back to work. I knew that the easiest way for me to overcome my homesickness was to get myself back into a routine. If you have a routine, then you could keep your mind busy which will help you forget whatever it is that is bothering you. In my case it was my thoughts of home that I needed to get past. When I got back Jones told me that he had already been back to work for a couple weeks since he didn't take the full 30 days of leave like everyone else. So Jones was lucky, he already figured out how to fall back into his routine. Of course, it wasn't much of a routine for him. He told me that since the main element of the unit was on leave he was pretty much doing sham work and going home early every day. Lucky him. I had a feeling that when I got back to work things wouldn't be as easy for me as they were for him.

When the rest of the unit came back to work, a lot of things changed. Some of these changes created a lot of challenges. One challenge was that the rear detachment Soldiers had to unite with us to come together as one unit again. That may sound easy to you, but in reality it wasn't. The Soldiers who stayed behind when we deployed had a reputation for being lazy and not performing at work. Since we had been through many hardships over the past year, a lot of us didn't really want to work with any of them. I hate to admit it now, but it's safe to say that we had a chip on our shoulders. Most of us didn't even respect a lot of them. Of course, hearing the rumors of some of the things that went on back there when we were deployed didn't help matters either. While we had to work almost every day in Iraq, we had heard through the grapevine that they were getting four day weekends all the time and going home early a lot too. Can you blame us for feeling a slight feeling of resentment? One time it got so bad that the rear detachment First Sergeant and our First Sergeant got into an argument in front of the whole formation. Our First Sergeant wanted to unite the two fractions of the unit, while the other one wanted to maintain the level of separation for a little while. The rear detachment First Sergeant even tried to "pull rank" and force our First Sergeant to adhere to his will. Ultimately, the Company Commander had to step in behind closed doors and set the whole thing straight. The truth was we were one unit. The disagreements and separation were unnecessary. The following morning, our First Sergeant announced that he was indeed the Company First Sergeant and from that morning forward there would be no more separation. We were one unit. We were Bravo Company, 101st Soldier Support Battalion, and we were proud of it.

Within a week of returning to work we were told that the entire 101st would be marching in a welcome home parade in the city of Clarksville. It was an honor to do so, and I could tell that many of my fellow Soldiers that returned from Iraq were also honored to be a part of the parade. The parade lasted well over an hour and it was quite a site to see, considering the entire division was out there marching. I never thought that I would ever see a 20,000 Soldier parade march through Clarksville. It was crazy. There were hundreds of citizens on the side of the road clapping and cheering us on the entire time. It was a little overwhelming to say the least. The event left a lasting impression on me of the city of Clarksville. It is probably the most patriotic "military town" I have ever seen. Marching in this parade was a great way to start things off on a high note after spending a hard year deployed.

Another notable event that took place when we returned to work at Fort Campbell was a visit from President Bush. This was the first time that I had ever seen a President in person, so I was excited. I wish I could say the same about a lot of my fellow Soldiers. As most people are probably aware, many people bear mixed emotions concerning President Bush's time in office. The day he came, the entire division was required to go to the parade field to see him. There were literally thousands of Soldiers out there and because of this I didn't get a very good view of the stage where he was speaking from. But just because I didn't get to see the man doesn't mean I didn't get to hear the man. His speech was what you would expect: he ran down some statistics of what was happening with the war, mentioned the capture of Saddam Hussein and that the US would continue to fight the war on terror, and of course he thanked the Soldiers of the 101st Airborne Division and stated that "the US couldn't have done it without you." Even though I was in awe of the fact that he was there to visit, the speech was still what I had expected out of a President during wartime.

One challenge that I had to face on a personal level was a major shift in my office structure. I was able to return to the evaluations section, but both Mehring and Defrates were moved to other sections in the company so they can learn a different aspect of our job. This is normally something that is done for the purpose of professional development. If a Soldier only works in one section while they are in a unit it will put them at a disadvantage when they finally get to move to another unit. Say the Soldier goes to a unit and they have no choice but to work in the promotions section, but for the past five years they worked in the evaluations section. It would create serious problems because the Soldier wouldn't know what they are doing, which would mean that someone would have to take the time to train them for the new job. It is a much better idea to try to cross-train your Soldiers while they are assigned to your unit. Anything else could be seen as "setting up your Soldiers for failure."

The new rotation of Soldiers proved to be a refreshing change. It's always good to change things up a little. I wasn't moved myself because everyone else was and when restructuring your unit you have to remember to maintain some continuity within the section. Now, while it was a refreshing change to work with other Soldiers, there was a leadership change that wasn't so refreshing. SGT Ramos was leaving the section to go work as the First Sergeant's training room NCO. Obviously after running the evaluations section for a few years SGT Ramos was more than ready for a change. Unfortunately for me, the NCO that ended up replacing him was a "lame duck" NCO, if you will. He wasn't much of a leader and didn't provide very much guidance to our section. This definitely created a problem because the Soldiers that replaced Mehring and Defrates were straight out of AIT. They didn't have the experience that I had, so they needed more guidance. Our new NCO wasn't just a lackluster leader; he also had no skills in our section whatsoever. I couldn't figure out how he knew absolutely nothing about evaluations; considering the fact that he is an NCO and all NCOs receive an evaluation at a minimum of an annual basis. As a result of our new leader's deficiencies, I ended up being the one that the new Soldiers would turn to for advice. On occasion they would ask me to teach them some things about the job, which I would. This wasn't much of a problem, but I did find it to be slightly comical when our NCO came to me asking to give him a quick class on evaluations. Of course I obliged and helped him out. He is the boss after all. The sad part was that I ended up having to re-brief him the same class quite a few times. I couldn't figure out if he either didn't care, or just couldn't grasp the material. I often considered throwing a stack of his reports on the floor in the same manner that SGT Ramos had done to me. That would teach him! Of course I didn't end up doing that because I was still just a Specialist and he was a Sergeant, so by regulation I did owe him a certain level of respect and courtesy.

I could remember that there were times that I would get so frustrated with our new NCO that I would take a ten minute break and head downstairs to SGT Ramos' new office to vent. He would always give me a shit-eating smirk and ask me, "How's your new NCO?" I could tell that SGT Ramos was being sarcastic and obviously knew that the new NCO wasn't going to last. Apparently, the other NCOs in the unit knew of his shortcomings and had even less respect for him than I did. He had absolutely no discipline in the office. The only thing that we knew about him was that he had recently been stationed in Korea and that he liked to drink a lot. I was very lucky to have the opportunity to vent to SGT Ramos during this trying time, and I was even luckier to have had the privilege to work and learn my job under SGT Ramos. Without SGT Ramos I wouldn't have succeeded as well as I had throughout my career. Thankfully my first impression of the NCO Corps wasn't this new NCO.

Before long, he made a huge mistake. The unit hosted the annual Adjutant General Ball. We all got into our Class A uniform and went to a ballroom just outside of Clarksville, TN. For me, it was my first military ball, and it was a cool experience. I sat at a table with a lot of the Soldiers that I had been deployed with and enjoyed dinner and there was also some dancing. There was also a video presentation with a bunch of slides that had pictures from our deployment. Along with all of the formalities and pageantry, there was also another thing available at this ball: alcohol. Like any formal event, if you are 21 years old you can legally drink. Because of alcohol use on this night, the remainder of my time in that unit changed forever . . . only it wasn't me using the alcohol. I didn't even drink at the time. It was my NCO. He started drinking at the ball, but didn't stop. I bumped into him at one of the award tables since we weren't actually sitting at the same table together. It was the first time that evening that I had actually spoke to him, and I could tell he was drunk. He kept telling people how much he missed Korea and how much Fort Campbell depressed him. A few of his superiors had asked him how he was getting home that night, and he claimed that he had a ride home. Someone was going to pick him up and everything was going to be fine. In retrospect I believe that his leaders should have followed up on his story, because his story ended up turning out to be a lie. On that night, my NCO made a horrible mistake and got behind the wheel. Luckily, he didn't get into a car accident and kill/hurt himself or anyone else. What did happen however became the new "talk of the water cooler" if you will. He got a DUI.

If you get a DUI it is of course a serious matter. There are all sorts of court costs involved, as well as the consequences of possible loss of drivers' license, fines, injuries, death, and even jail time. And that's just in the private sector. If you are in the Army and you get a DUI, it is way worse. You still go through all of the legal stuff that you would if you weren't in the Army, but you also have to deal with trouble at the unit. In almost every case, a Soldier who gets a DUI ends up getting an Article 15 which results in demotion as well as extra duty. The Soldier usually gets their on-post driving privileges suspended and they are forced to enter rehab. To say that the Army doesn't treat DUI offenses lightly would be an understatement. The NCO had to go and stand before the Commanding General and explain himself. See, as serious of an offense as it is when a Soldier gets a DUI, it is even worse if you are an NCO or an Officer and you get a DUI. As a leader in the Army you are supposed to set a proper example for your subordinates. Getting a DUI is not the way to do that. He ended up somehow not losing his rank, but the first sergeant treated him like he was a child for now on. The hardest part of this whole ordeal for me was that he was now forced to keep his Jeep parked behind the company while he was going through his case and his rehab program. His Jeep stayed parked for months. He had effectively lost his on-post driving privileges and he wasn't going to get them back any time soon. This became a problem for me because he relied on his Soldiers (me included) to pick him up and take him to work in the morning every day. It's a strange feeling when you have to pick up your supervisor for work every day because he is no longer legally able to do it himself. I can't imagine how embarrassing it must have been for him having to rely on one of his Soldiers to pick him up and take him home every day. I know that everyone makes mistakes, but if I was in his shoes I would have felt embarrassed and pathetic. To this day, I still don't drink and drive. I never have, and I never will. It is wrong, not just legally but morally as well. There is no way to measure the lives that you put at risk when you drink and drive. On his fateful night he is lucky that he didn't end up killing anyone. Considering he couldn't even get over missing Korea, I'm not quite sure that he could handle having someone's death on his conscious. Thank god no one was hurt in this incident.

The details of his incident spread like wildfire, especially since his Jeep was permanently parked behind the Company right next to the smoking area where everyone could see. There were jokes spread about him around the company. I remember at night in the barracks Jones would tell me stuff that he heard about him down in his section. The sad part was that my NCO didn't have any friends in the unit to begin with, the last thing he needed was to become the laughing stock of the unit. After a while he was finally transferred to another unit where he would complete his rehab and start over. To this day I have no idea how the rest of his career turned out. I do not know if he ever got his driving privileges back, and I don't know if he ever got the chance to go to Korea again where he was happy. What I can say is that the entire experience of not only working for him in the office but also witnessing the mistakes he made in his own life taught me a very important lesson. It wasn't just about the dangers of drinking and driving. That was only one part of the lesson. It was also about how not to act; how not to be when you are in a position of leadership. Maybe I wasn't as impressionable as the other Soldiers in our section because of my past experiences. The other Soldiers weren't as lucky. This NCO was their first leader they ever had in the Army (not counting the Drill Sergeants during training). As a leader he was a supreme failure and thanks to him I know what right looks like. I know how to set a good example and how not to act. This NCO went from being a new leader who didn't know the job to a new leader that had a pending legal case and needed his Soldiers to drive him everywhere; all the while he still didn't know the job. If I was to sum the lesson I learned from him into one sentence I think I would say, "Never underestimate the effect that your actions have on the lives of others."

CHAPTER 6

TNA

Before I get into the events of this chapter, I would like to take the opportunity to explain the meaning of the name of this chapter. This chapter is called "TNA", which as you can probably imagine is an acronym for many things. In this case, the acronym stands for "Total Nonstop Action" which at the time was the name of a new, up and coming wrestling organization. TNA Wrestling (as it was affectionately called) was the "number 2" promotion that was coming up in the early part of 2004. As a huge fan of professional wrestling I tried my best to follow Wrestling in all of its forms, not just the WWE. As a kid I was a fan of not just the WWE but also the WCW and ECW as well. Eventually the WCW and ECW organizations were bought out by the WWE which effectively made WWE the only Professional Wrestling program to watch. As a wrestling fan, the idea of a new wrestling organization coming into the scene was an exciting idea. As it turned out, TNA Wrestling was based out of Nashville, just a 40 minute drive from Fort Campbell.

One of the things I started doing again when I got back to Fort Campbell after my leave was going to the recreation center again to watch Monday Night Raw (a WWE program). After the long deployment it was good to be reunited with my old friends Jason Mays and AJ. Due to the fact that our units were in different parts of the country, I hadn't gotten to hang out with either one of them in a very long time. In fact, I only got to see Jason once or twice over the course of the deployment, and AJ I didn't get to see at all. That's the Army life for you though. Friends and family are always separated for the sake of the mission. Those two were my two best friends on Fort Campbell and it was great to be able to start hanging out again.

One night when we all met at the recreation center for Monday Night RAW, we saw that there was a stack of free tickets to TNA wrestling in Nashville at the front desk. They of course had the TNA logo on it with pictures of their wrestlers, but on the back there was a Fort Campbell stamp on the back to identify it as one of the tickets for the Soldiers. It seemed like a great idea to go to a free Wrestling show in Nashville, but the only thing was that the events took place on Wednesday nights. Back then that was how TNA ran their programming; a weekly Wednesday night Pay Per View. Unfortunately, since it was on a Wednesday and we all had full time jobs in the Army, both AJ and Jason couldn't go with me to that event. I honestly didn't want to go alone, so I convinced Jones to go. Jones was a wrestling fan but he wasn't as into it as me. If the tickets weren't free and I wasn't driving there was a good chance that I wouldn't have been able to convince Jones to go. There was a catch however, it was specified on the ticket that Soldiers should go in uniform. We didn't think anything of it, we figured it was a good thing since we had recently gotten back from a deployment and a lot of different organizations were going to great lengths to honor and take care of the troops at the time.

The event took place at the Tennessee State Fairgrounds in Nashville. When Jones and I got there to the event we were immediately shocked at how small the arena was. It looked like it could only hold about 1,500 fans. I guess when you watch it on TV the camera has a way to make the crowd and arena look much bigger than it actually is in real life. We looked around the arena and saw that we were the only two Soldiers in the room, or at the very least we were the only two Soldiers in uniform. If there were any other Soldiers there, they weren't in uniform. A woman by the name of Dixie Carter approached us and took us to our seats, which were in the front row. She asked us a lot of questions about the Army and wanted to know if we had been overseas. She was very interested in the fact that we had just returned from Iraq and thanked us for our service. We thought that maybe she was just a valet or perhaps a middle management company employee, but as the conversation continued she ended up revealing to us that she is actually the President of TNA Wrestling. We really didn't think that the president of the company would be there to greet us, but it happened. Right before the show started she summoned the ring announcer Jeremy Borash over to us and he took down our names. He then got in the ring and said, "Ladies and gentlemen in attendance, TNA Wrestling would like to extend a warm welcome to a couple of true American heroes that just returned overseas from the War in Iraq! Ladies and Gentlemen, I give you Ken Conklin and Jonathan Jones!" We couldn't believe that we were being given this kind of welcome. It was insane. We stood up and waived to the crowd. Everyone in the Arena had their attention focused on us, and the entire crowd was chanting, "USA! USA! USA!" Being in front of the patriotic crowd while everyone was chanting was a huge adrenaline rush. We felt like heroes. There is no other feeling like being in front of a crowd. I remember thinking to myself, "Wow, is this feeling what the wrestlers feel on the inside when they come to the ring?" If we had to leave the show right then I probably could have left a happy man after that experience. Fortunately for us, we still had a full wrestling show ahead of us to enjoy.

Dixie ended up sitting with us for the entire show, and all the while asked us what we thought of the action. As a passionate wrestling fan, I loved what I saw. One thing I was appreciative of was the fact that quite a few of the wrestlers that were there were former stars of the WWE and WCW. I grew up watching a lot of these guys on TV, and now here they were wrestling in front of me as we sat in the front row. TNA had a lot of young, up and coming talent that were also great wrestlers too. Overall, the show was excellent. When the show was finished, Dixie told us that we were welcome to come back any time we wanted and as long as we came in uniform we would always get into the event for free and we would be given preferred seating. We thanked her very much and told her that we would be back. We thought we were about to leave, but Dixie told us we couldn't leave yet, she had another surprise for us.

Dixie then took us backstage to walk around and actually meet the wrestlers. We couldn't believe it, there really aren't any words to describe just how much this excited us. The TNA heavyweight champion, Jeff Jarrett came up to us and talked to us for a few minutes. He told us that he knew exactly where Fort Campbell and Clarksville were because he was actually from Hendersonville, Tennessee. We thought that was cool because it gave us a bit of common ground with the TNA Heavyweight Champion. Jeff was probably one of the nicest guys we had ever met also. He even let me hold the TNA Championship belt. We also got to meet a couple of Legends from the old ECW promotion, "The Franchise" Shane Douglas and Jerry Lynn. I was a huge ECW fan in the 90's so it was a cool experience to meet them. Shane Douglas walked over to us and said something to the effect of, "Allright guys! Fuck what the French say, you guys are kicking ass!" Shane was apparently very patriotic and took the French's anti-war stance personally, as many Americans did at the time. Just as we did with Jeff Jarrett, we stood and talked with him for a few minutes and got a quick picture taken with him. When we got to talk with Jerry Lynn, I spent a little more time talking to him then I did some of the other wrestlers. Jerry Lynn had a historic feud in ECW with one of my favorite wrestlers, Rob Van Dam. I wanted his take on the feud because they had put on some of my favorite matches in wrestling history. Jerry had fond memories of the matches with Van Dam. He told us how much he missed the old ECW and how there will probably never be another place like ECW. He spoke of ECW like it was the "glory days" of his own career, and I guess in many ways it was. I felt that out of all of the wrestlers there, I connected with Jerry Lynn the most.

Along with the great matches, the hospitality, and the experience of going backstage, there was something else that happened that night. About halfway through the show a guy who was dressed up as the wrestler known as Sting approached us and asked us what unit we were in. We froze for a second because when you are asked that type of question in public it usually means that the person who is asking is not only in the military, but also possibly of a higher rank. It isn't uncommon to bump into an NCO from another unit out in public who may feel the need to try to bust on junior Soldiers for something that they may feel is unacceptable. It is a very petty thing actually, that some NCOs don't seem to know how to "turn off" the Army aspect of their lives when they are off duty. I always knew when and where to shut it off. Either way, the reason this man approached us wasn't to try to gig us on being in uniform in public or anything else. Instead, the reason he approached us was because he saw that we were wrestling fans who were also Soldiers. He had something to run by us, something that you would never expect.

The man's name was Duke. Duke was a Staff Sergeant in an Infantry unit who was obsessed with wrestling; far more obsessed than I was. Duke was so obsessed with his favorite wrestler (Sting) that he would often dress up like Sting and go to wrestling events. He would paint his face, wear the trench coat and boots, and carry a plastic baseball bat just like Sting would. Duke loved wrestling so much that he actually took professional wrestling lessons for a couple of years and subsequently purchased his own wrestling ring. This obviously led to the reason why Duke approached us in the first place. Duke was looking for other wrestling fans in the area (mainly Soldiers) who would be interested in learning how to wrestle. Once we learned enough wrestling skills we would wrestle; Duke had intentions on holding wrestling events for his neighborhood. In case you haven't put two and two together yet, the answer is yes, Duke did keep his professional wrestling ring in his backyard.

I have to admit that at first this entire idea sounded absolutely crazy. I did exchange phone numbers with Duke and I told him I may be interested and I might know a few other Soldiers (Jason and AJ) who may have been interested. Right off the bat Jones told me he probably wasn't going to get involved with the wrestling, and I understood. As crazy as it was, the idea of it did intrigue me. The funny thing was this wasn't the only offer I received that evening to learn to wrestle. Don West, one of the commentators at TNA, invited me to go to their weekend screening that they used to hold. It was called the "TNA Gut Check". You had to pay $150 and you would go in there, run through a few motions and exercises and then get evaluated by the TNA staff for potential future training. Since the TNA Gut Check would cost money I decided not to do it. A Specialist in the US Army doesn't always have $150 to just throw away on a screening to be a wrestler. Not to mention the fact that I probably couldn't be in the Army and be a TNA wrestler at the same time, so since I was contractually obligated to serve at least two more years in the Army, the Gut Check just wasn't an option. Still, the idea of learning to wrestle started to grow on me, so I gave Duke a call.

I talked with Jason and AJ about the idea of learning to wrestle and they both ended up being interested in doing it. We finally agreed to go over to Duke's place on one particular weekend to start training. We were shocked to see the wrestling ring when we got there. It was real. This wasn't a ploy, a joke, or a lie on Duke's part. No, Duke told us the truth when he said he had a wrestling ring at his house. It was a basic 15ft x 15ft wrestling ring which he had paid $3,000 for. It had a steel frame with a plywood floor that was covered in about an inch of foam to soften the fall. He said that some wrestling promotions use as much as 2 inches of foam, but you can't use too much because that will create too much of a crease when you walk around in the ring which could cause you to trip while trying to move around the ring and put on a show. You definitely don't want to trip and fall in the middle of a match. That would be embarrassing. The ropes of the ring were very basic too. They weren't real ropes per se, they just present the appearance that they are ropes. They are really just thick metal wire inside of a garden hose-like material which is then wrapped in multi-colored tape. The ropes are tightened at each corner of the ring, which provides the "bouncing off the rope" effect that you see on TV. The very sight of this ring was as real as it gets.

The training itself wasn't exactly easy either. Duke started off by teaching us how to fall and how to bounce off the ropes. You see, professional wrestling is an art. It's not a real fight, it is a show. The show does have to look real however and you have to convince the crowd that what you are doing in the ring is real and not a show. It takes a certain type of mentality to do this, as well as a lot of practice. In addition, there is a popular misconception that since professional wrestling isn't a real fight that there is no real pain involved. That isn't true at all. For one, every time you fall, there's only an inch of foam in between your body and the plywood. Continuously having to fall onto the wood over and over again over the course of a day starts to hurt after a while. This is especially true in a training session where Duke would have us fall over and over and over again just to learn how to fall properly. You have to land a certain way so that more of your body hits the mat to absorb some of the impact. There is also some pain inflicted from the constant bouncing off of the ropes. Keep in mind, there is metal wire inside of those ropes, and the rubber hose doesn't provide that much cushion to protect against the constant bouncing off of the ropes that wrestlers have to endure in order to put on a good show. Overall, there are a lot of skills that are required to put on a good match, and Duke was able to teach us at least some of these skills. I am not going to lie and claim that Duke was the greatest wrestler in the world. He wasn't. After all, if he was a great wrestler wouldn't he have gotten out of the Army and went on to become a professional wrestler? Either way as die hard wrestling fans we saw wrestling at Duke's house as a way to partially live out our dreams of becoming professional wrestlers, despite how stupid we may have looked at first.

Over the course of the next few months, the three of us spent a lot of our time doing "wrestling-related activities." We were going to the TNA shows in Nashville every single Wednesday night, and we were going over to Duke's house on the weekends and wrestling. It was probably one of the most fun summers of my Army career. There were so many great TNA shows that we went to. Every time we sat with Dixie Carter in one of the first three rows and got to meet even more of the wrestlers. One night I got to meet the wrestler known as "The Road Dogg" Jesse James.

He told us that he was an ex-marine and that a lot of wrestlers actually are former service members. It was cool to be able to stand there with a professional wrestler of all people and have an educated conversation about the military. I truthfully didn't expect that. Then again, we didn't expect TNA to be this hospitable to us on a constant weekly basis either. We met almost every wrestler on the roster. We met Jeff Hardy, AJ Styles, Ron "The Truth" Killings (who is now known as R-Truth in the WWE), Lash Leroux, Elix Skipper and so many others. Some of you who are reading this who are wrestling fans probably know who each and every one of these performers is. For those who don't, please bear with me. I remember there was one night in particular that we were standing outside with a bunch of other fans and we saw the wrestler named Raven get into his Chrysler Sebring with another wrestler. We overheard him say something that we probably shouldn't have overheard. He had found a winning scratch off ticket that was worth $40 on the floor and he said to the other wrestler, "Oh look we got a $40 winner! This is a huge break for us I could really use this!" This statement had an impact on Jason and I because we grew up watching this guy wrestle on TV, so we automatically assume that he is a millionaire. This entire scene was a wakeup call for us. Not only was Raven driving a Chrysler Sebring (not exactly the car you picture a millionaire driving) but he was also overly excited about a winning lotto ticket that was worth $40. Apparently, wrestlers are real people just like the rest of us. Sure, when Raven wrestled for bigger companies in the past he was probably paid more, but at this point in his career things were obviously different. I had always read stories growing up about how hard it is to become a professional wrestler and how the road to the top is a challenging one. Wrestlers usually have to pay for their training; there are no scholarships for wrestling school. They spend the first few years of their careers wrestling for smaller, independent promotions for very low wages. Then once they have had their run at the top and start "descending back down the mountain" so to speak, they end up earning less money and have to start pinching pennies again. This whole experience put it all into perspective for me. Maybe I made the right choice when I was in high school and I chose the Army as a career as opposed to following my childhood dream of becoming a professional wrestler.

There were a lot of great nights at TNA that I will be forever thankful for. On one night in particular the event ended with a six-man tag team match that featured three of their top "good guy" wrestlers taking on the three top "bad guys". I really don't remember who wrestled in the match that night, but it ended with every wrestler in the locker room flooding the ring for a big brawl. Eventually, all of the "bad guys" were cleared out and the winners stayed in the ring to pose for the crowd. The crowd on this night was a little more wild than usual, and didn't want to stop cheering. Every time the wrestlers would try to leave the ring the crowd would try to get them to stay for a little longer just to keep the show going that much longer. The wrestlers started to sense that the fans wanted more and they didn't seem to have a "good enough" ending for the fans. What happened next blew my mind. AJ Styles, who was TNA Heavyweight Champion at the time, pointed to me. (I was in the front row like usual). He pointed at me long enough for the crowd to turn their attention to me. AJ Styles then got on the microphone and said, "Let's hear it for the troops!" The crowd then erupted into a loud "USA! USA! USA!" chant. I was suddenly surrounded by hundreds of screaming wrestling fans, who were clapping and cheering for me. As this was happening, the wrestlers took the time to come over to me also and shake my hand and give me a high five in front of the crowd. Not to sound biased, but this was a very classy way to end the show, honoring a US Soldier. The funny thing was that after this was all over, some of the wrestling followed me into the parking lot and asked me for an autograph. I couldn't believe it. I am not a famous person and people were still asking me to autograph their wrestling merchandise. Of course, I went with it and signed the autographs, there was no way that I could break their hearts and turn them down. When the night was over I drove back to Fort Campbell feeling like a million bucks. After all the great things that the TNA wrestlers and staff had done for me I would have never expected that they would give me the honor of the cheering crowd at the end of a show. The one time they announced my name at the beginning was one thing, the crowd was just getting into the Arena. This time around, the fans were nearly rabid after a great show and going nuts. The "superstar treatment" that the crowd gave me that night will never be forgotten.

Things at Duke's house were starting to pick up a bit too. We were at the point where we were actually putting on whole matches at his house and recording them. We would also invite some of the neighbors over to watch the matches, which was funny because they actually were interested in watching. We would try our best to put on a good show but in all reality we weren't very good wrestlers. Duke was the best out of all of us, and he was mediocre at best. During the summer of 2004 I think the biggest crowd that we wrestled in front of was a whopping six fans. That didn't matter to any of us. It was the fact that we were having fun that mattered to me. The first few times that I wrestled I would wake up the next morning very sore and I made the mistake to mention this at the unit. The First Sergeant asked me why I was sore and I told him that I was doing professional wrestling training. Even though he knew that I was a huge fan of wrestling he still didn't take this very well. Since I was one of his Soldiers and I was technically accountable to him, he didn't want me getting hurt. If I got hurt it would cost the Army a lot of money in hospital bills as well as make me an ineffective Soldier. So he ended up ordering me to stop wrestling. Since I was such a huge fan and I was having so much fun doing it I didn't actually stop, I just told him I wouldn't do it anymore and I was careful about what I would talk about around the unit. I never mentioned wrestling in Duke's yard again while at the unit. Thank god I never got hurt. I would've had a hard time explaining myself to the First Sergeant then. I wonder if Duke's unit knew he was a wrestler. He was an NCO in an infantry unit too, so the consequences for him would have been much worse.

Over the course of this summer I was also finally able to shake the Neon and get a new car. By now I had paid off enough of the contract and was able to trade it in to a dealer for something new. I didn't have the qualifying credit to get a brand new car, but I would be able to get a car that was new for me; or at least newer than the Neon. God knows how much I needed to shake that damn Neon. In addition to God, my friends and I also knew how much I needed to get rid of that thing. I wish I could say that driving it was starting to get embarrassing, but it wasn't starting to get embarrassing it had been embarrassing for a while. By now, being embarrassed for driving the Neon was getting old. So I ended up going to a new dealer to see what kind of deal I could get. Even though I knew that I was going to be stuck getting a used car I knew not to go to a dealer on 41A. I had learned my lesson. I ended up getting a really good deal on a silver 2000 Chevy Cavalier Z24 convertible. It was a very nice car and it had always been my dream to own a convertible. To me there is a special feeling of freedom involved when you drive a convertible. The car had a lot more going for it than its looks too. It had low mileage and I ended up getting a great deal with a low interest rate. The car also had two years of its warranty left which was way better than the "30 day as-is" warranty that I had become accustomed to thanks to the help of Terry Harris. After owning the Neon this car was the greatest thing that had happened to me. I loved it. I loved showing it off and I loved driving around with the top down. I remember the night that I showed it to Jones. He thought it was funny because at this point he didn't think that it was possible for me to own a nice car. Honestly after owning the Neon I was starting to think the same thing myself. Thank God I didn't lose hope. Waving goodbye to that thing was the greatest feeling I had felt in a long time. I also promised myself that day that never again would I put myself through that. Mark my words I will never own a Neon again. I don't care how nice the modern ones may be. I'd rather walk.

Despite the fun I was having in my off time, things at the unit were starting to crumble. We had a change of leadership at the Battalion level which brought in a new Battalion Commander who was way too strict. There was also a scandal involving our Battalion Sergeant Major taking a PT test and ordering the graders to give him a better score on his test because he was the Sergeant Major. At first I didn't believe this and discounted it as a rumor, but then his NCOER came through my evaluations section and I saw it on his report with my own eyes. When your leaders at the top start messing up, it always erodes unit morale. That combined with the fact that we had a new First Sergeant in our company who didn't know what he was doing and dealing with my own NCO's issues involving his DUI. Things in the SSB were beginning to fall apart and I no longer wanted to be there. It was no longer the proud unit that it was when we came back from Iraq. Things were different. Luckily for me, there was a light at the end of the tunnel.

During the summer of 2004 I received orders for my next assignment, which was to Korea. The orders showed that I had a report date of October 10, 2004 which meant that if I wanted to take any leave I would have to leave Fort Campbell before October. I couldn't believe that my time on Fort Campbell was soon going to come to an end. I felt that I had grown so much while I was stationed there. Not only was it my first real duty station in the Army, but I had also endured my first deployment overseas while I was stationed there. Korea wasn't a deployment like Iraq. It was an actual duty station much like Fort Campbell. At first I didn't really want to go despite how bad the unit was becoming. I made a lot of friends at Fort Campbell and I didn't really want to leave. After a while I came to terms with it and started looking at the bright side. Korea would be a new adventure. It would be a new country that I could visit, as well as a new unit that I could work in. Maybe things in my new unit would be different than they were in the 101st. I knew I would also meet more people which would ultimately open more doors for my future. Before long, I was counting down the days before I would leave Fort Campbell.

Breaking the news to Jones and everyone else at the unit was the harder part than finding out the information myself. None of my friends wanted to see me go. We definitely built a strong bond between us during the course of the deployment and it would be hard to say goodbye to my friends in the SSB. I had built great friendships with Jones, Allison, Defrates, Mehring, SGT Ramos, and even Cursey. Having to say goodbye to them wasn't going to be very easy for me. I also couldn't forget about my friends there who weren't in my unit; Jason and AJ. The three of us had been through a lot together, between watching RAW Mondays at the recreation center to our adventures at TNA in Nashville and our matches in Duke's yard. All of this started to weigh on me. I also knew that Korea was a year-long tour, so I had to make sure to take leave home at Saint Johnsville to see my family for a little while before I left. Having to say all of these goodbyes at once wasn't easy at all.

I remember going to my last TNA event there with Jason and AJ in early September. It was the standard event, great matches, sitting in the front row with Dixie Carter and everything else. I broke it to Dixie that night that I would be leaving for Korea and she was sad to hear it. She told me that I could always come back to their shows for free when I got back to the US and that their doors would always be open to me. This really touched me because she made it seem like the great treatment that I had received there would never come to an end. I do regret today that I never stayed in touch with Dixie Carter. Sometimes I wonder today with all the changes that company has had if she would even remember us. I would hope she would. I also told "Road Dogg" Jesse James about Korea, and he told me not to worry. He told me that Korea is a great place to go when you're in the military and to trust him, that I would have fun. I don't know if he had actually been to Korea during his time in the military or if he was just telling me I would enjoy it, but either way I appreciated the gesture. He was just trying to make me feel better about having to leave the country again. The wrestler by the name of Lash Leroux actually wanted to stay in touch with me. Lash was a wrestler who had competed on the middle card of WCW before it was bought out by the WWE. He never went to work at the WWE however and instead he had been working the non-televised matches at TNA while we were going there. After his matches he would often come by and talk to me about life in general. It was like he actually wanted to be friends. We ended up exchanging email addresses and stayed in touch for most of my tour in Korea. Slowly but surely my last night at TNA went by. The show finally ended and I said goodbye to the wrestlers for the last time, never forgetting the great things that they had done for us. Even though I can never relive those times at TNA, I will always have the memories.

Aside from clearing and out-processing, there was one final thing that I had to do before I left Fort Campbell, my farewell dinner. There is a tradition in the Army that when a member of your unit departs for another duty station you send them away properly. It is done as not only a sign of respect, but also as a way to show the outgoing Soldier that their hard work at the unit over the years was appreciated by the unit. It is a way to say goodbye in case you don't get to see everyone during the last two weeks of clearing. Those two weeks are extremely busy and hectic which causes you to spend almost no time at the unit. Usually during clearing you take care of turning your equipment back into the post (once its cleaned spotless that is), out-processing the TMC for medical purposes, clearing the provost marshal to ensure you don't have any outstanding speeding tickets, and even last minute paperwork. It isn't uncommon to not see someone again when they start clearing, thus the need for the farewell dinner.

My farewell was unique because I had friends from not only my own unit in attendance but also my friends from other units, namely Jason and AJ. Some Soldiers don't actually make friends in other units but I obviously did. We held the dinner at a Chinese buffet in Clarksville. After everyone ate most of the NCOs and a few of the Soldiers got up and said a few kind words about me and my job performance. It was nice to know that the overall consensus was that Specialist Ken Conklin was a great Soldier and a hard worker. I did put a lot of effort into learning my job after all. I don't really remember much of what Jones had said, but I do vividly remember Cursey's speech. He started off by jokingly saying that throughout my time here I really got under his skin and that I was a major annoyance to him. To be honest this was the sort of behavior that I had expected out of Cursey by now. He would sometimes act rude and you couldn't quite tell if he was joking with you or not. After he got through with that he said, "Say what you want about Ken. One may say he's an annoying dude, one may say that he's a great worker. I would say that above all else, he's a great friend." As he said this he looked me in the eye and offered his hand. I really didn't expect that out of him, especially after the first half of his speech. It was moving. Of course, I jokingly said back, "I am?" That scene is probably how you could best sum up my time serving alongside Cursey in the 101st. We would go back and forth, bust on each other (sometimes joking, and sometimes not) but in the end we really were friends. Nowadays when I reflect back on my time in the 101st I find that some of my fondest memories involve Cursey, which is a good thing. In fact, I can't imagine what it would have been like without him there. Then again, what would my time there have been like without any of the people that I met there? You can never know. I made a lot of friends there and each one of them affected me in some way. You can never really know what it would be like without one person or another; you can just speculate. Things at Fort Campbell weren't always great. There were hardships on the deployment and there were issues within the unit itself both on the deployment and home at Campbell. I think having the friends that I had there at Campbell helped me to overcome those challenges.

I took the plaque that I received at the dinner and we all left. At this point I knew that I really only had one more day left on Fort Campbell. I had to final clear and sign out on leave. I had packed all of my stuff and said pretty much all of my goodbyes. That final 24 hours seemed to drag on. I was at the point where I knew I needed to go and I was ready to just get the 15 hour road trip back to Saint Johnsville out of the way. When the time to leave finally came, I signed out from the SSB duty desk and walked around the building one last time to say goodbye to whoever was at work that day. This was a weird day for me. It finally started to settle in that I was going to miss everyone. I had made so many friends at Fort Campbell and together we had been through so much. As I hit the road, I began to shed a few tears. Not many though, it's not like I was sobbing or anything. I started reflecting on some things for the first hour of the trip. I thought about the deployment and how we all made history. I thought about how much I had changed since I had arrived to Fort Campbell; how I had started there as a E-1 with no experience and now I was an E-4 who actually knew his job quite well. I reflected back on my experiences with TNA wrestling. I also thought about the friends that I had made and how I vowed to stay in touch with as many of them as possible. As it turns out, I was able to stay in touch with a handful of them over the years and still keep in touch with a few of them to this day. I've always been good at doing that. I did lose touch with some friends from Campbell but was able to reconnect with them during the process of writing this book. I believe that despite how many years go by without communication, it is always possible to reconnect. It may just require you to be a little more outgoing, but there's nothing wrong with that.

After the 15 hour road trip in my amazing new car was over it really settled in that I would probably never see Fort Campbell again. I would spend the next two weeks at home before boarding a plane in Albany to fly over to South Korea for my year-long tour there. I knew that I would be authorized to take leave halfway through my tour there. The problem was that since my report date was set for October 2004 I would not be allowed to come home for Christmas, thus making it the second Christmas in a row that I would not be with my family. Even though that didn't sit well with me I was still excited about the idea of going to Korea. It was going to be a new adventure for me. It always is when you are traveling to a new place. These two weeks of leave weren't very eventful for me but I was able to reconnect with one old friend who I hadn't spoken to in a long time; a childhood friend who I had lost in touch with by the name of Lauren. We had lost touch over the deployment over a personal argument that we had. I really don't understand why it happened but either way I wasn't comfortable leaving the country with unfinished business. I do not like making enemies out of friends. Legitimate enemies are one thing, but a disagreement with a friend should always be worked out before embarking on an important journey. That is a belief that I will take to the grave. Let's say I went to Korea and was killed in a training accident. I would hate to have died knowing that I didn't "right the wrongs" so to speak. I didn't agree with her on the decision to stop talking but that didn't change the fact that was willing to iron things out for the greater good. I was able to accomplish this about three days before my flight to Korea. It was good but obviously we didn't really manage to have any time to hang out but we agreed that when I returned to the US for leave that I would definitely see her then. Honestly it's not like there was anything else really going on in little old Saint Johnsville. It is probably one of the smallest towns in America after all, but I'm proud of that. We also agreed to stay in touch while I was in Korea too. In a place like Korea I wouldn't have to rely on "snail mail" at any time during the tour. I would have access to a phone every day as well as high speed internet at all times. That in itself was a major improvement over my previous overseas tour of Iraq.

The trip to Korea itself was an eventful one. I had to fly from Albany to Seattle, Washington for a layover and from Seattle I would board the plane enroute to Korea. What I didn't realize however was that I would have a 24 hour layover in Seattle. When I arrived to Seattle I decided to take the opportunity to go out and see as much of the city as possible. After all, I had a 24 hour layover so why waste it? This was my first time on the west coast. I was lucky to have arrived on a sunny day also. I hear stories that the Pacific Northwest is an extremely depressing place because it rains all the time. To this day I am still not sure if that is actually true or if that is just a rumor.

While in Seattle I decided to go to a Starbucks and have a cup of coffee. Seattle is where Starbucks was started and as an avid coffee drinker I felt it was one of the things that you "must do" while in the city. It's like being in Idaho and having a potato. Honestly the coffee was no different than any other part of the country but I just had to do it anyway. If I ever make it to Idaho, I'll have a potato. If I ever make it to Wisconsin, I'll have some cheese. That's how it goes when you're traveling the world. You try to sample whatever it is that makes that particular place famous. While riding around Seattle I also drove by Safeco Field. I decided to go and check it out, but not for the reason that most would think. Safeco Field is home to the Seattle Mariners baseball team. Now, I am not a Mariners fan (in fact I am a New York Mets fan). I am however a huge wrestling fan and Safeco Field happened to be the home of WrestleMania 19. That's right, you read that correctly. I stopped at Safeco Field for the simple fact that I was a wrestling fan and my favorite WrestleMania was held there. I was amazed that they could turn a ball park into a wrestling arena for a major event. There was someone inside that took me down and showed me the field when he found out that I was a Soldier. That was very nice of him, but it wasn't the first time that I had received any special perks for being in the military. It really made me feel good that there were so many people in the world that showed an appreciation for the military, especially during a time of war. It was also the first ball park that I had ever seen in person. (Later on in my life I would go on to visit two more ball parks: Citi Field; home of the Mets and Turner Field; home of the Atlanta Braves.) I should have thought to buy a shot glass or something while I was there as a souvenir, but I forgot.

After my sightseeing in Seattle I decided to return to the airport and have a few beers at the airport bar. Since I had recently turned 21 during the summer of 2004 I had started drinking lightly. I went to a few barracks parties at Campbell during my last few weeks there, but nothing major. I had also known that there was a lot of drinking and partying in Korea, but I really had no idea what the extent of that would be. Either way, I got back to the airport and checked on my flight status. Once I saw that there were no changes or delays, I went over to the bar and tipped back a few Coronas. There were a few other Soldiers there who were heading to Korea also so I had some company. They weren't coming from Fort Campbell but instead, they were straight out of AIT and were amazed to hear that I had just returned from Iraq seven months earlier. I guess it really hadn't settled in yet that I hadn't even been back on American soil for seven months and I was already being sent overseas again. I sat back and pondered that thought, finally fully accepting that the life of a Soldier isn't just a busy life, but also a life of travel and adventure. Either way this was an adventure that I had signed up for when I first met my recruiter years ago and it was an adventure that I was fully prepared to embrace. I patiently waited for the flight, knowing that Korea would be unlike anything I had encountered before.

CHAPTER 7

KOREA

The flight from Seattle to Korea wasn't as long as the flight from Fort Campbell to Iraq. This is obviously because Seattle is located along the Pacific Ocean. The flight was enjoyable for me because there was free alcohol on the plane since it was a civilian chartered overseas flight, unlike my flight to Iraq. A few cocktails and a good movie can make any flight go by fast. It also had a quick layover in Japan which was also cool. I was quickly adding up the list of countries that I had visited between actual tours and layovers. I know a lot of people don't like to count layovers, but I do. Some like to say, "Well on a layover you can't just leave the airport." While that is true, it still doesn't change the fact that you are still on that particular countries' soil. That's just my opinion, and I'm sticking to it. I also remember not being as jetlagged when I landed in Korea, which was also a huge help to me. Being jetlagged will often put you to sleep causing you to lose a day. I've never been a big fan of wasting days. I believe in the idea of seizing life, grabbing ahold of each day and making the best of it. You simply cannot do that by sleeping all day.

The first thing that I noticed when I stepped off of the plane in Korea was a strange odor. I couldn't quite tell what it was, and it definitely wasn't the greatest smell in the world. Soon enough I would learn that the smell I detected was something called Kimchee. Kimchee is a popular Korean food that is eaten with almost every single meal, including breakfast in most cases. It is made of a spiced fermented cabbage. Kimchee even has a history in Korea. When Korea was at war with Japan, the Koreans would put their cabbage and other vegetables into jars underground to prevent the Japanese Soldiers from finding it when they were busy pillaging their towns and villages. When the Koreans had the chance to dig up the food and eat it, the chemical composition had changed into the fermented version of the food. This food became known as Kimchee and became a part of Korea's heritage. There are literally hundreds of different forms of Kimchee, and if you spend any time in Korea it is virtually impossible to not try it because it is everywhere, thus the heavy odor in the air. Personally, I like the taste of Kimchee. I didn't care for it at first, but after a year in Korea it tends to grow on you.

My orders to Korea stated that I would be going to the 177th Finance Battalion in Camp Casey, Korea. Camp Casey is located up north by the North Korea/South Korea border and it is the home to the 2nd Infantry Division. The 177th FB was not a division unit however. It fell under the 175th FINCOM which was located on Yongsan Airbase just outside of Seoul. Because of this hierarchy any Soldiers who were reporting to the 177th FB would not have to go through replacement battalion in Camp Casey. Instead, they went through it at Yongsan. As a result, my first taste of South Korea was actually the capitol, Seoul. On our first night in the country I went out into the city with my fellow Soldiers into the neighboring district Itaewon. The place was packed to the brim with bars and clubs, as well as various places to shop. I couldn't believe the sheer amount of Soldiers that were out on the town getting drunk on a work night. Obviously this was my first night in the country so I didn't really know any better. I would soon learn that being drunk during the work week in Korea wasn't entirely out of the ordinary. Either way, walking around Itaewon was a fun experience. I had a few drinks with some of the other Soldiers until about 1 am in which we had to return to post due to the curfew. US Soldiers weren't allowed out past 1 am at the time due to agreements that were made with the South Korean government. These laws usually change every few years, often adjusting the curfew time for US Soldiers based on things like mission tempo, tensions between both Koreas, and even world events. I've heard of times when there was no curfew at all in Korea as well as times when the curfew in Korea was midnight. It changes often and I have no idea what the curfew is as of right now.

As far as going through replacement battalion itself, it was basically an uneventful process that only lasted about three days. We weren't issued our gear in Yongsan. We would instead be issued our gear in Camp Casey which was fine by me. It made my trip to Camp Casey that much easier. After all, who wants to carry three extra bags of gear onto a coach bus?

Before I knew it I was issued a bus ticket to take the two hour ride to Camp Casey where I would be working for the next year. Luckily for me, this would not be my last time in Seoul over the course of the year. Seoul is a beautiful city with all of the lights and pageantry that you would expect in any other major city or nation's capital. There's are many sights to see as well as tourist attractions which makes it a great place for a young Soldier to be stationed. And just like any other major city you can see thousands of people in the city streets walking to work every day. It is really a sight to see. Seoul has also been home to the 1988 Olympics which also helped cement the city as an attractive tourist attraction for the world to see. Of all of the cities I have been to, I have absolutely nothing negative to say about Seoul.

When I arrived to Camp Casey I saw that the area that surrounded the camp was not nearly as nice as Seoul. The town was called Dongducheon (sometimes spelled Tongducheon, or TDC for short). Dongducheon was a nasty, run-down area that had a bad smell in some parts of the town. The only thing that the town really had to offer was long strips of bars and clothing shops. This aspect made it seem a little more like Itaewon, but other than that it was very apparent that TDC was only surviving because of the money that the Soldiers that were stationed at Camp Casey were bringing into the local economy.

I arrived to the unit to find that I would be working in the Battalion S1 section. An S1 section takes care of all Human Resources functions for a unit. They process everything needed for the progression of a Soldiers' career, including awards, leave requests, promotion packets, memorandums of correspondence and evaluations. This was much different than my role in the 101st SSB. When working in an SSB you usually have one specific job function, which in my case it was NCOERS. I would no longer be working on NCOERS only. In an S1 you have to learn how to multitask and become a "jack of all trades" so to speak. You have to be able to take care of the needs of all Soldiers in your unit at any given time. If a Soldier comes to you with a question and you do not know the answer, you have to look it up in the regulation. Soldiers and Leadership alike often took to their S1 for advice and therefore you have to be ready at all times. Working in an S1 is a great experience for any Human Resources clerk because you not only learn more things about your job but you are also given more of an opportunity to get to know the Soldiers that you are taking care of. It gives you a sense of accomplishment when you make a positive impact on someone else's career.

My duties and responsibilities were also changed in the aspect of where my section sits on the "food chain" so to speak. In an S1 you have to submit your work to the SSB for review and they submit the work to the Department of the Army. Obviously I was aware of the process due to my previous experience of working in the SSB. One thing that I had to get used to was seeing people working in the SSB there that didn't know the job as well as I did. Sometimes you have to hold your tongue when you see something like this because they are now the ones who are in the position of authority. There was a few times where I would speak out of line to some of the Soldiers who worked there because they just didn't know what they were doing. I also learned that people tend to get insulted when you do that! Eventually I realized that there is a polite and tactful way to go about correcting the actions of another Soldier when in situations like this. Just like everything else in life, you live and learn.

At first, the new unit didn't seem as good as the SSB. This wasn't just because I missed my friends at Campbell. The morale of these Soldiers was legitimately in the toilet. You could tell the second that you arrived. There was a very strict Battalion Command Sergeant Major there who put a strong focus on enforcing Army standards. This is normally a good thing in a unit, but he did it to the point where it dragged everyone down. I think a lot of senior NCOs in the Army mean well when they do this but they don't realize how much their actions are despised by their subordinates. I agree that there should be a strong focus on the art of "soldiering" and military training, but I don't think you need to be an asshole when doing it. To me a unit with low morale is a bad unit, plain and simple. Not everyone is so proactive where they want to be eating, breathing, and sleeping the army all day, every day. I just wish more Army leaders would realize this. Maybe if they did the Army would be a better place and people would be a little happier.

To further explain the low morale in the unit, I saw that this unit had a Battalion Commander who was extremely overweight and would often come to work with her uniform looking shabby. This kind of thing can affect the morale of a Soldier because you are taught at the very beginning of your career in the Army that there are standards that have to be adhered to. Two of the most basic standards are physical fitness and wear and appearance of the Army uniform. You can't ask someone to do something if you are not willing to do it yourself. That's called being a hypocrite. So if you're in a unit and required to maintain a certain standard of fitness it tends to damage morale when your Battalion Commander is way out of shape. When I saw the Commander for the first time I found it funny that she was the exact opposite of the Battalion CSM. The CSM was so stuck on his Army standards that he would go running in shorts in 40 degree weather, while the Commander wouldn't run at all. This contrast may seem funny at first, but it does get Soldiers to start talking and thus it fosters bad feelings.

In addition to the issues concerning the unit morale and the Battalion leadership, there were also some internal problems as well. Our company had an overly-strict First Sergeant who was just as strict as the CSM. This really didn't help matters for the Soldiers whatsoever. There was also a lot of talk amongst some of the Soldiers that there was corruption in the unit. Overall, the unit to me really seemed like a huge step down from life at Campbell. I started to get depressed when I realized that I had to spend a full year there. I did have one saving grace however, which was the people that I worked with in my own section. I worked with a girl named Allison George and a really great NCO by the name of Staff Sergeant Stewart. George was a 42A who had a lot more experience than me in our MOS, as well as in the Army. Working alongside her would definitely help me to master my job. She also gave me a "heads up" right from the beginning that there were a lot of people in this unit that I couldn't trust (mostly senior leadership) and that I needed to watch what I said to certain people within the unit. To be honest she made the 177th FB seem like a "cut throat" environment in comparison to my previous unit. The sad part was this wasn't just George being paranoid, this was all true. I could just tell when I would walk by some of the NCOs there that they weren't people that I could trust. SSG Stewart on the other hand was much different than these NCOs. He was a great NCO who would always look out for his Soldiers. As a result of this some of the senior NCOs didn't like him and would often go behind his back on some things. Of course, since SSG Stewart was in charge of the S1 section he did wield a certain amount of power in the unit. When some of the crooked NCOs would need his help on their paperwork they would come into the office and be nice to him even though they didn't actually like him. Allison and I would actually find it funny how some of them would come in there and kiss up to him when it benefitted them. When it came right down to it, SSG Stewart was a guy who didn't just take care of his own Soldiers; he took up for other Soldiers as well, especially if they worked for those crooked NCOs in the unit. He was also an extremely knowledgeable NCO who knew everything there was to know about our MOS. I was relieved to finally be working for someone who knew their job; someone that I could learn from. After my last experience at Fort Campbell it was refreshing to finally work for a strong and competent NCO. He was truly a saving grace in the 177th FB. Without his guidance and leadership my time in the 177th would have been much worse.

I was also introduced to a type of Soldier that I hadn't encountered before, a KATUSA Soldier. KATUSA stands for Korean Augmentee to the United States Army. They are a Soldier assigned to the Republic of Korea (ROK) Army who gets to serve two years augmented into a US Army unit. In South Korea there is a law that all males must serve in the Military for a minimum of two years. This is a lawful requirement and there is no way out of this. The South Korean government does however allow them to put off their military service obligation for a few years if they wish to go to college to earn a degree. Once the individual earns their degree they are still required to complete their two years of service. Most of these Soldiers end up serving in the normal ROK army, but some are lucky enough to serve as KATUSAs in the US Army. There is a huge difference between the two. The ROK Army is far stricter on their Soldiers than the US Army is. The Soldiers who are allowed to serve as KATUSAs consider themselves very lucky since they do not have to deal with the problems within the ROK Army. As you can probably guess, ROK Army Soldiers don't like KATUSA Soldiers and have no respect for them. They look at them as if they are shamming and getting a better deal. The truth is they are getting a much better deal. There is also a misconception among the ranks that the only Soldiers who get to be KATUSAs are from rich families and thus pay their way into being a KATUSA. This isn't actually true, even though many KATUSA Soldiers do come from rich families. The real requirement isn't about money at all; it is about knowing how to speak English. Since these Soldiers will be working alongside US Soldiers for the duration of their service obligation it is important that they can communicate with the US Soldiers. If you can't speak English, how can you take orders from a US Army NCO? KATUSAs have a rank structure just like the US Army does, and since we are all working together a junior US Soldier must show the same amount of respect and courtesy to a KATUSA sergeant as they would to an American Sergeant. The KATUSAs also have their own customs that they keep to themselves. Once a week they have to meet with the ROK Army Sergeant Major for required training that the US Soldiers don't have to attend. Also, whenever a new KATUSA arrives, they are required to stand at the building exit every morning and greet every other KATUSA that comes along who may be senior to them in Hangul (their native language). We used to get a kick out of watching this; they would stand there at the position of attention not moving for at least an hour, not speaking either unless it was to greet their superior. If a US Soldier tries to speak to them during this ritual, they usually get ignored. Thank god we don't have a custom like that in the US Army. As far as I'm concerned I already did my time in the art of "standing around and doing nothing for no reason whatsoever." It was during reception and basic training, which you already read about in chapter 1 of this book.

There is at least one KATUSA Soldier assigned to almost every section in every unit within South Korea. In our S1 section, we had a KATUSA assigned to us by the name of Young-Chan Kim. Like many of our KATUSA Soldiers Kim was from Seoul. I didn't know it when I first met him, but I would end up doing a lot of partying with Kim and the other KATUSA Soldiers in the unit later on in the tour. In the office, Kim was put in charge of the leave and pass requests in our unit, as well as all basic memorandums of correspondence. Usually the KATUSA Soldiers are given basic responsibilities such as these because they are often pulled from the office for their mandatory ROK Army training. While it is true that both sides work together, it is well known that no US Army responsibilities can take precedence over ROK Army responsibilities. The relationship between the two nations proves to be at a disadvantage to both the US Soldiers as well as the South Korean Government. The goal of both sides is to protect the South Korean peninsula from North Korea and to continue to work towards the ultimate goal of peace between the two Koreas.

Between myself, George, Kim and SSG Stewart we had a pretty good working relationship within our section. We really meshed well as a team even though for a while I was the "low man on the totem pole" because of my lack of knowledge in other areas of Human Resources. I knew that while I was there it was my mission to learn the job as much as possible. Either way, having knowledgeable co-workers certainly helped me out a lot. There were a lot of cool people to hang out with in the other staff sections of the battalion also. There was another KATUSA down the hall in the automations section (also known as S-6) by the name of Dongnam Park. Like Kim he was cool to hang out with and would show me around parts of Korea later on in the tour. I found it interesting after my previous experiences in Iraq that I was now in a unit that was fully implemented with Soldiers of another country, and that we all could get along. Granted, I had worked alongside Youssef in Iraq but Youssef was only one man who wasn't even a Soldier. I guess I never even thought of the possibility of US Soldiers working alongside Korean Soldiers. Working alongside them gave me a newfound appreciation for other countries and I feel that any Soldier that doesn't get the chance to serve in Korea is missing out on a great opportunity. I can honestly say that I grew as a person working and hanging out with Kim and Park throughout that year.

Because of the low morale in the rest of the unit, I ended up staying to myself for the first month of my tour. Other than going to the gym and working out every day I didn't really leave the barracks very much except to go to work. I was extremely homesick and found myself missing my old unit at Campbell quite often. I stayed in touch with as many of my friends from Campbell as possible. I would often get emails from Jones, Mehring and Allison and I would also hear from Jason a lot too. It was good to keep in touch with all of my old friends. I've never been a fan of getting close to people and then forgetting about them. To me it makes it seem like you wasted your time getting to know a person if you are just going to forget about them and leave them behind in the long run. This is just my philosophy on the subject. I know that people choose to live their life in their own way; my way of living involves creating bonds with people and then keeping them in your life long after you move away. I did make plans with some of my old Fort Campbell friends to come back and visit for a reunion when my time in Korea was finished. Deep down I wasn't 100% sure if it would actually happen though. I knew that even though some of my friends back there meant well they would eventually have to leave Fort Campbell just as I did. As a result they would have to start anew elsewhere just as I had been forced to. I finally realized that even though I would still stay in touch with them as much as possible, that I should finally start making some friends in my new unit, or else risk spending the year miserable.

One Friday evening I got a knock on my door from a fellow Soldier by the name of Cariker. He wanted to know if I would go to the Class Six (that's army terminology for the liquor store) and pick up a few bottles of liquor for him if he gave me the money. He also invited me to party with them that night. Even though Cariker was of age to buy alcohol he wasn't able to at that time because he had exhausted his ration limit for the month. It was at this point that I got a crash course in the rules of rations while stationed in Korea. Every Soldier assigned to Korea is allowed to buy a maximum of three bottles of hard liquor on post per month. You can also buy unlimited beer but the beer often sells out quickly. If a Soldier buys more than their three bottle limit they will be reported to the provost marshal and subsequently get into legal trouble. Since I was new and hadn't bought any liquor yet I still had my three rations. I hadn't really started doing a lot of drinking yet but on this particular night I really had nothing to do so I told Cariker I would go ahead and get the liquor.

When I got back from the liquor store I headed over to the room where everyone was partying. Since I hadn't really made an effort to get to know anyone yet everyone thought that I was stuck up. That all changed when I walked through the door with booze in my hand. We partied all night long and had a blast. I got so drunk that night that it was the drunkest I had ever been. Before long he introduced me to everyone in the room and I made a few new friends who I ended up hanging out with for the duration of my tour there. Our main crew consisted of me, Cariker and three others named Reid, Dyson, and Pelletier. We all formed a tight clique and started partying together almost every weekend. Week after week I would be drinking more and more and before I knew it I was drinking all the time. Eventually it evolved to the point where we were drinking almost every day. While we wouldn't drink too much during the work week, we would definitely get out of control on the weekends. Before coming to Korea I had always heard stories about the high amount of drinking and partying there. Now I was experiencing it first-hand.

Sometimes things would get a little crazy when we would be partying. It started to get to the point where there was an incident every weekend. We would usually start drinking in the barracks and then head out to one of the two on-post clubs; the Warrior Club and Primos. There was almost always a report of an incident at either club on the blotter after each weekend. There were so many Article 15's issued to Soldiers in Korea due to alcohol related incidents. There was a saying that people used to say in Korea, "The best way to make E-5 in Korea is by showing up as an E-6!" The sad part is in a lot of ways that statement was true. It was only a matter of time before someone from our group got caught up in some sort of incident.

On one Friday night we were drinking at the Warrior Club and it was starting to get late. There was a 2 am curfew on post for all Soldiers to report to their barracks. At around midnight on this night Pelletier decided that he wanted to leave. He tried getting me to go with him and I just wanted to stay behind and keep drinking with the rest of the group. Pelletier was so adamant about getting me to go home that he even offered to buy me some Popeye's chicken if I walked back with him. I still didn't go back with him. I swear he must have been able to see the future that night, because after he left things started to get crazy at the bar. Some really drunk Sergeant First Class came over to me and started talking trash. We tried to show him a slight amount of courtesy because of his rank, but that didn't work. Now, it's not like any of us were drinking at the bar in uniform. Every one of us (to include the drunken Sergeant First Class) was in civilian clothes. The only reason that we knew he was a Sergeant First Class was because he made it a point to tell us his rank multiple times while he was drunk. He was definitely trying to "flex his beer muscles" with us. The guy also had someone with him who was equally as drunk, only he was trying to calm his drunken friend down. At one point we tried to just ignore the guy but he kept on pushing us. At one point I asked the guy, "What's your problem?" and he said back to me, "You guys showed interest in fighting us!" We obviously didn't, and his friend tried telling him that. Not only that, but his sentence didn't even make any sense. Who says, "You guys showed interest in fighting us!" anyway? This guy obviously didn't know how to handle his liquor and it was just another example that some of the NCOs in the Army aren't good examples after all. They aren't immortal. Often they do worse things than some junior Soldiers but they are just much better at covering up their tracks. I wasn't sure how this guy was going to cover his tracks since there was already a bar full of witnesses.

Just when I thought that the guy was finally calmed down, he walked up to me and attempted to grab me by the collar of my jacket. There was a step from the dance floor up to the bar area that we were all sitting at. I grabbed him by his shirt and I threw him down the step hard. I honestly couldn't care less about his rank since he started it. As soon as he hit the floor Dyson, Reid and Cariker all got up and rushed over to me in case a real fight broke out. The Sergeant First Class' friend got up and rushed over to him also. The drunken guy started yelling something at me but I couldn't tell what it was because his speech was too slurred from the alcohol. Eventually his friend got him out of there which was best for everyone. Then once they were gone Dyson decided to ring the bell above the bar signaling that he would buy everyone at the bar a shot. I guess he did it as a way to "celebrate" the fact that we just "won" the altercation. As he did this, someone else at the bar took that personally and next thing you know Cariker wanted to fight that guy. This one ended up getting broken up a lot quicker than the first one. Suddenly the bartender signaled last call. It was 0145 and we had to figure out a way back to the barracks which were a two mile walk away. We tried calling a cab but Dyson was so drunk out of his mind that he didn't want to leave. I guess we were all this drunk too. Eventually the bartender convinced Dyson to leave by giving him free beers. We got outside and immediately realized that this was a terrible idea. It was mid-November and freezing outside. We were drunk and now we had to walk two miles in the freezing cold, not to mention the fact that we were breaking the on-post curfew to begin with. We started to stagger down the road even with Dyson drinking his free beers as we walked. We couldn't wait to get this walk of shame over with, but at least we had plenty of time to come up with an alibi in case the staff duty NCO decided to bust us for breaking curfew. Depending on who was working the desk that night there was a chance that we could get off easy.

We got back to the barracks to find that the duty NCO wasn't going to be that merciful. He took us into the dayroom and yelled at us and said that the Battalion Commander had already been in there twice that evening. Of course, the Battalion Commander had no idea that we were out past curfew. The NCO was just using that as a tactic to try to scare us. We tried telling him that a senior NCO started a fight with us but that didn't work to calm him down. The thing that we found funny was that this NCO used to hang out with the gang, but that led to an alcohol related incident with him. He was let off the hook with a minor punishment. Since that happened he was now out to "prove himself" to the chain of command by being a hard ass to the Soldiers, in this case it was us. Normally we would understand if an NCO was going to be hard on us for a curfew violation but as far as we were concerned he was supposed to be our friend. Now he was turning on us just for the sake of benefitting his own career and pleasing his superiors. This didn't sit well with any of us. When he was finally done yelling at us he told us to all go to bed and that he would be reporting this in the morning. Suddenly, Cariker lost it on him. He started yelling, "Ya know what? Were supposed to be friends! Just a couple of months ago we were all getting down and drinkin' beers together and now you pull this shit!? Who the hell do you think you are? Ya know what don't even answer that question, Douggie! You do what you think you need to do, and we will do what we need to do! Me and my friends are gonna go upstairs and were gonna make some fuckin tuna casserole! I don't care what you do!" Then just when I thought Cariker was finished he repeated himself, "You do what you need to do, me and my friends are gonna go up and make some tuna fuckin casserole!" Cariker was drunk out of his mind and apparently he just wanted some tuna casserole, and thus he kept repeating himself. We stared the NCO in the eye and walked upstairs to our rooms. I was hammered. We all parted ways and went to bed. No one made any tuna casserole. All in all the night as a whole was a memorable one and I will never forget it.

The next morning I got a knock on my door from SSG Stewart. He was pissed off. I actually felt bad because SSG Stewart was such a good NCO that it was almost a privilege to work for him. I didn't want to be the Soldier that messed up working for him. He ended up letting me off as far as punishment goes. I didn't receive an Article 15 but I did have to sign in with him every time I entered and left the building for an entire week as corrective training. I can't remember what the other guys got for the whole thing. It would have all depended on the NCO that they worked for. I knew it was nothing serious though, and we never trusted the duty NCO as a friend again. I learned a few things that night: Senior NCOs aren't always the cleanest people in the world. They start bar fights too. I learned that walking two miles in the cold in Korea while drunk is a bad idea. Above all else I learned that you can't always trust everybody. Pelletier told me the next morning that I should have taken him up on the free chicken offer. I guess he was right.

There was also an incident we had one night that we went to Primos. Our gang went there and we had a lot to drink when suddenly Cariker just wanted to go back to the barracks. Luckily Primos wasn't as far away from the barracks as the Warrior Club so he took off. The thing was Cariker was having a rough night because of a recent breakup. He was madly in love with a woman in the unit who had left him for someone else and he wasn't handling it very well. He went back to his room and started to play his guitar. He was actually a good guitar player and would play his guitar when he was troubled. It would almost act as a form of therapy for him and he found it very soothing. For some reason he was so angry this night that he decided to smash his guitar right there in his barracks room mid-song. An NCO who was in the hallway heard it and knocked on his door. He went out into the hallway and ended up getting into an altercation with the NCO. It was a horrible night for Cariker. The next morning he didn't even remember smashing the guitar. He said it was a combination of his anger and his drunkenness. He also got in trouble for this, but luckily for him his time in Korea was almost over. A few weeks later he ended up leaving Korea for his next duty station. We all missed him since he was part of the gang but it was ultimately for the best. He needed a new start after the incident and the heartbreak. Unfortunately after he left I only heard from him once or twice and then I fell out of touch with him. The rest of our gang pressed on without him.

Because of my newfound habits I realized that I had start working out a lot harder. I needed to not only lose the extra weight that I had put on after my deployment but I also had to make sure I didn't gain any weight from all the drinking I was now doing. The unit did a lot of running during morning PT sessions (which was a big help to me) but I knew I needed to do much more than that. I started going to the gym immediately after work. I had a sweat suit I would wear in the gym while I was doing my cardio routine, which amounted to a full 60 minutes on the elliptical machine every day. I chose the elliptical machine over the treadmill because I was already a fast runner to begin with. Using an elliptical machine would not only offer my body a change but it would also take care of my knees since it's a low impact machine. Over the course of my first three months in Korea I ended up losing a little over 20 pounds with this routine. I was amazed that even with drinking every day I was able to drop weight. I started to create new goals for myself aside from just losing weight. There was a civilian who worked in our S-6 section who was an aikido master and was willing to give lessons to any Soldiers in the unit who took him up on the offer. He didn't have any students at the time so I decided to give it a shot and so I started taking aikido lessons once a week. I was amazed at how different it was than the martial arts that I had taken back in high school. This art was about technique and using your enemies' force against him. Through studying aikido I was also able to improve my flexibility, which had always been a problem for me. I felt like I could focus on getting in shape a lot more in Korea then I was able to in Fort Campbell. I guess it's because when you're overseas for a year you have a lot of time on your hands. If I didn't start training hard again I would have gained a lot of weight from all of the drinking I was doing. This would have been bad because I wanted to eventually go to the promotion board for the rank of Sergeant. I knew that I had what it took to become a Sergeant but as long as I was overweight I would never be able to get promoted. Thus I made the necessary changes to my lifestyle to make it happen.

I eventually went to a "Soldier of the month" board which is more or less a warm up for a promotion board. Sure, there are awards for the winners of the board but the true purpose of the monthly boards is to gain the experience of attending a board. If a Soldier goes to the promotion board, the score counts for promotion points towards the next rank. Therefore the object is to score as high as possible. I was very nervous going to the monthly board and I had to do a lot of preparation leading into the board. Luckily George helped me to study for it. There were so many questions on the board and they were all in a variety of subjects. Some of the subjects covered on a Soldier board are: wear and appearance of the military uniform, military customs and courtesies, physical fitness, chemical and biological warfare, weapons marksmanship and even questions about your MOS. Going to the board is a lot of work because you have so many different areas to study but in the long run it is well worth it because you learn a lot about the military in the process. You also have to memorize the Soldier's Creed for the board. If you don't know the Soldier's creed at the board than you will most likely fail. I probably couldn't have memorized the creed without George's help. It was a lot to learn and it always helps when you have someone else listening to you repeat the creed pointing out all of your mistakes. If you try to do this on your own you will develop a natural bias since you are grading yourself. It just makes sense. This is why any time a Soldier is required to appear before the board they always have a Sponsor NCO to prepare them. That's how you set your Soldiers up for success.

When the Soldier of the Month board finally came along I did very well. I did so well in fact that I won the board. It felt good to receive congratulations from our Battalion Sergeant Major since he was such a hard ass with things. When he told you that you did a good job, you knew that you really did a good job because he didn't hand compliments out that often. He was so hardcore and so into the Army lifestyle that he set standards so high. Of course there were perks with winning the board too. I received a Battalion Coin and a three day pass. Not too bad. The feeling of accomplishment from winning the board stayed with me and I couldn't wait to attend the promotion board in a few months when I was fully eligible. Now that I knew what a board was like I was ready to take the challenge head on. I was starting to realize just how bad I wanted to become an NCO. Deep down, I knew my day would come.

Christmas came along before we knew it. Since I had just arrived in October there was no way that I would be allowed to go home on leave for the holiday. At first I was upset because this marked the second Christmas in a row that I would miss out on being home because of being in the Army. I made sure to call home and talk to everyone but it still wasn't the same as being there. Things did end up getting better though, because every Soldier in the unit who wasn't on leave decided to band together to throw a huge barracks BBQ to celebrate the holiday. It was about 45 degrees out, which would be considered too cold for a normal BBQ. None of us cared about this though, we weren't about to let a minor detail like the cold keep us from having our fun. It wasn't like there was any snow on the ground or anything like that; it was just really cold out.

Everyone there did their part to make the BBQ a success. I made a homemade macaroni salad and a homemade potato salad that my dad had taught me to make when I was growing up. SSG Stewart did most of the grilling; he made ribs, cheeseburgers and chicken. All of which were purchased at the Camp Casey Commissary. And of course everyone brought beer. There was literally a case of beer there for every Soldier there. I remember going over to the grill to see how SSG Stewart was doing and he was pouring Corona all over the meat. Believe it or not it tasted good afterwards. We all stayed out there in the cold, eating out BBQ and drinking as much as beer as possible. This was just one example of making the best of a bad situation. No one wanted to be away from their families but because of the fact that we were stationed there we had no choice but to band together and do something positive. It was definitely better than my Christmas in Iraq a year earlier. And wouldn't you know that even with all of the drinking on that day, there wasn't a single alcohol related incident on Christmas. Everyone got along with one another and there was no fighting. I'd call that a success. When I look back on that day today I realize that even though I wasn't with my family, it was still a great holiday.

It wasn't long before I made contact with Duke. He had left Fort Campbell for Korea a couple of months before I did and I told him I would look him up when I got there. Obviously he didn't get to take his pro wrestling ring to Korea, but that didn't stop Duke from being obsessed with wrestling over there either. I remember people used to pick on me because they thought I was obsessed with wrestling. I wish those people had met Duke. After all, he owned a ring and dressed up like Sting all the time. If that isn't obsessed, I don't know what is. Duke was also stationed on Camp Casey like I was. I would sometimes go to his barracks and watch WWE on the Armed Forces Network while we had a few beers. This helped Duke a lot because he didn't make a lot of friends there and he was starting to get depressed. He missed doing the matches at his house and going to the TNA shows as much as I did. I guess hanging out with each other could be a way to comfort each other when you're missing home. I felt bad sometimes when I would show up to his barracks. He really didn't mesh with his new unit the way I had meshed with mine. But it wasn't just the lack of friends in the unit or missing the wrestling shows that was causing Duke some problems. He had some problems back home in the states as well.

Duke's marriage was starting to fall apart. When we were still back at Ft Campbell there were a few times that they would get into arguments in front of everyone. At the time none of us really thought anything of it. As I was starting to see now, things were way worse between Duke and his wife then they were letting on. There were a number of choices that he made in his life that she wasn't entirely happy with. He made a few mistakes with his money and created a large amount of debt. To his credit some of that debt was the mortgage for their house. Despite their financial concerns Duke was still able to provide her with a house for them to live in. She also had a son from another marriage that Duke treated well as if he was his own son. We also had reason to believe that she wasn't entirely happy with Duke dressing up like Sting every single weekend even though she acted like the was ok with it. After all, no offense to Duke, but who would be?

This was all starting to take a toll on Duke. He was starting to drink a lot more and he started going to the Juicy Bars out in TDC. A Juicy Bar is a term given to a strip of bars that are in most of the towns located just outside of the gate outside of any military post in South Korea. These bars are not like normal bars however. They are filled with girls who work for the bar called "Juicy Girls". A Juicy Girl is a scantily-clad employee who will approach an American Soldier at the bar and ask if he will buy them a drink. If the Soldier agrees, his drink costs the normal price for a drink while the Juicy Girl's drink is about $20. The drink that the Juicy Girl is given isn't even an alcoholic drink; it is just juice. Hence the name: "Juicy Girl." Sounds like a rip-off so far, doesn't it? It should sound like a rip-off because it is a rip-off. In exchange for this $20 drink the girl will spend time with the Soldier until the drink runs out. By "spending time" I mean that she will offer him fake companionship; putting her arm around him, acting like she wants to get to know him and so on. Once her drink is finished the Soldier can buy her a new $20 drink. If he doesn't buy her a new one, she gets right up and moves on to the next Soldier. As you can probably tell, the concept of a "Juicy Girl" in Korea is a terrible one. When a new Soldier first arrives to Korea they are briefed on the concept of Juicy Bars and advised to stay away from them. The reason for this is because most of these Juicy Bars are suspected of human trafficking. It had only been proven a handful of times; but the basic idea is that these Juicy Girls are not from Korea, they are contracted from other countries within Asia. If a Soldier goes out to see the same Juicy Girl over and over again and they start to fall in love with the girl they have been known to attempt to "pay off" the girl's contract to "free them" and take them to the US. The Soldier may think that they are doing a good thing but in reality it is illegal. When a Soldier gets caught doing this they are sent to jail and the US Army works with the South Korean Government to get the bar that she came from shut down. Often issues with Juicy Bars and Juicy Girls make news headlines there. They are disgusting places and I do not condone or support their existence.

Not only did I not support them, but I noticed that the KATUSA Soldiers didn't support them either. The KATUSAs look down on Juicy Bars just as I did. I don't believe in paying a girl for her time. Unfortunately some guys get so lonely that they turn to doing it as their own way to fulfill their inner desires and erase their loneliness. As I stated earlier Duke started to go to these bars as a way to cope with his problems. He was fighting with his wife almost every day either over the phone or via email and he wasn't sure if his marriage would last through the end of the tour. He started making acquaintance with one Juicy Girl in particular. I could tell that he was starting to have feelings for her because he wanted to go to that bar every night now. I tried telling him that going there was a bad idea but he didn't care. There were a few times that he took me there because he didn't have anyone to go with him and no one is allowed to leave post alone in Korea. Despite my objections I still felt bad for him so I went. This was the first time I ever went to these bars. I made it perfectly clear to him that I wasn't going to buy anyone a drink, just a drink for myself. And that's exactly what I ended up doing. I had a few beers that night and we got out of there. Before we left he introduced me to the girl that he was "courting." She seemed nice but I remember thinking to myself that it is her job to act nice. I left the bar that night sensing that Duke was not going to let go of this girl any time soon, especially if his marriage kept going downhill.

Soon enough it was time for Duke to take his mid-tour leave. He had a lot of mixed emotions about this because of all of the problems he was having with his wife. To add to everything, he got a message from a friend who was still at his old unit in Ft Campbell that he saw a man going over the house all the time to see her. Duke was pissed off about this and told me he was going to question her and try to do some investigating when he was home on leave. This was one of his arguments that he would use when I would try to talk him out of going to the Juicy Bars. As far as he was concerned there was a good chance that his wife was cheating on him so why shouldn't he try to meet someone else? I really felt bad for him through all of this and I had a feeling that Duke's problems were going to get much worse. I felt like I saw him change so much since the day I first met him at TNA in Nashville. He was much happier back then. The Duke I knew today was a shell of the Duke I knew yesterday. I tried my best to be a good friend to him through all of this, but there was only so much I could do.

When he got back from mid-tour leave he acted as if everything went ok. He told me that they fought at first and then they finally reached some common ground. He acted as if he left home this time around with a newfound hope that his marriage could survive. I was happy for him and I just hoped that they could survive the remaining months of his tour. You see, even if they didn't have things to fight about, a 12 month tour away from your spouse can take a toll on any marriage. Over the course of my career I saw many marriages fall apart because of deployments. Duke's situation was starting to look like one of those marriages and I really hoped that Duke could pull it together. The one thing that he wasn't sure of however was the matter of his wife cheating on him. He had addressed it with her (and I'm sure she denied it) but he still wasn't 100% sure. Secretly he was keeping in touch with his friend from his old unit at Ft Campbell who would keep an eye on her for him. He also wasn't going to stop seeing his Juicy Girl; he liked her way too much. That part I disagreed with. If Duke didn't trust his wife that was one thing but continuing on the path he was before leave definitely wasn't going to help the marriage. You either dedicate your time to fixing your marriage, or you don't. You can pick one choice or the other, but not both. I know that if his wife found out that would have been the final straw. Either way, Duke was a grown man who made his own decisions. He didn't have much more time left on his tour and so he lived the rest of it out his way. This was a lesson to me that once a man is set in his own ways you're just not going to change their mind. They have to learn things their own way, which is sometimes the hard way. Duke eventually did return home to the US to find his car at the Nashville airport waiting for him, without his wife. When he got back to his house he found that it was empty (with all of his furniture gone) and that his wife left. No letter, no email, no phone call, no nothing. I found out about this from him via an email that he sent me and to tell you the truth I felt bad for him. That had to be hard to endure. It pained me to see what this man had been through over the few years that I had known him. Eventually the girl that he fell in love with in Korea did move to the US and marry him, which in effect gave him a second chance at a happy life. Fortunately for me, Korea was not the last time in my life that Duke and I crossed paths.

Duke wasn't the only old friend from Fort Campbell who I met up with in Korea. As it turned out, Reynolds came over to Korea too. He ended up becoming a unit S1 like I did, so I would often bump into him at the PSB on Camp Casey when I was turning in reports and other work. Just like the old days we would greet each other with the customary greetings of "Hogan!" and "Booker T!" only this time it was in front of a new audience of people who also looked at us like we didn't know what we were talking about. A few times we got together for lunch at the local bowling alley to talk about the good old days. As wrestling fans the bowling alley was the perfect choice because they had a place called "Mean Gene's Burgers" which was affectionately named after the legendary WWF announcer "Mean Gene" Oakerlund. It was funny to see good old "Mean Gene's" face on a burger restaurant. It apparently was a small chain that never really caught on but for Reynolds and I it was our place to eat. Mean Gene, if you're reading this, thanks for the burgers.

Not everything I did in off-post Korea involved drinking and going to bars. The country itself was beautiful and there were a lot of sights to see. Tourism in Korea is huge, and as a US Soldier stationed there for a year it is in your best interest to go out and see as much of the country as possible. This is my advice for anyone reading this that hasn't gone to Korea yet: Go out and see as much as possible. Do not spend the whole tour in your barracks room or in the bar. Go out and see the country. Years later when you are reflecting back and telling people stories you are not going to want all of your stories to be party-related stories. Trust me on that one. There is a lot to see there and you won't regret it.

One tour I took while I was stationed in Korea was a tour of the DMZ. The DMZ refers to the De-Militarized Zone; which is the border that separates North Korea and South Korea. Every US Soldier that is stationed in Korea is required to take the tour of the DMZ at least once during their tour. We all got into a big coach bus to take the trip up to the DMZ. Even though Camp Casey is one of the northernmost camps in Korea the bus ride still took almost two hours. One of the rules of the tour is that everyone going must wear their Class A uniform; no exceptions. This was the few times that I rode on a bus in my Class A's. I remember being nervous that they were going to get wrinkled on the ride. Sitting on a bus for two hours in a suit can wreak havoc on the suit. You could end up getting off of the bus and look as if you store your uniform at the bottom of your closet. Nobody wants that. When you are required to wear your Class A uniform somewhere you tend to put a lot of effort (sometimes hours) into ensuring that the uniform looks perfect. If you show up somewhere wearing the uniform and it looks like crap then it looks like you're one of those Soldiers who don't take pride in himself. I'm not one of those Soldiers. Believe me if there's one thing I've got, its pride.

The tour itself was a true sight to see. They have a giant sphere-shaped rock shaped like the earth that is split in half. Inside you see the two Koreas. I had never seen a statue like this before in my life so I was sure to take a picture. Actually, I took pictures throughout the entire tour. There was a lot to see up there over the course of that day. There was a shorter bus ride around the area to show us some of the other monuments. There was also an underground tunnel that everyone walked through.

Apparently the tunnel was once used for people to escape from one side to another. The war between the two Koreas was devastating because it tore many families apart. I can't imagine what it would be like to not be allowed to see my family for over ten years just because one half of my country was fighting with another. Because of the existence of this tunnel, people were able to be reunited with their families. Since South Korea was the side that promoted freedom it was more common for someone to escape from the North to the South, but sometimes it would be the other way around just so the family could be back together. It boils back down to the old phrase, "family comes first." It was days like this that you become even more grateful that you live in America. In America you are free to travel to whatever part of the country you want to. That's just one of the many things that we as Americans take for granted. Nowadays the tunnel is part of the DMZ tour. We all walked the tunnel (which is over a mile long) in our Class A uniform. For those of you reading this that are or were in the military, you know just how unforgiving the Class A shoes can be. Walking a mile in them underground wasn't exactly the most pleasant experience and it gave me blisters. After all of the 12 mile road marches that I had endured at Fort Campbell I found myself going through more pain in a simple one mile tunnel. It didn't matter however, the tunnel was part of the tour and like everything else that I had seen in other countries it was an experience that I wouldn't trade for the world. That's the thing about traveling. You end up seeing another part of the world that you have never and probably will never see again. Thus you stay as positive as possible and you make the best of it. So what if I got a few blisters on this march. If you ever find yourself in these types of situations, remember to just embrace everything and live a little.

One other important part of the DMZ tour was the blue room. The blue room is a room at the border that the two sides meet in to conduct peace talks. From the room you can look out the window and see into North Korea. You see the North Korean guards that are standing at the position of attention ready to attack at all times. On the South Korean side you see the same thing. There is so much tension in the air that you can literally cut it with a knife. Both sides are ready to attack each other at any given moment. As if the view outside the window wasn't enough, there are also guards on the inside who are standing the exact same way. The tour guide advises every group that comes through not to touch one of the guards because they are trained to attack at even the slightest touch.

And of course in every group you have one dumbass that bumps into the Korean guard. In our case one of our guys lightly brushed up against one without realizing it and the guard snapped into a fighting stance but held back when the American backed off. It was obviously an accident, but it wasn't like it was totally unavoidable. They place the guard alongside a wall that stands near the peace talks table. There is only about two feet of room in between the table and the guard. When then tour guide tells the entire group to walk across the room there is a high chance that someone will bump into the guard. After all, there's only a two feet clearance. Come to think about it that guard is probably used to getting bumped into by now.

The table itself is the table where the peace talks take place, which are almost always hosted by the UN (United Nations). In the middle of the table there is a small yet elaborate placard for the UN flag as well as the flags of both North and South Korea. As I stated earlier the tour guide directs everyone in the room to walk from one side of the room to the other. When you get to the other side of the room the tour guide says, "You are now standing in North Korea." This room is the only part of the DMZ that you can get away with standing on the other side of the border. Anywhere else would result in immediately being shot by the guard towers on the other side. As you stand on the other side of this room it really settles in that the tensions and conflict in this part of the world are very real. It is nothing to joke about. I took quite a few pictures of this room and I'll never forget the experience.

Once we saw all of the main sights at the DMZ our unit boarded the busses to go back home to Camp Casey. The tour wasn't just a learning experience but it also served as a bonding experience between the US Soldiers and the KATUSA Soldiers that went on the trip. The US Soldiers learn so much about Korean history on the tour that they really start to understand where the Koreans are coming from, and some of the things that they have been through in their life. They have had to live their entire lives in conflict and their parents and grandparents have brothers and sisters who are still trapped on the other side. You gain a newfound understanding of them, and they also gain a newfound respect for the US Soldiers because it shows them that we are willing to learn about them and their struggle. Even though it is a mandatory requirement for all Soldiers to attend this tour I would still recommend it to anyone. Like many of the places I went to see while I was in Korea it was a great experience that you cannot put a price tag on.

Another cool tour that I took while in Korea was a tour of the Gyeongbokgung Palace. Like many of the tours that we took while I was in Korea, the tour arrangements were set up by the KATUSA Soldiers. That's one thing that was always beneficial to us; the fact that the KATUSA Soldiers were willing to act as tour guides to show us the country. The palace itself is located in Seoul and is actually the size of a small village. The main building of the palace (which is huge) has somewhat of a legendary story behind it that I will gladly share with you now: Many years ago Korea and Japan were at war. Japanese Soldiers that were fighting in Korea won a battle that took place near the palace. As an insult, they took down the Gyeongbokgung Palace and physically carried it back to Japan. Once they arrived in Japan with the hundreds of pieces of this giant palace they set it up on their own territory as a sign of disrespect to Korea. This action infuriated the Koreans and as a result they marched to Japan and fought them. This time the Japanese lost the battle and so the Koreans took the palace down again and marched it all the way back to Seoul. I found this to be an amazing story. Today in modern times, when wars are fought they are usually fought with bombs, tanks, planes, etc. Also in modern times you don't usually see an enemy army deconstructing an entire building in an effort to dishonor their opponent. The story itself serves as a lesson at just how much the world has changed. I stood there staring up at the center of the palace wondering just how it taken apart and then put back up again twice during the same war. It's mind boggling. The tour itself was a good tour and its one of the many experiences that I still tell people about. As a souvenir I bought a tiny replica of the main building of the palace. I keep it on a shelf on my book case along with all sorts of small things I picked up around the world. Today, when people see it they always ask what it is and every single time I tell them the story of that war. I still haven't met anyone who wasn't amazed by that story, a story of fighting for your countries' honor against a true rival.

We also took a unit trip to a few Buddhist Temples while I was there. I need to stress that I am not of the Buddhist faith and neither were most of the Soldiers who were in the unit. The reason of the trip wasn't to try to convert anyone to the Buddhist faith, but for the purpose of tourism instead. Some of the KATUSAs were Buddhists and they came up with the idea of taking the trip in order to further educate us on some aspects of Korean culture. The first thing that I had noticed when we arrived was that the temple had a symbol on the roof that resembled a swastika. Slightly irritated by it, I asked one of the KATUSAs why the symbol was there, to which he replied that the symbol was part of Buddhism before the Nazis adopted the symbol. He assured me that the symbol in Korea does not mean the same thing that it means in the rest of the world, notably Europe. I was astonished by this fact, especially when the KATUSA pointed out to me that the symbol itself is reversed. I guess to the naked eye you couldn't really tell, especially if you are an American.

The temples themselves on this particular trip were spread out over a few miles through a hilly region. This made it a long walk to and from each temple. The temples have been there for hundreds of years as well, and are made out of wood as opposed to modern buildings that would be made of steel, cement or rock. That in itself makes these buildings an amazing sight because you wouldn't think that a wooden building would last that long. Then again, the Gyongbokgung palace lasted all of these years too. Even still if you were to compare the architecture of a church in America to a Buddhist temple in Korea, there are so many differences. When you see a church in America that is made of rocks and cement it makes sense that it would be standing for so long, while the architecture of the temple is more thought-provoking. Upon entering the temple you see that there are Buddhist Monks inside silently praying. Throughout our whole tour of the temple those same Monks kept praying. They stayed there, silently kneeling all day. According to the tour guide there are times when certain Monks would come in there and pray for days on end. I am not going to speculate whether or not anyone does that in the US, but I will say that I have never seen that myself. Overall, the tour of the Buddhist Temple was an eye opening tour and served as a good way to further my knowledge and respect of the Korean Culture.

Not all of the tours that we took in Korea involved learning about the culture. Some of the tours were instead all about having fun. We took trips to the COEX Mall and Aquarium, as well as a huge amusement park in Seoul called Lotte World. The COEX Mall and Aquarium was located in Seoul and was one of the biggest malls I had ever seen in my entire life. There were all sorts of electronic shops and clothing stores and lots of international restaurants. They had Indian, Chinese, Japanese, Korean, and even Mexican restaurants. They weren't chain restaurants like you would see in the US however. Instead they were real sit-down style restaurants. This is much different than your average mall in the US where you would find yourself surrounded by Taco Bell and Burger King. Our group ended doing a little bit of shopping and then settled down at a Korean restaurant to eat before heading over to the aquarium.

I found the aquarium amazing since I had never been to one before in my entire life. They had all different sorts of species of aquatic life, ranging from sharks, fish, crabs and even eels. It was a really cool tour. There is even one room in particular where you walk in and realize that you are standing in a tunnel surrounded by water. I'm talking about being surrounded on all sides; to include underneath you. It was a funny feeling to look up at the ceiling and see fish swimming above you and then to look down at the floor and see the exact same thing. Something like this really takes the breath out of you. You can't even believe that you are seeing this, even though you are. For me, seeing something this amazing also made me very grateful that I was in the Army because if I wasn't in the Army I probably never would have traveled to Korea and I wouldn't have gotten to enjoy such an experience. Overall, the COEX Aquarium was probably the coolest trip I went on during the entire tour. I'd recommend it to anyone.

Lotte World is the mega-amusement park that is located in Seoul. It has indoor and outdoor rides, as well as water rides and an indoor ice skating rink. The park is huge; bigger than most Six Flags parks located in the US. I went to Lotte World a few times while stationed in Korea and all of the times I had gone there I went with Dongnam. Of all of the KATUSA Soldiers that were in the unit, I hung out with Dongnam the most. He didn't mind showing us around the country as much as possible. Usually we would go and eat and have a few drinks before hitting up the amusement park. It had become almost like a custom for us. One trip to Lotte World in particular sticks out in my mind the most, and it was because of something that Dongnam said to me in the middle of one of the rides. We were on this huge needle drop ride where you would sit in one of the many seats on the ground that wrapped around a needle. Once everyone was seated and locked into place the seats would slowly raise to the top of the needle, which was high enough in the air to see the entire park as well as a Buddhist Temple that was deep into the city. I remember the temple being there because I pointed out the symbol on the roof (the backwards swastika that I alluded to earlier.) After the seats rose to the very top they sat there for a minute so that everyone could take in the view. What comes next is what made the ride crazy. Knowing that we were about to drop to the bottom at a high rate of speed, (that's the point of the ride after all) Dongnam looked over at me and said to me in his Korean accent, "Hey Conklin. Fuck You." It was like the machine could hear him talk, because after he said that the seats dropped. I screamed at the top of my lungs as we plummeted to the bottom. It was the craziest ride that I had ever been on. Obviously Dongnam didn't mean any harm when he said that to me, he was just messing around because of the situation. We took a few other rides that day to include bumper cars and a water themed roller coaster, but none of them sticks out in my mind the way that his words did. It was hilarious, and I'll never forget that day.

Another cool experience from my time in Korea was trying all of the new food. Eating real Korean food in Korea doesn't compare to eating Korean food in a restaurant in the US. It doesn't even come close. There was so much food to try and so many places to try the food. Compared to American food, Korean food is very unique. The common foods in Korea that I tried were Bulgogi (beef with vegetables), Kim Bap (which is similar to a California Roll wrapped in spinach), spicy squid and Bip Bim Bap. Bip Bim Bap was my favorite Korean food. It consists of a big bowl of rice mixed with vegetables, beef, and a hot red bean paste. On top of the rice sits one fried egg. You are supposed to mix all of the items in the bowl together with your spoon. The different flavors blend together really well. While I was in Korea I would try to eat Bip Bim Bap every single time I went out for Korean food. To this day it is still my favorite Korean food and I try my best to have it when I can.

There was one other food that I tried In Korea while I was there that wasn't exactly as common as the other foods. The food was called Gaegogi, and it is essentially the same thing as Bulgogi, only instead of the main meet in the dish being beef it is dog. Yes, you read that correctly and before you puke please allow me to explain. Eating Gaegogi is actually a Korean tradition and is considered a delicacy. I guess I would consider it the equivalent to eating snails in France. Today, most of the younger generation has gotten away from eating it, but the older generation still embraces it. Therefore, eating Gaegogi is still part of the Korean culture. Now, I do feel the need to stress right now that I do have a dog, and I love dogs very much. Also, it's not like I eat Gaegogi every day or anything like that. I just wanted to try it once not only for the bragging rights but also as a way to further embrace the culture there. That is the only reason why I did it. One day at the office I had asked Young Chan to take me to a place that served it, since not all restaurants in Korea serve it anymore. He actually tried to talk me out of it, but I insisted. Young Chan ended up taking me to a place that served the Gaegogi in a soup. You would pick the pieces of the meat out of the soup and wrap it in a leaf. As far as the taste goes, it was horrible. It was very gamey and had a lot of fat marbled throughout the meat. I did not like eating it whatsoever but I still "Soldiered on." Like any challenge in my life, I embraced it. No other American Soldier in the unit was willing to try it, and when I told all of the other Soldiers at formation the next morning they just couldn't believe it. Some of them thought that it was disgusting, and some of them were impressed. The basic consensus was that none of the other Soldiers had the guts to try it, but I did. That didn't matter to me anymore. I tried it, and that was that. There was one lesson that I took from this experience, and that lesson was that you should never be afraid to try new things, despite any possible scrutiny involved. Once again, I will never eat it again.

Another thing that I did while I was in Korea that I will forever be proud of is I ran five half marathons while stationed there. I had come back from the gym after doing my usual 60 minute cardio routine and bumped into another Soldier at the duty desk by the name of SPC Pepple. I knew Pepple but at the time we weren't the best of friends or anything like that. It wasn't like we hung out; he was really just another Soldier in the unit that I knew. The one thing I did know about Pepple however was that he was an avid runner, and in fact ran more than me and ran faster than me. Usually I found that a runner that was faster than me was hard to come by. Up until now the only other runner I ever met that was faster than me was Jones, but Jones was still at Ft Campbell. Since Pepple was faster than me, I naturally respected him. On this particular day he asked me if I would be interested in running a half marathon (which is 13 miles) in Seoul with him. I jumped all over the opportunity because to me, knowing that the event was something that wasn't sanctioned by the US Army but instead the city of Seoul made it that much more special. By running in this marathon I would be representing my country on foreign soil in a foreign event. I agreed to run the race with him and I couldn't wait.

Race day came and I was astonished to see just how big of an event this truly was. There were about 1,200 people out there registered to run this race. While most of the runners were from Korea, there were also a lot of runners there from Africa. The one thing that I noticed was that there were only four Americans there, Pepple and I included. After the beginning announcements for the race (which were all in Hangul, not English for obvious reasons) the announcer fired the flare gun into the sky to signify the start of the race. I had my portable CD player (this was before IPODs came out into the mainstream) armed with fresh batteries and a few burned CDs with my favorite songs. I still remember the song that I started the race off with; a song that I stated earlier was very near and dear to my heart: I am a real American by Rick Derringer. Yeah, I admit if there is any song that will get me pumped up and ready to do something big it is that song. Throughout the race itself I was amazed at the scenery of the route. It started off in a metropolitan part of Seoul and at one point the route ran across a beautiful garden that rested along the Han River. It was amazing. I had never seen anything like this.

The further I ran the harder it got. This was the first time that I had ever pushed my body to the limit of running 13 miles. I pressed on, knowing that on this day the most important thing was to finish. That is the goal when running in one of these types of races; to simply finish. And that's exactly what I did. I finished running the race in great time too, 1 hour and 43 minutes for 13 miles. Considering the fact that I was of a slightly larger frame and I had worked hard to drop weight over the past few months I would say that was pretty good. When we finished the race we were given a medal for finishing along with a certificate. As it turned out, I finished 282nd out of 1,200 participants. I felt that was actually really good. As far as I was concerned, I outran over 900 other runners, in THEIR home country. It was something to be proud of and another accomplishment to add to the list. All in all it was also a lot of fun, so Pepple and I decided to make this a regular thing. I ended up running in a total of five half marathons while stationed in Korea. As an American, I'll never stop being proud of that. As a person, I'll never forget any of them.

Korea was also no stranger to USO tours and visits from celebrities. There was a few times where bands and musicians would come and play free shows on Camp Casey for the Soldiers to enjoy. Things like that always boost the morale of a Soldier. Of all of the USO visits that happened while I was there one stands out in my mind the most: a visit from Billy Blanks, creator of TAE BO. He came over as part of his "Mind, Body and Spirit" tour with the sole purpose of not just meeting and greeting the Soldiers, but to also put on a live TAE BO session, free for anyone who wanted to participate. I decided it would be a good idea, since I liked doing TAE BO anyway with the use of the DVDs. This was probably going to be the only opportunity that I ever had to actually do TAE BO live and in person with Billy Blanks. Let's be honest, I don't even know where these tapes are recorded, maybe in a studio in Hollywood some place but who knows. He put us through an incredibly hard TAE BO session, but just like on the tapes he was very supportive to the entire gang. If you have ever seen a TAE BO tape you know that Billy Blanks' style of motivation is that of positive motivation (unlike that of most NCOs in the Army). I feel that a positive style of motivation works better than a negative and I wish more NCOs would use that style, instead of making someone feel bad about things. For that and more I hold a lot of respect for Billy Blanks. When the session was over, he sat with us in the center of the gym and talked to us about a number of topics: the war, faith in God, physical fitness and positivity among others. This also gave me a newfound respect for the man because he just sat down there with us like he was still a normal person. Many celebrities wouldn't do that; they would do their show and then move on acting as if they are too good to talk to you. Billy wasn't like that; he knew that he was still a human being just like all of us and he didn't hesitate to show that. All he really wanted was to spread a positive message to us and I feel that he accomplished that. Over the years Billy Blanks continued to tour various military installations around the world, continuing to spread his message. Every time I break out my TAE BO DVDs today I think back on that experience. He was a true class act.

As the months moved on I realized that my turn to go home on mid-tour leave was coming up. I couldn't believe how fast time was starting to move. As the old saying goes; time flies when you are having fun. That statement couldn't have been truer. Between all of the partying with the other Soldiers and the sightseeing I started to lose track of the time. Still, there was one very important thing that I wanted to accomplish prior to going on leave. That one thing was attending the promotion board. I was starting to assume more responsibilities in my office and I craved the rank and pay that should come with new responsibilities. I knew that the only possible way that I could get promoted to the rank of Sergeant was to attend the board, so it was a no-brainer. I took this very seriously because I was tired of being a Specialist. I wanted to be a Sergeant, and badly. The promotion board would be just like the Soldier of the month board that I had attended earlier in the year so I was somewhat prepared for the task that lay ahead. And just like the last board George helped me study and get my uniform ready.

Before we knew it, the day came and I would rise up to the challenge. While I waited in the hallway to be called in by the CSM I didn't really think I was nervous. I felt confident and strong. I knocked on the door to the board room (which is custom) with three loud knocks. I heard the CSM's voice from the inside yell to me, "ENTER!" I entered the room, marched to the center of the room and rendered my salute and the customary greeting, "Specialist Conklin reporting to the president of the board!" The board members first had me enact a few facing movements, which I knew was also customary. As an S1 Clerk I had to sit in on many boards as the board recorder in the past so I knew this was part of the procedure. I knew that I would next be prompted to take my seat and prepare for the board questions. I had prepared for this also and I was more than ready. Suddenly, the CSM decided to throw me off. He didn't tell me to sit down right away like usual. Instead, he had me repeat the same facing movements that I had just performed. This actually confused the living hell out of me. I hadn't prepared for that, because I had never seen it happen before. I think the board members knew that I wasn't expecting something like that, because I could see the looks on their faces like they were happy about the fact that they got one over on me. I froze briefly and tried to find my thoughts again, to which after a few seconds I did. But even still, that slight hesitation cost me points on my final board score.

I did finally get to take my seat for my questions. I answered almost all of the board questions correctly, which wasn't exactly a surprise considering I had studied very hard. When the questioning was complete, I was dismissed from the board and I rendered my salute. About an hour later I found out that my board score was 139 out of a possible 150 points. That wasn't exactly the best score in the world, considering the cutoff score for my MOS is usually high. I would need every point that I could get in every area possible (the board is an area in itself) in order to ensure that I got promoted. Even still, I was happy to have attended the board because now I was considered a Specialist-promotable; meaning that now I am eligible to get promoted to Sergeant if I meet the cutoff score. The scores were released monthly, so each month that goes by it is now up to me to add points through various areas (board score, PT score, awards, education) and to monitor the scores as well. The monitoring part wasn't really hard since it was part of my job to monitor the scores for all of the

Soldiers in the unit anyway. I returned to work as usual, awaiting my time to go home on leave. SSG Stewart was proud of me and the fact that I was now promotable. I was too.

Finally I went home on leave. Just like on the way over to Korea I had a layover in Japan. The only difference was that this layover was longer than the first one. I had about six hours of free time on my hands so I tried to walk around and see as much as possible. I finally found the building exit near the baggage claim and decided to go and grab a bite to eat. I had some Curry Beef and headed back to the airport. I wish I had more time in Japan because I would have liked to have done a little more than just eaten lunch. I got back to the airport and picked up a souvenir just to prove that I had been to Japan. It was so unlike my layover in Seattle when I actually got to walk around the city. I think one day I am going to take a vacation to Japan so I can actually do some sightseeing. That way I won't feel as cheated.

Things in Saint Johnsville were business as usual and thus my two weeks of leave flew by quickly. I spent the two weeks hanging out with Hillary or Lauren; depending on the day. Hillary had just taken a job as a gym teacher/coach so I went with her to a few of the games she coached and watched. I was proud to see that a good friend of mine was doing so well. As far as Lauren, at the time her parents were going through a divorce and it was taking her toll on her. I spent a lot of my leave helping her clean her father's house because the place had really fallen apart since Lauren's mother moved away. It was a tough time for her and I was glad to be there for her while all of this was happening. I can remember us making jokes about some of the stuff that we found in the house just to lighten the mood. Because of everything that was going on I almost felt bad about going back to Korea and leaving her behind to deal with all of this. It was still good to spend some time with an old friend and catch up on things, especially considering the fact that every single time I called her from Korea I was extremely drunk. I could hardly remember half of our conversations. Nowadays when I'm drunk I try to stay off of my phone. If anything, it will save you some of your minutes.

When I got back to Korea I was re-acclimated to how much the unit sucked. I guess through all of the fun I was having before I took leave I didn't notice as much but now that I had been away for two weeks I realized again just how low the morale in the unit was starting to become. There were still crooked leaders, the CSM was still overly proactive, and the Battalion Commander was exactly the same as she was before I left. Not to mention the fact that SSG Stewart had been moved from Camp Casey to Yongsan for the rest of his tour in order to take a better position. He was taking a Brigade-level S1 position which would ultimately help him get promoted to Sergeant First Class (E-7). I understood why it was happening because career progression is extremely important in the Army. Also, he was such a great NCO that he really did deserve it. The main problem with him leaving though was the fact that he was a buffer to how bad the unit was. He would try his best to protect us from all of the crap that was going on. Now that he was gone, George, Kim and I were more or less on our own. That included the work in the section as well. There wasn't an NCO coming in to replace him. Therefore we had to take charge of the section. This was actually a positive for me because now I had no choice but to learn my job that much more. If George was gone, the customers would come to me. I had to be on my game all the time. Getting to that level would require reading regulations and really paying attention to my work. Sure enough over the next couple of months I did get a lot better at my job.

Over the first few weeks of being back I encountered a major problem that would prove to be detrimental to my career. I realized that while on leave I gained some weight. The problem with this was that I wasn't the only one who realized that I had gained weight, the leadership also realized it. One morning came along that I was asked if I wanted to take a PT test. I wasn't actually due for one for a few more months, but I decided to take it anyway. I was promotable and I knew that if I got a higher score on my PT test that it would increase my overall promotion points and thus increasing my chances of getting promoted to Sergeant. I did well on the test, but that didn't matter. It was what happened after the test that mattered more: after the test I was weighed in. I had completely forgotten that this would happen. I got on the scale, got weighed and taped, and I failed. I was 2% over on my body fat percentage. I felt like I was tricked into this because had I not taken the PT test I may not have been weighed in for a couple more months which would have been enough time to lose the weight. I was so angry with the system, and I was angry with myself.

The consequences of failing a weigh-in while promotable are clear. If you are promotable and you fail your weigh in you lose your promotable status. This was extremely depressing to me because I had worked so hard to become promotable and I knew that I could not get promoted to

Sergeant without being promotable. I called home to my Dad and broke to him what happened. He didn't agree with the Army's system of weighing and taping (for the record, I do not agree with it either) and the situation made him very upset. As a result, he decided to voice his concerns . . . to Congress. My father wrote a letter to Congress voicing how angry he was with this and in about three days the unit was contacted by an angry Congressman. I was proud of my dad for standing up for me when things had gone sour. That's the thing about family; you should always be there for your family through thick and thin. Above all else, family comes first. Granted, my dad's letter didn't force the Army to change its policies, but what it did do was it forced the unit to re-evaluate some of their practices and procedures concerning their weight control program. I knew that it was my own fault that I had gained weight, but it wasn't like the unit had an in-depth special population PT program in place to help Soldiers overcome this problem. All the unit did for their overweight Soldiers and PT failures was tell the Soldiers to go to the gym for an hour after work every day. I did that on my own anyway. What the Soldiers in that unit needed (myself included) was a skilled NCO to act as a personal trainer to these Soldiers to truly coach and mentor them and help them through this problem. Luckily that was soon about to start happening and I like to think that my Dad's letter to congress had something to do with that.

The Battalion Sergeant Major decided to start a special PT program that would be exclusively supervised by him. I was working out extremely hard in the gym almost every single day but I was missing direction. I admit that I really needed some help in this at the time, so I welcomed the idea that he was setting up this program despite the fact that most of the Soldiers thought he was too hard on people and wasn't very approachable. As it turned out he really wasn't all that bad once I got to know him. He put me on a special weightlifting routine that he called "drop sets." Basically the premise of the workout is you start off doing a set of any particular exercise with low weight and high reps. Then, for three sets you do high weight and low reps but immediately after you complete the third set you grab the light weight that you originally started with and pump it as many times as you can. This type of workout is designed to shock the body and promote the loss of body fat. He also taught me how it isn't necessarily important how much you weigh; but instead how much body fat you have. It made sense, but it also went against the normal PT routine that the Army normally puts forth. I had grown used to the Army's PT program and thus it was no longer helping me. The drop sets routine that the CSM put me on however was one of the better workout regimens I had seen in my entire life. Every single day I left the gym sore so I knew it was working.

I made it my personal mission to lose this weight as soon as possible and get back to the promotion board. I hated the lingering feeling of knowing that I was promotable before and now I wasn't. I wanted to achieve my goals and live up to the promises that I had made to myself. Every single day when I was in the gym I pushed it to the limit and it really helped to have the CSM coaching me. He supported my desire to go back to the board but he also was there to make sure that I earned the right to get another chance. Some units wouldn't have given a Soldier a second chance, so I was very lucky in that aspect. After just three weeks, I had worked hard enough to lose the weight. I was weighed in and I made tape with an extra 1% to spare. I was so proud of myself. It felt good knowing that I had it in me to make a comeback.

Now it was time to start studying and get ready for the board itself. Counting the previous promotion board and the Soldier of the month board that I had attended earlier this would end up being my third board appearance while In Korea. Because of the experience of having two other boards under my belt I really thought I had a grasp on things. I believed that there was no way I could do worse than my original score of 139 points. I don't think I was being too cocky, I was just being logical. When the board day finally came, I was pumped. My uniform was in perfect condition and I knew the answers to almost every question in the study guide. I knocked on the door, giving it three loud knocks and awaited to be called in. When the CSM yelled, "ENTER!" I stormed in, rendered my salute and shouted with confidence, "Specialist Conklin reports to the president of the board!" It was then that I made a crucial mistake. Instead of holding my salute until the CSM returned his salute I made a mistake and started to drop my salute. Halfway down I realized the mistake I made and started to bring it back up. Thinking aloud, I accidently uttered the words, "Oh Shit." Dropping the salute early was a big enough mistake as it was, but saying the words, "Oh shit" outright represented a total lack of military bearing. The CSM glared at me with an angry look in his eyes and said, "Get out of my board! I'll call you back in here when we are ready to see you. I felt like total garbage because I made a crucial mistake at a very important moment. I left the room and waited. I couldn't believe that I made a mistake like this. After about five minutes I was called back in. The five minutes felt like an eternity. When I got back into the board room, I paced myself, took my time and was very careful and deliberate in every single one of my actions. Whether it was answering a question, reciting the NCO creed or performing facing movements I made sure not to make any mistakes. As a result, I kicked that board's ass. I knocked this board out of the park, so to speak. I didn't miss a single question and I knew that had I not made the mistake earlier my score would have been higher than the last one. Now there was the simple question of how many points my mistake would actually cost me.

When the CSM informed me of my board score, he took the time to explain to me that given the circumstances he didn't even actually have to call me back in. I could have been disqualified right then and left the board as a non-promotable specialist. Obviously, that wasn't what I wanted and it wasn't what the CSM wanted either. He believed in me and wanted to see me become an NCO one day. With that said, I was once again awarded my promotable status but he had no choice but to give me a score of 117 points on the board due to that mistake. I didn't miss a single question (which was obviously good) but there was no way I could be allowed to leave with a high score. The mistake had proven to be a costly one because I now knew that I would have to work that much harder in the other areas in order to meet the cutoff score to get promoted. I took an important lesson from all of this to never lose my military bearing no matter the situation. As the saying goes, "always do what is right no matter where you are, even if you are alone on a deserted island." That quote came directly from the CSM. He had a good point.

Because of the fact that Korea is only a one year tour (unless you extend) many of my friends left the unit month after month. By the tour's halfway mark Pelletier, Cariker and Dyson had already left which meant the only ones left from our original gang were Reid and I. As a result, I started making new friends within the unit. I started hanging out with a few other Soldiers by the names of Corley, Mitchell and Vandever. Corley and Mitchell were a lot more like me than the previous gang in the aspect that they were big professional wrestling fans and they liked to drink a lot. It was good to be able to make new friends since many of my other ones left. The other cool thing was that they hung out with the KATUSAs a lot, while my previous group did not. Back when they were still around I usually didn't hang out with them and the KATUSAs at the same time.

This group would be different, especially because one of the KATUSAs was Corley's roommate.

There were a lot of times that I would go out partying with Corley, Mitchell and the KATUSAs too. Our partying wasn't limited to the barracks. Believe me, the barracks can get boring. There was one time that we went to a district of Seoul that was farther away from Yongsan then others were. It was so far away from the post that the Military Police didn't patrol out there, which meant for us that we wouldn't be subject to a curfew. Dongnam took us to a few different bars that night. We started playing a drinking game where we had an empty shot glass floating in a glass of beer. Everyone at the table would then take turns pouring a little bit of Soju (Korean Liquor) into the glass. Whoever ended up filling the glass to the point where it sunk to the bottom of the beer glass would have to drink the entire thing. We went around the table doing rounds of this game over and over again. I was amazed at how much the KATUSAs could drink. They really had a high alcohol tolerance. Apparently it's because they start drinking the Soju at a younger age then Americans drink in the US. Not to mention the chemical composition of Soju, it's only 22% alcohol . . . the rest is formaldehyde. When you combine Soju with other types of Alcohol the formaldehyde has a strange effect on you. It's almost like it makes you stay drunk longer. Trying to keep up with the KATUSAs when it came to drinking Soju was like going on a suicide mission. You just weren't going to keep up, and you would never be the same again.

After we played nearly a dozen rounds of the "Soju glass in the beer game" we started walking the streets looking for more bars. We stopped all over the place, bar hopping if you will. After a while we started to get hungry, so Dongnam took us to a bar that also served food. Even though it was 2 am we didn't care, we just wanted to eat. I guess you would call that "drunken munchies." Because of the time the only thing that they were serving at the moment was a weird tofu soup. They brought us a lot of the soup, along with even more bottles of Soju. Needless to say, we were really living it up that night. At one point I needed to go to the bathroom to relieve myself of all of the alcohol that we had been drinking all night long. There was an old Korean man who was standing at the urinal next to mine who started talking to me, but in perfect English. He seemed to know a little more about Americans than the average Korean, asking me strange questions like, "How long have you been here?" and "How did you know where to find this place?" Realizing that we were technically out past curfew to begin with, I decided to brush the man off and take my time in the bathroom, hoping he would leave first. Finally he left, and after I washed my hands I dismissed the entire incident as if it didn't happen. It was definitely an odd thing to have happened to me. When I got back to our table, I was startled to see that the old man was standing there. Not only that, both of the KATUSA Soldiers that came with us were now standing at the position of attention. Mitchell on the other hand, was just sitting there. I didn't fully understand what was going on, but what I did notice was that the old man was yelling at the KATUSAs in Hangul. As far as I was concerned this guy was being a total asshole to my friends and I took exception to this, especially considering I had no idea why. Finally he decided to leave, and when I asked my friends what the man's problem was they didn't speak right away. After a few minutes they finally broke it to me that the man was a Sergeant First Class from the ROK Army and he was pissed off at them because they were out so late with Americans. The man kept yelling at them about the fact that we were out past curfew and if we were actually caught we would all be arrested. I understood that the man was right; the rules are the rules, but these were rules that were enforced only by the Military Police, not the Korean National Police that patrolled that area. American tourists do not share the same set of rules as American Soldiers, and therefore the KNPs would have no idea which ones we were. Honestly, the old man would have had no idea that I was a Soldier if I didn't answer his questions. I felt he was overreacting, and so did everyone else. The incident served as a "buzz kill" and thus we went back to our hotel room to pass out and sleep off our drunkenness. The next morning we all laughed the whole thing off over a hung over breakfast. Even though the night had a crappy ending, it still goes down as one of the more fun nights I had out on the town with my KATUSA friends. They really knew how to party.

There were some other times that I went out with Corley and Mitchell that the KATUSAs didn't come with us. Usually these times were when they would want to go to the juicy bars. Now as I stated earlier, I did not condone these types of bars, but they would often go there just out of being bored and not having something to do. So since they were going out, I would end up going out there with them also. As long as I knew that I didn't hand a Juicy Girl a single dime in exchange for their "fake services" my conscious was going to be ok. As it turned out, they didn't really do that very often either. A lot of times they just wanted to have a place to go out to and have a few beers off post and since there were no regular style bars nearby the juicy bars were the only choice. We started going to this one particular bar called the head club. The head club was the only bar there that played rock music while the rest of them were playing hip hop and rap music all the time. We really didn't like hip hop and rap, so we made the head club "our place." We would go in there most weekends, drink a lot and have a good time. After a while the Juicy Girls caught on that we weren't paying for the "fake services" and so they started to greet us and treat us like regular customers. The bar was a basement bar also, so it got to the point where when I was walking down the stairs (which were at full view of the entire bar) all of the Juicy Girls and bartenders would yell "CONKLIN!" We always got a kick out of that, it was a sign we were making a good impression.

The other cool thing about the head club was that for music there was a computer hooked up to the stereo system. The DJ there would allow you to request a song to be downloaded via the internet to be played. That was a pretty good idea considering most of their customers were from the US. So I decided that one night when we were there that I would request a certain special song to be downloaded. I hope you can see where I am going with this, because Coley certainly did. I asked the DJ to download "I am a real American". Luckily he was able to find the song online, and when it played I couldn't believe what happened. Once the song hit, everyone at the bar simultaneously looked over at the computer. They were all drunk, and they all knew the song. Everyone started singing along. Up until then I had really thought that I had "seen it all" but apparently I hadn't. There is nothing like seeing a bar full of drunken US Soldiers sing along the words to Hulk Hogan's legendary entrance music in a bar in a foreign country. That's what I call patriotism. There's a good chance that someone could have gotten their ass kicked that night if they said something bad about America. And it wasn't like everyone was just sitting around singing the words either. Instead everyone was up and moving around, pointing the finger at people and doing the Hulk Hogan pose. Corley found it hilarious, and so did I. I've tried doing this a few times in American bars as well, and once in a while I'll get a small reaction, but I doubt that I'll ever see a reaction like the one I did in Korea.

For as much partying as we were doing, there was just as much hard training to match. There was a saying in Korea back then, "work hard, play hard." That's exactly what we did. Our unit went to the field a lot while I was there. During the year that I was there we went to the field five times, each time ranging from three to five days. Now, to an infantry Soldier this may not seem like a lot of time in the field. This is because infantry units have been known to send their Soldiers to the field for 30 to 45 days at a time. For them, that is the status quo but for a support unit that is excessive. Usually units like ours would go to the field once every six months for three days and that would be it. Our mission doesn't really cater to the long field exercise. That's just how it is. Usually some of the stuff out there that we did seemed very pointless considering our mission. Me being the sarcastic guy that I am, I always had something to say about this. It just would have been nice to have a friend out there that saw things the same way that I did. That's where Vandever came in. He believed in a lot of the same things that I did. He was a great Soldier and excelled at PT tests and Soldier of the month boards but at the same time he saw right through some of the political garbage that happened there. He shared the same sense of sarcasm that I did, and while we were on details that would involve heavy lifting we noticed a lot of the lazier Soldiers figuring out ways to get out of doing work. So Vandever and I would decide to go ahead and do the work, only after moving each heavy object we would stop right where we were and do the Hulk Hogan bow and arrow pose, as if we were showing off. A lot of people didn't like us doing this, but we didn't care because many of them were doing anything they could to get out of doing hard work. This ultimately forced us to pick up the slack so we decided to send them a message. If the rest of the Soldiers pulled their weight we wouldn't have had to resort to such actions. Today everything we did amounts to fond memories, and looking back, I'm almost certain that there were a lot of pictures taken of us doing these poses in the middle of work details.

Like me, Vandever also had a great deal of respect for the Battalion Sergeant Major and a great deal of disdain for the Battalion Commander. The lack of military bearing on the Battalion Commander's part was becoming so deliberate that even the lowest ranking Privates in the unit were beginning to see it. It was a shame, because we could all tell that the CSM wasn't on board with the way she acted and was counting down the days until she would finally leave Korea. When you have internal problems in a unit they always get worse if the Soldiers start to see them. Leadership would prefer that the Soldiers aren't exposed to problems because it does adversely affect morale. It's comparable to a kid watching his parents argue. The kid doesn't really know why it is happening all the time, but it still has an impact on the child's mind. Same thing, only instead of it being a kid, you're talking about Soldiers who are being trained to fight. The last thing you want on their mind is how their Commander is acting, and why they are acting that way.

There was one particular field week-long exercise that we went on where the problems became extremely apparent. While the positive aspect was the fact that we were getting some great field training with a night convoy exercise, (which ultimately landed me an appearance on AFN news in Korea) the negatives certainly outweighed the positives on this one. Spending a week out there was long enough, but there was an issue with the food. Instead of eating three MREs a day, the unit had coordinated to have hot food brought out to the field twice a day. It doesn't sound so bad so far, does it? The food that was brought out wasn't the best food available, but it wasn't like anyone was complaining because it was better than having to eat MREs. At least, no one complained yet. The complaining started when the Popeye's Chicken delivery car approached the field site. Apparently, the Battalion Commander ordered Popeye's Chicken to be delivered to her in the field. It wasn't like she ordered it for the entire unit as a treat; she ordered it all just for her and she had it delivered frequently. Understandably, this upset the Soldiers quite a bit for a few reasons. For one, there is no comparison between DFAC Caliber Chili-Mac and Popeye's Chicken. Seriously the DFAC food is garbage compared to the delicious hot fried chicken and biscuits that Popeye's provides. Also, it boils down to the impression a leader makes on a Soldier. When the Soldiers are in the field suffering you would think that a good leader would set a good example and do the same thing. It's just like when I spoke highly of 1SG Guffy back at Fort Campbell earlier in this book; he was someone who wasn't afraid to get down into the foxholes with the Soldiers at the range. That is what a good leader does. Fast forward years later to Korea and I am now serving under a Commander who has no issue putting her own needs above the needs of her Soldiers. That's not leadership. I honestly don't even know if she could see the impact that it was having on her Soldiers. Either way, it got the Soldiers and the NCOs talking. If you had reservations about her leadership style before, this field exercise transformed those reservations to outright hate. I really couldn't blame anyone because I felt the same way.

The week-long field exercise finally came to an end. We performed a lot of great training out there in addition to the nighttime convoy exercise. We did some NBC training out there and we pulled a lot of guard duty. For a non-infantry Soldier it would have been a good experience if it hadn't been for the actions of the Commander. When it was all over, the Commander had a formation and gave a speech about the exercise. You could tell she was doing this all for her evaluation report. She tried talking about the positive aspects of the exercise and mentioned how the Soldiers in our unit should be thankful to be in a unit like this one. During this speech she actually had the audacity to talk about how great the "hot chow" was that she allowed to be carted out to the field for us. You could look along this formation and see literally almost everyone (including the CSM) shaking their heads. The sad part was, she didn't make the speech quick. When she said the term, "Hot chow" she said it over and over again like we were at some kind of political rally. It was insane. It sounded a little bit like this, "Ya'll know what was great about the field, Soldiers? How 'bout that HOT CHOW?! Huh? HOT CHOW! HOT CHOW! GOTTA LOVE THAT HOT CHOW! I KNOW I LOVE ME SOME HOT CHOW! HOT CHOW!" I really wish that I was exaggerating right now, but I'm not. That is exactly how it all happened. She really believed that the "Hot Chow" was the highlight of our time out there, and I really don't think she caught on to the fact that we were all onto her selfish actions concerning her multiple deliveries from Popeye's. It was such a sad display. A true leader would have never done that. There is absolutely no reason why she couldn't have eaten the same food as us. One thing that this did do however was united the troops and the NCOs. We knew that the only thing we had there was each other because the Senior Leadership was just not going to take care of us at the time. As long as this commander was in charge we knew we had to stick together. The event also provided us with some comedy for a few weeks, and every time I saw Vandever for the next few weeks we would greet each other by shouting the words, "HOT CHOW!" It didn't matter where we were, outdoors, back at the unit, or in the barracks. If we saw each other, it was "HOT CHOW!" And every time that happened, it reminded us of what not to be. So, one more time, "HOT CHOW!"

About seven months into my tour in Korea, the unit was finally met with a piece of great news that would drastically improve the morale of the unit in so many ways. The time had finally come for the Battalion

Commander to leave Korea. This was seen as a "ray of light" to the darkness of the morale problem in the unit. The new commander that came in actually turned out to be a lot better too. He supported the Soldiers and afforded them every opportunity to succeed that was possible. He gave out a lot of awards that were well deserved that would not have been given out under the previous Commander. In addition, he came down on the bad leaders which pushed them harder to start improving. Despite being as nice and "people friendly" as he was, he still had a knack for being tough on the Army standards. This helped the transition even more because it enabled him to get along with the Sergeant Major. Overall, every single one of these changes improved the morale of the unit greatly. The funny thing was that now the CSM didn't seem so bad anymore. Looking back I think it's safe to say that one of the reasons that he was so hard on everyone in the first place was because the original Commander was so messed up. He had to over compensate. The Soldiers and NCOs had a lot of respect for the new Commander which also helped facilitate change. Gone were the wise comments and the "HOT CHOW" jokes. I now knew that the remaining months of my tour would be a lot more enjoyable at work. And that's how it should be.

By now it had been a couple of months since SSG Stewart left. George and I were taking care of business in the office and I was learning more about my MOS with each passing day. I was at the point where I didn't always need to ask her for help I could just look things up myself if I didn't know the answer. Also we were never late on a single suspense while we were running the section without SSG Stewart. That's impressive considering the fact that we were couple of Specialists without NCO supervision. Even though we were handling our business appropriately the unit continued to request an NCO to be transferred from Brigade to fill SSG Stewart's old spot. They never sent one. Instead they sent a Second Lieutenant to serve as our Adjutant Officer, a position that would technically supervise SSG Stewart's position. Although it was nice to have her around, (she was a nice person at first) her presence in our section didn't really do much for us. The reason for that is an Adjutant Officer isn't really supposed to do any of the work that the NCOs and Soldiers do. We needed someone to help us split the workload. The Lieutenant's main function there was to go to meetings, which I honestly I didn't mind doing in the first place. Her going to the weekly meetings did provide us a stronger voice as a section. We didn't always agree with policies and procedures that were in place, but

George and I didn't really have much of a voice in the meetings because we were only a couple of Specialists. Having an officer on our side helped a lot in that aspect.

By now most of my tour was complete. I only had about two and a half months left, while George only had a couple of weeks. For some reason or another, there weren't any projected replacements on the gains roster to replace either one of us. This presented a serious problem because the unit needed to have a functioning S1 at all times, which meant that they would need at least one of us to stay a little longer. I was on assignment to go to Fort Drum, NY after I was finished in Korea. I had specifically called my MOS branch to request this assignment. I could have chosen to go anywhere but I picked Fort Drum because it was close to home and there were a lot of problems at home while I was gone. The most notable problem was that my sister Jen was diagnosed with thyroid cancer. She needed surgery and radiation treatment to overcome it, to which she did overcome it before I returned from Korea. Even though she overcame cancer, the stress alone of dealing with the fact that I almost lost my 15 year old sister was too much to bear. I wanted to go home. Being stationed at Fort Drum would put me only 100 miles from Saint Johnsville, meaning I could go back home any time I wanted or needed too. It's always nice to be close to home in the event of an emergency.

My desire to be close to home didn't change the fact that it was becoming apparent that I would be needed slightly longer than a year in Korea. George was already out-processing and Kim had been promoted to Sergeant and assumed the senior KATUSA duties so I was basically a "one man show." I was working extremely hard and as a result of working totally alone I became a "walking encyclopedia" when it came to my job. So finally one day the Lieutenant approached me and informed me that there was a replacement lined up to take my place; a Sergeant who wouldn't be coming in until 3 weeks after my current PCS date. Because of this arrangement, that would leave the unit without an S1 for the three weeks between my loss date and the new Sergeant's gain date. After she informed me of all of this, the LT asked me if I would be interested in staying one more month until November 2005 if they could guarantee me that I would keep my assignment to Fort Drum. Of course, I was a little smarter than that. I had my branch manager on speed dial so I had already arranged for the branch to take care of this in case something like this happened. I explained to the LT that my assignment would stay intact, so effectively the unit wasn't really offering me anything that I hadn't already gotten on my own. I told her that the unit would have to offer me something else, something a little more lucrative if I was going to extend for the extra month. This, my friends, is called negotiating.

With everything going on combined with my newfound responsibilities of running the section, I was starting to get much more anxious about getting promoted. I wanted more authority, and I wanted to be paid more for my troubles. It was getting to the point where I wanted it so bad I could taste it. Obviously there wasn't much that the unit could do about getting me promoted to Sergeant because that is based on meeting a certain cutoff score that is set by Department of the Army on a monthly basis. What the unit could do however was laterally appoint me to the rank of Corporal. A Corporal is still an E4 just like a Specialist but with a major difference; that being that a Corporal is a junior NCO with NCO responsibilities and NCO authority. By regulation, the only thing that qualifies a Specialist to be laterally appointed to Corporal is that they have to be serving in an NCO position. Nothing else matters as long as you fulfill that one requirement; you do not have to be promotable, you do not have to have gone to the Warrior Leaders' Course. All you need is to be presently filling that position. So, when the LT asked me what the unit could do to convince me to stay 30 extra days, I made it very clear that I would do it if I was laterally appointed to Corporal. The LT seemed very much behind this (or so I thought) and told me she would convince the Battalion Commander to make it happen. Since we had gotten along so well on the deployment and she stood up for us on a number of things I trusted her, so I went ahead and signed the paperwork to extend my tour based on good faith.

That proved to be a huge mistake. My paperwork was submitted for me to become a Corporal, but it didn't go anywhere. I was starting to sense that there was something fishy going on. I would ask the LT about the situation (considering she promised that she would make it happen) and she would dismiss the question. She would change the subject. She would pull her cell phone out and act like she had a call. Something just wasn't right. She had acted like a good friend to us up until now, but suddenly she was acting very sketchy. Needless to say, I didn't like that. One day I was finally called into the Sergeant Major's office to discuss the situation. I told him my side of the story, to include the fact that I had been promised this. He started off by thanking me for staying the extra month, but the truth was the LT didn't really have the authority to promise me that. The most she could have really done for me was to ask the Battalion Commander and Sergeant Major, but that was it. He told me that his reasoning for not giving me the new rank was because I hadn't been to the Warrior Leader's Course. As an old-school Sergeant Major that didn't sit well with him. I explained to him that the regulation says that doesn't matter, and he understood that. For him it was a matter of principle not a matter of regulation. Once again he told me it was nothing personal. After all, he had helped me lose weight, and he allowed me to go to the board a second time. He had done a lot for me on that tour but he had to draw the line. I didn't see it that way however. I just wanted to be home, and I put going home off by a month to help the unit out, in exchange for something very specific. Not only that, I was promised it. As our meeting ended, the CSM admitted that the LT never should have promised me this, and that he was sorry. He told me to keep working on my promotion points because he believed that one day I would make a great Sergeant. I appreciated the compliment, but it changed nothing. It was then that I really started counting down the days until I left. I just wanted to go home.

As if I wasn't disgruntled enough about what had just happened to me, something else happened that really got on my nerves. About two days after my meeting with the CSM, there was a Battalion formation to laterally appoint George to Corporal. I was so angry with this for so many reasons. It was nothing personal against George, but when you take into account my whole situation combined with the fact that she was leaving in a few days, none of it made any sense to me. This was a little unexpected for me, and I really didn't like any of it. As far as I was concerned those Corporal stripes were supposed to be mine. I wasn't mad at George specifically, I was just mad at the situation. I was no longer even going to ask the LT about it. That wouldn't have made any sense. She obviously didn't look out for me and never really had any intentions on helping me out. I never spoke to her again for the rest of my time there. Out of anger I just couldn't bring myself to do it.

My replacement finally arrived and my time was just about up. Almost all of the Soldiers and NCOs in the unit took my side on the Corporal issue which did help me cope with things. Everyone in the unit also showed a lot of gratitude to me for my great job performance. As a one-man S1 I had a lot of work to do and I always made sure to take care of the needs of each and every Soldier assigned. Because of this, a lot of the Soldiers would tell me that I was the very best S1 that they had ever seen. That meant a lot to me coming from everyone. The only thing that I had left to do was out-process and go to my farewell dinner. The farewell dinner turned out to be one of the most emotional nights of the entire tour. It was held on a Friday night at an off post restaurant called Marty's. It was also conveniently scheduled during happy hour, which featured "buy one, get one free" drink specials.

The turnout for my farewell dinner was one of the bigger turnouts in unit history. Almost everyone assigned to the unit came out for it, and most of them bought me drinks all night long. I could tell everyone was really going to miss me, because at one point Corley told my replacement that he "had big shoes to fill." That actually meant a lot to me. When my time came to give my speech, I couldn't believe my ears. Everyone in the room started chanting the words, "PLEASE DON'T GO! PLEASE DON'T GO! PLEASE DON'T GO!" This wasn't just out of gratitude, but it was also a direct reference to my love of professional wrestling. There was one particular ECW DVD that I had watched with Corley and Mitchell a few times and it was the wrestler's very last show, to which the crowd started chanting "PLEASE DON'T GO!" It just made perfect sense that they were the ones who started the chant up. That got me a little choked up. It felt extremely good inside to know that the Soldiers in that unit were thankful for the contributions that I made. I was presented with my going away gift, which was a sword inside of a shadow box along with both the US and Korean flags. I still have it to this day. I gave a passionate speech and took the time to go around the entire room showing gratitude to each person there, with the exception of the LT. I said nothing about her and just moved right past her. I was still bitter about it inside, and since everyone was having such a good time at the event I didn't want to darken the mood by running my mouth. Also, she is an officer so saying something out of line would have cost me my rank anyway. So I took the high road and just didn't say anything. After my speech, we all continued drinking throughout the night, and we took the party back to the barracks. We didn't want the party to end, so once we drank all of the alcohol that was there and then we went back out. I had this strange urge to do something crazy so I put on a Tae Kwon Do uniform with a wrestling belt and a straw hat. Also, I was carrying a coffee pot. I really have no idea why. I was so drunk that I didn't care. We went off post out to a few bars with me dressed like that and with the coffee pot in my hand. A lot of people looked at me with funny looks, and many asked me, "Dude what's with the coffee pot?" I just said I didn't know, because after all I didn't know. I still don't know. The next morning pictures surfaced of me dressed like that in everyone's email. Not bad. If there was one thing I wanted, it was to be remembered. To be honest after those 13 long months that wasn't really a bad way to end the year.

The morning of my flight came and I was actually sad in a way. I was glad to be going home but I was sad to leave all of my friends there so I guess you would call it a "bitter sweet' feeling. I sat on the plane reflecting on everything; the good and the bad. Over those 13 months I accomplished a lot and I had a lot to be proud of. I lost a lot of weight and got back in shape. I became promotable. I got to see even more of the world and I made some good friends, many of which I am still in touch with today. Up until this point my career had become quite the journey, and I knew that this journey wasn't even close to ending. With that said, I knew that what I needed was some family time. Fort Drum awaited me.

Shaving in Iraq in 2003 . . . you wanted to bother me . . . therefore you get the finger point!

This photo was taken from the first person perspective during one of the convoys that i went on in Iraq. Sitting high up like this gave me a true perspective of what that country is really like for the people that live there.

At the famous Lottee World amusement park in Korea, 2004. This is definitely Seoul's version of DisneyWorld.

A view from my suite during the CMOC mission in Mosul. I have fond memories of this place.

Doing the bow and arrow pose in Kuwait. I just can't get enough . . .

Here I am standing in front of a CH-47 Chinook Helicopter on the day of my flight into Iraq. All of my comrades had previously crossed the border and I couldn't wait to meet up with them on the other side.

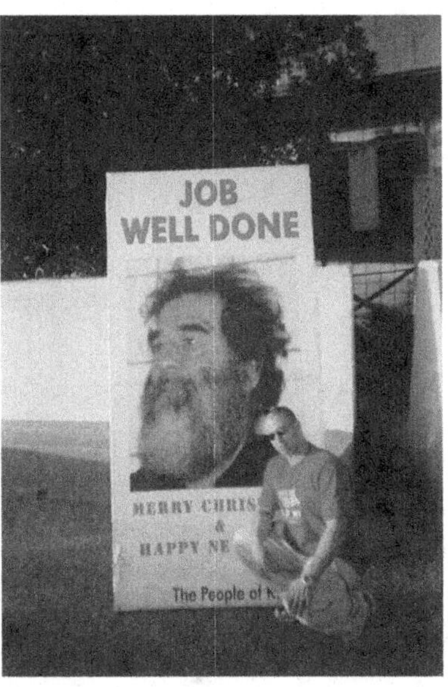

Posing in front of the Job well done poster in Kuwait that commemorated Saddam's capture in Iraq at the end of my first deployment. One of the proudest moments of my Army career was knowing that the US forced that dictator out of office and I was part of it.

Doing the classic pose in Mosul Iraq just before a convoy into the city. Sometimes all we had to keep our heads up was the very humor that we created.

This is where I had to sleep in Kuwait in 2003 while awaiting departure into Iraq. Notice the ever so comfortable cot.

CHAPTER 8

FORT DRUM, NY-
HOME OF THE 10TH
MOUNTAIN DIVISION

I arrived to Fort Drum, New York on November 16, 2005. For me it was a godsend to be stationed there because I now had the ability to go home to Saint Johnsville and see my family and friends almost any time I wanted to. Even though I am a native of upstate New York I was still astonished at just how cold it gets up there at Fort Drum. Saint Johnsville is 100 miles southeast of Fort Drum, which equates to about a two hour drive. Growing up in Saint Johnsville I had become accustomed to winters that were usually no colder than 15 degrees. Of course, you would have the occasional cold front where it would be much colder, but on the average it didn't get much colder than 15 degrees. Fort drum was so much different than that. Located just 30 minutes from the Canadian border, the temperature frequently drops below zero and stays that way for weeks at a time. To say that Fort Drum is cold is an understatement; you would be more accurate to say that it was bitter, freezing, or even deadly. The word "cold" just doesn't do it justice. This took a little bit of getting used to, but not much as it would have had I been a Soldier from the South.

Just like my previous two duty stations my first stop at Fort Drum was the replacement battalion. I immediately noticed that none of the Soldiers that were there were happy to be there. None of them were from upstate New York which would clearly explain that. You see, there isn't much to do in upstate New York unless you are from there. When you arrive to Fort Drum they immediately pitch the idea that the hunting and fishing there is some of the best in the country. What happens if you don't like to hunt and fish? Well the answer is simple. You'll have almost nothing to do there except drink, go to Canada, or go to Syracuse. Trust me, all of that gets old after a while. Obviously none of this applies to you if you are from upstate New York because being stationed here is a chance to get reacquainted with all of your friends and family that you perhaps left behind when you initially joined the Army. So, as I said earlier I was very happy to be at Fort Drum because it put me closer to my family. Being here guaranteed that I wouldn't miss a third Christmas in a row, and believe me I was ok with that.

Another thing that I noticed upon arriving to Fort Drum was how disorganized things were. By now I had seen my fair share of the Army; two actual duty stations including a deployment to Iraq and a tour in Korea. I knew "what right looks like". With that said, a lot of things that went on at replacement on Fort Drum didn't make a lot of sense and often Soldiers were left clueless with no idea what to do. Even though this didn't leave a very good taste in my mouth, (things in Korea were extremely organized when I left) I dismissed it at first because this was just the replacement unit. At replacement there is obviously a quick turnaround so you really shouldn't expect there to be much continuity. The unit's main purpose is to in-process you, issue your gear, and ensure you make it to your actual unit. Therefore I understood that not all of the pieces seemed to fit together. My time at replacement there ended up being a little longer than Korea; yet shorter than replacement on Fort Campbell. Apparently it's different at each place you go to. Before I knew it, I was on my way to my unit at Fort Drum: the 10th Soldier Support Battalion.

I welcomed the transition from replacement to the 10th SSB for one main reason. That reason was the fact that a good friend from Korea was there. Back in Korea I saw a lot of friends leave, but only one went to Fort Drum. That friend was Pelletier. While at replacement I called him and he was more than ready for me to get to the unit. He told me that he had a lot of friends there and he would gladly show me around and introduce me to everyone as soon as I arrived. For me, it was just good to have a friend there that I knew I could trust. I still remember the first night I got there. I pulled up to the front of the barracks building and Pelletier was standing there. It was freezing out and it was nice to have his help unloading all of my stuff from my car. I was shocked by the very first thing he said to me, but at the same time I appreciated it, "Hey bro, shit's grimy as hell here. You can't trust everyone. There are no Reids, Dysons, or Carikers here brother. We got to stick together. People here in this unit will stab you in the back." This statement immediately made me think. Back in Korea, our gang was tight. Pelletier, Dyson, Cariker, Reid, and I always watched each other's back. We were best friends and would do anything for each other. When Pelletier gave me this speech, it took me back because up until now I expected more out of the Army. Not only had I served in Korea with that gang; I had also served at Fort Campbell with a great unit. At Campbell I was part of a crew just as I was in Korea, so hearing from Pelletier himself that things here at Fort Drum were not as cut and dry certainly caught me off guard. Even still I was glad to have him around because above all else I knew we were tight. Pelletier was a dude I could trust. The good thing was that I had arrived on a Friday night so we went out and picked up a few bottles of liquor and caught up on things. This was also the first time I ever went with him to a liquor store where we didn't have some sort of restriction on the amount of booze we could by. And it wasn't the last either.

After the weekend my first day of work in the 10th SSB came along. It was nothing like the 101st SSB. This place was far more disorganized from the top all the way to the bottom. I couldn't believe it. I know I had my gripes with the 101st in the past, but in comparison the 101st was a perfect unit. Everything there at Drum just seemed screwed up, and I couldn't figure out why. Most of the NCOs did things backwards. Most of the Soldiers had attitude problems. Half the time the Soldiers would start running their mouth and not get busted down for it. When that kind of thing happens the Soldiers start to think that they can get away with anything, and so they continue doing that kind of stuff. Also, the DUI rate was high in the unit. That is probably because there isn't a lot to do at Fort Drum. Soldiers would get drunk and get behind the wheel to go to the next bar or party. That is a bad idea. Overall, I was disappointed with the 10th SSB within 72 hours of arriving there. I wasn't going to let any of that bring me down however. I wanted to do a lot of things with my career. I still wanted to increase my promotion points and get promoted to Sergeant. I didn't want to be a Specialist anymore. As far as I was concerned I had enough expertise in my MOS and enough experience to make it to the next rank. I started to realize that since I was surrounded by a bunch of underachievers that I would shine there. I would also later learn that I wasn't wrong about doing that either.

I was initially placed in the NCOER section, which was the exact section that I worked in at Fort Campbell. As you can probably guess, I did really well there because I had years of experience working on that particular task. What bothered me was the fact that I was put under an NCO by the name of SGT Griffin who didn't know a single thing about working on NCOERs. This reminded me an awful lot of when I returned from Iraq back at Fort Campbell and I was working for the NCO who ended up getting a DUI. He knew absolutely nothing about NCOERs and thus I ended up having to adjust. This situation would end up being no different; my skills showed and I was eventually asked to show the other Soldiers how to do the job because they weren't very good at it either. I didn't mind because I felt this would cause my stock to rise in the unit. What I didn't realize was that the underachieving Soldiers (and even the NCOs) in the unit would take exception to this and start talking behind my back. They would say things like, "Specialist Conklin is too cocky" or "Specialist Conklin thinks he's better than everyone" and similar things like that. This all got back to me through Pelletier because he was a good friend of mine. A lot of people didn't realize that and didn't know that we served together in the past. In my own defense, I was just "being me." I don't hate fellow overachievers and I don't try to stop others from succeeding. I believe that every human being has the capacity to achieve every single thing that they put their minds to. Unfortunately, I wasn't surrounded by people that felt the same way.

After a few weeks of working there in the 10th SSB, I was ordered to have my initial meeting with the First Sergeant. Everyone who arrives there is required to have this meeting with him, so it wasn't like I did anything wrong. It was a matter of formality. When I met with him he immediately told me that he was impressed with me. He told me that he had heard good things about my work ethic from some of the NCOs, and he was also impressed that in my few weeks of being there that I hadn't ended up on the police blotter yet. That in itself is an achievement at Fort Drum. I could have been a terrible Soldier in the office and still gotten compliments off of the fact that I hadn't been arrested yet since I was there. Things were that crazy.

Despite being happy with my performance the First Sergeant was still interested in my personal goals. He wanted to know exactly what I was doing in the Army; was I biding my time until the end of my contract or was I a "lifer" who wanted to give it my all? Did I want to contribute to the organization? Did I want to deploy? Did I want to get promoted? I was glad to inform him that I wanted to make the Army a career and serve 20 years or even more. I also told him right away that my goal was to get promoted to Sergeant. I wanted to become an NCO so bad and I wanted to contribute as an NCO. I knew I was so much more than an average Soldier and I wanted to prove that to not just him, but everyone. It really meant a lot to me. After I told him all of my goals he told me that he too was a "go-getter" just like me, and that he appreciated how proactive I was. He then warned me that everyone there in that unit was extremely lazy. No one there wanted to achieve anything, let alone get promoted. He warned me that there would be a lot of people there (to include NCOs) that would take exception to someone like me standing in the ranks. When he told me this he also told me that these same people would probably do what they could to make me look as little as possible. Apparently, misery loves company. Overall, everyone there was lazy and he knew it. At this time I informed him that I was already seeing that; there were certain people in the unit that had already given me the cold shoulder and I knew why. I told him that I wasn't a follower and that none of this would cause me to falter in my work ethic, goals, or beliefs. When I told the First Sergeant all of this, he was exceedingly glad to hear it and told me that he would do anything to support me. He ended the meeting by saying, "The Army needs leaders like you Specialist Conklin." God damn that felt good.

Over the next couple of weeks I continued to go to work as usual. I didn't go bragging about the adamant support that the First Sergeant had showed me, but at the same time I still worked hard enough to continue impressing him and the Company Commander. I knew that as long as the First Sergeant and Company Commander liked me that things were going to go well for me. I was doing ok. I kept on working hard, not only because I cared about my career but also because I cared about the mission. I took pleasure in knowing that all of the NCOERs were processed correctly. Sometimes when I had no work left I would help my fellow NCOER clerks out by reviewing their work, thus ensuring they had no errors either. As it turned out, they made a lot of errors that I caught and corrected. Obviously it benefits the NCO who the report belongs too when you make such a correction. Thus correcting any mistakes helps everyone involved. This was an important lesson that I was taught when I was at Fort Campbell and working in that NCOER section. It looked to me that this section wasn't taught that lesson and it was up to me to do so.

As time went by, there were even more comments and rumors about Specialist Conklin "being too cocky for his own good." I didn't get it. I just wanted to try my best. I just wanted to do my best. It got to the point where they started to alienate me and make me feel bad about the fact that I wanted to achieve things. I took great exception to this, so I decided to step my game up even more. Feeling like my back was against the wall, I intentionally got cockier. I was so angry with how I was being treated by my fellow Specialists that I thought were actually my comrades. Instead they acted like I was the bad guy. I wasn't. I just came from a unit where people wanted to achieve things. I wasn't accustomed to being around Soldiers who didn't care about that. Over the next few weeks I took things over the top, and every time that I felt slightly alienated I rubbed it in people's faces of how great I was doing. I knew it worked because people would complain to Pelletier about it, and thus it would get back to me. Hindsight being 20/20 I knew it was the wrong thing to do and I ultimately regret it. It is never good to intentionally rub it in to people when you are doing great. When I did it, it was merely a reaction of defense and I would never do it again.

I was working real hard at Fort Drum, but there was still plenty of room for play. I went home every other weekend, and on the other weekends I would party with Pelletier. We started hanging out with a group, much similar to the way we did in Korea. We ended up hanging out with a couple of people by the name of Bartz and Dioguardi. The four of us would throw some insane barracks parties that would actually rival some of the parties we threw in Korea. Part of that had to do with the fact that the weather was so bad at Fort Drum that a lot of Soldiers didn't venture too far from post. Some storms made it impossible to walk outside let alone drive. We would throw a lot of crazy parties. Dioguardi was an NCO who liked to get drunk and then attempt to freestyle rap. It was funny because Pelletier also knew how to freestyle rap and the two of them would get into "rap battles" in the barracks hallway. Often Pelletier would win because his rapping made sense, while Dioguardi's rapping consisted of a whole lot of filler like "yo yo" and "listen up, listen up, Dio in the house." Hands down there was just no way that Dioguardi could ever hang with Pelletier.

Bartz was another guy who was a lot of fun to party with. He had a knack for acting funny, unlike the rest of us. We used to think of Bartz like he was crazy. He would talk in a dialect that you wouldn't understand unless you knew him. This dialect was something that he came up with entirely on his own, and didn't always make sense. For one, instead of calling Pelletier by name he would call him, "PELLA!" He would rarely say it either, instead he would scream it. Also, when we would order pizza while we were drinking, he wouldn't call it pizza. Bartz instead called it "zaa." He would sit there and make a bunch of odd noises, and then he would just yell, "Pella! Let's get some ZAA!!" This always got everyone laughing, because we knew he wasn't mentally challenged, he just acted that way . . . all the time. Overall he was a lot of fun to be around and always made the party that much better.

Most of the time we would drink so much the night before that we would be severely hung over the next morning. There was a run-down diner in Watertown, NY (just outside of Fort Drum) that we would go to eat breakfast when we were hung over. This diner was called The Golden Unicorn. For the record, it wasn't a place that we ever went to when we were 100% sober. The place featured a pretty good breakfast buffet chock full of all of the typical greasy foods that one would crave the night after drinking heavy. The place was always packed with Fort Drum Soldiers on a Saturday morning for that fact alone. The Golden Unicorn featured something else that made it a "must-see attraction" to any incoming Fort Drum Soldiers. That "attraction" was a pancake special where if you ate two pancakes you would receive a free "Golden Unicorn" T-shirt. The only catch was that these two pancakes that you had to eat were no ordinary pancakes. They were two giant pizza sized pancakes. You had to eat every single bite, to include the two eggs, toast, and bacon that would come with it. Very few people had completed this challenge. It was next to impossible. Earlier in his time at Drum, Pelletier had been able to complete this challenge and thus he had the T-shirt. Since this happened before my arrival I wanted to see him do it with my own eyes, so one morning the four of us gave it a shot. Dioguardi failed early, while the whole time he claimed he didn't rap the night before (when in fact he did rap in his drunken state). That in itself was hilarious. I gave it my best shot, and finished about half of it but there was no way I could get it all down. Pelletier couldn't finish the dreaded giant pancakes this time around either. That left Bartz.

We had a lot of faith in Bartz' ability to finish eating the giant pancakes. Bartz was a bigger guy and was known for eating a lot. When we would order pizza (or Zaa as Bartz called it) during the barracks parties he would eat an entire pizza on his own. When we got there that day we assumed that out of the four of us Bartz had the best chance at finishing the giant pancakes. Unfortunately, that wasn't the case, but at least I've got this story to share. He tried his best, and really started that platter off with a lot of thunder. As he got deeper into it he started to slow down. Knowing that he was our only hope at scoring a free T-shirt, we started to cheer him on like it was some kind of wrestling match. We were chanting things like, "Let's go Bartz! Let's go Bartz!" As you can probably imagine the other people in the diner looked at us like we were nutcases. He struggled and struggled, slowing down with each bite. The time finally came where he gave up. He finished most of it and there was only about 1/6 of the pancake left. He got farther than any of us, and for that he deserved at least some congratulations. As we left the diner, we noticed that Bartz was walking a lot slower than usual. The big guy had clearly eaten too much. We thought he was going to be ok, but just before he could get into Dioguardi's Jeep he puked all over the ground. He puked right by the rear tire. It was disgusting. I felt bad for him, but not that much because his problem was self-inflicted. If that had been any of us I wouldn't expect much compassion out of Bartz. We would end up going back to the Golden Unicorn many times, but that was the last time any of us attempted the giant pancake challenge.

It was nice to have a few friends there at Fort Drum right from the beginning, because just like Pelletier had told me, there were a lot of backstabbers in that unit as well. I was starting to see this with some of the NCOs in the office, but in the barracks we had certain Soldiers to deal with. Some of these Soldiers would act nice to you to your face and then talk about you behind your back. It was terrible. We also had a lot of Soldiers in the barracks who would act like leaches. There was one in particular by the name of Jerry. All he ever did was he went from room to room trying to bum anything he could off of any Soldier that he possibly could. It didn't matter what it was either, he would take everything from food, to alcohol, to cigarettes, to CDs, even laundry detergent. He didn't care. He even took someone's car one time. Now, I have no problem with helping a fellow Soldier out from time to time, but he turned it into an everyday thing. There was one time that he reached onto Pelletier's plate and took some fries. Everyone just stared at the guy like he had a death wish. What made it worse was he had this grimy way about asking for stuff, he would say it like this, "Hey yo Pelletier lemme grab some of these fries" or sometimes he would say, "Hey yo Conklin lemme grab a beer." He was relentless and he just wouldn't stop. We all knew that he earned a military paycheck just like the rest of us, but he was acting like a homeless guy all the time. His actions caused us to give him a nickname, "Grimy J." We would then always make jokes about him at work, "Grimy J took this or Grimy J took that. Good old Grimy J." Even though it was all in fun, Grimy J was still a scumbag. That's my story and I'm sticking to it.

Back in the office things started to become routine and eventually my performance shined so much that I was put in charge of the NCOER section. This was a nice feeling and ended up giving me a nice flashback to my Fort Campbell days when I worked in the NCOER section there. The main difference here was that I was actually running the section, with two Soldiers working under me. It was a great feeling, especially considering I was still just a Specialist promotable. This experience in managing people would help me out greatly. I knew that my day to get promoted would finally come; I just had to keep on working hard. Becoming an NCO was inevitable. There was no reason why I couldn't start behaving like one now. When I took the section over there was a lot of work to be done as well as a lot of old NCOER errors that had to be fixed. I worked really hard to overcome all of these challenges, knowing that my work wouldn't just serve the purpose of making me look good; it would also help benefit the careers of the NCOs whose reports I was handling. As you can see, there was potential for my hard work to yield great consequences for a lot of different people.

Once I got the section caught up I began to monitor the online stats from EREC (enlisted records evaluation center) almost daily to see if my work was correct. I was hell bent on making sure I was doing the right thing. Finally I was able to see that I had reduced the EREC error rate to 0%. When I saw this, I was ecstatic because this had never been done before in the history of that unit. No one had ever brought the EREC error rate down to 0%. Considering I was a Specialist and the section was ran by various different NCOs in the past I felt this was a huge accomplishment. I decided to let my platoon Sergeant know what I had done, because it had been announced in past formations by our Company Commander that if you did something great, make sure someone above you knows about it so you can be put in for an award. Now, I need to stress that I didn't bring the EREC error rate to 0% for an award; I did it because it was the right thing to do but an award would help me get promoted to Sergeant and so I decided to bring attention to the fact that I accomplished this.

This brought about a problem however. The platoon Sergeant already didn't like me because I was already billed as an arrogant overachiever. I realized this one day at PT formation when he bragged about the fact that he scored a 181 on his PT test (the minimum passing score is 180) and that there is absolutely no reason to strive to do better. I didn't feel that this was the proper way for a Sergeant to conduct himself, especially in front of a formation full of Soldiers. His job is to coach, teach, and motivate enlisted Soldiers and to give them a positive role model to emulate. How could he possibly expect Soldiers to respect him if he was telling them that the bare minimum was good enough and there was no need to strive better? This was so much different than my time at Fort Campbell when NCOs would stress to Soldiers the importance of trying to excel. Since I had an issue with this, I made sure the Soldiers around me knew that I had a 300 PT score and that was the right thing to do. From that day forward the platoon Sergeant had a problem with me, but as far as I was concerned he brought that on himself, like most of his problems. That same Platoon sergeant ended up getting knocked out in a night club a few weeks later for running his mouth to someone that he shouldn't have. As the old saying goes, "what goes around comes around."

So fast forwarding back to the day that I had achieved the 0% EREC error rate and I reported it to the platoon Sergeant, he didn't act like it was anything special. I then showed him that it was special, because this had never been done before. Still, he wasn't buying it and said to me, "who cares, you're just doing your job, which you're paid to do anyway." I really didn't appreciate this. This guy was already rubbing me the wrong way (like most of the leaders in that unit) and by dismissing my accomplishment he just added fuel to the fire. I knew he had a bad attitude and was an extremely mediocre NCO, but I just had to know how mediocre he was. I went into the filing cabinet of old NCOERs and pulled out his last two reports. As it turned out, he had average reports with generic bullet comments, meaning that he was ALWAYS a mediocre NCO. No wonder he didn't like an overachiever like me. I now understood his standpoint, but that didn't mean I was going to take it. Since I wasn't given the recognition that I deserved, I intentionally gave the recognition to myself. I openly started bragging about that I had done in an effort to piss him off just to get even. Had he just given me the credit that I deserved I would have been ok, but that certainly wasn't the case. I will state for the record that this hurt my status with the NCOs even more, (with the exception of the First Sergeant, he was impressed and he thought my actions were hilarious) but it gave the Soldiers someone to look up to. The Soldiers thought this was funny and would come up to me out of the blue and ask me, "Hey Conklin, what's the NCOER EREC error rate? Is it still 0%?" I would reply with "Obviously." Then they usually would follow up with some sort of witty comeback like, "so is it true that no one has ever done that before?" I found this great, and I ate it all up. I was glad that I wasn't alone on this. As much fun as I was having it was heartbreaking to know that I had been cursed with this leadership. These were the worst NCOs that I had seen in my entire career. I started thinking to myself how I could possibly get out of this situation, but there only seemed to be one logical answer: another deployment.

Christmas 2005 came along, and in typical fashion I took about a week of leave. I didn't really need to take the customary two weeks because I was so close to home and I could visit anytime. I didn't really want to waste my leave. It was great to be home. I started doing a lot of partying with my brother Jason. This wasn't something that we really did before I joined the Army because back then neither one of us was into drinking. Now things were different. Not only were we both into it, but we were also both of age so there were no problems as far as the law was concerned. Quite often Joe Carter would throw beer pong parties at his apartment and pretty much the whole town would show up. Jason and I were no exception. I guess these times helped bring me and my brother closer together. Years ago when we were growing up we didn't always get along and we would end up getting into a lot of arguments. We had a lot of the same friends, but we had a lot of different friends too. So it was a relief that my brother and I could become a lot closer in our adult lives. I don't want it to come off like the uniting force between us was alcohol, because it wasn't. It just gave us something to do.

The holiday itself was great as always. Dad made a giant feast for the entire family like usual, and there were tons of presents under the tree as well. We always try our best to go "all out" for Christmas. For us, it is the most important day of the year. It was very special for me because it was my first Christmas home in two years. I hated the fact that I had to miss the last two because of being in Iraq one year and Korea the next, but at the same time it made me a stronger person to endure such sacrifice.

Overall I was just thankful to be home with my family on Christmas day. I told myself and I told my family that I would try my very best to never again miss Christmas at home . . . but deep down I had a feeling that the Army just wasn't going to let me do that.

As 2006 began, there were a lot of rumors circulating that the unit would be deploying to Afghanistan. No one seemed to know any of the real facts, and at the end of each day a lot of the NCOs would hold meetings and tell everyone to "stop listening to rumors." I don't feel this was really the right tactic. As a Soldier who has been deployed before, I would like as much notice as possible so I can not only "get my ducks in a row" but also so I can spend enough time with my family. When you know your days are numbered too much time with your family can never be enough. That's just how it is. I knew one thing for certain, and that was the fact that I was eager to deploy again. I wanted to go over for so many reasons, one being that I had never been to Afghanistan so I wanted the bragging rights and the experience, and also because the unit at Drum was really falling apart. I would take any chance to deploy. I knew that the hardships of a deployment would force some of the NCOs in the unit to change the way they acted. I hoped that this deployment would be just what the unit needed, and I also knew that I could be useful out there because of my experience. It would be a "win-win" for everyone.

In January 2006 Fort Drum hosted a special guest who came to give the 10th Mountain Division a speech in effort to motivate the division before the deployment. That special guest was then Vice President Dick Cheney. I remember at the time there were a lot of jokes and rumors going around that Dick Cheney was the epitome of evil and that he was really running the country. I never indulged these rumors/jokes, but I had to admit that they were sometimes funny. In addition, there was a lot of speculation amongst Soldiers that Dick Cheney's past with Halliburton had something to do with the Iraq war. I guess I can understand why some people would create a rumor such as this; KBR had set up shop after the invasion of Iraq took place. KBR's parent company was Halliburton. The rumor made sense, but that didn't make it true, it made it a coincidence. As the Vice President of the United States of America he would have had to surrender his control of that company and sign it off to someone else. Even still, I always got a kick out of the "Dick Cheney is running Iraq and America" jokes that used to surface while I was deployed.

Even with all of the rumors and jokes that were circulating, Dick Cheney's speech at Fort Drum was still a memorable experience for me. Soldiers from my unit were allowed to sit behind him while he gave his speech, which meant there was a good chance that we would all end up being on TV. The speech took place in a hangar near the airfield just outside of Drum, the Wheeler-Sack airfield. Everyone was filed into the hangar a few hours prior to the Vice President's arrival. Obviously when you have a VIP coming into your installation you want to have the crowd that will receive them in place hours before they actually arrive. Dick Cheney's actual arrival was a huge spectacle. There were cameras on the flight line that were airing a live video feed inside the hangar. When he finally stepped out of his plane, the song "Thunderstruck" by AC/DC hit and played the entire time as he walked the flight line into the hangar and eventually onto his podium. It was almost as if he was a professional wrestler with entrance music. As a wrestling fan, I found this funny. I understood that if the President was here he would enter the building to "hail to the chief" but that was procedure. There was no procedure in place that stated that Vice President Dick Cheney was going to enter the hangar with "Thunderstruck" playing. As a Soldier who served during the Bush Administration I will never forget this.

The speech itself was fairly generic. He spoke about the war on terror and patriotism. He talked about how great our country was doing; waging wars in both countries. The Vice President told us that above all else, the one thing that the American people could be thankful for was the Soldiers. The Soldiers were the ones who were out there making sacrifices for the American people and for that alone he was truly grateful. I know it may sound a bit cheesy, but his speech did make me feel good deep down inside. It reminded me of when President Bush himself visited Fort Campbell a few months after we had got back from Iraq. He was the Commander in Chief and he was showing his true appreciation for the sacrifices that we had made as well as the sacrifices that we would make in the future. As far as I was concerned, this was a true class act, despite what other Soldiers and Civilians may have thought about the entire situation. After the day of the speech I really did some soul searching about how the next few months would go. Did I really want to deploy again? Sure. Did I want to make a difference for America? Definitely. As far as I was concerned, it was only a matter of time before I heard something. Hopefully, it would be sooner rather than later.

The orders finally came down that the unit was deploying. There was a major catch however. Since the 10th SSB consisted of a Finance Company and a Personnel Services Company, (which I was a part of) it was policy that both companies did not necessarily have to deploy together at the same time. These orders showed the Finance Company (which Pelletier was part of) deploying but not the Personnel Company. This didn't make any sense at first because the entire 10th Mountain Division was deploying so the division would need both companies to support it. Then the word came out that the Personnel Company was going to send five Soldiers on the deployment. There would be one Warrant Officer, (which is a technical expert in the Army), three NCOs, and one junior enlisted Soldier. Still, this didn't even make sense to me. I knew there was no way in hell that five Soldiers could support the entire 10th Mountain Division. There had to be some piece of this puzzle that I was missing.

Finally the truth was revealed to me about why exactly the entire Personnel Company wasn't deploying to support the division. I found out that the mission of supporting the 10th Mountain Division was tasked to the 50th Personnel Services Battalion, which was part of the New Jersey National Guard. The reason that there were five Soldiers from my company going was because the Soldiers in the New Jersey Guard weren't 100% trained on the systems that the active component used. The Soldiers from my unit would be tasked with the mission of effectively training the NJ Guard while deployed. This seemed like a cool mission, and it made me want to go on the deployment that much more. Another thing that I had remembered was that my long lost friend Kathy was a member of the New Jersey National Guard. I wondered if she was still enlisted and if she was would she be on this deployment. So, just like in the past I took to the Army Knowledge Online (AKO) email system to contact her. Within a day, she got back to me. She told me that she certainly was going to be on that deployment, and that she already knew that there were some Soldiers from 10th Mountain that would be there. She had no idea that I was in the 10th Mountain and thought it was quite a coincidence that people from my unit would be embedded into her unit. She also told me that some things in her life had changed since we had last spoken, most notably that she had gotten married. I was happy for her, and the idea of her getting married was a wake-up call to me on just how much time had passed since I had seen her. I knew back in 2002 when we first met that we met for a reason and that we were meant to be friends forever. I know that is a style of thinking that not very many people subscribe to. I wholeheartedly believe that there are people in everyone's life that they meet for a reason. It doesn't necessarily have to be a big reason either. It could actually be a small part of a very large puzzle. Regardless of my over-thinking into this matter, I knew one thing for sure, and that was that I wanted to deploy even more so I can see my old friend again. I missed her.

It was at this point that I started lobbying really hard to deploy. I wanted to go so bad and I made this very well known to every single NCO and Officer in that unit. In addition, since I was so good at my job and I was far more proficient than any of the other junior Soldiers in the unit I knew that I was the best man for the job. Think about it, if you have to send your very best Soldiers on a mission to train other Soldiers, wouldn't you want to send your most proficient Soldier? You wouldn't want to send Soldiers who didn't know what they were doing, because they wouldn't be able to properly train the other Soldiers. It was just common sense. Still, that didn't seem to matter. The slots were already filled and it would take a miracle to get one of those slots. I was sad about this, but I didn't let it crush my hope. There had to be something I could do to get on this deployment.

Finally an order came down to run five more Soldiers through the readiness processing for deployment. The purpose of this wasn't because the unit was sending five more Soldiers; it was simply because they had a feeling that after being deployed for a few weeks they would realize that they needed a few more Soldiers. In other words, these five additional Soldiers would be back up in case they needed more help in Afghanistan. If needed, they would go over as "late deployers." Since I had done so much lobbying to deploy I was chosen to be one of the five that would go through the processing. Granted, it didn't mean I was deploying but I was still happy with it because it put me a step closer to my dream. So I took it in stride. People would see me in the hallway all of a sudden and approach me with rumors like, "so I heard your deploying now." By now I was used to the rumors circulating around in this unit, but I wasn't used to them being about me. I had to keep correcting them that this wasn't the case and as of now I wasn't going. Still, it sounded good and just hearing these rumors fueled my drive to deploy that much more.

It was at this point that I actually met the Soldiers who were going on the deployment for the first time. I had seen them all around the unit but I hadn't actually met them. The leader of the group was a man by the name of Chief Brandon Broadbent. He was a well-respected Warrant Officer who really knew our job well. In all honesty you have to know the job well to become a Warrant Officer. A Warrant Officer is expected to be a subject matter expert in every aspect of our MOS. If you ask a Warrant Officer a question, he should either know it right off the top of his head; or if he doesn't know the answer he should know EXACTLY where in the regulation to find the information. A Warrant Officer is exactly what I strived to be, and to be perfectly honest Chief Broadbent fit the bill perfectly. To this day, I still believe that there are only two people that I ever worked with who were better at my job than me; SGT Ramos from Fort Campbell and Chief Broadbent. Luckily for me, I had the opportunity to learn from both of them.

The NCOs that were going on the deployment were pretty cool as well. Their names were SGT Jack, SGT Johnson, and SSG Dugar. SGT Jack was a bodybuilder that worked out every day. I knew that if I ended up on that deployment I could count on him to be a good workout partner. SSG Dugar was a loving woman who everyone referred to as "Mama Dugar." What was funny about her was that when she would flip out and start yelling at people she just wouldn't let things go, she would keep going off on a tangent forever. So often times in the office you would hear people saying, "There goes mama Dugar going off at the mouth again." Just by meeting this crew I knew I would enjoy myself with them. They had a solid leader in Chief Broadbent and a good team of NCOs to boot. I really wished I could deploy with them. Unfortunately, I would soon find out what the unit's ultimate decision was.

I was home in Saint Johnsville for a four day weekend when I got the call. It wasn't just a call from anyone however; it was a call from my Company Commander. He broke to me the news that I wasn't going to be allowed to go on the deployment to Afghanistan. He also explained to me that he felt the need to call me personally and explain to me why I couldn't go. He told me that I didn't do anything wrong, in fact it was just the opposite. I was such a hard worker and so knowledgeable that he couldn't afford to let me go. The fact was he was already letting four of his best Soldiers go on that deployment, and he just couldn't afford to let any more technical expertise go. This was the very first time that the company Commander not only conveyed to me how valuable I was to his mission, but also just how invaluable the rest of the unit was. He said to me, "If you leave, I'll have no one left." I took this to heart, because you don't normally have someone as high up as your commander saying things like this about his other Soldiers openly to another Soldier. It just isn't proper procedure or even proper courtesy for that matter. We spent about a half hour on the phone, and he continued to explain to me how much he respected me and that he seriously admired the fact that I was both physically and mentally stronger than all of his NCOs, and here I was just a Specialist. All the while, it sounded like he was fighting back tears on his end. He told me that he felt like he was breaking my heart. The truth is that he was breaking my heart. All I wanted was to go to Afghanistan but here I had my Commander on the phone telling me it wasn't happening. When we were finished with our conversation, I hung up and did some thinking about the whole situation. First off, our conversation did make me feel honored, and I was honored to be part of the team. Despite this honor however, it still disappointed me. My dreams of going on another deployment were crushed.

The next few weeks in the office went by like a total blur. There were only two weeks left until the deployment and every time I saw the deployers they were doing something deployment related. This just broke my heart because it would cause me to think about the fact that I wasn't on the deployment every time. I hated having to dwell on all of this, but it wasn't like things at the unit were kept secret. One minute you would see the deploying Soldiers in the bay going through an inspection of their gear, and the next minute you would come across a flyer for their farewell dinner in the hallway. As I said before, it was like EVERYTHING was forcing me to think about the fact that I couldn't deploy. The unit sent me to NBC School for week so I could run the NBC (gasmask) room, but that wasn't enough. Getting away from the unit for that quick school just wasn't enough for me. I was so depressed about not being able to deploy that I realized that I just couldn't be there on the day they all left. I know that statement in itself sounds weird; but take a moment to picture the day the Soldiers leave in your mind: you would see various family members and spouses there crying that their Soldier was going away for a year . . . then you would see me over there crying (figuratively speaking) that I WASN'T allowed to be on the deployment. That didn't sit too well with me and I just didn't want to be "that guy" who was bringing everyone down out of envy so I decided to do the most logical thing at the time: put in a request to take some leave.

I did all of the paperwork, and I waited. It seemed like it took the commander forever to sign my paperwork. Eventually he called me into his office and asked me why I suddenly requested leave. I explained to him that I just needed to clear my head after everything that had happened. I had been on such an emotional roller coaster, from finding out about the deployment in general, to finding out that Kathy would be there, to meeting the great crew that I could have served with. The idea of missing out on everything took a toll on me and I knew deep down that I was far better than the junior Soldier that they were sending on that mission. Finally the commander understood my concern and approved my leave. I told him that when I returned from my leave that I would be 100% and on top of my game. I would be ready to come back to work and contribute to the mission, just as he wanted me to. I appreciated the fact that he approved my leave and made a promise to myself that when I got back to the unit after leave I would leave all of the bad feelings behind and start anew. Conveniently my first day of leave ended up being the day that everyone was supposed to get on the plane and deploy, meaning that when I returned they would have already been gone for two weeks.

I had a friend who was working at the duty desk the night I was supposed to sign out on leave at midnight. He agreed to sign me out on leave at midnight without me there (which isn't legal by the way) so I could head home immediately after the work day the day before. I didn't care; I just wanted to get away from Fort Drum as soon as possible. I was burned out and needed a break. Later that night I got home and my brother Jason and I went over to a friend's house to drink some beers. We made plans on what we would do for the two weeks I would be home. One of the plans involved throwing a huge party at our friend's house that upcoming weekend. It would have been something to do; anything for a good time. To be honest, I didn't really care what we did, as long as it took my mind off of what had happened back at the unit. After all, that was the whole purpose of taking leave to begin with.

I woke up the next morning feeling somewhat ok. I didn't have a hangover, since we only had a couple of beers the night before to unwind. It wasn't like we had gotten seriously drunk or anything like that. When I woke up that morning I also saw that it had snowed heavily overnight and a couple of feet of snow had come down. Being from upstate NY I personally enjoy snow so I didn't have a problem with this. I only have an issue with the snow if I have to drive somewhere, but since I didn't have to drive anywhere I was happy it snowed. My brother Jason on the other hand had to drive to work in a town called Herkimer (which is almost a 25 minute drive from Saint Johnsville). Since it snowed he left for work a little early and so when I got up that morning he had already left. I have to admit being on leave when everyone else around you has to go to work feel pretty good.

I grabbed my first cup of coffee for the morning and sat on the couch. My younger brother Jeremey (who was almost four years old at the time) stumbled over to me and wanted to play. I hoisted him up onto my lap and started tickling him, to which he started laughing hysterically. All of a sudden my phone started ringing. I looked at Jeremey and I asked him, "Should I answer it?" Knowing damn well that I would have to stop tickling him in order to answer the phone, he shook his head "yes." So I answered the phone, and I heard SSG Dugar's voice on the other end, "Conklin! Where are you?!" Shocked that she was even asking me this, I replied, "I'm home on leave, who wants to know?" What happened next changed my career forever. She said to me, "Yeah, well guess what? You're deploying! Get your ass up back up to Fort Drum! You have six hours!" I couldn't believe this. I knew I wanted to deploy really bad, but I wasn't prepared to have to deploy on a six hour notice. I was home, which was a two hour trip back to Fort Drum as it was. Two of my six hours would be wasted on travel alone, not to mention the fact that I had to pack up all of the stuff in my room on Fort Drum also. This was crazy. I franticly told my dad what had happened as I started packing my stuff. It was then that I realized that I was no longer happy with the fact that it snowed last night. To make matters worse, I looked outside the window to see that it had started snowing again.

There was just no way that I could handle a drive like that under those conditions in my Cavalier. I would have driven off the road and gotten into an accident which would have effectively ruined my chances of deploying. My dad ended up asking one of his friends that had a pickup truck if he could take us up to Fort Drum. The trip took nearly three hours because the snow got heavier and heavier the further north we traveled. During the drive I was franticly calling everyone that I could to say bye. I told a lot of my friends not to be worried, this was just a bye, not a goodbye. Goodbye means you'll never see someone again. I called my brother and told him what happened. At first he thought I was joking around, but when he realized I was serious he felt like crap about the fact that we didn't get to say bye in person. To be perfectly honest this entire situation was hard to swallow. Just the night before I was drinking beer and making plans for the next two weeks. None of those plans involved a flight to Afghanistan.

I got back to Fort Drum with only three hours to spare. Because I had so much to do before the flight I quickly said bye to my dad and got to work. I soon found out the reason why I had received such a short notice for this deployment. As I stated earlier, there were five Soldiers going; one Warrant Officer, three NCOs, and one junior Soldier. There was just one problem with that. The junior Soldier had gotten arrested earlier that morning at 3AM at a Denny's restaurant in Watertown. He was drunk with a few of his friends and a fight broke out. I honestly couldn't believe that he made the bad decision to get that drunk the night before a deployment. I wouldn't have made the same decision, but that's just me. I'm no stranger to having a good time, but I think doing that the night before a deployment is just pure stupidity. As far as the fight goes, I'll put it like this: getting into a fight at Denny's isn't exactly out of the question. It happens. Unfortunately for this Soldier his mistake proved to be my gain.

As I was franticly packing everything in my room the Commander showed up. He first wanted to express his gratitude to me that I was able to answer the call to duty on such short notice. He also asked if he could meet with my father real quick because he wanted to thank him for his sacrifice. I explained to the Commander that since we only had three hours left until the flight I had sent my dad back home. Looking at me with a startled look on his face, the Commander then explained to me that there must have been some sort of misunderstanding with the timeline. I had six hours to get back to Fort Drum, because everyone who was deploying was going to be on lockdown to the bay area awaiting the bus to the flight line. Then we would have a few more hours to wait for the bus in which we could spend with our families in the bay, so in essence we probably had at least 10 hours to go. I really wish that I knew that information prior to sending my dad home. It would have been nice to spend a few more hours with him, but as the old saying goes, "No sense crying over spilled milk."

When I got down to the bay for lockdown I met up with Pelletier. He couldn't believe that I was added to the deployment at the last minute and he was really glad to see that this was happening. It was good to have a friend like him around. We had known each other since way back in Korea and if there was anyone who I knew would watch my back on a deployment I knew it would be him. He was someone that I could trust. I also met up with Chief Broadbent and the rest of the Personnel crew that I would be working with out there. Chief told me that when he found out that the other Soldier was arrested and had to make a decision on which Soldier he should bring that he instantly chose me. If it was up to him he would have had me on the deployment from day one. That really made me feel good and I truly appreciated it. I had a lot of respect for Chief Broadbent not only as a leader but as an individual as well and I knew that I could learn a lot from him. As good as I was at my job I knew there was still a lot to learn, and Chief Broadbent would prove to be that mentor that I needed.

On the flight over to Afghanistan I had a lot of things on my mind. First and foremost I was still shocked about the fact that I woke up this morning in my own home contemplating going to a party later that evening and instead I was on a plane bound for Afghanistan. I guess I was still just a little bit in shock. However, I was extremely happy about the fact that this was happening. I couldn't imagine myself staying behind in that unit for any longer. Things were so disorganized that it was starting to get sickening. This deployment would get me out of that toxic environment. Then there were my own ambitions. I had already completed two successful tours in two different countries and I wanted the experience and bragging rights of adding yet another country to my resume. Could you blame me? I loved having stories to tell everyone that I knew about Iraq and Korea. I really wanted to have stories to tell about Afghanistan also. As of now I had a great story in the fact that I received my orders to deploy with just a six hour notice. That's actually a story I still tell people today; this book being just one example. I also knew that getting another deployment under my belt would help me professionally. I was still promotable and wanted to become an NCO very badly. I knew that by going on another deployment I would become a better NCO. Soldiers tend to look up to the more experienced NCOs more than inexperienced NCOs. Going on another deployment was a logical way to benefit my career. Furthermore, going on this deployment was going to ensure that I not only met a lot of new people, but also that I would be reunited with my old friend Kathy. I knew that it had been a long time since I had last seen her, but I was confident that we would pick up just where we left off without a problem.

We were friends for life, and it was time to start acting and living like it. I realized one very important thing on this flight that I had thought of many different times in my career; that being the undeniable fact that everything happens for a reason.

CHAPTER 9

AFGHANISTAN

After a 15 hour flight my unit finally arrived at Manas Air Base, Kyrgyzstan. By now I was at a point in my career where a 15 hour flight was starting to feel like a common occurrence. I wondered to myself just how many more flights like these I would have to take throughout my career. One thing I knew for certain was that every time I took a long flight like this it was bound to be followed by some sort of year-long adventure, as my previous tours in Iraq and Korea had proven. I was extremely excited to get this deployment underway. A year in Afghanistan meant new adventures to experience, new sights to see and new people to meet.

Before we could actually move into Afghanistan we had to spend at least a week on Manas to in-process and await a flight into Afghanistan (which from Manas is only about a two hour journey). I guess if you were to compare it to my first deployment, you would say that Manas is to Afghanistan what Kuwait was to Iraq. The environment in Manas was far different than that of Kuwait however. The cold weather in Kyrgyzstan was a far cry from the hot weather in Kuwait. Mountains surrounded the base and you could see snow on all of them. Unlike Kuwait it actually did snow there in the winter. The political and economic climate in Kyrgyzstan was different than that of Kuwait also. Kyrgyzstan was a former republic of the Soviet Union. Like all nations that were part of the Soviet Union during its downfall, Kyrgyzstan suffered from economic despair. When leaving the gate on the bus you could see this just by looking out the window into the city. The town seemed ravaged and run down. I couldn't imagine having to live there, unlike Kuwait which is an extremely rich country that has palaces in its capital.

Manas Airbase itself had a little more to offer the Soldiers than Kuwait did back in 2003. This is most likely because Manas is actually an Air Force Base as opposed to an Army Post. The Air Force is notorious for taking care of its troops way better than the Army does and thus offers many more amenities to its troops. Manas had a great morale building with movie nights, pool tables, and video games along with a basketball court outside. There was a nice gym and an internet café for Soldiers to use to email messages to home. Back in 2003 we didn't have any of that in Kuwait. All we had was a tent to sleep in and a small weight tent to work out in. The Airmen who were stationed or deployed on Manas were certainly luckier than I was in 2003.

Manas also had a bar tent called "Pete's Place" that would serve two beers a night to anyone who was stationed or deployed there. The problem with that was the fact that the Army didn't allow its Soldiers to drink on a deployment regardless; even if the Air Force said it was ok on an Air Force Base. Therefore those of us who were in the Army who liked to drink a lot (myself included) would get pissed off when we walked by there. As far as I was concerned it wasn't fair that I couldn't just have a mere two beers. Believe me it'll take a lot more than that to get me drunk, so I really didn't see the problem. We would also hear stories of some Soldiers who were deployed there in the past who would go to the Base Exchange and purchase an Air Force PT uniform and then put it on and walk into Pete's Place and attempt to drink. They got caught almost immediately. Dealing with the no booze rule that the Army imposed on us was just something that we were going to have to endure. It wasn't changing any time soon; or in fact ever.

The 10th SSB pawned us off on the NJ National Guard unit (the 50th Personnel Services Battalion-PSB) almost immediately. We stood in maybe two of the 10th SSB's formations before they decided they wanted nothing to do with us. In a way I understood this because we would be working with the 50th PSB for the entire deployment, but at the same time the five of us felt a little slighted about this because the 10th SSB was our real unit. We were part of them at Fort Drum and we didn't see why we couldn't still feel like we were part of them on this deployment. Apparently, the 10th SSB didn't really feel the same way. What was confusing to us was the exact description of our mission. We knew that we were supposed to train and supervise the New Jersey Guard when it came to personnel services functions, but we weren't 100% clear on how long we would be there.

Back on Fort Drum our Company Commander told us that we would not interfere with the way the 50th ran their unit as a whole, just how they handled the mission for the 10th Mountain Division. In other words, the Soldiers in the 50th weren't actually going to be answering to us, and we wouldn't be answering to them. Of course, this all proved to be 100% false. We would be attached to the 50th for the entire deployment and we would take orders from them. I remember this becoming a huge dispute/confusion various times throughout the deployment. Finally we caught on and fell in line with the 50th but it's just too bad that our Company Commander at Drum (who in fact didn't even deploy with us) gave us misinformation from the very beginning.

As far as the flight schedule was concerned, that was also thrown slightly into disarray because of the actions of the 10th SSB. You see, the 50th PSB had arrived to Manas just a few days before us and thus were scheduled to fly into Afghanistan a few days before we would. Now, this wouldn't necessarily have been a problem if the 10th SSB had booked us to fly with them, but since they decided to immediately hand us over to the 50th they just assumed that it was the 50th's responsibility to book our flights. As the old saying goes, "You know what happens when you assume things, right? You make an ASS out of you and me." And that's exactly what happened. In the end, it was Chief Broadbent who booked our flights out of Manas. Chief was someone that you could really count on. He was a true leader that never thought he was too good or too high up in the "food chain" to mentor a Soldier. There were a lot of leaders in the SSB that could have learned from the example that Chief Broadbent set. This was just one example of that leadership.

One day when we were still waiting in Manas I finally bumped into Kathy at the internet café. I knew that at some point I would see her there; it was just a matter of time. This was the first time that I had seen her in about four years; since April of 2002 when we graduated AIT to be exact. Things had changed in her life since I had last seen her, as she was now married to a guy named Mike who was also on the deployment. He introduced himself to me quickly and then went to use one of the computers. Kathy and I spent a few minutes catching up on things and then she had to go to a formation (which for some reason my crew didn't have to be a part of). Although we didn't get very long to sit and catch up it was still really good to see her after all these years. Back in AIT she was basically my best friend and I knew that with enough time things could be that way again. We parted ways but I made a promise to myself that this would not be the last time that I saw her. (I really couldn't break a promise like that if I wanted to . . . we were about to spend a year on the same deployment; of course I would see her again.)

After a few more days the 50th PSB finally flew off to Bagram Airfield where they would begin their mission. We knew that our flight was coming any day, thanks to Chief Broadbent doing all of the coordinating. Chief finally decided where each one of us would go for the deployment; we wouldn't all be going to the same camp because the mission was split into different locations. The reasons for this were quite obvious, there were 10th Mountain Division Soldiers deployed to various regions of the country, there was just no way that the entire PSB could be located in one location. (Back in Iraq in 2003 the circumstances were very different, as you read earlier. Back then the entire PSB/SSB stayed in one location. Since then the Army had obviously gotten smarter.)

It was decided that Chief Broadbent himself would initially be going to Forward Operating Base (FOB) Salerno where a small detachment would be located. There he would oversee the operations of that camp on a day to day basis, as well as take any of our concerns via phone or email. He was confident that there wouldn't be many concerns because he knew that we were a competent crew that all excelled in something. My expertise was in NCOER Evaluations, while SGT Jack's and SSG Dugar's expertise was in promotions. It made sense that he could trust us to be spread out across the country without his constant supervision.

The rest of would also be split up, but not evenly. I would be going to Kandahar Airfield with SGT Jack and SSG Dugar and SGT Johnson was going to be deployed to Bagram Airfield with the main body of the 50th PSB. The reason the decision was made in this manner is that Chief (along with the 50th leadership) believed that the mission in Kandahar was far greater than that of Bagram. I wasn't entirely happy with this because I knew that Kathy would be at Bagram which meant that it was the place that I wanted to be also. There was no chance that Kathy would be going to Kandahar because the Soldiers who would be stationed there weren't even from the New Jersey National Guard; they were actually from the Tennessee National guard. Apparently, a detachment from Tennessee was also going to be attached to the 50th in the same manner that our crew was. Honestly, this was the first time in my career that I had ever been introduced to something like this. I was used to doing things the "old way;" meaning that if the 101st SSB deployed, then just the 101st SSB deployed. There wasn't going to be various detachments from various places glued together to make one big "cluster-fuck" of a unit. It didn't make sense to me to do something like this, but that clearly wasn't important because it did make sense to the Army. So much for common sense, right? Either way, going to Kandahar was still a challenge for me because I knew absolutely no one there. I had mentally prepared myself to be deployed alongside the New Jersey National Guard for the year. I really didn't like this sudden change, but I had no choice but to deal with it.

There ended up being a ton of flight delays for our departure from Manas. It started to take forever. Since our crew was going to three different places we were obviously booked for different flights. After being stuck there for quite some time, SGT Jack started making jokes about the situation. That was the thing about SGT Jack; he was one hell of a comedian. He could turn almost anything into a joke, and he was very good at it. He was great at making some people look like an idiot with some of his jokes also. This time wasn't as drastic as others, but I can still remember what he said about us being stuck there in Manas. All he did was he simply restated a fact, that fact being that we were stuck in Manas. In this case, it wasn't the words that he used that made things so funny; it was the manner in which he said the words. Instead of saying the phrase, "dammit, were stuck in Manas!" he would instead say, "dammit, were stuck in MAN-ASS!" In doing this he would take the extra time and consideration to put emphasis on the two words: MAN and ASS. So in effect he was saying that we were stuck in a man's ass, which didn't exactly sound right. Then again, that was the point of the joke. He would also make sure that he would say it in front of random people who were usually passing us by, or while we were standing in line at the DFAC. Almost every time that he would do this we would end up having people looking at us funny. Sometimes we would even get a few people to laugh. I guess that was SGT Jack's best asset, the fact that he could create comedy out of almost nothing. Having him around definitely made that deployment that much better.

As the days went by, Chief Broadbent and SGT Johnson eventually flew to their respective locations. Jack, Dugar and I were the final three that were waiting for a flight. I remember Chief telling me before he flew out, "don't worry, you guys are going to be fine, I'm sure that SSG Dugar can network her way into a flight." To this day I still don't know what he meant by that, but I sure did use my imagination. As you can see, all of us were using humor to get by those first few weeks.

The day eventually came that we would fly out of Manas to Kandahar. I was glad that the flight day finally came along because we had been in Manas forever and I was ready to get to work. Not only that, but SGT Jack's "MAN ASS" jokes were starting to get a little bit out of control. It was at the point with him where it was the first thing he would say when we woke up every day in the tent. We would wake up in this dirty, nasty tent and before I could even go outside and brush my teeth, Jack would say to me, "Hey Conklin, were still stuck in MAN-ASS" . . . every single damn morning. There was no end to it, and believe me it wasn't exactly the visual that one would want first thing in the morning, every morning. I was eager to get on this flight to Kandahar because I knew it would put an end to the "MAN ASS" jokes, or at least I hoped it would.

When I got to Kandahar I immediately noticed how hot it was there compared to Manas. Kandahar is located in the southwest region of Afghanistan in the dry dessert, as opposed to Bagram which is located in the east near the mountains. Once we settled in, we took the time to introduce ourselves to the Soldiers of the Tennessee National Guard. We found it funny that every single one of them was a "country redneck." They talked with a country accent, used a lot of tobacco chew, and even spoke in the country dialect using such terms as "ya'll" and "I tell you what." Now, I don't want to offend anyone reading this that may be a "country redneck," believe me that isn't my goal here. In fact, there are plenty of "country rednecks" in my home town of Saint Johnsville. I have many friends who are "country rednecks". The thing was we just weren't prepared to deal with so many "country rednecks" at once, in Afghanistan of all places. We tried our best not to laugh at a lot of the dialect that was used, but it was irresistible at times. Before you knew it, SGT Jack was running around saying things like, "I tell you what son" and "Hey Ya'll!" It was funny to say the least.

Even though they were the way that they were they were still good people. They were down to earth and good natured and appeared genuinely interested in learning the job. Unlike the NJ Guard crew, they didn't have the advantage of having Chief Broadbent visit them for a week at Fort Dix, NJ to give them a few classes, therefore when we were working with them it was like starting from scratch. Only a few of them were AGR Soldiers or had Active Duty experience. This obviously would make our mission harder. Anytime you are starting from scratch as opposed to starting off with a solid foundation of knowledge you will clearly have a harder time, and that goes for anything in life. It didn't take long for the Soldiers of that unit to build a certain level of respect for me. They were all very laid back, and didn't get uptight about anything. This can be a concern with some people; there are people in the world who will take offense to things when someone tries to teach them the proper way to do something. Instead these Soldiers valued my opinion, took notes when I would give classes, and never show the slightest sign of disrespect. I was delighted to know that the National Guard and Active Duty Component could co-exist after all.

The Tennessee Guard unit had a Warrant Officer by the name of Chief Payne assigned there who was responsible for overseeing all of the personnel functions, similar to the role that Chief Broadbent played back at Fort Drum for the 10th SSB. Chief Payne was an interesting person to work with. While he didn't possess the same level of knowledge in the field of Human Resources that Chief Broadbent did, he did have a lot of a different type of knowledge: military knowledge; meaning that he had spent many years serving in various positions at various ranks. Now, you may be thinking, "Isn't that what every Soldier in the Army has to do?" To elaborate on my point concerning Chief Payne, I will explain: Chief Payne somehow managed to serve as an enlisted NCO, a Warrant Officer, and a Commissioned Officer. This is not something that is common in the military, especially on Active Duty (which would explain why I had never encountered someone like this before). Apparently taking a career path such as this isn't as uncommon in the National Guard. Also in most cases when someone does that in their career they would start at the lowest ranks(enlisted) and move their way up to the highest ranks (Commissioned Officer) with the Warrant Officer ranks falling somewhere in the middle. That makes sense considering the rank structure: Warrant Officers are senior in rank to NCOs/enlisted Soldiers and Commissioned Officers are senior to Warrant Officers. Chief Payne on the other hand didn't follow the conventional order, he started as an enlisted Soldier (and subsequently was promoted to Sergeant) and then became a Commissioned Officer. At some point, he decided that he wanted to be a Warrant Officer, which is technically going in reverse. To me, it made absolutely no sense.

Despite his perplexing career choices Chief Payne was still a very nice person to work with. Just like the rest of the unit he had the laid back country attitude and would always value my opinion. He didn't know very much about the job itself, but that wasn't really a problem. He didn't let his rank go to his head; if he didn't know the answer to a question he wouldn't try to use his rank to cover things up and he wouldn't be ashamed to ask someone junior to him for help. I really respected him as a result of his actions and attitude. I've never been a fan of Soldiers thinking they are smarter or better than anyone just because the hold a certain rank. Chief was so down to earth that you would forget he was a Warrant Officer at times. He would try to make jokes with the Soldiers and get along with everyone. He was a clear example of a man being able to use his great personality to overcome other issues. There will always be a special place in my heart for Chief Payne.

Not everything at Kandahar was laid back. Just like my previous deployment to Iraq in 2003, there were a lot of rocket attacks that we sustained while there. Once in a while we would get an attack during the day, but in most cases the attacks came at night when we were sleeping. At one point we were getting at least four rocket attacks there a week. Every time we sustained an attack we had to run to the bunkers to take cover, just like in Iraq. The only difference was here in Afghanistan we had real cement bunkers to hide in, while back in Iraq we had bunkers made of dirt and sandbags (covered in plywood) that we dug into the ground on our own. There was also an actual siren that would go off any time a rocket entered the airspace above the camp. These were just two of the things that I saw change since my last deployment. Everywhere I looked I could see something that was a huge improvement over Iraq in 2003; there were housing bays to live in as opposed to tents, a bigger PX to buy amenities, laundry machines that actually worked, and upgraded security features. It had become very apparent to me that the US Government wasn't afraid to invest loads of money into the War on Terrorism. Every single improvement that I saw was just another sign that we were "in it for the long haul" as Chief Payne would put it.

Sometimes during the rocket attacks we would crack jokes and make fun of each other just to pass the time. We almost had no choice; someone had to lighten the mood. If you walk around bitter for an entire deployment I can promise you that it's going to be a long year. Usually during our attacks SGT Jack became the comedian. He was always hilarious. He used to make Sergeant's time training back at Fort Drum a lot funnier just with his comments alone, which is why I knew that deploying with him would be fun. There was one night in particular that SGT Jack decided to make fun of Chief Payne because he wore a sleeveless under-armor shirt outside, which was exactly what SGT Jack was wearing too. Now, to put it into perspective for you, SGT Jack was a big time body builder, while Chief Payne was an out of shape older man. He wasn't elderly or anything like that, but he had at least 20 years on SGT Jack. Knowing that Chief Payne could take a joke he looked over at him and said, "Damn Chief Payne! You been pumping iron at Venice Beach?" while he started flexing his own arms. "God damn chief, I aint got shit on you! You could win Mr. America today!" It was hilarious and it had everyone laughing. Chief tried to say something back, but there was really nothing he could say without breaking out and laughing. You could tell that Chief Payne thought it was funny because he couldn't even keep a straight face. Just when you thought it was over, SGT Jack kept it going, "Damn man, I bet Arnold takes tips from you, huh?" That was the thing about SGT Jack and his comedy routines, he would get a good laugh out of everyone but then he wouldn't know when to let it go. After a while it would come off like Chief's feelings were a little hurt and even though it was for the good of the group's morale I guess I could see where Chief would be a little upset . . . SGT Jack taunted him for about 45 minutes straight that night. The dude was relentless. And it wasn't even like Chief Payne was his only target. There was one Soldier who for some reason, carried around a teddy bear and acted like a kid. Do you think SGT Jack let that "kid" off the hook? Nope. That was just how he was. He did make it clear to everyone that it was just in good fun. If you could figure out a way to dish it back to Jack he would take it all in stride just like you did. He wasn't sensitive by any means, which was a good thing considering some of the crap that would come out of that man's mouth.

After spending about a month on Kandahar, Chief Broadbent sent down word that I would be moving from Kandahar to Bagram for the remainder of the deployment. The original assessment that there would be a larger workload in Kandahar proved to be wrong and so Chief Broadbent made the decision to move me to Bagram to assist SGT Johnson and the NJ Guard unit. To be frank, this made a lot of sense to me because there were a lot of days in Kandahar where we would get finished with all of our work by 11 am. There were even times when we wouldn't have work for two or three days. This type of thing is ok sometimes, but I can't stand it on a long term basis. I'm a person who always needs to be working on something and always needs to be working towards accomplishing some type of goal. One of my goals on that deployment was to become even better at doing my job, that way when I finally got promoted I could be the most reliable NCO possible. With the limited workload at Kandahar I just wasn't being challenged and therefore I wasn't going to get any better at my job.

On a personal note I was very happy to be moving to Bagram because, as I mentioned earlier, Kathy was deployed there. Granted, I was happy being deployed with the Tennessee Guardsmen and I made friends with them quickly but that still didn't compare to being able to spend the deployment with someone that I basically knew my whole career. When I finally got to Bagram Airfield it was great to see her and we started to hang out a lot. At one point our desks in our office were connected and were directly across from each other. I remember thinking to myself that years ago in AIT I never would have guessed that we would ever end up deployed together in this type of situation. To be perfectly honest I never even knew that the National Guard and Active Component would even deploy together. I guess you can never really know what sort of scenarios that you can find yourself in until you actually experience things.

While it was great to be able to hang out with Kathy again, things at Bagram weren't exactly as I thought they would be at first. The Soldiers from the NJ Guard were a lot different than the Soldiers from the Tennessee unit and it showed. They were younger Soldiers and thus they had just a little more attitude than the laid back "country rednecks" that I had dealt with before. I don't know exactly what it was, but I didn't really seem to "click" with anyone right away. I guess I should take this time to highlight the fact that in most cases, Active Duty Soldiers are conditioned to have a very low opinion of the National Guard. This is a feeling that is felt amongst most Active Duty Soldiers right from the very beginning. You are made to believe such things as: the National Guard is just a bunch of lazy, incompetent weekend warriors, they are trouble makers, they don't know their job, they don't care about rank, etc. There are just so many bad stereotypes in the Active Army in respect to the National Guard. It really is sad to believe that, but there are even cases where a Soldier will cross over from the Guard to Active Duty and during that Soldier's first few weeks in their new unit they are treated like they don't know anything about the military. Simply put, National Guard Soldiers are usually treated like second class citizens, and that just isn't fair. I am very ashamed to admit that in the beginning I felt the same way about the National Guard. It would end up taking me a while to believe otherwise, but in the very beginning of this deployment I was stuck on these messed up beliefs that had been drilled into me since the beginning of my career. As a result of that I decided to come into that unit and start acting like a total asshole to everyone there with the exception of Kathy. I know now that it was a bad idea to do so, but at the time I didn't care. I treated them all bad. I called them names, I walked around like I was better than them, I ran my mouth, I intentionally told them that I was a Specialist Promotable as opposed to just saying I was a Specialist, as if there was really a difference. I would intentionally say that they didn't know their job, and I would say to them that they were lucky to have me around to teach them. I would even go as far as to claim that since I was active duty I wasn't taking orders from anyone in the guard. Does that sound a little conceited to you? Of course it does! I still don't know to this day why I acted this way, and today I truly regret it. I was a total asshole, and it wasn't like anyone in that unit wronged me or anything like that. I'm not going to sit here and try to justify my actions by saying they started it . . . because they didn't start it. I did. Before long I was finding myself getting called into the Detachment Sergeant's office to get chewed out for acting this way. There was only so much protection that Chief Broadbent could provide me. One day he and SGT Johnson took me to lunch at the Korean restaurant that was there to try to talk some sense into me. They told me outright that I had to stop. People really didn't like me, and it was my fault. Most of the Soldiers in the unit would ask SGT Johnson who the hell I thought I was and why did I have to act so "hardcore." I had no choice but to change, or I would end up spending this deployment friendless (aside from Kathy). Did I really want to spend the deployment this way? No, I didn't. I knew deep down that I had to change, but at times it was like I didn't know how to turn the "asshole button" off. I was so good at being an asshole, and to be honest it felt good even though it wasn't actually good. I guess I was partially stuck on the asshole kick that I was on back at Fort Drum when dealing with the 10th SSB. The only difference was that back there they provoked me; here in Afghanistan I was the one doing the provoking. I agreed with Chief and SGT Johnson that day that I would try my best to change and be more personable. It would just take me some time.

The section that I ended up being assigned to train in was Evaluations. This was fitting for me since I had so many years of experience of working on Evaluations by now. To be perfectly honest, if there was anyone who would be considered a subject matter expert when it came to that it would have been me. There were two other Soldiers in the section; Billy Wade and Leon Coleman. They were good guys, real easy to get along with. They spent a lot of time talking about what most guys would talk about: sports, women, cars, TV shows, etc. Coleman had actually been deployed before, and Wade had spent a couple of years mobilized to Fort Dix, NJ following the September 11th terrorist attacks. So it was good to see that they weren't really inexperienced. I'm sure they were a little weary of me at first, considering I had come into that unit acting like such an asshole but eventually we all became friends. Sometimes I would get frustrated with them when they wouldn't do the reports as quickly as I would, which was technically wrong considering I had so many years of experience. That was just another mistake I made with people on a personal level on that deployment. I admit that there were a lot of times that I said things during the work day that I didn't really mean and shouldn't have said. Eventually I did mellow out and I stopped having so many attitude issues. I'm just glad that we were able to get over our differences. The three of us are still friends to this day.

I wasn't limited to only getting to know the Soldiers in the Evaluations section. Across the hallway from the Evals/Promotions office there was another office that took care of the other personnel functions that the unit needed. There was a Soldier in that office by the name of Timothy Jardinico, (also known as JD) who happened to be a "jack of all trades" if you will. JD did everything that was ever asked of him, and he did it well. He processed passports for Soldiers (to include my own) among other things. In addition he went on almost every convoy mission that the unit went on during that deployment. Many of the other Soldiers weren't really "into" doing that, but he was. Over time he built a reputation of being a "Super Soldier" due to not only his contributions but also his versatility. I was glad to see JD on any of the convoys that I went on throughout that deployment because I knew he took the job seriously, and therefore I knew that if anything happened out there I would have a dedicated Soldier watching my back. That's all that you can really ask for in situations like that.

I was told one day that the 50th PSB was going to be sending a three Soldier team to Kabul to provide personnel support to the Soldiers that were stationed there. Chief wanted me to give them a quick class on how to handle the Evaluations while there. The group consisted of two Soldiers and one NCO. It was at this point that I made my first real, new friend during this deployment. Her name was Maria, and when I started showing her what needed to be done she informed me that she would be the one handling the reports anyway and that there was really no point of me giving the class to the other two Soldiers. I admired her brutal honesty, as that is a trait that I have myself. As the day went by I realized that I had actually made a connection with her, which was good. I needed a new friend out there anyway. I also admired the fact that even though she was in the National Guard, she had come from a unit where she was working full time so she was used to doing this type of work. She just needed a level of brushing up on processing active reports. You see, even though most National Guard Soldiers only serve one weekend a month, there are some Soldiers in the guard that work full time for their respective state. This type of duty is called AGR, which stands for Active-Guard Reserve. Usually the mission of an AGR Soldier is to provide support to those Soldiers who only go to drill one weekend a month. An AGR Soldier earns the same rate of pay and benefits that a normal Active Duty Soldier earns. Simply put, there really isn't a difference between AGR and Active Duty, aside from the fact that one works for the State and one works for the Federal Government.

After a few days of teaching the Kabul crew they finally left Bagram. It was really good for me to meet Maria because making a new friend softened me up a little, which was good because as I stated before, I really did need to stop being such an asshole. Since it was known that the command team would be making regular visits to Kabul to check in on them and possibly provide support I knew that I would see her again at some point during this deployment. Mission-wise I had to stay in touch with them at least once a week because Chief Broadbent had put me in charge of reviewing all of the Evaluations for the entire country. This was a great honor for me and it showed me that he really valued my opinion and work ethic. What this meant was that before any camp across the country sent their reports to the Department of the Army they had to be reviewed by me first. This included not only the old Tennessee Kandahar crew but the Kabul crew as well. It got to the point where I had to call both of these camps almost every day to discuss some errors on the reports or procedures. In Kandahar the problems were more error related, while in Kabul the problems had more to do with "red tape" then anything else. Apparently Kabul was packed with senior officers that wanted to try to control that section. Sometimes Maria would be asked to do things that weren't actually in accordance with regulations or even within her scope of duty. What none of those senior officers at Kabul understood was that I worked for the PSB and therefore I was the one who was put in charge of this; not them. I sent these reports directly to the Department of the Army, they did not. Therefore, the authority was mine as a matter of position. Granted there were probably times that this newfound authority may have gotten to my head, but it didn't change the fact that there were certain procedures in place that needed to be followed. I knew it was only a matter of time before I would have to take a trip to Kabul myself to set the record straight.

When the day came to take the trip to Kabul we convoyed there from Bagram. It was my first time convoying in Afghanistan, and it was a lot different than convoys in Iraq. For one, the vehicles here were completely up-armored, as opposed to the Humvees that we used back in 2003. This change would obviously provide us with a lot more safety. Part of the reason for this was that there were now vehicles that stayed in country for every rotating unit to use. It was a simple matter of just signing them over to the next unit when your time there was up. This made things much easier on units when they left their home station. Units no longer had to go through the extensive cleaning, packing, and rail load process that I had to go through in the past. I was very glad to see that we were using better equipment this time around. It really made me feel like we were making progress in this part of the world.

The convoy itself took about an hour, and I found it funny that Afghanistan looked much "dirtier" than Iraq. Up until now I hadn't seen any place that looked worse than Iraq. Finally that had changed. The streets just looked so dingy. There were a lot of fields that were just nasty brown mud, not even the beautiful sand that I had become accustomed to in other countries. I've always heard the rumors that Afghanistan is the "opium capital of the world." After convoying through that nasty country, I wouldn't be entirely surprised.

When I got to Camp Eggers, Kabul Maria briefed me on what was happening there. They had a lot of work to do, and the main problem was that the Senior Officers kept trying to get involved in their business and enforce their own procedures. I didn't appreciate this; after all it was me that was reviewing their work every day. If anyone should have been setting procedures in place (which I did) it should have been me. I didn't want to be reviewing stuff that was being manipulated by people other than those who I had actually trained. Another problem was they needed a refresher class from me since I only really had about three days to train them before they left Bagram. That made sense to me since years ago at Fort Campbell it certainly took me a lot longer than three days to learn the job! The tasks were divided amongst the three Soldiers there and Maria was the one who was doing the Evaluations, which was my specialty. During the week that I stayed there in Kabul I taught her many things on a professional level but we also connected a lot more on a personal level. We would hang out after work, head to dinner at the post DFAC and then usually head to the coffee shop. (Funny that there was a coffee shop on a deployed post, this was a luxury I didn't have on my first deployment!) Overall we ended up getting close and became good friends. We really made a positive connection, and it was good to know that I had another good friend out there. Aside from Kathy, she was the first close friend that I actually made out there. The only real difference was that I had known Kathy for years, but who says you can't make close friends on a new day?

Camp Eggers itself was a rather interesting sight. The camp appeared to be an old resort for Afghan royalty (I couldn't be 100% sure on that however, it was just a hunch) and was now covered with KBR buildings used for work and living. It was really an odd sight but the camp had an elite feeling to it and thus I enjoyed being there. Camp Eggers was a joint base for all of the services (Army, Air Force, Marine Corps, and Navy) and most of the Soldiers who were stationed there were high ranking officers. If you walked down the main road in the middle of the day you would pass by various Generals, Admirals and Colonels. While walking down the street you would be best served by rendering a salute and just holding it up because if not you would be raising your salute every other second. I know that sounds like I am exaggerating but there really were a lot of officers there. It was extremely rare to see enlisted Soldiers there as there were only a few of them there and this somehow made the enlisted Soldiers more valuable than normal. Enlisted Soldiers, while obviously not high in rank usually do have a higher level of work experience than many officers, and rightfully so. Enlisted Soldiers are the "worker bees," the ones who are actually down in the trenches trying to get the mission accomplished, so it made sense. Up until this point in my career I had never seen a place in the Army where the Officers outnumbered the Enlisted Soldiers by this high of a margin. It almost seemed odd.

After a week in Kabul I had to get back to Bagram and get back to work. Things there were business as usual but I was definitely acting like less of an asshole to everyone. The more time that went by the more I loosened up and before I knew it I was making friends with everyone. I just didn't really see a real reason to keep acting that way. I was still hanging out with Kathy almost every day too. We would go to eat lunch at the DFAC and the Korean restaurant to eat and catch up on things. We would take smoke breaks at the same time, as I re-ignited my old love for cigars from my first deployment. It got to the point where we were hanging out just about every day, and I was perfectly fine with that.

A few months went by and the deployment was really starting to flow. As I learned on my previous deployment, time always starts to fly once you've got the first month knocked out. Finally on June 1, 2006 my big day came. I met the cutoff score to get promoted to the rank of Sergeant with a score of 715 points. I had worked so hard for this and waited so long that when it finally happened I couldn't believe it. There were so many mixed emotions running through me: excitement, honor, even a hint of cockiness. I dreamed of this day ever since I first went to the promotion board back in Korea and now it finally arrived. Since this event was so important to me, I wanted the day to be as special as possible.

As with any promotion, a big ceremony took place. I wasn't the only Soldier getting promoted that day, as there were a few of the junior Soldiers from the NJ Guard getting promoted also. I was the only one getting promoted to Sergeant however. Since I was still technically part of the 10th SSB I wanted both the 50th PSB and the 10th SSB there to witness my promotion. I don't know how many Soldiers request to have two units attend their promotion ceremony, but I do know that it doesn't happen often. Usually when someone gets promoted there will be someone who goes up to the front of the room and says a few words about the person. They may talk about the person's accomplishments, what type of challenges they overcame to get to this point, their duty history, etc. Usually when this happens it is a very positive message, but it is still usually coming from one person. What I didn't expect was that four different people came up to speak on my behalf as opposed to just one. SGT Johnson came up and spoke for me and he talked about what it was like to work with me. He mentioned how I was the first to bring the Evaluations section to a 0% error rate. I thought it would end with him, but then a Warrant Officer that I served in Korea with came up and talked about how years ago in Korea my S1 section was the best one out of all the units. I honestly didn't expect him to come up and say that and to be frank I was surprised he even remembered that. Then when he was finished, LTC Alvarado (the 50th PSB Battalion Commander) came to the front and expressed his gratitude also. He mentioned how he was truly grateful to have me, an active duty Soldier working alongside his troops. Hearing him say that meant a lot to me. Last but not least, the 10th SSB Battalion Commander (who was my Commander at Fort Drum) also came to the front and talked up my accomplishments. I'm not sure if I've ever seen someone get promoted and receive this much fanfare. It felt like one big Sergeant Conklin tribute show. It seemed to drag on forever, and at times it felt like they were eulogizing me at my own funeral. I can't fully describe the emotions that I felt during all of this, aside from telling you that I felt great. The only thing is, the word "great" just doesn't seem to give that day justice. After my rank was placed on my chest, there was only one thing left to do, and that was that I had to recite the NCO Creed, which I have included below in its entirety:

> ***"No one is more professional than I. I am a Non-Commissioned Officer, a leader of Soldiers. As a Non-Commissioned Officer, I realize that I am a member of a time-honored corps, which is known as the backbone of the Army. I am proud of the Corps of the Non-Commissioned Officers and will at all times conduct myself so as to bring credit upon the Corps, the Military Service, and my country regardless of the situation in which I find myself. I will not use my grade or position to attain pleasure, profit, or personal safety.***
>
> ***Competence is my watchword. My two basic responsibilities will always be uppermost in my mind—accomplishment of my mission and the welfare of my Soldiers. I will strive to remain technically and tactically proficient. I am aware of my role as a Non-Commissioned Officer. I will fulfill my responsibilities inherent in that role. All Soldiers are entitled to outstanding leadership. I will provide that leadership. I know my Soldiers and I will always place their needs above my own. I will communicate consistently with my Soldiers and never***

leave them uninformed. I will be fair and impartial when recommending both rewards and punishment.

Officers of my unit will have maximum time to accomplish their duties; they will not have to accomplish mine. I will earn their respect and confidence as well as that of my Soldiers. I will be loyal to those with whom I serve; seniors, peers and subordinates alike. I will exercise initiative by taking appropriate action in the absence of orders. I will not compromise my integrity, nor my moral courage. I will not forget, nor will I allow my comrades to forget that we are professionals, Non-Commissioned Officers, leaders!"

As you can see by reading the above paragraphs, the NCO Creed is extremely long and it took me a long time to memorize. I had been studying and practicing it ever since I first went to the promotion board back in Korea. For so long I had anticipated the very day that I would recite the NCO Creed while getting promoted. I blurted it out, loud and proud and didn't make a single mistake. That was impressive, and the crowd's round of applause showed that my efforts were not in vain. When it was all said and done, everyone from both units came to the front and congratulated me. I was extremely proud of myself and I was glad to see that everyone else was too. When I look back fondly on this day I realize one very important thing: the day that I was promoted to Sergeant was the greatest day of my entire career. I was now ready to start leading Soldiers.

Time continued to flow by on the deployment and things were pretty much business as usual every day in the office. By now I had dropped my attitude problem and was getting along with everyone in the office. Our group was really starting to build a strong bond amongst each other. It was almost like we were becoming our own brotherhood if you will. There was even a time when SGT Johnson went on leave for two weeks and thus I was left in charge of the office since I was now the senior ranking Soldier there. That really made me feel good, and I considered it to be my first true leadership experience as an NCO. I knew enough about the job by now to perform well as a leader; any questions that the Soldiers or the customers had I was more than able to answer. It was good to know that I was starting to come into my own. During the work days I was all business and when off duty I either hung out with Kathy or I went to the gym. I was striving to keep in shape throughout the whole deployment. I knew that I was getting older and at times I would gain some of my old weight back a little quicker, and then since I was getting older it would take longer to come off. This would get frustrating to say the least so I would make sure to work out as much as possible throughout the deployment. I ran faster than almost all of the other Soldiers, but that really wouldn't matter on a weigh in. I did not want to fail tape. Luckily for me, I never ended up having to do a weigh in that deployment, so it didn't become a problem. The last thing I would have wanted would be old demons coming back; especially after recently getting promoted. That would look bad to say the least.

One thing that we used to have to endure at Bagram was the fallen comrade ceremonies. Basically any time a Soldier was killed outside of the wire they would hold one last ceremony to honor that Soldier before flying the body back to the US. Every Soldier's casket would ride through on a long motorcade all the way up the main road that runs through Bagram. After a while we were starting to have these ceremonies at least once or twice a week. As you can probably imagine, it saddened us every single time. In fact, they were outright depressing. Bagram had a loud, overwhelming giant voice system that was controlled by Base Operations that would signal that there would be a ceremony within the next hour. Every time a fallen comrade ceremony was announced a sad, bitter mood would just fall over the office and it would put a terrible feeling in my stomach, knowing that there was a Soldier involved; that it could have been any one of us. The entire office would have to flow out into the road for the ceremony, as a sign of respect. I can remember standing at most of these ceremonies with Kathy and each one of them was extremely depressing. It was never an easy sight to witness. They never got any easier to watch, and watching them also puts things into perspective for you. For one, that could have been you or someone you knew well in that casket, and that in itself is a horrible feeling. When you know that the box that rode by you contains a fellow American Soldier, the feeling inside is just terrible. Back in 2003 when I was in Iraq these ceremonies weren't done on Mosul Airfield where I was stationed, so the first one I ever saw took me a little off guard. Every time I think back on those days it still makes me sad and I'll never forget the brave sacrifices that those brave men and women made for their country. When the ceremony was complete and everyone would go back to work for the rest of the day things wouldn't be the same. There would be an underlying feeling of sorrow for the rest of the day. At times like this there would be only one thing left to do; go back to work. We would go back to doing what we were doing before, accomplishing our mission. Maybe having a mission to accomplish helped some cope with the scenario. Either way, days like this would always leave a lasting impact on everyone involved.

Throughout the deployment there were a few more occasions where I had to go back to Kabul and provide support. I became the designated Soldier to fill in for any one of the three of the Soldiers there when they would go on leave or pass. There was one time in particular that will stick out in my mind forever. I went down to there to replace Maria as she went on pass to Qatar for four days. For some reason, the Lieutenant who was in command of the detachment went on the convoy with us for this particular trip. When we got to Kabul, I was notified that the LT made a serious mistake; she forgot her plates for her vest. These plates would obviously protect someone from shrapnel, bullets, etc. Now, it isn't my fault that she forgot her plates, (I just wanted to make that clear) yet when they were getting ready to depart back to Bagram she asked me for my plates. She claimed that I wouldn't need them, since Kabul is such a safe place and never gets attacked. I really didn't want to give up my plates because after all, I would need them if something actually did happen. In the end, the LT ordered me to surrender my plates and there was nothing that I could do about it. Do you really think that it's ethical for an officer to order a subordinate to surrender their plates? Of course it isn't. Leaders in the Army are always supposed to put the needs of their subordinates above their own. If it was me, I never would have ordered a junior enlisted Soldier to hand their plates over to me. That's just common sense. This was a display of some of the worst leadership that I had ever seen; which was surprising considering some of the other Leaders in that unit were actually really good. But, as the old saying goes, "There's always a bad apple in every bunch."

I was infuriated with this turn of events, but not so much for the fact that I was no longer considered safe. It was more so from the fact that this was such a bad display of Leadership on the part of a Commander. I took her bad display of leadership very personally, even more personally than the fact that I had no protection without my plates. As a leader I would never do something like that to one of my Soldiers. I remember being so angry with this officer that I didn't even want to look at her. The feelings were unlike any feelings that I had ever felt before. This wasn't like the times at Fort Campbell when SGT Ramos embarrassed me in front of other Soldiers by throwing my reports on the floor—that was child's play compared to this. This was personal.

Knowing that I was now vulnerable, I can remember actually thinking to myself that it was a good thing that this place hadn't been attacked in a while. I figured that we could hold out without an attack for the few days that I would be there, but I turned out to be wrong. Of all the times for something to happen, this was the time. During the course of the week a massive riot broke out in Kabul that had stemmed from a recent hit and run auto accident. It was all over the news, a US Humvee accidently hit an afghan civilian one day. The locals obviously didn't take too kindly to this, and thus a riot ensued.

Things during these next few days became frightening out there. Afghan police cars were being tipped over and dismantled, there were shootings in the streets and people chanting in protest. Soon enough, things escalated and people started shooting at our camp. There were only a few rockets, but you could hear a lot of bullets as well. Usually you would hear the sound of a bullet bouncing off of something nearby; perhaps building walls. Base Operations immediately issued an order that everyone would have to wear their vest (which would include plates) and Kevlar helmet any time they were walking around the camp. I remember calling home over the course of the next few days and telling my dad what had happened, not just about the riots but also the situation concerning my plates. Upon hearing this, my dad got extremely pissed off. I thought about asking him to write a letter to congress but I ultimately decided that this was not the best course of action available. I didn't want to hurt the unit's integrity over the actions of one bad leader; and I knew that writing a letter to congress would bring some negative attention to the unit. I didn't want that. I remember my dad giving me one piece of advice: find a frying pan, cut it into pieces and use that as your plates. What a great idea . . . only one question remained: where the hell would I find a frying pan? There weren't any frying pans out there, so I just had to deal with this problem on my own.

The riots finally came to an end the day before I left Kabul but things out in the city were still shaky. It would take a while for the locals to come to terms with their tragedy, and rightfully so. When I got back to Bagram I informed some of the other Leaders in the unit about what had happened, about how I was ordered to surrender my plates. While everyone sympathized with me, they really weren't going to be able to do anything about it. While she wasn't as high in the rank structure as the Battalion Commander, she was still the Detachment Commander and thus no one was really going to be able to do anything about her bad choices. To my knowledge a few of the other NCOs went to her and told her she was wrong for what she did, but it didn't go anywhere past that. I guess I was glad about the fact that I wasn't the only one who saw her for the bad leader she was; most of the other NCOs saw it too. Therefore, I wasn't alone. My fellow NCOs had my back and that was good to know.

The sad lesson to be learned here is that in the Army you will encounter various types of leaders. There are great leaders, decent leaders, and outright bad leaders. I believe that there are plenty of leaders in the Army that do want to do the right thing, but for every one of them you have one that is the opposite, that puts their own needs first or prefers to "lead from the rear." I don't believe in that. I believe in "leading from the front." A great leader will never ask their Soldiers to do anything that they wouldn't do themselves. A great leader will also never put their own needs above the needs of others. Unfortunately there will always be an influx of bad leaders, and sadly enough that's just the way it is. What's even sadder is that some of these bad leaders believe deep down inside that they are actually "doing the right thing". That is the true underlying problem, not the existence of the bad leaders, but the existence of bad ideals. I know that I was raised to take care of others, to always stand up for the weak and to never give up. And the funny thing is, while I have had a number of leaders that were senior to me tell me that they didn't agree with my leadership style; I've never once had a junior Soldier tell me that they didn't look up to me. Whose word do you think matters more? Once again, it boils down to ideals. Some would favor what their boss tells them just so they could get ahead in their own careers. Some, like me just aren't built that way.

So much time had flown by on the deployment by now, and before I knew it my R and R leave came up. It was August 2006, I had been deployed to Afghanistan for over five months now and it was time for a vacation. Like every deployed Soldier, I needed to take a break. Being allowed to take leave halfway through the deployment was a blessing. From a procedural standpoint, things had greatly improved in the R and R leave program for deployed Soldiers and as a result every deployed Soldier was now allowed to take leave at some point during their deployment. I was extremely excited because I had been away for a while and I needed some time to let loose. I knew Saint Johnsville didn't have much to offer, but I didn't care. It was my town, and by god I missed my town.

I did so much during these two weeks of leave. I reunited with some old friends that I hadn't seen in a while and of course caught up with the ones that I had recently seen. I partied a few times with Joe, and we also ordered that years' WWE Summerslam event at his apartment. I really looked forward to seeing the event because it marked Hulk Hogan's return to the ring. Watching that event home on US Soil meant the world to me. Hulk Hogan's entrance music was still the famed favorite song, "I am a real American" and it was still one of my favorites too. And for those of you reading this who do not watch wrestling, I'll just go ahead and let you know now, yes Hogan did win that night.

I really wanted to cram as much as possible into this vacation so I decided to take my brother Jason and a few friends to a Korn concert in Darien Lake, NY. It was all day long event and we had a blast. I believe there were 11 bands on tour that played that day, making it an all day long festival in the summer heat. So what do you do when you're outside at a concert in the middle of summer? You drink! I remember they served Southern Comfort smoothies at the show. They were delicious and between me and my brother we put down a lot of them. Every time you bought one, they would give you a set of gold Southern Comfort beads. Since I was wearing a black hoodie, my huge collection of beads stuck out even more, so much so that people were calling me Mr. T (I was so drunk that I took this as a compliment). When the show was over, we passed out in the car as one of my sober friends drove us back to Saint Johnsville. It was one of the more memorable events of my time on leave and more importantly it was the first time that I went to a concert with my brother.

The Korn concert wasn't the only major event I attended. I also went down to Poughkeepsie, NY (where I was originally born) to see an ECW (Extreme Championship Wrestling) wrestling event with Joe Carter. Well, it was almost an ECW event. The WWE had recently brought the ECW name brand back after buying it out years ago. When the WWE re-launched the brand in 2006 they made sure to bring back all of the classic ECW wrestlers, even though it wasn't the "real" ECW. The show still had all of my favorite wrestlers from the past, and it was held in a small enough arena in Poughkeepsie to still have the same old gritty ECW feeling. It was a great time, and I even managed to give a "high five" to my favorite ECW wrestler, Rob Van Dam.

I also bought a lot of cool stuff while I was on leave. I earned a lot of money so far on the deployment so I figured why not, right? I firmly believe that if you don't occasionally reward yourself and enjoy the finer things in life then you aren't really living life to its fullest potential. There was no reason why I couldn't (or shouldn't for that matter) reward myself. I bought a paintball gun and went paintballing a few times while home. I used to play paintball in high school and I really missed doing it. It's a lot of fun and extremely competitive. I guess I didn't "need" the gun, but it made me feel good to buy it. I also bought a new digital camera. That was something I really did need. Throughout all of my years of traveling I had always used cheap disposable cameras. As a person who travels a lot, it was only logical that I own a nice camera. I hadn't really taken any pictures while in Afghanistan yet since I didn't own a camera. I wanted to make sure I took some pictures, it's not like it was a nice looking country or anything (it was a dump after all) but I just wanted to be able to take a few for my memories. Years later I would probably want to look at them, so it all made sense.

While the paintball gun and new camera were both very nice and expensive as well, neither one of them ended up being the most expensive thing that I bought during that vacation. No, there was still something that trumped both of those things combined. I was riding in my car with my dad one day, and we passed by a Jeep dealer. He mentioned how nice Jeeps are, and I agreed. I liked Jeeps a lot. Jeep is not only a durable, reliable car but it also has a long standing military heritage. The US Army used Jeeps years ago before it switched over to using Humvees. I'll always appreciate the Jeep for that fact alone. Also, Jeep is an American car and I only buy American cars. Nothing against foreign cars, I just believe in buying American. That's my prerogative, and everyone is entitled to his or her own, right? As we rode by the Jeep lot, Dad jokingly said that I should consider buying one. By now, I knew I didn't have enough money saved up anymore, but I had a feeling that I could get credit approved for one through financing, maybe with a down payment. I knew I had good credit, so I decided to pull into the lot just to see what happened.

At first I test drove a Maroon 2006 Jeep Grand Cherokee. I really liked the truck, but I didn't like the color. The only reason that I test drove one of that color was because it was an automatic transmission and

I can't drive a manual; almost all of the other trucks there were Manual transmission. Even though I didn't like the color I was really considering getting it because a Jeep Grand Cherokee had always been my dream car. Yes, you read that correctly. A lot of kids growing up through high school fantasize about owning Corvettes or Ferraris, but for some reason my dream car had always been a Jeep Cherokee. I think that also boils down to the military heritage that the Jeep has. Sure, you could like, or even love a Corvette. They're great cars and would obviously outdo a Jeep any day of the week; however, there is a certain respect factor that comes with a Jeep. They just look tough, and that's what I've always wanted in a car.

So we headed up to the showroom to work out the financing paperwork on the maroon 2006 Jeep, and I was startled to see that there was another Jeep Cherokee in the showroom that was also an automatic for half the list price of the one that I just test drove. I asked the salesman why the price was so much lower, and he explained to me that it was actually a 2005. He explained that due to the rising gas prices, they were having trouble selling the 2006 models and the 2007 models were scheduled to start rolling onto the lot shortly. Therefore, they had to get the 2005 off of the lot as soon as possible. I told them to never mind the maroon Jeep (which I didn't like the color too much anyway), I'll just take this one. The salesman looked at me and said, "Are you sure?" I looked over at the man like he was an idiot and said to him, "Yeah I'm sure, you just told me it's the same Jeep, only a year older for half the price. Yes, I'm sure." In addition to the amazing price, there was something else that attracted me to this particular Jeep: the color. It was silver with black trim which matched my Cavalier. During the time that I owned the Cavalier the color silver had grown to be my new favorite color for a car and I absolutely loved how the Jeep and Cavalier color schemes matched. When I saw the Jeep, the color scheme was all I needed to see to know that it was my fate to buy it.

After the paperwork was done (which took hours) I drove my new Jeep home while my Dad drove the Cavalier home. I still loved the Cavalier and I had no intention of getting rid of it. For now, I took pride in the idea that I owned two cars. Sure, I didn't really need two cars but it sure as hell felt good to own them. I could drive the Jeep in the winter during snowstorms and the Cavalier in the summer since it was a convertible and great on gas. When I got home, my brother Jason couldn't believe it. He thought it was a joke until he got into it and I took him for a ride. For a second I think that he thought that I was going to give him the Cavalier, but that just wasn't the case. The funny thing was that this all took place four days before my leave ended, so I didn't really have enough time to enjoy it before I had to fly back to Afghanistan. I told myself that my new Jeep could be my motivation for coming home in one piece. If I didn't come home, I wouldn't be able to enjoy my new Jeep again so I had better do my best to be careful! I'll never forget that day; the day that I bought a Jeep Grand Cherokee on a whim without any real thought.

Knowing that my vacation was almost over, I decided to slow down a bit and just take the rest of my days to relax and breathe. I really tried to squeeze in as much as possible on leave; between the Korn concert, the parties, the ECW Wrestling show and buying my new Jeep I definitely had my fair share of good times. I guess I could see how my leave flew by so quick, it wasn't like I sat around and did nothing while home. I knew that I had to get back on a plane and head back over. There was a lot of work for me to do out there, and I had to get back to it. To be honest, I was used to this routine by now anyway. When a Soldier is faced with multiple deployments they are forced into the fast paced tempo of flying overseas to work long days for six months straight, fly back to the US for two weeks of leave only to fly back overseas for another six months of long, hard days. That's just how it goes, it is the very "nature of the beast" and as a Soldier you just roll with the punches.

I flew out of Albany to Atlanta, GA to await my flight back to Afghanistan. There were various other Soldiers in the airport waiting at the USO area for their flight. When we were formed up by the liaison NCO to walk to our departure gate, we were surprised with the warmest farewell that I had ever seen. Literally hundreds of people who were in the airport stood up and gave us a huge round of applause. Everyone was clapping and cheering, and I even heard a few "USA! USA!" chants break out. It was such a patriotic display, and it made me a bit emotional. How could it not? A farewell like that is more than enough to remind you that the cause still meant something; that we were appreciated. It was also more than enough to get me ready to go back to work. I can't fully put that feeling into words, but it felt good.

I felt like it took forever to get back to Afghanistan. Between the long flight and a layover in Kuwait that lasted a few days it seemed like an eternity. It didn't really take that long to fall back into my routine at Bagram. When I got back, everyone told me that they missed me, and it made me realize that the Soldiers in the NJ Guard actually liked me. It felt good to know that I was actually appreciated, especially considering my conduct at the beginning of the deployment. I was nice to know that I had some friends out there. The only thing that I really had to worry about now was finishing out the second half of the deployment. I was amazed at how quick the first half went by, and I knew that as long as I could fall back into my old routine the days would start to fly by quicker. What I didn't know was that fairly soon I would be forced to change my routine, and so would most of the other Soldiers in the unit.

The unit leadership wanted to change things up a little, meaning they wanted to shuffle everyone around to different sections in an effort to "cross-train" everyone. I wasn't exactly happy about this because I was doing so well in the evaluations section by maintaining the 0% error rate for six months straight . . . deep down what I really wanted was the bragging rights of knowing that I maintained that error-free performance for the entire year. Unfortunately it just wasn't meant to be, and all of us assigned to the Evaluations section were shuffled around. I was placed in the Casualty Operations/ID Card Section, and Wade was put at the airport terminal to run flight manifests. Everyone kept telling me to stay positive because on a professional level learning how to work a new section is a great thing, but to me that didn't matter. All I really wanted was the 12 month long error free deployment. That had never been achieved before, and I verified this fact by pulling old statistics from the Department of the Army website. I could have become the first one to ever do this. Reluctantly I fell into swing into my new section and reverted from teaching people things to being taught myself.

It was during this time that I also came down on orders from the Department of the Army to attend Recruiting School after the deployment. I was given a report date of April 2007. This idea actually excited me for a number of reasons. One being that since I hadn't been stationed at Fort Drum for very long it offered me an opportunity to leave Fort Drum before getting "stuck" or "fenced in" as one would call it. Fort Drum had a reputation of keeping people for way too long and it is viewed at one of those places in the Army that is nearly impossible to leave. There was actually a Sergeant First Class from the 10th SSB years ago that ended up serving 17 years at Fort Drum and retiring there. While I am still not sure if he was 100% happy with that or not, I knew damn well that I didn't want to be one of those Soldiers that got stuck on Fort Drum for that long. If I took the orders for recruiting school my time on Fort Drum would be just under a year and a half (if you factored in the 12 month deployment to Afghanistan) and would be considered one of the shortest tours on Drum. That kind of opportunity was just too hard to resist.

Another positive aspect of going to recruiting school was the fact that in most cases you are allowed to request where you want to go upon graduating school. There are the rare occasions that the Army does have to force you to go somewhere based on the "needs of the Army" but in most cases they try their best to send you where you want to go. In most cases Soldiers will request to go somewhere close to home. Seeing how recruiting duty requires you to do a lot of marketing and selling of the Army, you would need to be a "people person." What better way to do that than to be stationed close to home, where you already know people? It just makes perfect sense. In addition, recruiting is very hard and can often result in long, miserable work days so having the freedom to live where you want while you do recruiting can make the days a little easier. You may not be happy during the work day, but there's no reason why you shouldn't be happy during your off-time.

Recruiting was a great chance to benefit and further my career, but as far as I was concerned, I really didn't want to go be a recruiter close to home for so many reasons. For one, I knew that I was from a very small town and that there weren't many people from there that actually joined the Army. Being a recruiter there would be very hard because from a young age most parents in upstate NY drill the idea of going to college into their children's heads. For most kids it isn't even an option, it is just assumed that you will go to college after high school. As a result, joining the Army is rare in that kind of an area, especially if you were to compare it to the south. Therefore I probably wouldn't have been a very good recruiter had I worked in upstate NY, and believe me being a bad recruiter is no way to benefit your career! Up until I served with the NJ Guard in Afghanistan most of the Soldiers that I met in my career were from the southern states and it was seldom that I would come across a fellow northerner.

So once I decided that recruiting in upstate NY wasn't an option, I had to figure out exactly where I wanted to go. The point came where all signs started to point to the idea of being a recruiter in New Jersey. For one, I had made a lot of friends on this deployment and I wasn't exactly interested in the idea of saying goodbye. I've always been a person who put a legitimate effort into getting to know people and I didn't want my efforts to go in vain. In addition, I was very thankful for the fact that I was able to "revive" my old friendship with Kathy and I also didn't want to throw that away either. Overall, going to NJ was a chance to get away from NY for a while but still go somewhere where I knew people that I could hang out with. It's also close enough to NY that if I did have to go home in the event of an emergency I could do that at the drop of a hat with no problem. When I told everyone that I was going to go to New Jersey to recruit they thought it was a great idea, but I don't think that everyone believed me at first. Either way, everyone in the unit thought it was cool that I actually willing to do that. I guess if there needed to be some sort of indication that I was part of this team this would definitely be it. I knew that my actions earlier in the tour were forgiven and forgotten by now because if they weren't I don't think that everyone would have been cool about the prospect of me moving there. Needless to say, it felt good to know that I was welcome.

Another thing that made me feel extremely welcome in that unit was being invited to be a part of COL Alvarado's cigar night. He knew I was a cigar smoker so he invited me to come out on Friday nights and enjoy a cigar with him and the rest of the cigar smokers. There weren't many of them in the unit, but there were enough smokers to make things interesting. Obviously the Sergeant Major was out there, but there were also a few senior NCOs that were part of it. Even Chief Payne joined in on cigar night when he eventually made his way to Bagram. Cigar night turned into a regular thing and to tell you the truth it was a great concept. It was an opportunity for military men to get together and air their grievances and just "mellow out" in a way. Sure, COL Alvarado was the Battalion Commander, and we all knew that, but the act of him hosting a cigar night was a sign that he not only respected us as Soldiers but he also respected us as men; as comrades on the battlefield. As time went by, those of us who enjoyed COL Alvarado's cigar night built up camaraderie together. It became an unspoken rule that Friday nights were reserved for cigar night; so much so that when I ended up moving to night shift later on in the deployment that Chief Payne would stick around late to enjoy a cigar with me. I appreciated that. My personal love for cigars also deepened as the deployment went by. I got to the point where I was ordering specific brands and varieties from internet websites. I developed a taste for one cigar in particular; Oliveros Long Lady Cognac cigars. They were the perfect smoke, the tobacco leaves were steamed in cognac prior to being rolled. The taste was simply amazing. Also due to their size they only took about 20 minutes to smoke as opposed to a larger cigar that may have taken 35 to 40 minutes. Sure, I enjoy a good long smoke but when you are in the middle of a work day you don't always have 40 minutes to spare. The Oliveros cigars perfectly accommodated the idea of having a cigar in the middle of a work day. Other people liked them too. I would regularly order boxes of them and pass them out to everyone; the Soldiers, the Officers, it didn't matter. COL Alvarado enjoyed them, the Soldiers enjoyed them, I even let Kathy try one and she liked them too. It was unanimous! They were the best cigars available and I'm glad that I not only discovered them but also that everyone around me enjoyed them.

As a Battalion Commander I had the upmost respect for COL Alvarado. For one, he always supported me and was quick to tell me what a good job he thought I was doing. I appreciated that, considering he knew about my conduct when I first showed up. He knew how I came in with a chip on my shoulder in the beginning, and he also knew that I had cleaned up my act and changed. So I guess when I look back on things he respected the fact that I was able to make a change in my own life. Often he would remind me that I was a part of "his unit" and not "that other unit" (referring to the 10th SSB). He would remind me that the SSB didn't really take care of us when we got there and instead just pawned us off on the 50th PSB. He was right; that actually did happen. Sometimes when I would be at the front desk at the gym signing in, he would be standing behind me. He would see that under the "unit" column I wrote "10th SSB". Right then he would stop me and ask, "Hey SGT Conklin, don't you mean 50th PSB?" At first I didn't know how to take that, but eventually I understood. He wanted to make sure I knew where I stood, that I was part of the unit and part of the 50th family. Sooner or later, I was writing "50th" in the unit column.

COL Alvarado also vowed to me that if there was ever any time that I needed help, he would "go to bat" for me. He would often tell me that if I ever needed a letter of recommendation for anything that I could always go to him for help and he would be there. I appreciated this; let's be honest here for just a second, he was a Lieutenant Colonel at the time, and I was a Sergeant. In all honesty he owed me absolutely nothing. In offering me his help he showed to me that he was gracious, which is a quality that isn't found in every officer or Commander that you come across in the army. That is a clear fact. Sometimes officers don't even want to have anything to do with the professional development of an enlisted Soldier. They just leave it to the NCOs to handle that. While it is true that senior NCOs are supposed to play a key role in the development of junior NCOs, I can tell you that it never hurts to have a LTC in your corner. Even I, with my arrogant attitude in the beginning, knew exactly where I stood in relation to a Battalion Commander. It's just that simple.

There was one other thing that COL Alvarado consistently mentioned to me when I was deployed, that being the possibility of me crossing from the Active Component to the National Guard. He almost always asked me if I would ever consider switching over. Every time he assured me that he would love to have me on the team. To tell you the truth, I found this to be the most flattering thing ever, however at the time my loyalties were with the Active Army and I just couldn't see myself in the Guard, but I did assure him that when I moved down to NJ as a recruiter that I would drop in frequently to see him and the rest of the unit. Today I find it funny that I once had such a high degree of caution towards the National Guard and I can tell you that I also find it amazing how much things can change with time.

After a few weeks of working in the Casualty Operations section I received word that I was going to start going on missions to some of the other camps in the country for ID card missions. The primary purpose of these missions was to go around from camp to camp and either issue new ID cards to certain Soldiers or to update the PIN numbers for Soldiers to sign into computers with their cards. At the time the Army was moving towards a more "electronic, paper free, password free" way doing things, and being forced to reset a bunch of ID card pin numbers fell right in line with that. Honestly I found the whole thing to be utterly pointless but at the same time I did welcome the chance to leave Bagram for a few days. Things on Bagram were ok, but I liked the idea of traveling and seeing more of the country. What I also found funny was the name of the mission. It was probably the dumbest name for a mission that I had ever heard, and I'm almost reluctant to reveal it, but in the interest of full disclosure, the name of the mission was "Operation Mountain Reset." I know that you're probably reading this and thinking it is a dumb name as well. Don't worry, I agree with you 100%! The name was almost as redundant as the job itself, but I rolled with the punches anyway. As I stated earlier, it was an opportunity to leave Bagram for a little while so ultimately I was happy with the idea.

When I got to each FOB and got to work I found things to be extremely mundane. The task of resetting a PIN number on an ID card takes maybe five minutes, and that's if the system is running slow. I don't want to sound like an asshole by saying this, but I found the work to be below my level of intelligence. The lesson that I learned on these missions wasn't really about the PIN resets, but rather it was about putting things back into perspective for me. I probably traveled to a minimum of six different camps to perform these resets, and on each one the living conditions were far worse than Bagram. Sometimes I would be on a camp that didn't have a decent PX and food court and didn't even have a working DFAC. The Soldiers there would have to eat MREs all the time, and so did I while I was there. Other times I would be on a camp without working phones and slow internet, so communicating with home was harder which severely affects Soldiers' morale. Sometimes I would find myself on a camp that sustained many rocket attacks over a short period of time. That itself reminded me of Iraq back in 2003. By going on all of these missions I was reminded of how easy we had it on Bagram, how easy Maria had it in Kabul, and how easy the Tennessee Guard had it on Kandahar. Life was outright harder on these camps. The Soldiers at these camps made so many sacrifices for their country. By going out into these places I seemed to find a new sense of self; a part of me that went away when I returned from my first deployment. I understood their sacrifices. Many of them would come up to me in the ID card line and tell me that it was their first deployment. They would see my 101st Airborne Division combat patch on my right arm and they would ask me about my experiences. Some of them were clearly straight out of high school, 18 or 19 years old. I tried my best to offer words of advice, and even though I was just 23 years old I felt like an old man talking to them. Finally when I returned to Bagram I felt like a new man, ready to take on any challenge. Unfortunately none of that mattered, because I was about to face one of the hardests moment of my life.

On this particular day I returned to Bagram after being gone on a mission for a ten day stretch. The mission itself was business as usual, and we did have internet and phones at this particular camp. What was odd to me was that every single time I called home I couldn't reach my dad, and he didn't return any of the emails that I sent him while I was out there. That really didn't make any sense to me; it just wasn't normal for my dad to NOT return emails for a period of ten days. For our family, that is a long time. We are a close family and we wouldn't normally go ten days without being in touch. Needless to say, I was a little concerned that I couldn't reach my dad while I was on the mission. In fact, while on this particular mission I witnessed a few extraordinary things that I wanted to fill him in on, so when I got back I made it my personal mission to get ahold of him. I called the house multiple times a day, and after two days of being back on Bagram I finally got ahold of him.

When I finally spoke to my Dad on the phone, I learned that he wasn't in good shape at all. In fact, he had just spent ten days in the hospital. He sounded very weak on the phone, and he told me what had happened to him. His intestines burst inside of him, and caused him the highest degree of pain that he had felt in his entire life. The burst caused various chemicals to run through his system, and he almost lost his life. The pain was so crippling that he couldn't move, he couldn't crawl to a phone or do anything. His saving grace was the fact that my sister Jen happened to be home. If she wasn't home, my dad would have died alone right there in the house. I can't even begin to explain just how scary the idea of losing my dad is to me. It is something that I never want to go through, and just hearing that it almost happened made me cringe.

I was a little upset about the fact that no one informed me when this all happened, that dad waited until after he returned from the hospital to inform me of the situation. Dad explained to me that he wanted it to be kept a secret because he didn't want me to worry. He knew I was in a dangerous situation in Afghanistan and he didn't want my mind to be occupied with thoughts of his emergency. What he didn't realize was that his emergency could warrant an excuse for me to go home on emergency leave, to help him out. At this point I realized that I needed to be home, I couldn't handle being out there anymore. Even more importantly, my help was actually needed. You see, when I left home a two months ago I could tell that there were some issues with my dad's marriage. Simply put, I didn't trust my dad's current wife. The problems and trust issues were so serious when I last left home that I now felt that she would neglect his care, or even worse attempt to kill him. Normally my dad was a big, tough man that didn't need protecting, but in his weakened state he might not have been able to defend himself. He was attached to an Ostemy bag and couldn't even get out of bed or even climb stairs. A bed was installed in the living room for him to sleep in, and a nurse had to come to the house two days a week to check on him. That just wasn't good enough for me, my dad deserved better. I needed to go home on emergency leave to not only help take care of him, but also to make sure no foul play occurred on the part of his wife.

The only way to guarantee a trip home for this emergency was to get my family to file a Red Cross message. Typically when a Soldier's family has an emergency they will file a Red Cross Message and that will be more than enough to warrant the Soldier a trip home. The only problem for me was that since I had always viewed my Dad as immortal, I never briefed him on the procedures of how to bring me home in case he had an emergency. I admit that I should have planned for this type of situation a lot better. This time around, he was in no shape to file a Red Cross message, so I had to walk my brother Jason through the steps on how to do it. He was a little reluctant at first, until I explained to him that this was absolutely the only way that I could come home. I don't know why he was shying away from the paperwork involved at first, but that didn't matter. I gave him the required phone numbers, and told him exactly what he needed to say to the people when he called. Before I knew it, word came down at the unit that I had an official Red Cross message and I would be permitted to go home. A flight was booked and I was well on my way. In order to make the flight quicker, I was booked through civilian channels as opposed to military, which would ultimately take me on an entirely different route than a normal R and R flight. I found this funny in a way because it was a way of admitting that the military wasn't as efficient as civilian channels when it came to flying Soldiers across the world. Eventually I was flown to Qatar to receive my official flight itinerary. I was set to fly from Qatar to London, and then from London to the US.

The flight to London went off without a hitch. When I got there I realized I had an eight hour layover ahead of me. This wasn't really any different than my other extended layovers in Seattle and Japan that I had experienced earlier in my career (aside from the fact that my dad's emergency was on my mind). Since I was stuck there, I decided to treat this layover like any other one. I had a few hours to kill, so why not make the most of it? I went to an actual English pub in the airport and had a real English breakfast: Eggs, fried green tomatoes, and a Newcastle Brown Ale. I found it funny that the English that everyone around me spoke sounded nothing like American English. Everyone, to include the bartender spoke with a different dialect and an accent. I guess I should have expected that. After all, I was no stranger to visiting foreign countries.

When I finally got home I saw for my own eyes just how bad shape my dad was in. Everything that I was told over the phone was true; he could hardly walk, let alone climb stairs and he was confined to the living room. I also noticed that he lost a significant amount of weight from the surgery, which was scary. He didn't look healthy anymore. Seeing him like this was one of the saddest moments of my life. Once I saw him I couldn't imagine being anywhere else during this tough time. Over the next few weeks I did everything that I could to make things easier for him. I did work around the house. I bought groceries, helped take care of the kids; basically anything that I could do while I was there. I realized that coming home just after the surgery was probably a better idea then coming home while he was in the hospital. Sure, I wanted to be able to be at the hospital with him, but realizing the fact that the Army was only going to allow me to take two weeks of leave made me see that I was more effective in this capacity. There wouldn't have been much to do at the house while he was in the hospital for obvious reasons. I was glad that I was able to do what I could do when I was home. The only thing was that two weeks just didn't seem like enough time. Dad wasn't recovering very quickly and there was still a lot to be done. This prompted me to contact the unit from home and request to have my leave extended. Thankfully the unit had no problem extending my leave for a week to continue to help out at home. The unit leadership didn't have to do that either; they could have turned down my request and ordered me to return. I would have had no choice and I would have felt bad about leaving home while my dad was in such bad shape. That's one thing that I can always say about the 50th PSB: they were always flexible and willing to work with me. You don't see a lot of units like that in the Army and it was just another testament to why I was starting to believe in my own mind that maybe the National Guard was a much friendlier place to work than the active component.

Not everything that took place on emergency leave was sad. I worked as hard as I could to help out, which was a positive. There was also a day where some flowers were delivered to the house for my dad. They came from Maria, who was obviously still in Afghanistan. This really made me feel good, and showed to me that she was a true friend. She didn't have to do that, especially considering that she's never even met my dad. I seriously couldn't believe it and I made sure to send her a thank you email from home. I'll never forget that.

I didn't really do much partying while I was on emergency leave, which was obvious because I went home with a purpose during an emergency. I wasn't there to have a good time. Still, there was one night that I just couldn't resist. Jason and Jen were home anyway, so I knew if anything did happen they could just call me on my cell phone. So with that said, the local bar Central Hotel used to throw an annual Halloween party the weekend of (or before depending on the year) Halloween. Half of my friends were going to the party, so I really wanted to go also. I didn't see anything wrong with taking just one night to let loose. So while the idea of going to the party itself wasn't a question at all, there was just one question that did remain: what or who would I dress up as for the Halloween party?

I decided that there was only one option. I had to go dressed as the Hulkster. There was no debate; I was going to dress up as Hulk Hogan for the Halloween party. As you read earlier in this book, this wasn't the first time in my life that I had dressed up as Hulk Hogan, which made it convenient because I still had the entire costume: the "Hulkamania" T-shirt, the yellow bandana and the old 1980's WWF Heavyweight belt. The only thing I needed was a fake blonde moustache and I would be good to go. When I told a few of my friends that I was going as Hogan they thought it was funny, but not nearly as funny as when they actually saw it.

I walked into that bar in character, meaning that I wasn't "Ken," I was "Hulk Hogan" on that night. I did the Hulk Hogan bow and arrow pose when I came in, I started talking trash like only Hulk Hogan can, shouting to the bar, "Let me tell ya somethin' brother!" It was hilarious. Everyone there thought it was great, and there was even a live band there called the Karg Brothers who kept making Hulkamania references on the microphone in between sets. That showed me that I really did have the best costume in the bar. And isn't that what's important, the fact that I can dress up like Hulk Hogan better than someone else can dress up as a vampire? I would say so. I got extremely drunk that night and had a blast. The only setback was that every time I would take a drink my moustache would fall off, so I had to keep re-gluing a fake blonde mustache to my face all night long. Other than that it was a great time and it proved to be a great way to wrap up those few weeks at home. My flight was scheduled for the next morning. I knew I had no choice and I had to go back. My dad was doing considerably better (even though he wasn't 100% yet) so I could go back to Afghanistan confident that he was going to make it; that he was going to keep improving. I'm just glad that I was able to make an impact and be there for him during one of his darkest hours. All of these thoughts flowed through my slightly hung over mind as I boarded the plane to head back overseas.

My flight took me through the exact route that I flew through a few weeks ago. I passed through England and then eventually landed in Qatar. When I got there to the Air Base I was told that I had a layover ahead of me and would probably be there for a few days, maybe even a week. I actually liked Qatar based on my past experiences there so I really didn't mind, especially because I was on the Air Force Base, as opposed to the Army post where the R and R trips take place. This was a blessing in disguise because I was in the Army, not the Air Force and because of this the Air Force personnel who were in charge of the base there didn't actually care what I did with my time. Now compare that to being on the Army post, where someone would have taken accountability of me and I wouldn't be allowed to leave post at all, and probably be restricted to drinking three beers a night (since those were the rules). On the Air Force base I had zero restrictions, as long as I didn't get arrested.

The only question that remained now was what would I do with my few days in Qatar? I knew there was a small contingent of Soldiers from the 50th PSB who were working in Qatar so I decided to get together with them and see if they wanted to go out on the town and do some partying. There was an NCO there by the name of SSG Tuck who I was already cool with so it wasn't going to be a problem. Also, Chief Broadbent just happened to be there that week for an inspection which was also great. They had access to an SUV so there was literally nothing that could stop us from going out and having a good time.

The laws in Qatar regarding alcohol are nothing like the laws in the US. Alcohol isn't served everywhere in the country and is considered outlawed in many places, but not everywhere. You can't get served alcohol in a normal restaurant but if you decide to eat dinner at a hotel bar you can get served every night. So for those of you reading this that may have a trip to Qatar lined up in the near future, be sure to hit up the hotel bars. They will take care of you. I think the reason that it is legal there is they probably assume that since it is a hotel bar that you also already have a room there. In theory you could drink as much as you want there and then head up to your room to sleep it all off. I guess it makes sense. Of course, the bar has no way of verifying if you have a room or not. And if they ask you, just tell them that you're going to get a room after your dinner. The restaurant there wasn't some cheap fly-by-night continental breakfast style place that you would see at a Holiday Inn in the middle of Watertown, NY either. No, it was a five star restaurant. This place was amazing. There were crystal chandeliers everywhere which really added an element of class to the place. Once you ordered your dinner they would wheel out a cart and cook some of it in front of you. This was especially good if you ordered a flambeau because everyone at the table would be treated to a fiery show. It was amazing, and slightly reminded me of my time in Korea when we would be able to cook our own food at some places.

As I stated earlier, alcohol was served there and there was no limit to what you could order. This actually became funny in a way because after we ordered a few drinks our food still hadn't come out yet. We had no clue of this at the time, but apparently the idea is that they won't actually bring your food to you for a long time while you are drinking, because they know that you are spending a lot of money on the booze. That makes sense when you really think about it; why not try to make as much money off of a table full of people as possible? I kept on ordering drinks, knowing that this was going to be the last time that I would be able to drink for a few months. I think the rest of the table started to notice because at some point Chief Broadbent just ordered a bottle of wine for us all to drink. There's a good chance that was a tactic to get me to stop ordering so our food can come out. I really can't remember how the night ended, but I do know that our food eventually did come and I ended up crashing in a bunk in the R and R tent on the Army post for the night. They didn't want to take me back to the Air Force base that night because it was late and they would have to explain at the gate why four Army personnel were coming in that late. That makes sense to me now, but I remember being confused when I woke up the next morning. I had no idea where the hell I was and could barely remember even leaving the hotel bar the night before. Some people may look at this as taking things too far, but as far as we were concerned you only live once right? When else are we going to have the opportunity to do something like that? The chance to party in the middle of Doha, Qatar may never come again so why not have the best time that you possibly could? I will say this much though: when I checked my bank account the next morning I found that last night's "good time" cost me well over $200, including dinner. Good thing that I had a few more big deployment paychecks ahead of me to cover that! As I said before, you only live once.

After spending a week in Qatar I was able to make my way back to Bagram to finish out the tour. A lot of things changed in the few weeks that I was gone. For one, the unit leadership decided that I was no longer going to be going on the ID Card missions and instead I would be staying there at Bagram to work the night shift in the Casualty Operations section as the NCO in charge of the section (NCOIC). I remember being told that doing this would be good for my evaluation report because it was a leadership position but at this point I didn't really care about any of that. I just wanted the deployment to end already. There were just a few months left and I was just ready to go. At first I thought that working the night shift would make my days drag by because all of my friends were working on day shift. I'm a firm believer in the idea of "time flies when you're having fun." How the hell could I have any fun for the remaining few months of the deployment if all of my friends were on day shift? It didn't seem feasible but at the same time I had no choice in the matter.

I also found out some news when I got back to Afghanistan that Kathy and her husband Mike were going to be moved to Kuwait to fulfill a mission for the remainder of the deployment. That really didn't sit well with me at all; over the course of the deployment I had greatly appreciated the fact that I was able to re-unite with the best friend that I ever had in the military, not to mention I made friends with Mike as well. So now I'm sitting here faced with the idea that I'm not only being moved to a shitty shift but also two of my friends are being moved out of the country too. It was almost like things were falling apart for me day by day. I promised that I would stay in touch with her and I would obviously see her again when I became a recruiter in New Jersey. I was not about to let this sudden departure create the same set of circumstances that happened back in 2002 at the end of AIT. Back then the decision to stay in touch or not was in my hands and I made the wrong decision. Almost five years later in late 2006 the decision was still mine, only this time I wasn't going to make the wrong choice. We were going to stay in touch, plain and simple.

The job of working in Casualty Operations isn't an easy one. The responsibilities of the job are immense and require a certain level of secrecy. In the interest of not releasing any classified information, I will not reveal many details here. Those of you reading this that served on that deployment alongside me know exactly what I am talking about. With that said, I will say this much: working that section in the final few months of the deployment got depressing after a while. There are some nights that would go by quickly and some that would just drag on by. Even worse there were sometimes incidents that would happen that would make us a bit emotional, even though we weren't directly involved in the incidents per se. I've heard some people say that working in that section "builds character." What I will say is that unless you've worked there you cannot fully grasp just how hard it can be, and I promise you that I never want to work in that section again. I also understand that like any job, somebody had to do it and at the time that somebody was me. That is all that I will say on that particular subject.

When Christmas 2006 came along I pretty much treated it like any other day. I knew the deployment would be coming to an end shortly so I tried my best not to let the idea of being away from home for Christmas bother me. Like any other holiday that I was away from home I made sure to call home and talk to the family, but other than that the day was nothing special. In fact, I had to work in the CASOPS section that day with Chief Payne of all people. COL Alvarado and the rest of the command team came through the office and presented us with coins for making the sacrifice of working on Christmas day (which was fine) but there was only one thing that I actually wanted to do on that Christmas. All I wanted was to be able to enjoy a cigar outside in the snow. That would be enough to put me at peace with the fact that I wasn't home in upstate NY because growing up there provided me with many white Christmases over the years. A white Christmas would have been great. Sure enough, that is exactly what I got. Just before the end of my shift it started snowing and we went outside to enjoy that Christmas day cigar. About six inches of snow ended up coming down, which was more than enough for me. As I stood outside and looked off into the mountains that surrounded Bagram Airfield I felt an inner peace that I hadn't felt in a long time, almost like a feeling inside that everything was going to be ok. I suddenly had a carefree feeling that nothing that would happen for the rest of the deployment even mattered any more. This deployment was going to end soon enough, and in fact I would soon find out that it was going to end sooner than I ever realized.

After a year of ups and downs 2006 came to its end and 2007 came roaring in. I knew deep down that 2007 was probably going to be a crazier year than 2006, simply because of the fact that every year that I had been in the Army so far had brought me some sort of adventure. Therefore it stood to reason that 2007 had a lot in store for me. I knew that the deployment was going to soon come to an end and on top of that I was going to go to recruiting school and start a new life as a recruiter in NJ. That subject in itself would soon lead to a change in my redeployment date back to the US. I had talked about the subject with Chief Broadbent and a few others, and it just seemed that since I had a class start date of April 2007 it made absolutely no sense to leave Afghanistan in March. That would leave me only a month to take leave, pack my gear and get all of my personal affairs in order; not to mention the fact that I had to attend the required 2 week Warrior Leaders Course (WLC) that Sergeants have to attend. There was just no way that I could make all of that happen in 30 days, so a request was put in to release me from Afghanistan and send me back to the US as soon as possible. Everyone in the 50th PSB was going to miss me and was very sad to see me go, but I had no choice. In order for me to reach my personal and professional goals I had to get back to the US sooner, that's just all there was to it.

I was actually ok with the fact that I was going to leave early. I was so burnt out from the deployment. It was a long year and I feel that I had not only accomplished a lot but I had also endured a lot. It got to the point that every single day that I woke up in Afghanistan felt like a long one. Deep down inside I felt so much older than my age. I was 23 years old but my experiences made me feel like I was 50. I knew I needed some "me time" and I wasn't going to get that in Afghanistan. It took a few weeks to get the approval paperwork signed for me to leave early but it eventually came back with a flight date of January 31, 2007. That would effectively make the deployment an 11 month deployment instead of a 12 month one. Honestly there isn't much of a difference and I viewed it as a trade-off for the 13 month tour I served in Korea. When asked today how long I was in Korea I usually don't say 13 months, I just round it off and say I was there a year. The same thing goes for Afghanistan. I don't say I was there 11 months, I just round it off. The date of January 31st was also the date that I was officially going to fly back to the US, which meant that I would have to fly back to Manas air base a day or so earlier than that just to make sure I made the flight in time, which meant that my days on Bagram were truly numbered. Now that I knew what my official date was it felt like there was actually a light at the end of the tunnel; a solid day to look forward to where I could put behind all of my worries and stress and just get on with my life.

My last few days in Afghanistan were eventful. Everyone in the CASOPS section threw me a small farewell party (probably the best that could have been thrown given the circumstances of a deployment). They had one of the unit T-shirts from the deployment and everyone in the section took the time to sign it. I remember Chief Payne signed it saying, "Hope to see you wearing Warrant Officer Rank in a few years!" That really meant a lot to me. As I started getting ready to say my goodbyes to the entire unit I realized that I really bonded with most of the Soldiers there. Saying bye to some of them was hard, but I knew that I would see them again one day. I was ultimately happy that the deployment proved to be a good experience that will stand out in not only my mind, but also in my heart forever. I had so many ups and downs and above all else I grew as a person. I changed. That deployment helped me to mellow out and to give people more of a chance in life. It taught me not to judge people based on what they did for a living or what organization that they belong to, but instead to judge people based on what type of person they truly are. With that said I knew that I just spent 11 months deployed with a great group of people and it was a true honor. I sat on the plane out of Bagram knowing that I was about to put one chapter of my life behind me and that a new one was about to begin.

Eventually I arrived back to Fort Drum to a small ovation at the unit area. Some of the rear detachment Soldiers were there to welcome me. It was nice to enter the room to a round of applause and it was even better to enter the room to see my Dad and my sister Jen there. After that long deployment with many ups and downs I found it extremely refreshing to see my family. What I found funny was the fact that my Dad was over there telling the First Sergeant that there was asbestos on the ceiling and that it was wrong to make Soldiers work there. I remember thinking to myself, "good old Dad, not afraid to tell anyone what he thinks." I think the First Sergeant tried to blow him off at first because I heard my Dad re-iterate it to the man a few times. When my Dad needs to make a point he sure knows how to do it. It's a good thing that this confrontation didn't accelerate past words because I'm about 99% certain that my Dad would have beat that man's ass if it came down to it. This display showed me one thing: my Dad was back up to full strength again; or at least close to it. Not a bad way to start off my comeback to the US.

I was allowed to go home for a three day pass, which was fine but I didn't think it was enough time. After all, when I came back from my last deployment we were given a four day pass. Apparently it was 10th Mountain Division policy that redeploying Soldiers only received a three day weekend instead of a four day pass. I know that I've said this many times in my career in the past, but this was just one more indication that the 10th Mountain Division wasn't half as good as the 101st Airborne Division. There was just no comparison between the two divisions and this was just another sign of that. I would think that after a year-long deployment the least that I could have been given was a four day pass, but not this time. At least I knew that after the three days I would be able to knock out my reintegration requirements and then allowed to take leave. So I guess that part was good enough for me.

The three days went by quickly and I really can't remember much of what I did during that time, but I do remember one very important thing. I had taken the time to email a few of my friends that were still back in Afghanistan as a way to touch base with everyone. I was so glad to be home but that didn't change the fact that I made a lot of bonds with a lot of people on that deployment. The last thing I planned on doing was severing the ties that I had made. I sent emails to just about all of my friends there and waited to hear back from them. Upon receiving an email from Kathy, I learned that just after I left Bagram Airfield actually sustained a rocket attack. It was the first (and only) time that entire deployment that Bagram sustained an attack. The good news was that no one was hurt and everything was ok. I still found it to be absolutely shocking because that camp seemed so safe when we were there. The place was surrounded by mountains and the perimeter was heavily guarded by Soldiers. By virtue it just didn't seem like an attack would happen there, and after such a peaceful year I just couldn't picture an attack happening. Yet there I was at home reading her email describing the events of the attack, and I had just missed it.

CHAPTER 10

2007

Just like when I returned from my first deployment, I had to go through a re-integration process upon returning to Fort Drum. It was more or less the same old process as before; a few shots and various classes ranging from suicide prevention to DUI classes and spousal/family abuse classes. There were really no surprises here. This was all just the same protocols for any Soldier coming back from a deployment. And just like the last time I returned the process went by quickly. Before I knew it I had free time at the unit and I was being approached with the idea of going to the Warrior's Leader Course (WLC). I knew that it was necessary for me to attend the class before I departed for recruiting school but deep down I knew I wasn't ready yet. I needed a few weeks to catch my breath. Here I had just returned from a deployment and I hadn't even been afforded the opportunity to go home on leave. Taking a week of leave was part of my plan upon returning and I really didn't appreciate the fact that my Battalion was attempting to force me onto a different path. I understood at the time that ultimately the Army will make your decisions for you, but that didn't mean that I had to agree with it. Such is the case with most enlisted Soldiers and NCOs that serve in the Army. They rarely get to make their own choices, especially in matters like this.

The other reason that I wanted to put off going to WLC for a few weeks was that I knew that I was slightly overweight. Since I spent the last three months of the deployment working night shift in Casualty Operations I was unable to attend PT sessions and I couldn't get myself into the gym during the day because my sleep was messed up from all of my roommates coming in and out of my room and waking me up all the time. Naturally, I gained some weight during those months. It wasn't like

I gained a ton of weight however, it was just a few pounds and I knew that if I hit the gym hard for the next few weeks that I could drop the weight and be ready to go to WLC in no time. I assumed that if I pitched this idea to the unit leadership that I would have more ground than if I simply stated that I was burnt out and wanted to take leave. After all, no one could really care less about me taking leave but if I failed weight at WLC I could possibly be thrown out which would make the unit look very bad. Logically there was no way that the unit would want to look bad so I figured it was a no-brainer.

Unfortunately nothing that I could possibly express to the unit would matter to them. They were going to send me to WLC anyway, regardless of my concerns about gaining weight and not having the time to clear my head after a deployment. When I told the unit First Sergeant all of my concerns, his reply was that "as an NCO I should just suck it up and drive on." I really didn't like this response and to me it showed me what was really wrong with the Army. By telling any Soldier to "suck it up and drive on" you are effectively telling them that their problems don't really matter to you. That is just bad leadership. There is no way around it. The idea of "suck it up and drive on" can maybe be applied in a simple situation, such as having a minor cold or missing some sleep the night before PT. That type of scenario I would agree with, but forcing someone into a rigorous school and/or training program immediately upon coming back from a deployment is just outright wrong. It wasn't even like I was trying to skip WLC altogether either. I knew that I needed to go and to be honest I wanted to go really bad, just not right then. All I would have needed was two weeks but the First Sergeant was just too stubborn and wouldn't grant that to me.

The morning that I reported to WLC was probably one of the most tedious days that I ever served in the Army. I had to report to the school at 4 am (0400 hours in military time) with two huge bags of gear, a pair of night vision goggles, and my assigned weapon. Since I had to report at 4 am I obviously had to report to the unit arms room even earlier to sign out the pair of night vision goggles and my weapon. This kind of timeline makes your first day at WLC an extremely long and tiring day. The course itself was two weeks long at the time, and every day is a long day but from what I am told the first is the very longest day of them all. What else would you expect if you had to report in at 4 am?

The first thing that I had to do upon arriving there was get into a formation so the instructors could call attendance. This is a protocol in every single Army school or event so I understood that this would happen. Of course, it didn't happen without incident as there were a few Soldiers that were late which resulted in the instructors yelling and screaming at them for a few minutes. So far this was just like basic training all over again, except for the fact that I couldn't understand why the Soldiers were late in the first place. Every Soldier that attends WLC is required to report there with a "sponsor" from their unit who is responsible for their every action while in school. The sponsor more or less has to make himself available for anything that the student could possibly need for the two weeks that they are in WLC. In most cases the sponsor is appointed by the unit First Sergeant or Command Sergeant Major meaning that the sponsor is also answering to them. In other words, if that Soldier messes up due to fault of the sponsor the leadership will most likely come down hard on the sponsor. With that said, a Soldier couldn't possibly be late to WLC unless their sponsor made a mistake somewhere along the line. I didn't understand how someone could allow that to happen. Granted, I knew that I wasn't really ready to go to WLC because of my weight issue but I knew that above all else I needed to be on time. I had a good sponsor (which helped) but I knew deep down that I wasn't the type of NCO to arrive late for things. I never wanted to be the one who was getting yelled at in front of a formation full of Soldiers who were required to stand outside in the cold just because I was late. I didn't want to be "that guy". Apparently these late Soldiers didn't share that same sentiment because we didn't have to stay outside in the ten degree cold for longer than necessary just to watch these Soldiers get yelled at. Needless to say, I've never been a fan of the idea of mass punishment.

After the accountability formation we were all filed into the building for our next task: an in-depth inspection of our gear. Everyone was provided with a huge checklist of things that we were required to bring with us to WLC, even if we were certain that we wouldn't even need some of it while we were there. (Usually Soldiers only need about 30% of the things that they are required to bring. The rest is just an annoyance.) If the instructors find that you are missing a particular piece of equipment during this inspection it is documented and your sponsor is required to bring the item to you within 48 hours. If your sponsor fails to bring you the items within the given time then you will be kicked out of WLC, which will ultimately make you and your sponsor look bad. The thing is it doesn't matter how your sponsor obtains your missing gear, as long as they get it back to you in that time frame. They could do any number of things; loan you their gear, borrow someone else's gear, search your barracks room for the missing gear, buy you the gear out of their own pocket, even steal the gear if they have to. As long as your sponsor gets the missing gear to you everything will play out fine. The situation almost creates a bigger sense of urgency then attending the school itself in most cases. Since I had just returned from a deployment I didn't even have half of my gear so I had to borrow some of it from one of my friends at the unit by the name of Rios. Rios was the motor Sergeant from the unit and a good friend as well. I appreciated the fact that he loaned me his stuff. It put him in a tough position but at the same time he understood that I had just returned from the deployment so it wasn't an issue. Thanks to Rios I passed that equipment inspection with flying colors. As fate would have it, none of that would matter because the hardest challenge of that morning was yet to come: the weigh in.

When the time came to step onto the scale things went EXACTLY as I knew they would: I failed. I was overweight. There's really only one remedy for this problem, that being to just lose the weight (which takes time). As I stated earlier, two weeks of preparation would have been enough time to get my act together but the unit just wasn't going to allow that. Fast forward to today and it is me that is standing here on this scale and failing his weight. Too bad the First Sergeant couldn't come along and fail the weigh in right alongside me. That would actually have made this trip worth it. (I really hope that you can sense the sarcasm in that last statement). To be perfectly honest even though I was upset about the whole situation I had a strange feeling of satisfaction inside of me because now I could go back to the company and use the good old "I told you so" routine. I know that probably doesn't sound like the proper course of action/proper thought pattern, but I was outright forced to go to this school even though I stood up for myself and voiced my concerns. This failure (as bad as it was) was almost like a way for me to throw it back into the unit's face.

I was given one of two options: I could have either stayed at the school and receive a bad 1059 report that would reflect that I did pass the class but it would still be a negative report, or just go back to my unit and return to the class at the unit's discretion when I lost the weight. I knew that if I stayed and received the bad report that it would hurt my career in the long run. There was just no logical way that I would want to have a negative report on my record. By going back to the unit I knew that I would probably be yelled at and even talked down to but that was just paperwork; it didn't really matter. There were no permanent effects of a good old fashioned "ass chewing", but I would still make sure to squeeze in my "I told you so" rhetoric at some point during that ass chewing. After weighing the pros and cons of both courses of actions I decided that it was the right thing to just go back to the unit. That decision may have hurt more immediately but would be much easier to deal with in the long run.

When I arrived back to the unit the First Sergeant (as well as all of the rest of the leadership) was pissed off at me. I expected all of this from the very beginning, so I just let all of his words go into one ear and out of the other. Throughout my life I have learned that if you prepare yourself for an "ass chewing" then you will be more likely to handle it better than if it was unexpected. (Trust me; I've taken many "ass chewing's" in my day). I was given the typical "I would expect much more out of a Sergeant" line as well as the "NCOs are better than this" line. To tell you the truth none of them were in a position to judge me because I knew deep down that even though I was slightly overweight I was still a great NCO and they weren't. I had previously seen some of their evaluation reports over the years and I knew what they were really made of so I just took it all in stride. Had they listened to me from day one none of this would have been a problem anyway.

The funny thing was that no one was really angry with me about coming back for the sole reason that I couldn't make it and "wasn't good enough" in their eyes. I would soon find out that it was much deeper than any of that. Apparently the unit had to send their graduation statistics to the next higher headquarters (Brigade) on a weekly basis. I hadn't realized this before, but my dropping out of the course had hurt the unit's statistics which were conveniently reported on a Microsoft PowerPoint slide on a weekly basis. Therefore it became painfully apparently to me that someone in Brigade Headquarters had come down on someone at the Battalion (most likely the First Sergeant) about my weight failure. What this showed me was that it was NEVER about me or my success in passing the class but rather about the unit's statistics. That's all it ever was for me and probably for any other Soldier. This really pissed me off and showed me a selfish, heartless side to the unit. Even though I had seen a lot in my career so far I had no idea that most of what I (or any other Soldier) had done was chronicled on a PowerPoint slide and viewed in a meeting by people that have no real connection to the Soldiers in the first place. I had no idea who half of these people were, but they knew who I was: SGT Conklin, the NCO who failed weight at the Warrior's Leader Course. Last time I checked I was actually SGT Conklin, the NCO who went on not one, but two deployments to Iraq and Afghanistan including one deployment that I had a six hour notice to deploy. Sarcastically speaking I was really glad that the unit overlooked my previous sacrifices for the sake of their weekly slide shows.

Once everything was said and done the unit's next step was to "flag me" under the provisions of the Army Weight Control Program. What this "flag" meant was that as long as I was overweight I couldn't get promoted, receive an award, or attend any type of school. Although the initiation of this flag was proper procedure under Army regulations, (and I understood that to the fullest) the unit didn't follow proper procedures in initiating the flag. As a Human Resources NCO I knew that there were certain procedures that the unit was supposed to follow, to include sending me to a nutritionist to learn about eating right and also a doctor ensure that there was nothing wrong with my thyroid. People with thyroid disorders can have issues losing weight and thus the Army is supposed to ensure that it's overweight Soldiers do not have that issue. The problem here was that the unit leadership didn't want to even give me the chance to see if that was an issue; they just wanted to "flag me" as soon as possible in order to make themselves look better in their staff meeting. The sad part was that since I came home early from Afghanistan the rest of the unit was still deployed; I had actually only been dealing with the rear detachment leadership. I couldn't wait for the real leadership to come back. I knew they would do things right. There was just no way that Chief Broadbent would have allowed me to be treated this way. For one, he probably would have listened to my input when it came to sending me to school early. He also would have advised the unit to follow proper procedures when it came to flagging me. Even though things were really starting to look bad for me I started to look at the unit's return to the US as a "light at the end of the tunnel." The forward element of the 10th SSB did have some good leaders assigned and I just knew that things would get better when they came home. I started counting the days until their big comeback.

I needed a job to do at the unit while I waited for the SSB to come back. Since everyone was deployed there was no PSB element and the Battalion S1 job was already taken. I knew that I would do a good job if appointed as the Battalion S1 since I did that job in Korea but the section was already full so it wasn't in the cards. The acting First Sergeant ended up appointing me as the company Barracks NCO, which was a very simple job. All I really had to do was ensure that the junior Soldiers that lived in the barracks mopped the floor every morning and kept the place neat. From time to time those duties may have to be extended to something a little more serious but at the time that didn't mean anything. I realized immediately that this type of work was below my level of intelligence but at the same time I needed a real job in the unit; they couldn't just let me sit around and do nothing for a few weeks. At this time I made it perfectly clear to the First Sergeant that I did live relatively close to Fort Drum (or at least a two hour drive anyway) and that I would be heading home most weekends. Therefore, even though I was the "Barracks NCO" during the week I wasn't going to be there to be anyone's babysitter on the weekend. If the Soldiers in that barracks building got out of hand there would be a staff duty desk to handle it, and if that didn't suffice then the duty NCO could just call the Military Police. In other words, don't try to reach me on a weekend that I am not already scheduled for because I will not be there. And I stuck to that. During the work week I handled the duties accordingly, and on the weekend I was off the hook. Every other day the First Sergeant would mention to me my weight problem to which I would tell him that I was working on it. The funny thing was that this First Sergeant wouldn't even be in charge in two and half weeks so I really couldn't understand why he was taking such a stand on the issue. Granted there was the issue of those PowerPoint slides, but they wouldn't be his slides to brief anymore in two weeks anyway.

Soon enough the SSB finally came home from their deployment. After spending nearly a month with the rear detachment it started to seem like the SSB was gone forever. I went to their welcome back ceremony on Fort Drum along with everyone else. It was so good to see everyone and I was extremely glad to see everyone come home alive. Chief Broadbent was glad to see me and he told me the story about Bagram getting attacked right after I left. Of course I already knew the story, which I ended up telling him after he was done. I also found out on this day that I would immediately be going back to work for him once he got back from leave.

I was glad to hear about this because I wasn't really happy about being the Barracks NCO. I needed a real job that would actually benefit my career, not a garbage job that would land me nowhere.

When I returned to work for Chief Broadbent I found that there was a very specific mission that needed to be accomplished. There was a huge box of evaluation reports that were left over from the deployment that didn't get finished while they were still in Afghanistan. It would now be my responsibility to get those reports processed and submitted to the Department of the Army. I knew I could get the mission accomplished but it still bugged me that we had to do this. It felt like we were backtracking; doing work that should have been done two months ago in another country. The other reason that it bugged me to say the least was I felt that had I not been taken out of the Evaluations section out on Afghanistan that I wouldn't have to do these reports now. I would have finished them out there. There's no way that I would have let this happen had I still been working in the section. Granted, working in Casualty Operations was an interesting experience but looking back I probably wouldn't have chosen to switch sections had I known that this would have happened. Ultimately like most things that happen in the Army I really didn't have a choice in the matter, so I just got to work. There were enough reports there to keep me busy for a few weeks. After that I really didn't know what my job would entail. The remainder of the PSB Company at Drum ended up deploying to Iraq a few months after we went to Afghanistan so there wasn't even a PSB unit at Fort Drum. Most of the Brigades at Fort Drum had switched to a new concept called "PSDR" which more or less meant that they would be doing their own Human Resources work from now on. Therefore I knew I would have to do something, it just wasn't clear to me what that something would be. I really didn't want to leave the SSB and go down to one of the units and work as their S1. I had already done S1 work earlier in my career in Korea and I viewed doing that again as taking a step back. I wanted a job that was "higher up on the food chain" so to speak, not lower. I patiently went to work for the next few weeks, awaiting word on what my fate would be.

I wanted to have my fair share of fun upon getting back from Afghanistan also. Even though I was close to home and could go home any weekend that I wanted I still had a lot of friends at Fort Drum who were going to be leaving soon so I wanted to try to have fun with them before they left. Specifically, SGT Johnson, SGT Jack and SSG Dugar were all scheduled to leave Fort Drum soon, just as I was. The only difference was that they were going to normal duty stations while I was tentatively going to a school that I had to lose weight to even get into. None of them had to do anything special to qualify for their assignments, which made theirs "set in stone" in comparison to mine. Because of their upcoming departure Chief wanted to put together a trip for us as a group. That trip ended up being a trip to Montreal which would be my first time in Canada. That idea alone made me that much more excited to go.

The trip itself was like a four day long party. Since Chief was technically in Command of us remaining PSB Soldiers he put us all on a four day pass while the rest of the unit (the finance company) had to work. That alone was funny to me. He picked us all up one at a time at around 9 AM and the party started right then. SGT Johnson broke out a bottle of Jack Daniels and the two of us started drinking in the back seat of Chief's SUV while he drove. In the interest of full disclosure I will admit that this wasn't my first time drinking on a road trip. I'm not saying that it's legal but that didn't stop me and SGT Johnson.

When we got up to Montreal there was so much to do. There were actually so many sights to see that a four day trip just wouldn't be enough to see everything. We went everywhere we could; nice restaurants, strip clubs, the Montreal Casino, night clubs and bars. On the day that we went to the casino we had a blast. The place was amazing, one of the nicest establishments that I had ever seen. There was a beautiful water fountain outside the window near the bar area that was mesmerizing. Like any Casino the place was jam packed with flashing lights and sounds to attract gamblers to each area. The downstairs area had a glass floor with an aquarium underneath it, so if you walked on the floor you could literally look down and see fish underneath you. That added a certain level of class to the place. While we were there someone was filming a cooking show on that floor as well which I thought was even better, especially if they were cooking fish. The whole experience was overwhelming to me because it was the first time that I ever went to a Casino. With everything going on there you could certainly have a good time, but since I was in a Casino I did feel the need to do some sort of gambling. You have to try everything once, right? Now, I am not normally a gambler and to be perfectly honest I've really only played poker once or twice in my life so I didn't even bother with any of the high stakes poker tables. Instead, I hit up the slot machines. That may not sound like a lot of fun and probably not a very good way to win any money, but within 20 minutes I did win some money . . . 500 dollars to be exact. If winning $500 on a slot machine isn't considered lucky, then I don't know what is.

The Casino wasn't the only fun place that we hit up in Montreal. We also hit up a really cool night club called Thursdays and the Hard Rock Café. Thursdays was a great club that had a rotating dance floor as well as a stage with an illuminated floor. After making my rounds on the rotating dance floor I decided to head to the stage. I don't normally dance, it's just not something that I do very well but I had so much alcohol running through my veins that night that I didn't care. I ended up getting on the stage and for some reason I broke out the MC Hammer "typewriter" dance. Today I am pretty sure that I made a fool out of myself because in no time Chief was bribing me to get off of the stage with a bottle of wine, to which I grabbed and started guzzling right there on the rotating dance floor. For the record, I've tried to replicate the typewriter dance many times since then and I haven't been able to do it. I guess it was a one-time only thing.

The Hard Rock Café was pretty cool too. My whole life I always wanted to visit a Hard Rock Café so it was great to finally get my chance. Like all of the other Hard Rock Café restaurants worldwide, the place featured various memorabilia from different bands and musicians. This one in particular had a KISS drum set and a Jimmy Hendrix jacket, both of which I took pictures of. I loved the experience and I have made it a habit since then to visit as many Hard Rock Café's as possible. Since then I have been able to visit the Hard Rock's in Atlanta, San Antonio, and Philadelphia but the one in Montreal will always stand out in my heart the most; not only because it was the first one that I visited but also because it is now closed.

Before we all knew it the four days were up. We checked out of our hotel and hit the road to head back to Fort Drum. We definitely had a blast during this memorable weekend and we agreed that every couple of years we would try to get together and do this all again. For me it was nice to know of a new destination to go and party and I planned on going back up there a few more times before I left Fort Drum. The question now was exactly who would I go up there with since some of my closest friends were now leaving. I would be left to figure out all of that over the next few weeks. It was time to get back to work.

About a day into the new work week, I was approached by the Battalion Sergeant Major who had a job proposition for me. Well, it wasn't really so much of a proposition or a request; it was really an order. I was told that I was going to be working in the Battalion S1 section until I left for recruiting school. By now my school date was pushed back until the fall due to the fact that I wasn't losing weight as quickly as I wanted to so I had plenty of time left to work the section. To be honest I was half-expecting this to happen since I knew that both of the NCOs assigned to that section were on orders to leave Fort Drum. What this meant was that I would be running the section; it would be my section and I would be completely in charge. I embraced the responsibility for a number of reasons: for one, going to that section meant that I didn't have to leave the SSB and go work for the S1 section in a lower level battalion. I really didn't want to do that. The SSB was a division-level unit and I wanted to stay there in that environment. Also, I took a lot of pride in helping people out for a living and I knew that working as the NCOIC of the S1 would give me that opportunity. One of my fondest memories of Korea was my job in the S1; back there I was responsible for the careers of everyone in the unit. If they succeeded, it was because I did my job right. I missed that feeling, that level of involvement with Soldiers.

I found that the NCO who had previously ran the section had literally "run it into the ground." There were just so many things that were messed up that needed fixing. The file cabinet was a wreck, half of the evaluation reports that were due weren't even started and the duty appointment memos hadn't been updated in forever, there was no tracking system in place to track any of the unit's awards. I wondered if my predecessor had any real Human Resources training at all. It sure didn't seem like it. The office itself was even physically dirty and needed to be cleaned. I wondered to myself why it was always me that was getting called in to clean up the messes that were created by other people. What was even worse was the second that I took the section over he didn't even want anything to do with me or the other NCO who was leaving the unit. He stopped coming into work and just spent all of his time doing all of his out-processing. This pissed me off to an extremely high degree. At this point in my career I was so good at my job that I actually took it personally; if I saw someone in the exact same position as me but was screwing up on purpose I would nearly lose my mind. I knew that the job could be done so much better if they would just put a little bit of effort into it, and if you're not putting any effort into your job than what the hell is the Army paying you for in the first place? I reported all of his actions (or lack thereof) to the Sergeant Major, who was now my first line supervisor. There was really nothing that he could do about it, considering the fact that the other NCO was leaving. Ultimately I ended up just having to "suck it up" and get to work at my new job as the S1. I liked the job itself anyway but I will forever be disgusted by the terrible display of professionalism that my predecessor showed.

Over the next few weeks I really fell into my new job well. It was like I found my old flow again. The one NCO with the attitude problem finally left and the section was all mine. For a little while I was really starting to enjoy myself and settle in, but then I realized that it was time for me to take another trip. Ever since I left Fort Campbell I had stayed in touch with Jason Mays, AJ and Duke. We had been planning out a reunion of sorts for years. This planned reunion would take place at Duke's house in Clarksville and would obviously feature the wrestling matches that we had so much fun with so many years ago. The plan was that we would all meet up at Dukes and have some matches, only this time in front of a crowd. Duke himself had been bugging me about this for a while because he had went back to wrestling school to learn more skills since I had departed Fort Campbell. Yes, you read that correctly. Duke did go back to wrestling school, only this time he was able to compete a few times in front of a live crowd. The only catch was that he didn't wrestle as "Duke," but instead he wrestled as "Stung" the Sting impersonator. This was a perfect fit for Duke considering his obsession of Sting. What made it even funnier was the fact that his only matches took place against a guy who impersonated the wrestler the Undertaker, only that guy's name was the "Underfaker." So in other words, Stung vs. the Underfaker was a match made in heaven. I still don't know if they were booked as a joke match, and if they were did the two of them know that they were a joke? It didn't matter. What mattered was that Duke wanted to somehow turn his previous success into success in his front yard, and I was all for that.

I bought my plane ticket to fly down to Nashville and started planning things out with Duke and everyone else on exactly how the weekend's events would go. Duke wanted to make this into as big of an event as possible. Unfortunately as it got closer to the date of my flight, both AJ and Jason had to pull out of the trip due to personal reasons. This really sucked because I was not only looking forward to a group reunion, but also because of the fact that them not being there meant that there would be one less match on the card. Event-wise I didn't know how this would play out. I wasn't sure if Duke had other "wrestlers" lined up for this event, but I had a strange feeling that me and Duke would be working more than one match. I didn't really have too much of a problem with this because I did enjoy the wrestling. Furthermore, this was something that I said that I would do a while ago. I've always been a man of my word and because of the fact that I agreed to this a while back I wasn't going to back out of it. That just wasn't in me. Even if it wasn't fun for me anymore that still didn't change the fact that I had given Duke my word and that was that.

When I got down there I saw that things in Duke's life weren't exactly 100%. He did end up married to the girl from Korea and things with his marriage seemed great but that didn't mean that Duke's life was care-free. In fact, in all of the years that I have known Duke I can't say that I have ever known him to not have some sort of problems. In this case, Duke's problems were that of a financial nature. He had recently left the Army because he was put on orders to become a Drill Sergeant. He wasn't interested in doing that so he signed what is known as a Declination of Service statement, which effectively ended his career in the Active Army. Now he was working as a security guard in Nashville and serving in the Army Reserves once weekend a month. I didn't understand how he would be able to continue paying his mortgage payments and all of his other bills on a security guard's salary. Things looked extremely bad for him; looking through his cupboards you would see that there was almost no food, just barely enough to survive. Seeing one of my old friends reduced to this state was heartbreaking. He went from earning over $4,000 a month in the Army as a Staff Sergeant to earning only about one third of that amount. Throw in the fact that Duke had to support his wife as well as himself and things just seemed impossible. Still, he kept his spirits up by investing a lot of his personal time into his favorite pastime; professional wrestling.

The idea of me paying Duke a visit for the purpose of cultivating his love for professional wrestling really brightened things up for him. Since I left all he thought about was the idea of getting the old gang back together to do one more event. We still had no idea if he was going to get anyone else together for the matches so we more or less prepared ourselves to make this a two-man show. We ended up doing the actual matches on the third day that I was there, which left us with a few days of time on our hands. We rode around Clarksville, TN to see a lot of the old sights. Since it had been a few years since I left the Fort Campbell area I really wanted to take the tour and see what I had missed out on since I left. As the old saying goes, "Some things never change." This was true of Clarksville. It was exactly the same as when I left, which was fine by me. Clarksville was still the same patriotic, welcoming, homelike-feeling town; the kind of town that will just reach its loving arms around a Soldier who is far from home and just take them in as one of their own. Deep down I missed it, even though I knew that going to Fort Drum was the right thing to do. There was a part of me that thought that if I were to ever leave Fort Drum one day that I might try to go back to Fort Campbell. Maybe the feeling was just nostalgia, but going back there to visit made me feel great.

There was one thing about visiting Duke that did "creep me out" so to speak. He made me sleep in his "Sting room." Due to the man's obsession with the wrestler Sting, he owned a lot of Sting merchandise that he purchased over the years. He had everything; ranging from Sting action figures, Sting bed sheets, matchbox cars with Sting's likeness on them, the Sting costume, a life-size cardboard standup of Sting, even magazines with Sting's face on them. He decided that the best thing to do would be to put all of this stuff into one room and plaster everything all over the walls and even the ceiling. That way, when you walked into the "Sting Room" the only thing that you could see in there was Sting. If that doesn't qualify as obsession, I don't know what does. Since this was Duke's guest room I was forced into sleeping in there. Even though Duke didn't see the problem with having to sleep in there I did. This was just like when you see the little kid walk into a room full of clown stuff; he gets scared, not necessarily because he's afraid of clowns, but because it's creepy to be surrounded by them at all times. I wasn't scared of Sting per se, but that didn't mean that I was comfortable being surrounded by his merchandise for a week. Some nights I would turn to alcohol, just hoping that I would get drunk enough that I wouldn't notice the Sting stuff that I was surrounded by when I stumbled back into the room at night. It never worked. There may not be enough alcohol on earth to erase that memory. What was even worse was waking up in that room. I would almost forget where I was while I was asleep, peacefully dreaming my night away. The morning light would shine into the bedroom, naturally causing me to open my eyes, just like on any peaceful southern morning. And every time I opened my eyes, I was greeted by Sting, Sting, and even more Sting. I've been a fan of wrestling my whole life and probably will be forever, but as a grown man I don't think that I could ever dedicate an entire room to a wrestler, or wrestling in general. The lesson to be learned here is that if you ever have a guest flying across the country to visit you, don't put them in the Sting room. 9 out of 10 guests don't like it. That one guest who does is probably Duke, who wouldn't be coming to see you in the first place because he knows you don't have a Sting room for him to sleep in.

The day of our much anticipated wrestling matches quickly approached. This was the one day that we were waiting for; the main reason that I flew down there in the first place. Once the ring was completely set up and the whole neighborhood was informed that there was going to be a wrestling event tonight, Duke and I had to sit down and iron out the details of the matches. We did end up being the only wrestlers who would compete that night so we ultimately decided that we would do two matches. He also wanted them to be gimmick matches, meaning that instead of wrestling as ourselves Duke would be competing as Sting, and I would be competing as a wrester as well, that being Hulk Hogan. So far things hadn't become that much of a problem, but as we discussed the layout and outcome of both matches I noticed that Duke was starting to get a little hot under the collar, especially when I would suggest things that I would do in the match. He had this idea that I would win the first match of the night and then he would win the second match, which in effect would be the last match of the night. I guess Duke had to close the show as the ultimate winner to appease his own ego. I really didn't care about any of that; I just wanted to put on a good show for the people who were actually going to come to this. The details of the first match were pretty much set, we would go back and forth for about 20 minutes, taking turns beating each other up. Then, at the end of the match I would "Hulk up" (in typical Hulk Hogan fashion) and give Duke the classic big boot followed by a leg drop to win the match. Sounds simple enough, right? The match would pretty much be a 50/50 exchange with me winning at the very end. After that we would go into the house for a brief intermission and discuss what went right or wrong and then head out for match number two. That would effectively give the crowd a 20 minute intermission.

When we started planning out the second match things started to turn a little sour. Since I was set to win the first match Duke was obviously going to win the second match, which was only fair. The problem didn't come in the idea of him winning the match itself; but instead in the fact that he didn't want to hear any of my recommendations for the match.

He wanted free reign to call every single step of the match. It started to seem like he wanted to have a squash match, where "Sting" would just outright crush "Hulk Hogan" in front of the crowd for everyone to see. I didn't really think that was a very realistic outcome and I also didn't think that would make for a very good show so I kept on trying to throw my ideas out there. At no point did I really care who won or lost the match, I just wanted us to put on a good, competitive show. At one point Duke snapped at me and yelled, insisting that this was his call. When I looked into Duke's eyes, I could see a legitimate look of anger; like he wanted to hurt me for real in order to defend Sting's legacy in wrestling. Right then and there I remembered that Duke did have a gun in his home (since he worked as an armed security guard) and something told me that he wouldn't be afraid to pull it on me if I refused to comply. He was clearly taking something that was meant to be fun a little too personally. And here he invited me down to Tennessee to do these matches with him. Ultimately I decided that arguing with him just wasn't worth it; I was just going to go out there and do the matches and get it over with.

We pulled the first match off without incident. I entered the ring to the customary Hulk Hogan entrance music (I am a Real American, which if you can't tell this late in the book that's more or less one of my favorite songs). While pandering to the crowd I got a fairly decent reaction. We had attracted a whopping crowd of about 25 fans (which was a lot for Duke's front yard) and they were eating the whole experience up. Duke eventually came to the ring to his music and we got things underway. Throughout my various experiences of wrestling with Duke through the years I had been able to perfect a lot of the basic moves that he taught me, which he learned in wrestling school. We did the basic spot for starting a match; the collar-elbow tie-up. We did the test of strength. We did the pose-downs. We did virtually every single wrestling move we knew. I even pulled off a body slam on Duke, which looked really good on tape. The entire time we wrestled we were motivated by the crowd chanting for us. They were yelling things like, "Hulkamania! Get 'em Hogan!" There were a lot of "Stinger!" chants too. Overall I would say that they really enjoyed it. When the time came to end the match, we did it exactly as we had planned: I was getting beat down for a few minutes, and then I suddenly started to "Hulk up" just like the real Hulk Hogan. Duke acted scared as I hit him with the signature three punches, the big boot, and the Hogan leg drop. What I didn't know at the time was that my leg drop was probably the most miserable looking leg drop in the history of wrestling. But what more could you ask of me? After all, it's not like I was an actual professional wrestler like Duke was. (Years later the video tape of me performing that horrible leg drop surfaced at various parties in Saint Johnsville, thus becoming the laughing stock of the party for a little while. All the while I just wanted to know who else from that crowd had the balls to fly down to Nashville and get in the ring with Duke.)

Once I pinned Duke for the three count and held my replica WWF Heavyweight championship belt above my head (the same one that I wore to the bar when I dressed up as Hulk Hogan during the previous year) I posed for the crowd for a few minutes and told them not to leave, we would be back for round two. When we got inside, it seemed like Duke had a number of complaints about the match. Personally I thought it went well; no one got hurt, the crowd loved it, and it wasn't even like we messed up on too many moves (aside from my horrendous leg drop). We ran through the plan for the second match again, just to make sure that we weren't going to leave anything out. Duke seemed to be a little over zealous about the outcome; even though I made it perfectly clear to him on various occasions that he was going to get to win the second match. Deep down I wished that the real Sting was here to tell Duke that things just weren't that serious. When we got out there, I thought we were having a pretty decent match, but Duke just kept whispering to me things that he wanted to happen in there. (That is a technique that wrestlers do use.) After about ten minutes I just couldn't take it anymore. Duke was really starting to piss me off and I was getting sick of it. There was one spot in particular in the match where I was supposed to bounce Duke off of the ropes and then give him the classic big boot. I would then go for my famous leg drop, only to miss and have Duke lock me in the scorpion death lock submission move. I would eventually "tap out," thus giving Duke the victory. That was exactly how the ending of the match was planned out. So when the time came for me to give him the big boot, I was so pissed off at him that I kicked him in the chest for real. I just couldn't take his crap anymore; I had to get that out of my system. After I kicked him we still went ahead with the planned finish but I could clearly tell that he was feeling the kick. He never said anything after the match, which was probably for the best. We were friends; I really didn't want to turn this into some sort of altercation.

After the match we catered to the fans for a little while, to really give them their "money's worth." We allowed some of them to get into the ring to see what it was like. Duke briefly went into his house and came out with a handful of Sting action figures and handed them out to the some of the children in the audience. That was a classy move; he really didn't have to do that. Overall the fans really enjoyed the show and had a good time. A lot of them asked Duke when he was going to throw another wrestling show, to which he replied that he didn't know because I had to fly back up to New York. He didn't have any other wrestlers up there to hold regular events like we did back in the "old days" when I was stationed at Fort Campbell. While that was a true fact, Duke was leaving out one important detail: the fact that he was hard up for cash and was considering selling the ring. This event that we put on for that crowd proved to be the very last wrestling event that we hosted for the town of Clarksville, TN. That crowd would be left with memories of a great time, but the disappointment of never getting to see another show there again.

Duke had a buyer lined up in west Tennessee to buy the ring. There was a small, independent wrestling promotion out there and the promoter was willing to give Duke $3,000 for the ring but he would be paying him in installment payments. Duke would only be receiving $1,000 cash up front on the night that we dropped the ring off. Since this was a promoter that Duke had previously wrestled for a few years back he went into the deal knowing that the promoter was "shady." In other words, this promoter had screwed people over in other types of deals in the past (to include wrestler's pay) and there was a possibility that Duke would get screwed over. I still don't know why Duke didn't just hold out for another buyer considering the fact that he knew that this buyer may not be such a good idea. I guess when someone is that desperate for cash they will take any offer that they can get.

I can still remember taking the ring apart that night with Duke and loading it onto a U-Haul. (Which I was surprised that Duke didn't have to pay for considering the buyer's reputation). As we dismantled the ring piece by piece all that was going through my head were the memories; great memories of the matches we used to have when I was still stationed at Fort Campbell with Jason and AJ. There were just so many good times to reflect on. When we put the final steel beam into the truck and shut the doors I had a feeling deep down inside of me that this was the end of an era. Duke kept on trying to be positive about the situation, claiming that "he would be buying a new one with his taxes next year" and "we'll even make sure it's a better ring." I knew why he was trying to act positive, because by selling that ring away it was like he was selling a piece of himself. It was a sad display and to be honest I even got a little choked up about it. It's amazing what kind of effect some things in life can have on you. You often don't realize just how important something is to you until it is taken away. That was exactly the case here.

We hopped on the road to drive to the wrestling promotion to pick up Duke's $1,000 payment. The very idea of getting paid was probably the only thing that was keeping his spirits up by now. We got there at the beginning of one of their events and the promoter told Duke that he would pay him after the event, which meant that we had to stay and watch the matches. It was the absolute worst wrestling show that I had ever been to. There were maybe 100 fans packed into this place, the ring was tore up all the way to hell (obviously the reason why the guy wanted Duke's ring), and most of the wrestlers weren't even that good. At some points during the event we found ourselves heckling some of the wrestlers. There was a guy dressed in a blue luchador costume who I kept yelling, "Let's go Blue Ranger!" at. I don't think he appreciated that. During some of the matches Duke would look over at me and say, "Ken, we could have pulled off better matches than this." The sad part was that was actually true for a few of them. When the event was over, we went to the "backstage" area (which was just a couple of tables behind a big black curtain) to collect Duke's money. Duke did get paid, but something just wasn't right. I could just sense it; I could feel it in the air. The man agreed to the installment plan which would have ended up in Duke receiving the rest of his money over the next few months. On the way back to Duke's house he said to me, "See, he's going to keep up his end of the bargain, you just watch." Then he continued to bring it up for the rest of the night, as if to reassure himself. That showed me that he was thinking the exact same thing that I was thinking, which wasn't very good. Either way, I didn't matter much to me anymore. My return flight to NY was scheduled for the next morning. I knew I had a lot of work to get done when I got back to Fort Drum, so it was time to turn my focus back to that. Reflecting back on the past few days I knew that I had a great time, but I knew it was time to "wrap things up" so to speak. That trip ended up being my final trip to Tennessee. I haven't been there since. That was also my last wrestling match. I'll probably never wrestle again; I wasn't that good at it in the first place and it was really just for fun anyway. What remains now are the great memories that I have from that part of my life and the stories that I can tell. Those I will cherish forever. By the way, Duke never got paid the rest of his money for the ring and I never saw him again.

When I got back to Fort Drum I got back to work like usual. Once again I found myself running the S1 section completely alone, much like I did back in Korea. This was fine by me, it just forced me to become better and better at my job as each day went by. It was during this time that I started to work with a new group of people. Most of the Soldiers who were on the deployment to Afghanistan ended up coming down on orders to leave Fort Drum, which meant that they would all have replacements come in. This happened throughout the entire unit; friends of mine left; NCOs and Junior Soldiers alike. You really can't hold it against them either, no matter how much you will miss them. In many cases Soldiers leave Fort Drum for professional development purposes; for the betterment of their career. It just happens, that is how the Army works.

It was only a matter of time before I started to gain a certain amount of respect from the new Soldiers that were coming into my unit. Many of them were coming from units that didn't have a very good S1. In some cases their records hadn't been updated in well over a year and by taking care of business and fixing their records they really started to appreciate me. There were even a few new Staff Sergeants (E6) that came into the unit who were appearing before the Sergeant First Class (E7) promotion board and needed to have their records updated in a quick and accurate manner. While updating a lot of their records they were telling me how they "couldn't believe how easy I made it look." Apparently any time they ever needed the help of an S1 in the past they would have to make an appointment and wait forever to get the work done. I didn't believe in that. I took my customers on a first come, first serve basis regardless of rank. That is honestly the best way to do it for so many reasons; one being that you ensure the work actually gets done and doesn't sit around for a while, and also by doing this you tend to build up a very good reputation amongst your fellow Soldiers. It is nice to be known as someone that can be relied upon when the going gets tough. After a while it became very apparent that there was no task that I couldn't handle. I was simply that good at my job. I knew regulations like the back of my hand. There was never an answer to a question that I didn't know. Even though I took a lot of pride in this, it still made me sick that there were so many S1's in the

Army that didn't take their job that seriously. All it took was a little bit of extra effort but apparently there are some that just don't care about that. When you hold a position like this, the careers of others are in your hands. It is your responsibility to make sure certain tasks are executed properly and if you don't ensure that then plenty of other people will suffer the consequences. That is one of the problems in the Army; there are just too many Soldiers that don't take pride in their job. I didn't understand it back then and I still don't understand it today.

As time went by the Army started to change in ways that I never thought possible. One of the changes that took place was the restructuring of certain units, my unit being one of them. We were changed from a Battalion to a Company, which effectively meant that our unit would not only get smaller, but we would have less authority to perform our own functions. What this also meant was that we would now fall under a Battalion who not only didn't understand our mission, but also didn't even respect our mission. All they were really interested in doing was micromanaging our unit and changing things to fit their own vision. This became a serious problem amongst all of the NCOs and officers within our unit because we knew that the new Battalion didn't really know what they were doing. This change affected me greatly because I actually did know what I was doing when I came to work every day; I didn't need someone from another unit who knew absolutely nothing about me or my work ethic bossing me around or trying to "teach me" anything. With my level expertise it should be me doing the teaching. Naturally every single one of us resisted this change and decided the best thing to do was to put on an act that we were doing what the Battalion wanted but in reality we were doing things the way we did them before, which was the right way. The transition proved to be very hard, especially when the Battalion would try to book week long field exercises for our unit. Our unit was a Finance unit that had a very specific mission, that being to support all of the Soldiers in the 10th Mountain Division. When you book the entire Company to a week-long field exercise you end up taking them out of their office, which means that the Division has zero support for an entire week. As you can imagine, that is a bad thing. There is nothing like having Colonels from other units who need help from the finance office getting upset because the finance unit was ordered out of their offices. That usually creates a "ripple effect" and after enough phone calls some of the Finance Soldiers are sent back to work. Now, for all of you reading this that may have held a combat MOS (job): I imagine that you're probably reading all of this and either laughing about it or asking yourself something like "What gives them the right to complain?" Well, I will simply put it like this: the Army structured Finance and Personnel units to work like this. That is how it goes. I am the last person to dodge a field exercise (as you read previously in the Korea Chapter) but the mission must always come first. If the Army says that the mission is to take place in the Office, then who is anyone to judge? With that said, I will restate this simple fact: any time a support unit is ordered to stop performing their mission for an entire week it is a true detriment to the Army as a whole.

Throughout all of the crap that we had to deal with due to the influence of our new Battalion, a new First Sergeant took control of our unit. A man by the name of First Sergeant Gudger took charge and I will state for the record that he was the absolute best First Sergeant that I ever worked for. He was very strict and believed in Army standards, but at the same time he truly believed in taking care of his Soldiers. As one of his Soldiers, if you messed up it was pretty much going to be the end for you. You would not only suffer some sort of consequences (be it through actual punishment or just corrective training) but you would also NEVER hear the end of it. 1SG Gudger could (and would) talk forever, sometimes behind closed doors, or sometimes in front of everyone. Sometimes he would hold company formations and just talk for hours, often running down certain Soldiers for mistakes that they made. He also didn't hesitate to use "colorful language" as he called it, which basically meant that he swore a lot, making him the least politically correct First Sergeant that I had ever met. (There were many times when the things that he would say would actually make the formation laugh, which lightened the mood.) At first, I thought the guy was a total asshole and a lot of other Soldiers did too. But through time everyone started to gain respect for him. For one, there is nothing wrong with upholding standards and demanding the very best out of your subordinates. In addition, First Sergeant Gudger really believed in standing up for your Soldiers, which is a character trait that not all leaders seem to share anymore. If he saw that an NCO was wrongfully punishing their Soldier or not giving the Soldier the proper level of mentorship he would not hesitate for a second to jump all over that NCO and set them straight. I really respected the man for that. He also didn't like the idea that we had to answer to the new Battalion and thus he would not only stand up to them as often as possible on our behalf, but he would also give us any tools that we needed to get the mission accomplished in the event that the Battalion was hindering that. At the end of the day what the Battalion was doing was creating a lot of "red tape" and 1SG Gudger HATED "red tape." He was all about getting the mission accomplished, through whatever means possible.

Since 1SG Gudger was now effectively in charge of the Company and I was the S1 for the Company that made him my new first line supervisor. This was great for so many reasons, one being that since he was the most powerful man in the company he provided me with a certain amount of "backup." If someone didn't agree with what I was doing, he would back me up and make sure that they understood that I answered to him, and only him. By doing this he gave me the ability to work freely and make my own decisions without the involvement of the Battalion, providing I didn't mess up. Battalion Headquarters still made an effort to breathe down my neck as often as possible, but with 1SG Gudger around I had a legitimate ally who would do his best to make sure that no longer happened. When it comes right down to it, that's all you can really ask for in a leader.

Soon enough I received word that my recruiting assignment was deferred until early 2008. I had been trying my hardest to lose the weight and had lost a few pounds each month since I returned from Afghanistan. Unfortunately, it wasn't enough. I was really putting forth a lot of effort into losing the weight, but I didn't really have any guidance. 1SG Gudger finally took me aside one day and asked me exactly what was going on. I had explained to him that I was going to the gym every day and trying my best, but there wasn't really a good Special Population PT program in place. Since he had just recently taken control of the unit he still needed to iron out a lot of areas, this being one of them. He also found out at this point that when I initially failed my weigh in the rest of the procedures weren't followed properly either. Anytime that a Soldier fails tape they are supposed to be sent to a thyroid doctor to ensure that they don't have a health condition that would cause them to gain weight. Once it is found that the Soldier doesn't have a thyroid problem they are then supposed to be sent to nutrition counseling and enrolled in a Special Population PT program. All of these steps are listed in Army Regulations and must be followed to the letter before a Soldier can be flagged for overweight. When he found out all of this, he immediately lifted my flag as an erroneous flag. He was a little upset that it had happened, since that flag was exactly what was keeping me out of recruiting school. Had I arrived to school and failed, they would have kept me at school and just allowed me to lose the weight while I was there. The flag just kept Fort Drum from releasing me.

Of course, the previous errors didn't stop 1SG Gudger from putting me through the proper procedures; that being the thyroid appointment and the nutrition counseling along with a great PT plan. The thyroid test wasn't actually a real test per se; it was a simple drawing of blood. At the time I didn't really think that it was a valid or legitimate test, based on the experience that my sister Jen went through when she had thyroid cancer. Back then, her actual thyroid glands were examined, as opposed to a simple blood drawing. It didn't really matter to me at the time however, since I knew that I gained the weight through not doing PT for a while on the deployment I just assumed there was no reason to kick up a fuss over what I believed was a faulty thyroid test. I just pushed onward for the rest of the year and made the best effort that I could to lose the weight and make tape. Some months I would do really well and drop eight or nine pounds, and then some months I would do not so well and drop maybe three pounds. I really didn't think that the process would take this long, and it was starting to teach me an important lesson about aging. We all age; there's no way around it. When it starts to happen, our bodies change and our metabolism slows down and things will never be the same again. I knew that I was still in my 20's, (so I was young) but at the same time I wasn't 18 years old anymore. While I did recognize the facts in reference to aging, I did not let them get me down. I just kept on working every single day.

By June I decided that it was time to take another trip. It had been about two months since my trip to Nashville. Since I made a vow that I would not lose touch with Kathy ever again, I decided that it was high time that I took a trip to New Jersey. It was my first time going down there, so I didn't know what to expect. I had stayed in touch with many of my friends from the deployment and I knew that we were all going to get together and throw down some drinks. I was really looking forward to the trip to say the least.

When I got down there things were great. I stayed at Kathy and Mike's house for a week and they showed me around some of the state and took me to a few great places. We met up with our old detachment Sergeant and took a trip to Atlantic City to see the Casinos. Since I had previously visited the Montreal Casino with Chief Broadbent this wasn't my first time in a Casino, but it was definitely a more fun time. In Atlantic City the casinos have a policy where they will allow you to drink alcohol for free all night long, provided that you gamble. It doesn't matter what type of gambling you are engaging in (blackjack, poker, craps tables, even slot machines) or how low of an amount you are gambling, as long as you are gambling your drinks are free of charge. Needless to say, we took complete advantage of this idea. We started off at one of the bars that had touch screen shot machines built right into the bar. These types of machines are also known as "nickel slots" because each game only costs a nickel. Each one of us put a $20 bill into the machine and spent a little over an hour playing. Every few games I would win some money (usually around twenty cents) which would prolong the games. All the while I am drinking mixed drinks for free. When we finally moved from the bar to the casino floor I had consumed nearly $75 worth of alcohol, while only spending $20.

The rest of the Casino proved to be enjoyable too. Mike took me over to a blackjack table and taught me how to play. It was only a $5 table, just enough to blow to learn the game without losing your shirt. I know I won some money that night, but I can't remember exactly how much. I just know that the next morning when I woke up I had an extreme hangover and a bunch of crumbled up $5 bills in my pocket. That was enough assurance to tell me that I had a great time.

We also took a long walk on the boardwalk that night. The four of us were completely drunk, and I was surprised about the fact that I was able to freely walk around the boardwalk with a drink in my hand and not get busted by the cops. I still don't know if it is considered legal/proper to do that down there; or if I just got lucky and didn't get busted. Either way that didn't matter, because I didn't get busted. Going to Atlantic City proved to be one of the best times of my life and I knew that if there was one place I would want to visit again, that would definitely be the place.

Since Kathy lived in South Jersey (which borders the city of Philadelphia) it only made sense to go there also. Considering the fact that I had never been to Philadelphia or New Jersey it was almost as if I was killing two birds with one stone. I wanted to go and do a little sightseeing, and there was one sight in particular that I just had to see in person: the Rocky steps. Ever since I was a child I was a huge fan of the Rocky movies. Throughout my life they provided me with a certain amount of inspiration, just as they do for many people. The idea of going to physically see those steps where Rocky Balboa heroically ran before his big fight with Apollo Creed was just too good to pass up.

In the years since Rocky 5 came out the Rocky Statue itself was moved off of the top of the steps to the ground off to the side of them. I didn't understand why this was done considering the statue was put there in the movie Rocky 3; by now the statue has been "immortalized" into history so to speak. Not only that, but considering the steps lead up to the Philadelphia Museum of Art it just seemed fitting that the statue would still be there. After all, a statue is a work of art, is it not? I really found the size of the statue to be amazing in person. Even though I saw it in the movies many times there is just nothing like seeing it up close. Words can't do it justice.

After taking a few pictures of the statue I decided to make one of my lifelong dreams a reality. It was probably the same dream that many people who saw those movies had when they were growing up: running the steps. I couldn't resist, up until now the largest staircase that I had ever ran up was the stairs leading up to my high school in Saint Johnsville. Trust me; those steps do not measure up to the Rocky steps. They don't even come close. I climbed the steps with ease, and when I got up there I turned around and gazed into the city of Philadelphia, raising my arms in the air just as Rocky did in the movies. It felt good. The funny thing was that I wasn't the only one who was doing this. People often come to those steps to do the same thing, which has more or less turned it into a tourist attraction. I've heard that those steps get more tourists than the Liberty Bell, but there's no real way to fact-check that rumor.

Finally after a few days it was time to go back up to Fort Drum. I had an absolute blast visiting and I knew that I would go back at least one more time before recruiting school. Going there to visit really made me look forward to my future of moving there. It was nice to know that I was indeed welcomed there; that it wasn't just an illusion due to the circumstances of a deployment. I have seen many people become friends (or even more than friends in some cases) over the course of a deployment for the very sake of necessity and convenience. That wasn't the case for any of my friends in New Jersey. Visiting there validated that for me.

The next few months seemed to go by in a blur. I was working hard every day and doing the very best that I could in the office and in the gym. The constant battles with Battalion were still in existence too, but they were a lot easier to handle with 1SG Gudger leading the company. Outside of my office life I was going home at least every other weekend and catching up with friends and family. There were a ton of parties at Joe

Carter's apartment over the course of the year and I would almost always end up at one, provided I came home that weekend. I started to develop a nice rhythm for myself between work, visiting home, and hanging out with my remaining friends at Fort Drum on certain weekends. While we were deployed Bartz and Dioguardi both left Fort Drum, so that left me and Pelletier. We eventually began to hang out with Rios as well. Sometimes when we would drink together we would give each other stupid nicknames; Pelletier pretty much stuck with "Pella," and I usually went by either "King Conklin" or "Optimus." After watching the first Rocky movie one drunken night we decided to start calling Rios "Spider Rios," after the bum boxer that Rocky fights in the opening scene called "Spider Rico." It just sounded good. So those became our drunken nicknames for any and all parties that we threw or went to on the weekends that I stayed at Fort Drum.

It was only a matter of time before they wanted to really get out of the area to do something fun. For a minute I considered bringing them home to Saint Johnsville for a weekend of partying, but then I remembered that a small town like that is only actually fun if it's YOUR hometown. Since it wasn't their hometown, I pretty much just dropped the idea in the interest of a better time elsewhere. It was then that I remembered back on the great time that I had in Montreal with Chief Broadbent and the crew from the deployment. Most of that crew had left already (with the exception of Chief) and I knew that I wanted to go back up there again. So we started going up there throughout the summer. We used to get crazy up there. I showed them all of the sights that I saw the first time I visited. We went to Club Thursdays, the strip clubs, the fancy restaurants, the Casino and the Irish Pubs. It didn't matter what was going on back at the unit or how depressing things got at work; when we were in Montreal we lived like kings and that was all there was to it. We would stay out partying until 4 am most times. Before we went back to our hotel we would always go through the McDonalds drive through in a taxi and order a bunch of crap that we knew we weren't really going to eat. Pelletier used to call it "Mickey Sleaze." The only thing was he would just say the words Mickey Sleaze, he would yell them at the cab driver the second we got in the car. Then when we got to the drive-thru to order our food, we would scream "Mickey-Sleaze" into the intercom as loud as we possibly could. I can't explain why we all thought that was funny; I can just choke it up to the fact that we were drunk and having a good time. What was worse was after we left the drive through I had this dumb idea that I would roll the window down and start shouting "Carl Winslow!" at anyone who happened to be walking the streets of Montreal at 4 AM. Just like the "Mickey Sleaze" idea, I don't know where the idea of yelling "Carl Winslow" came from. I know that "Carl Winslow" was the name of the Cop on the show Family Matters, but I have no idea how or why that computed to something that I should shout at an innocent passer-by while I was drunk. Either way we meant no harm and it was all done in good fun. Those trips were some of the greatest times that I had while I was stationed at Fort Drum. They continued for the duration of the summer and partially into the fall until Pelletier and Rios left Fort Drum. Pelletier got out of the Army altogether while Rios was moving to a new duty station, thus leaving me back at Drum all by myself. It was heartbreaking to see them go, but I was starting to get used to this pattern in the Army. Besides, I knew that my time to leave for recruiting school was soon coming. I just had to wait a few more months. Today when I call those guys to catch up on things, I sometimes throw a "Carl Winslow" into the conversation out of the blue to get a good laugh, which it always does.

Fall of 2007 came along and things at Fort Drum were becoming too "routine" for me. I am not sure why, but because of the fact that I had crammed so much into 2007 so far I would come down with a case of "cabin fever" relatively quickly; meaning that I didn't want to sit in upstate New York all the time. I decided that it was time that I took yet another trip to New Jersey. I had the leave saved up and 1SG Gudger didn't really have a problem with me taking a few days off so I packed my bags and headed down there. This trip would be a little different than my first one however. I still stayed at Kathy and Mike's house, and we still took a trip with our old Detachment Sergeant to Atlantic City to party it up, but we did some other things too. One night came along where we went to a place called "Dave and Busters" in Philadelphia to meet up with most of the old crew from the deployment. Now, for those of you who don't know what "Dave and Busters" is, I will gladly explain: it is more or less a Chuck E. Cheese for adults, meaning that it is a place where you can go play video games and drink alcohol at the same time. It's actually a really good place to visit or hold a party. On this particular night everyone met up and it was the first time that I had seen some of my friends since we were in Afghanistan. In addition to Kathy, Mike, and me, Wade and Coleman were also there. While I don't remember all of the details of the evening, I can remember that after we left Dave and Busters we decided to do some "bar hopping." On the way to one of the bars, I saw a parking meter and yelled, "I'm the Incredible Hulk!" and tried to rip it out of the ground (unsuccessfully). It was all done as a joke, and I can hardly remember doing it today but at the time everyone thought it was the funniest thing ever. The sad part is I can't even remember why I did it. That evening went down as one of the highlights of that particular trip to NJ.

In the spirit of trying to catch up with as many of my NJ friends as possible I decided to take a day to hang out with Maria on this trip as well. Just like in the case of Coleman and Wade, I hadn't seen her since our deployment to Afghanistan either. At the time she was working a new AGR position and she was also living on Fort Dix, NJ. We hung out for a day and caught up on a lot of things. Since we hadn't heard from each other in so long I had to explain to her exactly why I hadn't left for recruiting school yet. I had to fully explain to her that sometimes in the active component you don't always have the freedom to just do what you want. My recruiting assignment was postponed by forces that I couldn't control; I couldn't just get into a plane and fly down to Fort Jackson for the school. Granted, one may argue that it was my own fault that I gained a little bit of weight, but as far as I was concerned it wasn't my fault that I was put into positions and shifts where I wasn't available to do PT. In addition, it wasn't my fault that the unit didn't follow proper procedures when administering my flag when I first returned; it wasn't the fact that I was overweight that was keeping me from going to school, it was the fact that I was flagged for overweight that was keeping me out. Still, notwithstanding the technicality I was still bound by the ruling of individuals other than myself. After explaining all of this to her, I realized that this may not have been something that she was accustomed to due to the fact that she was a member of the National Guard . . . I, however was not a member of the National Guard despite the fact that I wanted to join my friends in NJ as soon as possible. When the weekend was over I returned back to Fort Drum, vowing to work as hard as I possibly could to drop this weight so I can just move down there once and for all.

November finally came along, which marked the end of Chief Broadbent's time on Fort Drum. He was on orders to go back to Korea for a few years. Although I knew that I was going to miss him a lot I was happy for him considering the fact that he really did want to go back to Korea. Hell, I probably would have gone back too if I had the chance. Although I didn't actually tell him this to the fullest degree; seeing him leave made me emotional. He was only the third person that I encountered in my Army career (the others being SGT Ramos back at Campbell and SSG Stewart back in Korea) that was able to mentor me as a Human Resources Soldier. He was one of the few that I ever encountered that knew more about my job than I did, and was always able to teach me new things. Knowing that he was leaving was hard because I knew that there wasn't going to be another one like him for a long time. What that meant is that I would no longer have a mentor there on Drum. I had to do things completely on my own for now on. Sure, I had been working as the S1 for the unit on my own for a few months now, but Chief worked right downstairs from me. Any time I had a serious issue I could just go down and vent to him. It had been a while since I had needed regulatory guidance from him; at this point he was there as more of a confidant; a shoulder to lean on if you will. He had gone from being just a leader to being a friend as well. That's not a line that a lot of leaders cross in the Army. So needless to say, the idea of him leaving wasn't exactly easy.

He didn't have a traditional farewell dinner either. Instead, he decided to hold Thanksgiving dinner at his house and invite people that he wanted to say goodbye to. Many of the people that he was actually close to had left Fort Drum already, so I guess I understood why he did that. If he had a traditional farewell it would have just been a bunch of bureaucratic nonsense; a bunch of new, young Soldiers forced to go to a dinner because he was a Warrant Officer, to say goodbye to someone they hardly knew. He didn't want to go out that way, and I understood that. So in a way I was honored to be invited over because that showed me that I was one of the ones that he actually knew and liked. What made this unique was the fact that since I was so close to home now I could go home any time I wanted. With that said, there was absolutely nothing that could or would keep me from going home for a holiday to spend it with my family, until now. If I was put on the duty roster to work on a holiday, I would just pay someone to pull the duty. In other words, there was just no way that I was going to miss out on being home with my family for Thanksgiving . . . well almost no way. In order to willingly skip out on a holiday with my family it had to be a special occasion. This was definitely that occasion.

It was on this night that I first tried deep fried turkey. He had the deep fryer set up in his garage and we all stood around it drinking beer and talking about things we did out in Afghanistan. I also filled him in on the trips I took to NJ too, since he wasn't able to get down there to visit since we came home. It was weird in a way, because just standing there with him made me feel like I would still see him tomorrow; like this was just another day. The reality of things was that it wasn't just another day: this was it, the last time I would see him. I had no choice but to bid my mentor farewell. As hard as it was for me, I accepted it. We agreed to stay in touch, and he reassured me that if there was anything that he could do for me in the future that he would be there.

With the end of the year 2007 drawing near, I started to do a lot of reflecting. It had been a "bittersweet" year in a lot of ways. I had to suffer the inconvenience of having my recruiting assignment deferred until the following year and I was forced to say goodbye to many of my longtime friends and faced the idea that I may never see some of them again. At the same time, I knew that 2007 was a great year in many ways too. I did a lot of traveling during that year; I went to Tennessee to wrestle my last match, I had priceless trips to Montreal, and to top it all off I went to NJ a few times and had a blast. I guess 2007 wasn't so bad after all. With my recruiting assignment on the horizon, I knew that 2008 could only get better, right?

CHAPTER 11

LOYALTY OVER VICTORY

The New Year at Fort Drum opened up just like any year up there: cold. And it wasn't just regular cold, it was extreme cold. Fort Drum has a reputation for being the coldest place in the entire Army, even colder than Alaska. The winter of 2008 proved to be no different than any other winter. The temperatures were well below freezing, sometimes hitting 25 degrees below zero. The snow was unforgiving as well. We would often get hit with "flash blizzards," where one minute it was perfectly sunny out and then the next minute the snow was coming down quicker than you could even utter the phrase, "I think it's going to snow today." For obvious reasons, storms like this would make it next to impossible to travel and thus the post would be closed early because you couldn't even travel on the roads. At times it seemed as if there was no end to the winter and that it would go on forever. There are a lot of "inside jokes" about the winters at Fort Drum, and by "inside jokes" I mean jokes that are only shared and understood by Soldiers who have actually had to endure the conditions there. One such joke is that Fort Drum is lucky if it gets two weeks of summer weather, usually taking place in August. To be honest Fort Drum does get more than two weeks of summer, but it is usually a mild summer at best.

Despite the challenges that the brutal winter brought to everyone, I was still working hard at my job as the unit S1. I was still able to make it to work on some of the days when the weather was bad due to the fact that I drove an SUV. I never used that as an excuse to partake in reckless driving, but it allowed me to not fall behind on days when all of the other Soldiers couldn't make it to Clark Hall (that's the building that we worked) on time. I also began to take on a plethora of new responsibilities in the unit, to include Key Control for all of the offices at the Clark Hall building, as well as maintaining the accounts for any Government Credit Cards that needed to be issued within the unit. My new duties would often include walking Soldiers through the process of applying for a Government Credit Card (only if their mission required it that is) and then monitoring their account activity on a monthly basis to ensure that they were not using it on anything that wasn't duty related. Needless to say, the addition of new duties not only broadened my scope of knowledge and made my work day harder, but also improved the appearance of my NCO Evaluation report. The more duties that you can list on your report, the better you will look. Aside from the blemish of having to mention that I was slightly overweight, my evaluation report was shaping up to look exceptionally well. This was good to know because even though the Army places a bit too much emphasis on the overweight bullet I knew that it wouldn't matter if I ever had to leave the Army and find a new job. I could use those evaluation reports as references to verify some of the things that I would put on my resume. While I don't think that a civilian employer would really care about the idea that I was overweight, I do feel that they could or would care about the fact that I was a highly competent Human Resources NCO who also had experience with the issuance of Government Credit cards and possessed a valid Security Clearance. It was nice to know deep down that my experiences thus far could benefit me in the long run.

Another new task that I picked up was I now had to attend the weekly staff meetings at the unit level. Since I was the only one working in the S1 and effectively running the section I would have to sit in on these meetings and brief the Company Commander and the rest of the unit leadership on everything HR related. Sitting in a meeting all morning may sound like easy work, but trust me it isn't; especially when you are briefing information to various people who may not understand everything that you are trying to brief. In other words, when you are a Human Resources NCO trying to brief to Finance NCOs and Officers, they don't always understand what you are saying and therefore you have to break it down for them. And that is to be expected; if any one of them was trying to brief Finance information to me I probably would end up lost too.

It was during this time that I started working alongside some of the other staff NCOs in the unit, especially in the meetings. Usually I would have to brief my slides right before the Supply NCO, SGT Terrance Cappe. I had first met him before our deployment to Afghanistan, but

I didn't really have a lot of time to hang out with him while we were deployed since we were both working for different units at the time. Now things were different. Like me, he had to deal with a lot of the bureaucratic nonsense that Battalion would push off onto our unit just like I did, so we developed a certain level of understanding with each other and eventually became friends. Like me he also worked directly for 1SG Gudger, and the two of us subsequently became almost like two of his "right hand men" if you will. Being from New York, Cappe was also a fan of New York sports teams like I was; although he favored the Giants while I was a Jets fan. He didn't mind the Jets like some other Giants fans do, so we would still be able to talk football often without getting into an argument. He ran his section with a very high degree of attention to detail, meaning that he always tried his best not to miss suspense's or deadlines. He commanded the upmost respect from his Soldiers but at the same time was very approachable, which made him a good leader in my book. I was never a fan of NCOs that weren't approachable. Your Soldiers should respect you, not fear you. If they cannot approach you without fear then how can you truly lead them? You can't. I would take respect over fear any day of the week. If someone respects you there is a good chance that they will follow your orders and try their hardest; if they fear you they will probably leave your side when things get really tough. That's because respect is an emotion that is grounded inside of you, deep down into your soul. Fear on the other hand is only based on external situations, like having someone yell in your face for example. When that person loses the ability to scream at you they just lost all they had on you; and therefore you would have no further reason to follow that person. Respect doesn't work that way. Respect follows you to the grave.

I also started working alongside the unit Training Room NCO during this period too. The only thing was that in this case there was a Specialist filling the Training Room NCO slot. This is a very possible scenario; according to Army regulations Soldiers can always work "two up, one down," meaning that an E4 could potentially work in either an E6 slot or an E3 slot. The Soldier's name was SPC Brizzee, and he was a hard worker who never complained about the fact that he had to handle an NCO's workload. Just like Cappe and I he had to report directly to 1SG Gudger, who demanded nothing but the best out of Brizzee. One of his duties included the actual set up and administration of the staff meetings, which obviously had to be done before the meeting started. What this meant was that if we had an early meeting then Brizzee would have to come in even earlier and get everything set up, which would often cut into his personal time.

Brizzee could always be relied upon, no matter what. I had a lot of respect for him as a Soldier considering the fact that he was working at somewhat of a disadvantage. While we were deployed to Afghanistan he sustained a major back injury and was in constant pain. He often had to take painkillers that would hinder his duty performance. The problem with this was he still had to come into work anyway. He was working in a section all by himself and someone had to handle his workload. Another problem that Brizzee faced was the fact that he was a Finance Soldier, which meant that often times when the Finance NCOs were holding Finance-related training they would attempt to force him to attend the classes. This became a problem because it cut into his work day, and a lot of the NCOs refused to understand the fact that Brizzee worked directly for the First Sergeant just like I did. In cases like this he would have to bring the situation to the First Sergeant's attention. Granted, it always worked but it presented a problem in the fact that it wasted everyone's time. Had some of the NCOs just taken Brizzee's word from the beginning things would have worked out fine. Usually when this happened some of the NCOs would make comments towards Brizzee about always "trying to get out of stuff" because of his position or because of his injury. As far as his injury goes, it was 100% legitimate and it deeply saddens me that in the Army the instant you become injured you are suddenly treated like garbage. No one ever seems to put themselves in the shoes of the injured Soldier, and instead tries to figure out a way to label that person as a "malingerer" or even worse. That mentality always made me sick and I always tried to talk some sense into some of those NCOs, but to no avail. At the end of the day Brizzee was there to do his job, as commanded by the First Sergeant. Simply put that was his responsibility there, a responsibility that I feel he carried out exceptionally well. While his time there seemed to last forever, he finally was put before a medical board and granted a medical retirement for his injuries, and rightfully so.

I still had a while until my recruiting assignment, as it had been pushed back yet again, this time until the summer of 2008. This gave me a lot more time to drop the weight. I knew that I could get the job done. I worked out every single day after work. I never took a break, even when I was home in Saint Johnsville for the weekend. I would often get up on a

Saturday morning and go for a run around town. It didn't matter what I had done the night before, whether I stayed home and relaxed or if I went out partying the night before; either way I would still go out and run in the mornings. Weather conditions were no deterrent to me either. I would run in heat or cold, rain or shine. I would even run in the snow. Back at the unit everyone could notice the difference in my weight loss month to month and I started to develop a reputation for having one of the best PT scores in the company. I took a lot of pride in that and I choked up my weight issues to genetics and my height. Had I just been a little taller (I'm only 5 ft. 7 in tall), I would have been able to "make tape." While I never once stated that I agreed with the procedures of the Army Weight Control Program I still understood that I was subject to have to work within the system. I didn't have a choice. As far as not agreeing, how could I ever agree with it? Putting my natural bias aside, the Army Weight Control Program takes a measurement of your height, waistline, and neck. Your actual body weight doesn't really factor into the occasion, it only determines if you have to be taped or not. The measurement of your waist supposedly measures your fat while the measurement of your neck supposedly measures your muscle mass. Both of those ideas are tremendously flawed. When it comes to measuring your waist it could be extremely inaccurate depending on who is doing the actual taping. Some people will allow you to "suck in" while others will not. To be honest, the regulation states "normal relaxed position" but most NCOs will give you the benefit of the doubt and allow you to suck in. That helps because the standard is so incredibly unrealistic. The charts were developed decades ago; society has clearly changed since then and thus many Americans are now heavier as a whole. I am not saying that it is a "great idea" to be overweight, but what I am saying is that I feel that it is wrong to attempt to enforce a standard that is unrealistic for many people due to the conditions of our society. As far as the neck measurement is concerned, the very idea that the measurement of your neck is an accurate representation of your overall muscle mass is simply preposterous. What if you are a person who doesn't work their neck out at all but you work your chest and your arms? I know many weightlifters but not all of them take the time to work their neck. Does that mean that since they have a small neck that they are either not physically fit or they don't have a lot of muscle mass? Of course not. Does that mean that the Army would use common sense and change the way body fat composition is measured? No. There are many other ways to measure someone's body fat percentage. As a matter of fact, I have consulted various doctors and personal trainers about this very issue on many different occasions. Two examples of alternative methods are the electric method (where electricity is rippled through your body by standing on two metal plates and holding two metal handles) and the water displacement method. I have personally tried the electric method (no, it doesn't hurt) and I found that it is extremely accurate, more so than the administering a taping. While I have never tried the water displacement method I have heard positive things about it. Both methods were available at most of the duty stations that I served at during my career, and I am sorry to say that every time that I recommended them to a leader to use in lieu of the taping method the idea was shot down. Therefore it is safe to say that the Army as a whole has willingly used a method to measure a Soldiers body fat percentage that has been proved to be slightly inaccurate. To me that makes no sense and it never will. Unfortunately, it doesn't appear that the Army will change that method any time soon.

Since I was going home most weekends now, I had more opportunities to catch up with more of my old friends from high school. The parties at Joe Carter's house allowed me this opportunity. Since almost the entire town would show up to his apartment on the weekends it was only a matter of time before I touched base with everyone that I had fallen out of touch with over the years. On one such night, I finally met back up with one of the best friends that I ever had growing up, a man by the name of Josh Richard.

Joe's apartment was directly above a bar called Godfathers. The name Godfathers was just one incarnation of the bar, through the years it had been bought and sold by various different owners and changed names each time. Usually at the parties everyone would filter down to the bar to take a shot in between games of beer pong. On one particular night I walked over to the bar and I saw an old familiar face that I hadn't seen in a while. It was Josh Richard. The last time I saw him was at his high school graduation in 2002. His mom had asked me to attend and wear my Class A military uniform, to which I did. His mom liked me so much that she hand knitted me a blanket when I came back from the Army, which I still have to this day. Josh and I were the best of friends in high school, and due to me joining the Army we had fallen out of touch. I guess that's what traveling the world can do to a friendship.

Josh and I caught up over a few beers. Over the years he had went to college for a little while and since then he had been working jobs and doing pretty well for himself. He had also grown his hair out and looked like a 1990's era rock star by now. Back in high school he always kept his hair short, so it was quite a change to see him like this. When I told him that I was still in the Army but I was stationed at Fort Drum he was very glad to hear it. What it meant to him was that since I was coming home every weekend that we could hang out again, just like the "good old days." I told him that Joe threw parties every weekend upstairs and that he should start coming, to which he did. That night proved to be a great one and a true testament to the fact that there's nothing like re-uniting with an old friend after a long time.

Since I brought him back into the fold I figured it would be a great idea for Josh and I to be beer pong partners every week. I know that probably sounds juvenile, but this became our weekly tradition. It was what we did for fun. Everyone had a partner that they usually chose, and thus certain teams would win more than others. I really wasn't very good at beer pong, and neither was Josh. But that didn't matter. It was all for fun anyway but we always made sure to be partners. We would win some, but we would lose so many more. The times that we won against a good team we would just chalk it up to good luck. There was one night on the table where he brought up the fact that we lose all the time. He said he was surprised that I hadn't picked a better partner by now, to which I dug deep and responded to him with something insightful. I looked him dead in the eye and I said, "Loyalty over Victory." He thought about that for a second and asked me what it meant. I explained to him that sometimes you are going to embark on endeavors in your life that are going to look like a loss right from the start. Sometimes, your friends will be involved in that and at the end of the day it doesn't really matter if you won or lost because as long as you stick by your friends (which is loyalty) then who cares if we win or lose. You should always stick by your friends right until the bitter end no matter what. That's what Loyalty over Victory means. Before he actually told me that he liked it I could already tell just by looking in his eyes that my words had captivated him. Somehow even while I was drunk I was able to dig down and pull out something that insightful. From then on we adopted the words "Loyalty over Victory" as our motto, both on the pong table but in life as well. We still say it to this day. Years later Josh ended up getting those words tattooed on his arm. That really meant a lot to me. Today when people at parties hear one of us utter those words I still take the time to explain it to them because after all, the phrase really does have a special meaning for me. In most cases whoever asked about it leaves that conversation with a true understanding of what it's supposed to mean. That's all I can hope for. If my words can influence someone in a positive manner than I consider that an accomplishment and I have nothing to complain about.

Out of all of the parties that Joe threw in 2008, one stands out in particular. It was a mid-summer night, and there was more than just the usual crowd there. In fact, it seemed like there were at least 10 to 15 more people there that weren't regulars. On this night Joe (who was considered the rule-making commissioner of beer pong) made a rule that no one would be teamed up with their usual partners. Instead, everyone would have to draw names out of a hat to determine who their partner would be. This would make things a lot more interesting than the usual parties. When you have been teamed up with the same person over and over again (as me and Josh normally did) you tend to build up a certain understanding with that person's playing style. I can see why Joe did this. By changing things up a little bit things wouldn't get as boring. After all, we almost always did the exact same thing on a Friday night which meant that it could tend to get boring for some people. I never had an issue with it myself considering that I had missed out on so many years with my friends, but some of the others didn't feel that way. To them, the boring culture of Saint Johnsville was their life seven days a week so I guess I could understand why they would get bored with things.

When it came time to draw the name to see who my partner would be, I was shocked to see that I drew the name of none other than my brother Jason. Now, we had never actually been partners before, partially because he usually teamed up with our friend Larry and partially because Jason and I didn't always get along. We weren't really sure how we would function as a team, but at least I knew that he actually had some skill on the beer pong table, more so than I did. Unsure of how things were going to go, we approached the table ready to make history.

Even though we were actually doing pretty good and hitting most of the cups, we still needed a little "something extra" to pull through this night. We decided to start rallying up the crowd behind us any way that we could. Jason would start talking shit, which would get a few people laughing, and then every time that I would hit a cup I would break out and do one of my classic Hulk Hogan poses. (Ok, they were never really my poses to begin with, but you get the idea.) Each and every time we would get a few people to either laugh at our joke or cheer us on. Either way it was a sign of support which greatly helped us because we would use this crowd support to "psych out" our opponent and make it to the next round. As each game passed, our support grew more and more. When we won the semi-final round we celebrated like we had just won the super bowl. We were jumping, yelling, and screaming and all the while there were people who were joining in and celebrating with us. It was a surreal feeling, like we had actually won something worthwhile. Even though in reality it was just a beer pong tournament it still felt like we were doing something important. Now we had just one game left, the final round. Whoever won that would win the tournament. Jason and I knew that we needed something extra to win this one.

After a five minute intermission the last game finally began. Standing on the other side of the table were our opponents. One of them was none other than Joe Carter. Joe, who was an excellent beer pong player, was also the "commissioner" of the beer pong league as well. Not only that, we were standing in his apartment. In other words, playing against Joe Carter meant that the odds were stacked against us. Instead of letting this bother us, we decided to stick to our strategy from the last few games; getting the people in the crowd rallied up behind us. There were at least 25 people crammed into Joes little kitchen, crowded around this high stakes game to see who would come out on top. As I landed my first cup and broke out my Hulkamania pose, Jason decided to yell something that would go down in Saint Johnsville history. He looked to the crowd and yelled "FUCK JOE CARTER!", and then followed it up with the five clap sequence that you hear at sporting events. Looking to capitalize on this momentum he decided to do it again, only this time I joined in with him. The next thing you know, members of the crowd started to join in, and every time Joe would try to throw the pong ball his concentration would be broke by someone chanting the words, "FUCK JOE CARTER!" Eventually everyone in the apartment joined in and Joe's kitchen was filled with the chants of 25 people, all chanting "FUCK JOE CARTER!" As the game continued on, Joe eventually found his stride and started to make a comeback. He still appeared to be phased by the loud chanting, which just wouldn't stop. The next thing you know, the Cops crashed our party. We still aren't sure who let them in, but either way the cops came in and told us we needed to shut the party down because we were getting too loud. Apparently, people across the street could hear the "FUCK JOE CARTER" chants. While the Cops didn't actually arrest anyone (which is a good thing) they still killed almost everyone's mood and thus people started to go home. While we will never really know who would have won that game, we know deep down in our hearts that it was probably one of the most fun nights that we ever had at Joe's apartment. Years later everyone still remembers that party too. I don't think anyone will ever forget it, and I certainly know that my brother and I won't forget it anytime soon, if ever. We will always have the memories of that night. That's all I can really ask for.

Although most of my partying in 2008 took place at home in Saint Johnsville, there were still a few times that I didn't go home on the weekend. This usually took place on weekends where there was a blizzard and the weather conditions were just too extreme to attempt to drive home. Since Pelletier and the rest of my friends left I had slowly started to make new friends up there, so it wasn't like I was spending these weekends alone. I don't know what I would have done if I didn't have any friends up there. I can't stand being alone and not having anyone to hang out with. It isn't a pleasant feeling and things could start to get lonely. I could see it if it was a long work day, but if I am off all day long I can tend to get bored quick if I don't have anyone to hang out with. That's just how it goes for me, and I'm sure that I'm not the only one in the world who feels that way.

Some of the barracks parties that I would throw on these blizzard weekends would get a little out of control. By "out of control" I don't mean that the Military Police ever had to get involved or anything like that; I really just mean that we would have a good time. This wouldn't happen all the time, but when it did no one would ever actually get in trouble at my parties, and in fact 1SG Gudger would sometimes jokingly tell the formation to stop by my room and take a shot of Hennessey, since there were so many liquor bottles in my room. I think deep down he would rather the Soldiers be in my room instead of out in Watertown getting a DUI. Hell, I felt the same way. I would never want to see a Soldier get a DUI. It's dangerous and it can ruin their career.

I would pick up a few bottles of liquor on a Friday night and invite everyone in the barracks over. Some of the Soldiers who would come by would bring something with them. One Soldier who I was friends with used to make this homemade ceviche and bring chips with it. He would also occasionally take trips to Belize (since he was from there) and bring back this special rum that tasted like candy. That stuff was delicious. There was also a Soldier in the unit by the name of Victor George who was from India used to come over and hang out with us after he got out of work from his second job at Pizza Hut. If he had cooked food earlier in the day he would bring over some of his food for us to try, and if he didn't make any food he would just bring over a few dozen wings that he would get from work for free at the close of his shift. There was another Soldier there named Dantes that would sometimes order the group some Chinese food. Either way, everyone that came would try to contribute something to make the party that much better for everyone else. A lot of times that is how it goes in the Army. It doesn't matter what type of unit you are in; after a while you start to change from just being a unit to almost being like a brotherhood. When you hear the term "brothers and sisters in arms" it is referring to a real feeling that Soldiers do often share. We shared it just the same. When you start to foster that "brotherhood" feeling it no longer matters who buys what or who does what. Everyone is there together as a group and that's all there is to it.

Every time that we put together a barracks party we had a blast. I guess deep down inside I was trying to relive the party atmosphere that I had back in Korea. We wouldn't just sit around and drink either. Sometimes I would blast music as loud as possible and turn on my disco ball light which would cause drunken people to start dancing. Then when new people would want to come into the room they would have to shout the password at the door before entry. The password thing was a joke, almost everyone knew what the password was; it was Tony Montana. This was because of the fact that I had invested in a cardboard life-size standup of Tony Montana from the movie Scarface and put it in the corner of my room. Because of its location it was pretty much the first or second thing that you would see when you came into the room. When it was purchased it was purely for shock value purposes and believe me it lived up to its desired purpose. The standup only added to the party-like image that my room portrayed; there were empty liquor bottles that covered all of my shelves and the window sill. There was also the disco ball and my old Wrestling belts from Korea on display. And just like in Korea, those Wrestling belts did come off the wall and go around my waist during some of these parties.

I also had a Nintendo Wii in my room which we would use during the parties as well. Sometimes I would hold Wii boxing tournaments through the "wee hours of the night" (no pun intended). It was just another added element to our good times. There were just so many things that we would do with the limited resources that we had. Sometimes the snow would get so bad that you couldn't even drive to the PX which was only a few blocks away. In other words, we often found ourselves confined to the barracks building for the weekend during those blizzards. There were even a few times that I got extremely crazy and put my Gasmask on and started running up and down the hallway with a canister of coffee creamer. (Again I resorted to coffee and coffee-related props when I was drunk, and yet again I really don't know why I thought that was funny).

When I look back on those few weekends that I stayed up at Drum in 2008 I realize that they were a lot of fun. When I would go back home to Saint Johnsville for the weekend and come back to Fort Drum afterwards I would always be told how boring the barracks were without me staying up there for the weekend. That always touched me in a special way; knowing that deep down I was capable of entertaining those Soldiers on what would have otherwise been a depressing weekend. At times the work day and the unit itself was depressing enough, the least I could do was help them to unwind and have a good time on the few weekends that I stayed up there. Granted, alcohol-related activities may not be looked at as the most noble of ideas, but at the same time I never once served an underage Soldier and there was never once an alcohol related incident as a result of my parties. When it boils right down to it those parties did help boost morale in that unit, so as far as I am concerned they were a good thing. That's my story, and I'm sticking to it.

As spring came approached things at the unit hadn't changed very much. There was word that 1SG Gudger was going to be leaving during the summer, but that wasn't going to happen for a few more months. I was still working my ass off and as a result I was very close to making tape. At this point I was also the very best at my job that ever served in that unit, and I was told that by a few of the NCOs that were around for a while. Being told that really made me feel good. I knew that if I just worked harder for a few more weeks that I could make tape and hopefully get sent down to recruiting school before the new First Sergeant showed up. While I didn't know much about the new 1SG, I did know that I wasn't exactly a big fan of change, so in an effort to avoid being there for the "big change" that was coming I just started working that much harder in the gym. I had a weigh in coming up during the first weekend of May and I knew that if I played my cards right I could finally make it.

When the weigh in day came along, I finally got my wish. I weighed in at 202 pounds (the lightest that I had been in a while) and made tape. I didn't just barely make it either, I made it with about 3% body fat to spare. What this meant to me was that all of my hard work over the past year was worth it. I could look into the mirror and see a "new me," a man who worked his ass off and legitimately looked like it. I felt like a "million bucks." My improved appearance wasn't the only thing that excited me; the idea that there was no longer a restricting factor keeping me out of recruiting school gave me a newfound motivation and a newfound hope. As far as I was concerned I had been stationed at Fort Drum long enough and it was time to go. The other NCOs in the unit shared my victory with me, as they had watched me through this incredibly long journey. I had a couple of months until my assignment, so I knew I had to wrap things up relatively quickly at Fort Drum. Months earlier I found out that WLC wasn't actually a requirement to attend school at the time (it was a huge misunderstanding from the start) and thus I didn't need to waste two weeks of my time in WLC while waiting for recruiting school. As far as I was concerned I would just go ahead and get WLC knocked out when I got back from school. It made sense because after recruiting school I would have to return to Fort Drum to wait for my orders to be cut, which could take anywhere from a few weeks to a few months. Either way, I wasn't about to let past misunderstandings or mistakes break my stride. I had succeeded at reaching my goal, and aside from waiting to leave for school there was only one thing left to do: celebrate.

I decided that the best thing to do was to take a trip to New Jersey. I hadn't been there since late 2007 and because of the fact that I was going to school soon I knew I wouldn't be there for a while. It seemed like the most appropriate thing to do. I put in for a week of leave and went down there, only this time with the intent to celebrate my recent win. Just like all of the other times that I visited I stayed at Kathy's house, and we met up with as many people as possible. We seemed to go out partying almost every night that I was there, pretty much drinking wherever, whenever, and whatever. Like usual we went to Atlantic City and had a blast there too. It was a celebration after all; a celebration of the idea that I was soon going to be moving down there. The entire week went by great and had a real positive feeling until the final morning came along. I was sitting in a diner in Atlantic City drinking coffee and eating breakfast with a few of my friends. We stayed out the night before partying at one of the Casinos and we were just trying to recover from our hangovers. All of a sudden my phone started to ring. It was one of the Detachment Sergeants from my unit, and he was calling with some bad news. He informed me that while I was away on leave for the week the unit decided that they would be sending me to WLC almost immediately upon return, and because of this the Battalion had sent down guidance that I had to take a PT test and get weighed in the following morning. I couldn't believe this. This seemed like the absolute worst thing that could happen to me. Here I had just spent the past year working my ass off to achieve a goal, and all I wanted to do was celebrate just a little. Now, considering the fact that I had been on leave for a week and not doing any PT whatsoever in addition to drinking every day for that week there was just no way that I could make tape. For one, I know my body. If I take a week off from exercising I am sure to gain a few pounds. That's just how my metabolism works. In addition, if you drink a lot of beer for an entire week you are sure to be bloated and carry around a few extra pounds of water weight. When I first left for this particular trip I had no idea that I would be weighed in upon return. I figured that any water weight that I did gain from the booze could just be lost through a good week or two of doing some cardio. Had I known that any of this was going to take place I just wouldn't have went on leave in the first place. I would have put my career first and just stayed at Fort Drum, but since I had no idea that this was going to happen all of that seemed like a moot point now. The whole thing seemed like one big "screw job." Deep down it felt like the Battalion was almost out to get me; the Army as a whole always seems to have a thing with screwing with people who are overweight. I have never felt that it was fair, and I never will. I asked myself the question, "If I was a Soldier who was thin would this issue even come up?" The answer was simple: of course not. I've seen many Soldiers go on leave in my career and most of them were NEVER weighed in upon returning. Why was I any different? Why the double standard? When I got off the phone and I told Kathy, Mike and our former Detachment Sergeant what had happened they were all disgusted. They couldn't believe that a unit would treat one of their own that way. They shared the same sentiment that I did; that I was not only being set up for failure but the whole thing also seemed "rigged." They knew that I wasn't required (by regulation) to attend WLC before recruiting school, the requirement was really just an imaginary one set by higher headquarters. It wasn't like their opinion/input didn't mean anything because Kathy and Mike were both Sergeants (E5) and our Detachment Sergeant was a Sergeant First Class (E7). All three of them had years of experience and the very fact that they shared the same ideas as me was even more of an indication that the unit had an ulterior motive in forcing me into this horrible situation.

The next morning the weigh in and PT test took place, just as I was told that they would. The PT test itself was a little messed up; for one it didn't even take place on the normal track that all of the other tests took place on and the graders weren't even in the right place at the right time. The graders didn't send someone to the halfway (1 mile) turnaround point and thus when I got to the supposed point I didn't know if I was supposed to turn around or not. What pissed me off about this whole thing was the very fact that I had just taken a PT test a few weeks ago, meaning that I wasn't actually due for one for another six months. Being forced into doing the PT test made even less sense to me than being forced into the weigh in itself; throughout my entire career I had consistently had a high PT score, usually a 270 or above (out of 300 possible points.) There was no question among the unit leadership about whether or not I could pass a PT test. It was well known that I could not only pass, but I could nearly max it and outscore almost all of the other Soldiers in the company as well. That was a fact and I will swear to it to this day.

The weigh in went down exactly as I thought it would as well. I failed the tape with about 2% body fat percentage over the allowable amount. I knew that would happen, since I just spent an entire week drinking beer. When I was waiting to be taped, there was a smug feeling in the room; I could almost "feel" that this was a plan set forth by some of my superiors. I know that sounds paranoid, but please put yourself in my shoes for just a second. How would you feel? All of this just seemed like one big ploy to force me into going to WLC before I wanted to, not for the sake of benefiting my career but for the sake of the Battalion's slide show, which I alluded to earlier. That's all it ever was in that unit. I knew deep down that I could lose this weight in a week, if I was given the chance. None of that mattered to the unit however; I wasn't going to be given any chance. My flag was going to be re-instated and I wasn't going to go to recruiting school anytime soon. Heartbroken and depressed I returned to the company area, because I had received word that 1SG Gudger wanted to see me, and he wasn't happy.

When I got down to the company, he immediately started to yell at me. He was clearly unhappy, and every time that I tried to reason with him and explain to him my side of the story he just didn't want to hear it. There was nothing that I could say to him that could make him listen to me, and there were few times that he just told me to "shut the fuck up." What made all of that worse was the fact that there were other Soldiers and NCOs in the immediate area that heard every word that we said to each other. SGT Cappe was even there, and he couldn't believe what he heard next. 1SG Gudger shouted the following words at me, words that will stick out in my head forever, "SGT Conklin, take your fuckin ass to Clark Hall, and fuckin flag yourself!" The meaning of that statement was simple: the act of "flagging" a Soldier is what takes place when a Soldier fails either their PT test or weigh in or gets into some sort of legal trouble. These flags prohibit a Soldier from going to school or getting promoted. These flags are administered by the unit S1/Human Resources representative, which happened to be my job. Clark Hall was the office that I worked at. In other words, when 1SG Gudger told me to "take my fuckin ass to Clark Hall and fuckin flag myself" he was doing this in an effort to humble me. Think about it; how humbling would it be to type up and input your own flag into the system? Luckily for me, it is prohibited for an S1 to input any transactions on themselves into the system, so I was limited to the humiliation of just having to type the form up. That in itself was still humiliating and either way 1SG Gudger got his message across in front of a large group of people. Although SGT Cappe and I tend to look back and joke about that day nowadays that still doesn't mean that I appreciated it when it happened because believe me, I didn't appreciate it. It pissed me off to a high degree and what made it worse was that I now knew that I was going to be stuck working in that unit that much longer and my dream of moving to New Jersey was going to be put off yet again, all because of something that appeared to me to be something that took place not for my interests, but for the interests of the unit leadership and their slide shows.

The next few weeks were an extremely depressing time for me. I didn't want to do very much in my free time during the week, and as a result I started drinking more. Things started to seem very dark for me for a long time. Everything that I had worked for had been taken away from me and it just didn't seem right. I was so bitter because I didn't feel that I was given a fair chance at things. Before I knew it I received some even worse news from Battalion headquarters that my Recruiting assignment was just outright deleted. That in itself was a dream crusher. Ever since I returned from the deployment all of my energy was focused on the idea that I would get to leave Fort Drum and eventually get to move to New Jersey where I knew I had a lot of true friends. Now that all of that had come crashing down all around me I felt stuck, like my back was against the wall. For the next few weeks I no longer tried hard during PT. I was no longer motivated in anything that I did, with the exception of my day to day job in the office. Honestly, the only reason that I didn't start letting my performance slip in that area was because I knew that the careers of other Soldiers were in my hands. I didn't want to make others suffer because of a problem that I was having. That would have been selfish.

I knew that I couldn't stay depressed forever. I had to find things that would make me happy again. Slowly I cut back on my drinking and made sure that I went home every weekend. I couldn't stand the idea of being there at Fort Drum anymore, so I made sure not to be there any more time then I absolutely had to. As of now there were no more of the barracks parties on select weekends; since I no longer wanted any part of that place I just made sure to go home every single weekend. If the Soldiers in those barracks wanted to have fun I am sure that they could find a different party, they did not need me to always be the one hosting it. I just hated that place so much that I couldn't even stay there and party. On the weekends at home it didn't matter what I did; one weekend I might have spent a lot of time partying with Josh and the others, and then the next weekend I would lay low and just spend the weekend hanging out with my Dad. Either way, being away from Fort Drum was what made me happy so I just distanced myself from there as much as possible. I remember thinking about all of the things that I had done while I was there and thinking about all of the sacrifices that I made. I was still the same guy who deployed to Afghanistan on a six hour notice, so after all of those sacrifices why was I treated this way? Didn't I deserve better? Realizing that things may not ever get better up there I decided to set out to work my very hardest at my job (like always), but with a different goal in mind. My goal was to always be as good as possible and to be known as one of the greatest S1 NCO's that they had ever seen. Realizing that those types of ideas no longer sufficed, I decided that my new goal in life should be to take my talents and use them to help as many Soldiers as possible, not for any form of recognition or personal gain but simply to help those out who had to suffer the hand of the crooked Battalion headquarters. Since I had the ability to do more types of transactions than the average S1 that meant that I could do more for Soldiers at a quicker rate, provided that the Company leadership didn't stop or hinder me. As long as I knew that my immediate supervisor was ok with this (which he was) I would do everything possible to help Soldiers cut through the same red tape that had been used to hold me back. Now that I had a newfound focus and purpose, my depression quickly faded away. There was just one question left that remained a mystery to me: exactly why was my assignment deleted when it could have just been pushed back again? I did need an answer to that question, and the mystery would linger in my mind for a little while longer.

Summer finally came along and it was time for the change of leadership that the unit had been anticipating for a long time. Many of the Soldiers were upset about the idea that 1SG Gudger was leaving, and rightfully so. He was a tremendous leader and did a lot for so many of the Soldiers as well as the company as a whole. Before he left he told me that when he lashed out on me it wasn't personal, he was just extremely pissed off. He wished me the best of luck, and I wished him the same as well. I was actually glad that he said this to me, because I hadn't spoken a single word to him since the day that he told me to "take my fuckin ass to Clark Hall and fuckin flag myself." It was a good way to "bury the hatchet," perhaps a hatchet that didn't really need to exist in the first place. Either way, I did end up staying touch with him and there were a few times later on in my career that I was able to call him for professional advice. As a leader he never failed me, and that's all I could really ask for.

Now that he had left the company things steadily started to get worse. 1SG Gudger's replacement came in, and right from the start she created a ton of problems. For one, she outright voiced that she had no desire to be our First Sergeant. She not only voiced this to the higher headquarters, but she also voiced it to the Soldiers. As you can probably imagine, this created a lot of problems. A company First Sergeant is supposed to be the standard bearer; the leader of the Soldiers and the "face" of the company. The last thing the Soldiers needed to hear was that their new leader didn't want to be their leader under any circumstances. This put a bad taste in the Soldiers mouth and caused a lot of them to lose respect for her right from the start. That's an easy way to "get off on the wrong foot" so to speak.

In addition to stating that she didn't want to lead us, our new "leader" caused a lot of other problems in other areas as well. The most notable one that had a direct influence on me was that she started micromanaging me to a high degree. That made me sick for so many reasons. For one, I knew my job extremely well and everyone in the company KNEW that I knew my job well. It was common knowledge, and I was the last person that needed to be micromanaged. In addition, I was a Sergeant; an NCO. You don't micromanage an NCO unless their performance is "piss-poor." The new First Sergeant didn't seem to care about any of that, and now demanded me to start following some of the dumbest protocols that I had ever heard of. Every single document that I now processed had to be run through her office, regardless on if it needed her signature or the commander's signature. (Usually if something needs the commander's signature it is common to go through the First Sergeant's office.) She also forced me to send her a courtesy copy of all emails that I sent to the Battalion. That really wasn't necessary and it seemed like she wanted to read every word that was said to them. There were so many other problems that were created as a result of her micromanaging me, and at the end of the day it amounted to more "red tape," only this time it was being applied at the company level. This ultimately slowed down my work day which I didn't like whatsoever. I went from working for a First Sergeant that hated "red tape" to a First Sergeant that created it. Since she just arrived it was painfully clear to everyone that these problems weren't going to go away any time soon. I wasn't the only one she micromanaged either. She made every attempt to micromanage everyone that she possibly could. To this day I still don't know why she did it; maybe it had to do with her own insecurities as a leader. If you ask me, as a leader I would prefer NOT to micromanage someone. Not only would it create a lot more work for everyone involved, but it also displays a lack of trust. By micromanaging most of her NCOs the new First Sergeant was sending all of her NCOs an underlying message: I don't trust my NCOs.

As a member of the company staff I was privy to certain information before the rest of the Soldiers in the company were. The day came where a certain piece of information was brought to my attention; a piece of information that would not just change my life but would also finally explain to me exactly why my recruiting assignment was deleted. I found out that our unit was being put on order to deploy to Iraq in early 2009, meaning that since I was part of the unit that I would have to go as well. This news put a lot of things into perspective for me, for one the idea that I wasn't ever going to have to deploy again was now gone. Also, in my own mind I started to deduct that this may be exactly why my assignment was deleted; after all there was really no reason why it couldn't just be postponed yet again. As far as I was concerned there was a slight possibility that someone requested that assignment be deleted for the good of the unit. If you knew that I was the best Soldier for the job why wouldn't you want to take me on the deployment? From a leadership standpoint that idea makes sense, but here is the thing: if my theory is correct then that means that my feelings/desires for my career were never taken under consideration when deleting my assignment. Deep down I believed that was the case, so of course I was a little hurt about this situation. Now, is there any way to ever prove my theory to be correct? No. I will never know if these ideas were based in fact, or if they were just conjured up by my own mind. Many Americans today believe in conspiracy theories, ranging from high-level conspiracies transpired by major corporations all the way to personal-level conspiracies that may take place at their own workplace. I will not say that today I believe there was, or wasn't for that matter, a "conspiracy" because to be quite frank at this moment in my life it doesn't really matter. All I will say is that AT THE TIME it certainly seemed that way to me. And just like all of the other stories that I have told so far, that's my story and I'm sticking to it.

At this point things at the company were getting worse and worse by the day. None of the NCOs were getting along with the new First Sergeant, and the idea of having to deploy and work under her almost seemed like an impossible task. No one wanted to do it, but everyone knew that they had to. Morale in the unit continued to dwindle and almost no one was looking forward to this deployment. On a personal level, all I wanted to do was turn a negative into a positive. I looked at a deployment as an opportunity to drop all of the weight and make tape once and for all. Then I would look into the idea of calling my branch manager to request to finally get orders to leave Fort Drum once the deployment was over. Even though none of us wanted to go on this deployment I still knew deep down that adding a third deployment to my resume would not be a bad thing. All that we had to do was to make it through the deployment, with our sanity intact.

Christmas 2008 came along, and like any other time that I was home in the US I went home and had the best time possible. Because of my newfound deployment orders I knew that I wasn't going to make it home for Christmas 2009, so I tried to make this one count. Our family had a great Christmas and I am very thankful for that. Unfortunately, I can't say the same for New Year's Eve. While all of my friends threw an awesome New Year's Eve party back at home, I was required to head back up to Fort Drum and pull 24 hour staff duty at the barracks that night. As you can probably imagine, that greatly upset me and added an insult to the injury of the idea that I was about to deploy with this unit in a few months. Granted, I went to a ton of parties at home in 2008, but let's be honest about one thing; there is only one New Year's Eve. Earlier I alluded to the possibility of a "conspiracy" to keep me out of my recruiting assignment. When I alluded to that, I was careful to state that while I believed it at the time, I don't exactly share that sentiment now; that there is just no way to ever know the truth. When it comes to the New Year's Eve matter however, I know for a fact that I missed it due to the First Sergeant's doing, and that it was intentional. (Notice that I did not use the word conspiracy because a conspiracy insinuates that there is more than one person involved.) How do I know that the First Sergeant intentionally caused me to miss out on New Year's? Well, the answer is simple, and I will gladly explain: the First Sergeant is in charge of compiling the duty roster on a monthly basis. Usually, when the Soldiers name's come out on the roster they have an opportunity to get off the roster through one of two different methods; one being they could simply trade duty dates with another Soldier or they could also outright pay a Soldier cash to take your duty off your hands. The idea of paying a Soldier may or may not be ethical and it really isn't for me to decide if it is ethical or not. What I do know about paying Soldiers to take your duty is that the idea of doing it isn't covered in Army Regulations, which doesn't necessarily make it illegal, and in fact I have seen various Soldiers do that throughout my career at every duty station that I ever served at have partook in this practice. This includes Fort Drum. I will state for the record that I have NEVER seen a leader not authorize their Soldiers to pay another to take their duty. I have witnessed Soldiers make a good $200 to take a weekend duty, especially during a four day weekend? Is that a problem? No it's not a problem! It presents a great opportunity for a Soldier to make some quick money. I don't think that there's anything wrong with that. With that said; when

New Year's Eve approached I attempted to pay another Soldier to take my duty. The First Sergeant quickly shot the idea down and claimed that she didn't think it was ethical. I couldn't believe it. I tried to reason with her, citing that various Soldiers have done this in the past and it was never a problem. She felt that it was a problem; that it shouldn't be happening and wasn't going to be happening anymore. This not only upset me, but it upset many of the other Soldiers when I conveniently broke to them the news that the new First Sergeant was no longer going to allow us to sell our duty away to other Soldiers.

What made all of this even worse was what transpired the following week. A Soldier had duty in the barracks and didn't want to pull it. So, what do you think they did? They sold the duty to another Soldier, like usual. And who do you think allowed this to happen as if it wasn't a problem? The First Sergeant. That's right, you read that correctly. The First Sergeant, who put a ban on selling your duty when I had to pull duty on New Year's, was now allowing Soldiers to sell their duty just a week later. Can you honestly blame me for feeling like this was all done intentionally to ruin my New Year's? It had to be. If she hadn't "brought back" selling duty spots the week after I would have just choked it up to a bad leader making a bad decision. Instead the practice of selling your duty was re-introduced into the company immediately following New Year's, which made things seem not only "too convenient" but personal as well. I feel that I had every right to take that as a personal attack, and thus I did. So I say this, to all of my friends back in Saint Johnsville (this one's for you, Josh and Joe) who were heartbroken because I couldn't make it home for that New Year's, it wasn't my fault. I was treated unfairly, and I apologize for not being there.

As 2009 began everyone in the Company started to realize the harsh reality that the deployment was coming up quick . . . a little too quick actually. I was still going home every available weekend so I could spend as much time with my family and friends as possible. I knew that I was going to miss them an awful lot and departing on this trip may even be harder than the last two times. It wasn't just because I had built closer bonds with all of my friends at home. The day to day life and morale in the unit had deteriorated so much to the lowest level possible, so much so that I could remember that when I did go home it was almost therapeutic for me. I felt that I could take anything that the messed up leadership could throw at me, provided I could go home and "recharge" on the weekends. Things may not be making any sense at Fort Drum, but I knew deep down that everything made sense at home. Saint Johnsville was my town, my home; that special place that I could always go where things would always be ok. The very idea that I had to endure working in that unit for an entire year without being able to go home was a hard idea to comprehend. What was worse was that the First Sergeant was constantly coming down on me for going home all the time, claiming that it displayed "bad leadership." I took an exception to that because if you were to take a poll amongst the Soldiers in the company at the time about who was the worse leader, me or her, she would certainly win "worst leader" by a landslide. When it came right down to it, I was one of the NCOs that the Soldiers actually respected there. Every time that the Soldiers came to me and displayed that it served as my own personal validation; a little feeling inside that told me that I was doing the right thing. That's all I ever cared about; if the people that were under my charge believed in me and respected me that was all I needed. I didn't need the validation from a First Sergeant who blatantly stated to the Soldiers that she did not want to be their leader. That type of validation meant nothing to me. The only time that I went home was the weekends anyway; it wasn't like I was skipping work call, PT formations, or any other types of activities or duties that were happening at the unit. Had I been skipping out on work days I would have understood the complaint and fixed the issue. As far as I was concerned, what I did in my free time was my business, not anyone else's. If there were any other Soldiers who were in my shoes that were fortunate to be close to home I am sure that they would have cultivated the opportunity as well. When it came right down to it, the ability to "forget about the Army" on the weekends was just too good to pass up.

Part of the issue that everyone had with the new First Sergeant was that she wasn't like our former leader, 1SG Gudger in any way, shape, or form. Aside from all of the issues that she displayed in front of the Soldiers, there was also the issue that she wasn't exactly the type of leader who believed in standing up to Battalion when they were wrong on the issues. 1SG Gudger always stood up for us, every single time. This worried us because we knew that we were not going to be falling under the same support Battalion from Drum during the deployment. We would be falling under a different unit altogether. With any new unit there comes a new set of rules and a unique set of circumstances and subsequently new problems. The general consensus amongst the NCOs in the unit was that our "leader" may not be able to handle the pressure of answering to a new unit. It was obvious that 1SG Gudger would have been able to handle this task but unfortunately the "glory days" of working for him were long gone.

Before I knew it I was home for my final weekend before the deployment; my "farewell weekend" if you will. I rallied up the entire gang for one last hurrah. I knew that they would all carry on without me, and next weekend when I was sweating in the dessert they would still be here in Saint Johnsville but that didn't matter right now. This was my weekend. We started off the usual way; "pre-gaming" at Josh's house drinking a few beers and playing drinking games. After we were finished with all of that we filtered down to the local bar. Josh and Joe pretty much bought all of my drinks that night, and like usual I did get drunk. There were a lot of toasts for me that night and I'll never forget one of Josh's toasts. As he raised his bottle in the air he yelled, "This one's for you Kenny! LOYALTY OVER VICTORY!" That was touching and it meant the world to me.

At one point in the night I was too drunk to continue, so I went home. Most of my friends weren't ready to go back yet so they made sure that my beer that I left on the bar stayed there so that every time they took a drink they could toast my beer, as if they were toasting me in person. Looking back on things I wish I stayed out the rest of the night like everyone else, but what could I do? I was too drunk to continue so my instincts kicked in and I went home. When that weekend was over I definitely was emotional about having to leave, but at the same time I knew that I had a good final weekend and went out the right way. It was a great feeling to know that I had so many friends behind me that cared and would stay in touch. When I arrived back to Fort Drum I knew that was it, the end of having a good time for a year. There were only a few days left until we had to deploy and we would spend those days going to formations and packing our gear. I pretty much came to terms with the fact that the deployment was here and there was nothing that was going to change that. When the morning finally came to leave we boarded a coach bus that took us to Baltimore-Washington International airport (BWI) where we would board the plane and embark on our journey. The eight hour bus ride to Baltimore afforded me one final opportunity to reflect on the events of the past few years as well as things to come in the future. I thought about my friends and my family and vowed that I would stay in touch. I thought about the challenges that were ahead; I needed to get my ass in shape during that deployment so I could leave Fort Drum the second I came back. I also thought about the deployment itself; I didn't know a lot of these Soldiers very well at the time (with the exception of Cappe.) Would I be able to get along with everyone? I hoped so. Finally I thought about the greatest challenge of all, keeping my sanity while having to work directly for someone that I knew was a bad leader. I was going to try my very best out there, but deep down inside I had a funny feeling that this was going to be my worst deployment ever.

CHAPTER 12

BACK TO IRAQ

We arrived to Kuwait early one April morning. Just as expected the temperature was hot in comparison to Fort Drum. That's the main reason that a lot of units tend to rotate in and out of there in the Spring as opposed to the Summer; it gives Solders a chance to acclimate themselves to the environment and the heat before the real heat (the Summer heat) settles in. Although the temperatures in Kuwait were exactly what I had expected, Kuwait itself was not. The camps had changed so much since I was last deployed there in 2003 and it was almost like I was looking at an entirely different place altogether.

Camp Buering was the name of the place that we would spend the next few weeks while we awaited our trip into Iraq. The funny thing about the place was that it wasn't always named Camp Buering. Its original name was Camp Udarri. Camp Udarri was the exact same camp that I was deployed to six years earlier on my first deployment. Back then the camp was a baron wasteland with few amenities. Survival on Camp Udarri was an actual challenge. Camp Buering on the other hand was a built up camp that had everything. There were not only basic necessities but also plenty of entertainment/morale related activities there. Camp Buering had a huge MWR center that had about 100 PlayStation 3 and Xbox 360 video game systems with HDTV's there for the Soldiers there to enjoy. As if that wasn't enough, there were also basketball courts, a movie theater, and two built up Dining Facilities. In comparison to Camp Udarri in 2003, Buering seemed to have everything. In 2003 there was nothing there except sand, circus tents to sleep in, and a makeshift trailer to eat at. It was amazing just how many things had changed, and it made it hard to believe that I was standing on the same camp that I stood on years before.

Another main difference between Kuwait in 2003 and Kuwait in 2009 was now every Soldier was required to go through certain training exercises before entering Iraq. Obviously on my first deployment there wasn't any infrastructure whatsoever, but since then there were various training areas set up all over the country. There were weapons ranges set up on camp and every Soldier was required to qualify on their assigned weapon in the dessert heat before the unit left Iraq. There was also a machine set up called a HEAT trainer, which is a machine that simulates accidents that could take place inside of a Humvee, to include rollovers. The machine, which looks like a Humvee without wheels attached to a giant frame which allows Soldiers to enter, buckle up and simulate a Humvee rollover. Once the machine "rolls over" the Soldiers are required to exit the vehicle while it is still positioned upside down. This provides an extremely valuable training experience. Back when I was deployed the first time we didn't have special equipment like that, and the only way to experience a rollover was to actually be involved in a real rollover. The problem with a rollover is that it can cause someone to panic, obviously because it is a dangerous experience but also because it is a new experience that you haven't encountered before. By putting Soldiers through a simulation they are actually becoming subject to this horrible experience in advance which mentally prepares them in a much better manner than just reading about it on a PowerPoint slide show. On a personal level I not only understand why this training takes place in Kuwait but I agree with it as well. As you can probably tell by reading this far, there are a lot of things that take place in the Army that I don't agree with but I will say that I feel that US Soldiers should be trained to the fullest extent possible prior to entering a combat zone, regardless of what their MOS or position may be. Seeing all of these new requirements in Kuwait really made me feel like the United States of America was making great strides in the war.

My time in Kuwait wasn't free of leadership-related incidents however. The First Sergeant was up to her usual tricks of not only making my life a living hell, but also making the other Soldiers around her miserable. She expected me to be proactive and call the rear detachment back at Fort Drum to talk about work, even though they were all set on their own and none of the other Soldiers that were with us were required to work. While in Kuwait the only thing that we were required to do was attend the training exercises and await our flight into the country. There were no work requirements whatsoever, but the First Sergeant just had to try to push my buttons. I couldn't just enjoy my off time like the rest of my Soldiers. Sensing that this was all deliberate, a lot of the officers would comment to me about how the First Sergeant was treating me. I was glad to know that officers (who were not only senior to me, but senior to her as well) saw that there was a problem. It sent me a message that I wasn't alone, and I wasn't judging her from a position of bias. It also showed me that things at the time were not a "conspiracy" whatsoever, because as I stated earlier a conspiracy requires more than one person to conspire. Knowing that certainly helped me sleep at night, but that didn't mean that dealing with the First Sergeant got any easier. There were a number of issues/stories that resonated from the female tent where the First Sergeant lived. Apparently, many of the female Soldiers in the unit had an issue living with her because she not only made their lives miserable all day long, but also complained to the Soldiers as much as possible about how much SHE hated life. As a leader, you should never complain about your problems to your subordinates; especially to the junior enlisted Soldiers. It is a severe sign of weakness and causes your Soldiers to lose respect for you. If you absolutely have to vent or complain to someone at least have the decency to do it to a fellow NCO; someone of a comparable rank or very close to it as opposed to 18 year old Privates who have been in the Army for seven months. Trust me; those junior Soldiers will thrive on the fact that their leader has problems. I guess none of this logic was ever conveyed to the First Sergeant because if it was I am sure that she would have acted differently. Every single act that she committed was relayed to me first hand because of the fact that a Soldier was finally appointed to work for me for the deployment who happened to live in the female tent. Her name was Specialist Rivanna Cummings, and she wasn't actually a Human Resources Soldier. Her MOS was 74D, which is code for NBC Specialist. In other words, she maintained gasmasks and planned, coordinated and managed all NBC related training for the unit to include the gas chamber itself. The reason that she was appointed to work for me wasn't just because of the fact that no chemical weapons were found in Iraq, but also because she had experience working as an HR clerk in the past. She worked in what was called an "Orderly Room," which meant that she had to perform certain HR functions at the Company level. Obviously it wasn't comparable to the amount of experience that I had, but it was enough experience to know that she certainly knew her job. Over the course of the deployment she proved to be "more than reliable" and even took charge of the section a few times in my absence. She was so good at doing the job that at times you would swear that she was an HR Soldier herself. Either way, we hadn't started our official mission yet because we were still in Kuwait so all I really had to do was make sure I took accountability of her on a daily basis and make sure she was doing ok. Each and every time she (along with some of the others in the tent) would have a story about what messed up action the First Sergeant committed that day. It got to the point where some of us NCOs (to include myself and SGT Cappe) would just shake our heads and say "wow." It got to the point where nothing surprised us anymore. It was like what happened yesterday was the worst thing that ever happened . . . until something happened today. So in other words, every day brought us a new challenge. When you are preparing to go into a combat zone it isn't exactly the best feeling in the world when you know that the "leader" of the company is behaving this way.

The First Sergeant wasn't the only NCO in that unit who "had a few screws loose." There were a few more NCOs who I would encounter on that deployment who consistently caused problems and just never really seemed to get along with anyone. There was one NCO in particular who had caused a lot of problems in the past back at Fort Drum who came along on this trip as well. He had built up a reputation for being a guy who liked to run his mouth a lot, even when he made a mistake and even when he was wrong. He took his rank far too seriously and thus he didn't get along with a lot of the Soldiers either. Since he made so many mistakes the company leadership didn't really like him very much either. This deployment would prove to be no different, and to be honest with the reputation he had everyone expected him to mess up anyway. His first mess up of the deployment came in the form of a road march that he decided to take out of the blue on the second day that we were in Kuwait. Now, he had a reputation for always being heavily involved in doing PT yet not being in very good shape, if that makes any sense. Part of that had to do with his age (as he was almost 50 years old) and part of that had to do with the fact that he did drink a lot of alcohol; which not only meant that he wasn't in the best shape but he also was dehydrated often. Being dehydrated can severely demean your performance when working out. This is a documented fact and has been proven by doctors, yet every morning when we would do PT back at Fort Drum he would still smell like booze. I couldn't understand how he got away with it for so long. If we were in Korea that would have been one thing, but this was the 10th

Mountain Division, things were far tougher and even stricter here. If that was a junior Soldier he would have gotten in a lot of trouble, yet this NCO never got in trouble. If you were to ever speculate that this man was drinking on the deployment, this road march would have been the time to do so.

He departed the tent to embark on his road march during the early hours of the morning. The sun wasn't out yet, but considering the fact that we were in Kuwait it was still hot out, even at night or in the early morning. When he didn't come back right away, the officers in the unit started to worry about him yet didn't send anyone to find him. If that fact doesn't send you a "red flag" that you aren't assigned to the best unit in the world than I don't know what is. Finally after being gone for hours he stumbled back into the tent and fell right asleep, without going out to take a shower. No one seemed to think anything of it, he was just exhausted from being outside in the sun and it took him a lot longer to finish the road march then we all thought it would. Doesn't seem like too much of a problem so far, does it? Everyone in the tent should have seen the signs that the man was in fact suffering from heat exhaustion, but no one did. The news came the next morning when he tried to wake up, and he couldn't even get out of bed. Furthermore, his speech was severely slurred and you couldn't understand half of the words that he was saying. It was clear that he had to be taken to the TMC for medical treatment immediately. Out of everyone that lived in the tent, I was the one that was chosen to take him. I thought to myself, "Great" as I took him over there. I didn't really get along with him at all back at the unit, and the only reason that I cooperated was the very fact that I felt that his life was in danger. I assumed that I would take him over and he would receive the treatment that he needed and the day would be over. Unfortunately for me and everyone else involved, that just wasn't the case.

When we got to the TMC he immediately started running his mouth, saying things to people that he shouldn't have. He would make a comment to a young female Soldier that was there that could have been taken way out of context, if you know what I mean. He would look at the doctors and laugh and start touching things on the shelves at the doctor's office. It was almost as if he was a drunken man. I knew that one of the signs of heat stroke is acting irrationally, but with him you really couldn't tell because he was acting very similar to the way he acted back at the unit which obviously made things a little more difficult for me to deal with.

He was connected to an IV by medical personnel in an effort to hydrate him. The doctors thought that it wasn't enough because his behavior hadn't really changed since they administered the IV. Before they were able to hook him up to another IV, problems started to ensue; only I could tell that they were problems that he was creating on his own. There was an Army medic and a Navy doctor working on him, and the Navy doctor stepped out of the room for a brief second. It was at this point that he looked up to me and the Army medic and said, "I'm glad you guys are here. I can't stand that Navy doctor. He doesn't know what he's doing. Fuck the Navy. I hate the Navy and that man is an idiot." Now, as far as I am concerned a doctor is a doctor; it doesn't matter if you are in the Army, Navy, Air Force, Marine Corps, or if you are a civilian. If you are a doctor by profession then you have obviously passed the required tests to become a doctor and you are fine by me. This NCO didn't feel this way however, he simply felt that if you were not an Army doctor then you weren't really good enough to work on him. The problem was not just the fact that he made such a statement, but that he made the statement within earshot of the Navy doctor. When the doctor "left the room" earlier, he wasn't really leaving the room at all. We were actually in one big room, which was sectioned off by blankets which meant that the Navy doctor that was being badmouthed was just standing behind a curtain the whole time and could hear the whole thing. The doctor emerged from the curtain and looked me dead in the eyes. I could tell that he was pissed off, but then again he wasn't pissed off at me because the words hadn't come out of my mouth. I looked him dead in the eye and raised my hands in the air, as if to say, "It wasn't me." At this point the doctor still hadn't made himself visible to the NCO from my unit, which was even funnier because he was still preaching his anti-Navy sentiments. Suddenly, the doctor blew his cover and said, "Everything seems fine, just drink a few bottles of Gatorade and you will be ok. Now, if you don't mind I would like you to leave my office." Again I made eye contact with the doctor, and I could see the amused look on his face. He took exception to what was said about him and his branch of service, and quite frankly so did I. I didn't have any issue with the Navy whatsoever. In fact, one of my good friends from Saint Johnsville by the name of Daniel Murray was in the Navy. We never fought over the fact that he was in the Navy and I was in the Army. That's just stupid. When you look at the big picture, you realize that we are all on the same side. This is the United States of America. Was Dan part of China's Navy? No. Perhaps Russia's Navy? Definitely not, he was part of America's Army and that's all there is to it. I don't know why some Soldiers in the Army had an issue with the Navy; our missions almost never crossed paths so it all seemed immature to me. On the way back to the unit, I can remember the NCO from my unit saying to me, "I can't believe that after everything all I needed was some Gatorade. God that Navy guy was an idiot." I quietly smiled to myself, knowing that this nutcase needed a lot more than a Gatorade. Aside from the medical help that he probably needed, it seemed to me that he wasn't entirely ok, and that he would have to suffer the consequences of his own actions. Had I been in his shoes I probably wouldn't have said the things he did; but the funny thing about that is I am not in his shoes, I am in my shoes. From the perspective of a man who stands in my own shoes, I can promise you that it was funny to watch him make a fool of himself. Over the course of the next 12 months he would continue to make a fool out of himself, but none of those occasions were as funny as the time he decided to say that the Navy sucked within earshot of a Navy doctor. As the comedian Bill Engvall would say, "Here's your sign."

After two weeks of good training and mundane incidents our unit was finally ready to board a C-130 Airplane enroute to Iraq. Even this was a difference from when I was deployed here in 2003. Back then, almost the entire unit took the trip via convoy which left only me and a few other Soldiers to have to fly into Iraq. Nowadays, everyone would fly in and the unit that we would replace would just provide us with vehicles that stayed with whatever unit was deployed at the time. This was so different to me because it posed the possibility that some Soldiers may actually endure a tour in Iraq without having to go on a convoy. Back in 2003 that idea was inconceivable, everyone went on a convoy. That's just how it was. It was amazing how many things had changed since the last time I was here, and that was just in the first two weeks. Time would only tell what kind of things would come my way over the duration of the year. I knew that the most important thing to focus on was keeping a level head and a steady mind. Our arrival into Iraq signified that it was time to get to work.

We were set to work and live on a place called Tallil, also known as Contingency Operation Base (COB) Adder. Upon first looking around, COB Adder looked like a deserted wasteland that fostered sad feelings. Everywhere that I looked I could see nothing but sand, gravel, and dreary tan buildings. I guess I expected this because Tallil is located in Southern

Iraq where most of the country resembles a baron dessert as opposed to the city of Mosul, which had a lot of grass and lively palm trees that gave the place a much better look as well as a better feeling. Tallil did have a few palm trees scattered throughout the camp, but they were all dead. I don't know if you have ever seen a standing dead palm tree or not, but I can promise you that I didn't find the sight to be very inspiring to say the least. COB Adder was also a lot hotter than Mosul due to its location in the southern part of the country. It wasn't unheard of for temperatures to reach 125 degrees in the spring, let along the summer. The winters did get a little chilly, but nothing near the 40 degree winter that I endured in Mosul.

Aside from the aesthetic and weather differences between the two different camps that I worked on during both deployments there were a lot of other changes as well. Just like on Camp Buering, COB Adder was fully stocked with amenities. There were two huge KBR dining facilities that served four meals a day, to include midnight chow. These DFACs ran on a 21-day menu schedule, meaning that every 30 days you were eating the same food with the exception of holidays. Granted, the same old meal schedule did get tiring after a while but it was still better than having to eat MREs every day. If you didn't want to eat at the DFAC that was perfectly fine, because it wasn't the only option available. COB Adder was home to a food court area which featured various fast food trailers to include Burger King, Taco Bell, and a Pizza Place. There was also a restaurant called 6-Pazzi that served burgers and fries, pizza and Italian pasta dishes among other things. 6-Pazzi also served fake, non-alcoholic beer and hookahs as well. Soldiers would order a hookah and smoke it over their meal in peace. The place really had a nice feel to it and I would sometimes head over there for a meal and a hookah. I stayed away from the fake beer for almost all of the deployment because after all there's nothing like the real thing, right? It wasn't until the last month of the deployment that I lost it and finally decided to try one. Just as I suspected it tasted horrible.

Units had different (and subsequently better) amenities as well. Most units were issued anywhere from two to four Chevrolet Trailblazer SUVs to get around the camp. On a personal level I felt that many of the junior Soldiers abused the privilege of having these vehicles by using them for absolutely everything that they wanted or needed to do. It didn't matter if it was going to the PX (which Tallil had a nice one) or if they were going to the DFAC. They would take these vehicles each and every time.

I didn't agree with this because I felt that it fostered a feeling of laziness. For them, walking to the DFAC was unheard of. Maybe it was because I had deployed to Iraq in 2003 and they had not; in 2003 the idea of taking an SUV to the DFAC would have been considered insane. It just wouldn't have happened. The constant use of the vehicles utterly disgusted me and as a result I decided to question the junior Soldiers about it every time they would get ready to leave with one of them. I knew that I didn't have the authority to stop them from using it, but I hoped that if I talked about it enough something in their conscience would come to life. As far as I was concerned, these were government vehicles and it was wrong for them to use them for personal use. Too bad I was the only one who saw it that way. To further my efforts I would even make it a point to tell them that I was walking whenever I would leave the room. I know that after a while I probably came off as an asshole, but sometimes that's what believing in self-reliance will get you. Many people prefer to have things handed to them, I do not.

Iraq as a whole had also changed. Gone were the days of the initial invasion and the troop surge. With the change from the Bush Administration to the Obama Administration the mission in Iraq seemed to change as well. Soldiers were no longer kicking in doors and taking over new camps. Instead, most units were sitting on huge camps such as COB Adder waiting to leave. Everyone knew that this was going to be one of the last years in Iraq since there had been talk of the US Government pulling all troops out of Iraq over the next year. Sure, there was still some action out in the cities, and we would still get a rocket attack from time to time but it was nothing like the deployment in 2003. Due to my position as the S1 for the unit it became painfully apparent to me that I would have to spend this entire deployment on the camp as opposed to getting to go on missions like last time. I know that some people may look at this as a blessing, but I enjoyed going on missions in 2003. For one, going on missions gave the deployment an element of adventure. It was something that I could do that would possibly give me some stories to call home about. In addition, going on missions always seemed to make the deployment fly by quicker. Prior to our arrival I had secretly hoped that there would be a few convoys that I could go on so I didn't have to deal with the First Sergeant every day. Now the future seemed bleak and I realized that I was doomed to stay on the camp and work my desk job every day. Furthermore, since the official time frame to for US Forces to start pulling out was scheduled for late 2010 there were no way that we were leaving early. Our 12 months would be up in April 2010. Upset with some of the changes that I had seen so far I realized my fate and decided that I would just work as hard as I could at my job and get the year over with. Deep down I hoped that this would happen without incident, but I just knew this wasn't going to be a great year whatsoever. I remembered the old saying, "it isn't the place that makes the place; it is the people that makes the place." That was so true. Our year was looking like it was going to be a miserable one due to the actions of one person. The only thing that helped me keep my head up was the fact that I wasn't the only one that felt that way.

Weeks earlier while we were still at Fort Drum everyone was told to decide who they wanted their roommate to be in advance which would make the process of moving into our rooms a lot quicker and easier upon our arrival into Iraq. SGT Cappe and I mutually agreed that being roommates with each other would the best idea because we knew each other for a long time and we could trust each other. Throughout my career I have witnessed many instances of theft where Soldiers actually stole from other Soldiers. I am not saying that anything like that took place in that unit recently, but I am saying that Cappe was someone that I could trust that would never do that. If someone was going to get robbed, Cappe was the last guy that I would ever suspect. In addition to the trust factor, I knew that I got along with him to begin with so there really wouldn't be any kind of arguments or anything like that. Being fans of New York teams it was pretty much a guarantee that we would always have something to talk about. Living with him also guaranteed a sanctuary where we could talk about the issues with some of the unit leadership without any fear of being caught. Some of the leadership in that unit (the First Sergeant in particular) would hassle both of us on a daily basis. By being roommates we now had the ability to almost "compare notes" about some of the problems that were circulating within that unit. Overall it was nice to have a friend there that I could trust to watch my back on that deployment.

The very housing itself was a far cry different than the way I lived in 2003. Instead of the tents that I lived in during most of the first deployment, we were able to live in two-man Containerized Housing Units (also known as CHU's). They were very similar to the ones that were brought onto Mosul airfield towards the end of my first deployment, only these were a little bigger and were upgraded with better locks, better air conditioning and cable TV and internet access. Hands down the living conditions were 100% better than my first deployment which meant that I had nothing to complain about in that aspect. That didn't stop many of the younger Soldiers from complaining though. Since they hadn't experienced anything worse in the past this all seemed like the "end of the world" to them. They really had no idea how good they had it out there and no matter how many times you explain to them how much worse it could be they just never seemed to get it. It was almost like some of them enjoyed moping about it all day. Not me. You get nowhere by sitting around and dwelling on your problems all day, especially when the problems you are dwelling on aren't even serious problems to begin with. Instead I choose to take the high road and focus on the positives. Honestly if you can't rationalize the little problems as meaningless in your mind then how the hell could you possibly handle a major problem? These Soldiers used to complain about how hard they thought they had it, but what if we did have to live in tents? What would they say then? What if our camp sustained a major attack? From my perspective you should be thankful for what you have when you are a combat zone. Personally I thought it was a blessing to not only live in a room to begin with but to also have internet access in my room so I could communicate with my family any time I wanted. When you compare a deployment in 2009 to a deployment in 2003 the first thing you would think of are these types of basic changes that generally boost the morale of everyone. Granted, being away from home does suck, but it would suck even worse if it took you three weeks to get them a hand written letter, as opposed to an email that takes minutes to send.

We got right to work on our first day on Tallil. We spent the first two weeks doing a "left seat-right seat" exchange with the previous unit, which was more or less a matter of assuming control of all of the databases and learning all of the procedures that were in place there. I was amazed at how much had changed even in that aspect; in 2003 I was deployed with the 101st and therefore everything I did went through the 101st. This time around I was deployed from Fort Drum but most things went through a theater-level command and that was it. I really wasn't used to this newfound command structure for the individual units and to me it didn't make any sense. I am sure that at the Department of Army level there was someone who thought it made sense but from my perspective doesn't it make more sense for Fort Drum Soldiers to process paperwork for those same Soldiers? The funny thing was that many of the other NCOs in the unit shared that same perspective, but that just didn't matter. Things had changed in Iraq and we had to adapt, plain and simple. Even with some of these procedural changes, the First Sergeant was up to her usual tricks and attempting to micromanage the entire office. She micromanaged all of the staff sections but my section took the hardest hit. Every single morning she would go out of her way to critique my emails that I sent to other people and to also pick through my work with a "fine-tooth comb" just to find a mistake. Even though she almost never found a mistake in my work, it still got to be a bit annoying to me and day by day I started to resent her as a result of it. After all, she didn't do this to the same degree with the other Soldiers. It was clear that she was doing this just to me, and it even got to the point where the other NCOs in the office would take notice and either console me or make jokes about it. I took exception to this fact because I knew my job extremely well, and I figured that I had proved that by now considering she was doing the same micromanaging back at Fort Drum. To me it was even more of a testament to her terrible leadership skills. She lacked the ability to know talent when she saw it and give me the ball. Had I been a bad NCO then her actions would have been justified but that just wasn't the case with me.

Another issue that I had on the deployment was in the form of the support battalion that I had to answer to in Iraq when it came to work related matters. As you read earlier I took great issue to the fact that we had to fall under the support unit back at Fort Drum because they didn't really know, understand, or care about our mission in the way that I felt that they should have. This battalion out in Iraq was no different; they also showed a lack of understanding for what I did for a living which made my life very hard. In addition to the typical crap that I had expected, they were a reserve battalion that only had one AGR Soldier. To be blunt, they were nothing like the hard working Soldiers from the NJ National Guard that I was deployed with in the past. Instead, these Soldiers were lazy and careless when it came to the job. To top it all off, two of their NCOs had severe attitude problems which also didn't sit well with me. They would often try to talk to me like I didn't know what I was doing. Who the hell did they think they were? After all, I had accomplished things as an S1 that many others had not and I had received praise from various senior NCOs and officers over the past few years for my dedication and work ethic. I had an excellent record so as far as I was concerned these "weekend warriors" were in zero position to judge me. Things all came to a head one day when I was over there for a briefing on their procedures for flagging Soldiers. The way that they wanted it done didn't just conflict with my method, but it also conflicted with Army regulations. Therefore, I told them that I wasn't going to do it their way, I'll just do it my way (the right way) instead. That was how things went back at Fort Drum and that was how things were going to go out here as far as I was concerned. I thought that the Company Commander and the First Sergeant wouldn't have an issue with this because they had always given me that type of freedom in the past. Even when the First Sergeant was micromanaging me back at Drum she had enough common sense to know that the battalion didn't know what they were doing and thus I called a lot of my own shots. Therefore, common sense told me that things would be no different out here. I would soon learn that it wasn't the case whatsoever.

When I got back to the Company I was called in by the First Sergeant to see both her and the Company Commander. They were extremely pissed off at me for my actions across the street at Battalion headquarters. Apparently the Battalion Commander himself had heard everything that I said and decided to yell at the Company Commander for it. As the old saying goes, "shit rolls downhill" and therefore it was time for me to get yelled at. I couldn't believe it because while I had come to expect this type of conduct from the First Sergeant, I didn't expect anything like this out of the Commander. I usually got along with him and as a result this was the first time that he ever actually yelled at me. For a minute I actually felt bad about my actions, after all if it was serious enough to force the commander to yell at me then maybe I was the one at fault. For the next few days I rethought my actions, asking myself such questions like, "If the Battalion had a problem with me why didn't they tell me to my face?" and "Was I really in the wrong?" The more I thought about it, the more I started to realize what the "big picture" here was. Actions that were condoned at Fort Drum weren't going to be condoned here because the leadership was already accustomed to dealing with the battalion at Drum, as opposed to the "walking on eggshells" feeling that we had out here with this new battalion. In other words, the company leadership was a little bit more concerned with not upsetting the battalion, when instead they should have been a little more concerned with standing up for them (in my opinion.) This entire experience gave me a true picture of what this deployment was going to be like and what type of things to expect, which wasn't a good feeling at all. It was at this point that I knew that it was going to be a long year whether I liked it or not.

While on a professional level I was starting to understand what was going to be expected of me on this deployment, things were a little different on a personal level. On a personal level, there was only one thing that I needed to accomplish, and that was that I needed to lose this weight once and for all. I felt that I had bounced back from the horrible incidents that cost me my recruiting assignment and now all of that was truly behind me. I now had a whole year in the dessert in front of me to get the job done. It was time to get to work. I had to find the "eye of the tiger" again. Immediately I began watching what I ate and I starting exercising hard and running for almost an hour every day. There was nothing that would stop me from going to the gym; not the heat, not a long work day, not an emotionally bad day, nothing. I was focused on the task at hand I knew that losing the weight was my only true ticket out of this horrible unit. After the first month of being deployed I was weighed in and saw that I had dropped 12 pounds in the first month. That's what hard work and dedication can get you, results. I was so proud of myself but I knew that there was still a lot more work to be done. I kept it up and kept training throughout the deployment, knowing that on a monthly basis I was going to be weighed in and most likely judged on my performance as well. I did not want to give that First Sergeant any real reasons to come down on me, and working towards my weight loss goals was a personal way of rebelling against her on the inside.

As the first couple of months flowed I fell into a steady routine just like I did on my previous deployments. The routine was simple: PT in the morning, work all day long, and then I would hit the gym at night. Every single day the routine was the same and by establishing the routine the days started to flow into one another. A Monday morning would come along and before you knew it Saturday was here. There was always a constant flow of work coming into the office since I had to process the work for three other detachments that were spread out on other camps in Iraq. This wasn't the first time that I had to do the work for other camps from a different location via the internet so I was very much used to the idea. Often times there would be a lot of issues with processing the work from some of these camps because they didn't know what they were doing half the time. There would be so many errors that would make you swear that a five year old filled out these reports. Obviously the work couldn't be submitted to Department of the Army in this condition so I would be the one stuck correcting other people's work half the time. I didn't mind doing it to an extent because it was my job, but I still expected a little more professionalism out of the senior NCOs that were turning this work into me. As far as I am concerned, if you are a 41 year old Sergeant First Class in the United States Army then you shouldn't be making spelling errors on memos and reports, but that's just my opinion.

By late June 2010 I decided to take my leave for that deployment. Even though it was extremely early into the tour (we had only been deployed for two and a half months by now) I really needed a break. I missed home a lot and so I took my leave at the earliest possible time. I think I missed home as much as I did this time around because I had gone home so often prior to the tour that it became second nature again. On my other two deployments I wasn't really going home all the time so back then I didn't miss home as much since I wasn't as used to being there. Believe it or not I was already feeling a little burnt out because of the long work days and the constant battles with the First Sergeant. I just wanted to get as far away from that place as I could. It was such a monotonous two months with no adventure whatsoever. At times it felt like a hot, sandy jail. The last place I ever wanted to feel like I was at was a jail.

I didn't really do too much on leave for those two weeks. My vacation consisted of a lot of relaxing and drinking beer. The only two major events of my leave were the fact that Transformers 2 was coming out in theaters and I also went to a concert in Saratoga Springs, NY called the "Big Day Out" concert. As far as the movie goes, the Transformers movies were, still are, and will always be my absolute favorite movies. I saw the first one on the day it came out in theaters and there was no way in hell that I was going to miss the second one when it came out. I didn't care if I was deployed or not. I guess when I look back on things the release of Transformers 2 played a major role in deciding to go home as early as I did on that deployment. I took my whole family (as well as a few friends) to go see it at the IMAX Theater at the Crossgates Mall in Albany, NY. What made the experience special was that it was the first time that I had ever seen a movie in IMAX. I'll never forget it.

The "Big Day Out" concert was a blast too. We loaded a bunch of friends into my Jeep, to include Josh Richard and we went out there for a day of loud music and drinking under the hot July sun. Like usual we tailgated in the parking lot before the show and thus we all put on a buzz before we even went in there. That's the way we always did it. There were a lot of bands that played that day to include Staind, The Offspring and Shinedown among others that I simply can't remember as of this writing. We all had a blast and it was a good way for me to "close out" that particular vacation. Two days later I had to fly back to Iraq, amazed at how quick my leave actually flew by. It was always like that however; by now I was used to my leave always flying by at the speed of light. The important thing was that by taking leave I was able to clear my head again and focus that much more. I was now ready to return to Iraq and get back to work. I just hoped that the rest of the tour would fly by as quickly as the first few months did.

I returned to Iraq to find that a few things had changed since I had left, and they weren't for the better. Granted, Cummings had done a fantastic job running the section in my absence, which was impressive considering she wasn't actually an HR Soldier. The problem was that she was left all alone to not only deal with the bureaucratic crap that the battalion liked to dish out, but also the crap that the First Sergeant liked to dish out. She had a number of stories about some of the things that the First Sergeant put into place while I was gone and none of them were good. Every one of them involved even more micromanagement than before. The worst change that was made was the First Sergeant made an executive decision to have Cummings and I move our section down the hallway and share offices with the First Sergeant. This was a horrible idea. Now that I had to share an office with her (at this point I outright considered her an enemy) created a lot of tension and arguments. I still believe that she only did it to make our lives that much harder. This took away my ability to call friends of mine on the office phone and vent about how bad it was because the person I would be griping about was sitting in the same room as me all day long! It also became a problem with the day to day mission as well. As if there wasn't enough tension in the room, there's nothing worse than having someone intervene every time you give your Soldier (who works directly for you) a task to complete. As a leader you sometimes have to delegate certain tasks to your subordinates while you work on something bigger and while sharing offices it just didn't work out. I would assign a task to Cummings, and almost every time the First Sergeant would chime in and say, "That's something you should do, you're the NCOIC." It was getting bad because this was MY section, not the First Sergeant's. Day after day there were arguments and after about a week we were finally moved back down the hallway with the rest of the staff sections. When we were given the official word that we would not be sharing offices with the First Sergeant anymore we felt as if we won the lottery. It was honestly one of the better days of that deployment, which is sad when you really think about it. When your best day involves the fact that you don't have to sit in the same room as the person that you feel hates you the most then you know there is a serious problem in the unit, plain and simple. Moving down the hallway didn't mean that we wouldn't have to deal with her anymore, because we certainly did. It just became a little easier when we got out of there.

Between the issues with the back to back office moves and the tensions in the office I suddenly realized that it actually was a mistake to take my leave so early in the deployment. I now had to face the reality that I had nine more long and grueling months ahead of me before I would see United States soil again. I fell back into my routine of working hard all day and then hitting the gym at night relatively quickly upon return. I was doing very well in the gym and after four months I had dropped over 25 pounds. Seeing progress on each of my monthly weigh-ins kept giving me a new motivation to keep trying harder. Even still, it was all part of the routine, and I knew that the routine itself was what I really needed because that technique had helped me burn so many deployment days easily in the past. When you have to spend an entire year in the dessert there tends to be a lot of thoughts that flow through your head; therefore you have to try to keep yourself as busy as possible to suppress those thoughts. Sometimes your own thoughts can eat you up inside; making you constantly think back to how great things are at home, or maybe forcing you to think about an argument that I got into with a friend before I left, and now that I was away I really couldn't rectify the situation. It's those types of thoughts that creep up on you when you least expect it, when you're stuck out in the dessert for all that time and you know that you can't just go home right now and fix it. You have to wait. There isn't a choice. Just your thoughts alone make a deployment even harder than it needs to be, and that is the truth.

Aside from my position as the NCOIC of the S1 section, I did have a few other responsibilities out there, not to include the additional duties that all of the other Soldiers had to pull. One of my additional responsibilities was that I was assigned to be the assistant squad leader for one of the best groups of Soldiers that I will ever meet. (I'm not just saying that because there is a chance they are reading this right now either, they were legitimately good Soldiers.) There were four Soldiers that fell under me, and I answered to the actual Squad Leader, Staff Sergeant Darnell Tisby; affectionately referred to as "DT." SSG Tisby was a hell of a leader who really knew how to lead Soldiers. He wouldn't hesitate to tell a Soldier when they were wrong and would often "smoke" them if they needed it. Obviously there were a few Soldiers in the unit that feared the guy not only because of that reason, but also because he resembled Mr. T, both in his look and the way he spoke. I don't think that I ever told him that, but when I would hear SSG Tisby yelling at Soldiers it felt like I was listening to Mr. T. That's not a bad thing by the way; Mr. T was a hell of an actor that always played that "tough guy" role in movies and in television. SSG Tisby fit that character to a "T," no pun intended. He was still a fun loving guy too, and loved joking around with not only the NCOs, but also the Soldiers. Most importantly, he believed in defending his Soldiers and always stood up for them, no matter what. To me, that has always been the shining character trait in all good leaders and SSG Tisby had it. I knew that if I kept not only my own act together but also the Soldier's act together everything would be fine under him. As an assistant Squad Leader there really weren't many responsibilities, especially considering the fact that none of those Soldiers actually worked for me in the office. All I really had to do was take accountability of the Soldiers at formations and inspect their rooms for cleanliness from time to time. From an office standpoint they worked for SSG Tisby anyway so my duties in that aspect were limited.

As I stated earlier, the four Soldiers in the squad were good Soldiers as well. Dantes fell in our squad, which was cool because I had already known her for a while. We spent a lot of time hanging out and partying in the barracks so it was nice to have someone else there that I knew for a while. Dantes wasn't even actually supposed to be on the deployment either. Prior to the deployment it was found that she had a neck tumor that needed operating on. She made a recovery, but she was never 100% and needed medication and treatment. She didn't actually have to go on the deployment, but after lots of pressure from the unit and a little soul-searching of her own she decided to go. As far as I'm concerned, that act in itself took a lot of courage. Of course, there were others that didn't see it that way. Over the course of the deployment there were many Soldiers and NCOs that would often say things about her; making such claims that she was either malingering in order to get out of doing certain things or just outright faking the injury altogether. When I would hear some of these things said by leaders within the unit it would make me absolutely sick. There were others that believed her injury was legitimate and treated her badly because she was hurt. As crazy as that may sound to someone who has never been in the military, it's true. Many leaders seem to share an unfair, biased opinion against Soldiers who are either injured or overweight. I've not only seen it with my own eyes, but I have felt the wrath of such treatment myself. Basically, once you fall into one of those two categories you are treated like a second class citizen, no matter how hard you work at your job or even in the gym. Some of the hardest workers that I have ever come across were Soldiers who fell into one of those two categories. It was no different than back in 2008 when SPC Brizzee was still in the unit and he was treated the same way (by the same people no less.) SPC Brizzee's injury was caused in the line of duty and he was treated badly; so why wouldn't someone with a neck tumor (obviously not something that a person causes on their own) be treated any different? That was actually a trick question, and the real answer is simple: they shouldn't be mistreated at all, and it has to stop. Unfortunately for Dantes she spent that entire deployment always having to second-guess if the unit leadership liked her, let alone respected her. Personally I can't say that I would have gone on a deployment if I was in her shoes. I may have "sat that one out" so to speak. When the deployment was over SSG Tisby (who actually did look out for her and sympathize for her) recommended her for a Meritorious Service Medal, as well as a battlefield promotion to the rank of Sergeant. Both of which were approved and I was extremely proud of her, yet even then I could hear whispers amongst the ranks that she didn't deserve it. I hated that. Often times I would hear Soldiers in the hallway talking about it and I would have to correct them. I wasn't going to let that stand. If I could change one thing about the Army, it would be that I would put an abrupt end to the mistreatment of injured, overweight and other disadvantaged Soldiers.

Dantes wasn't the only Soldier that I was held accountable for during my time as assistant Squad Leader. There were three other Soldiers, a married couple by the name of Dexter and Ling Lanuza and a young kid from Michigan by the name of Charles Daily. They were all young Soldiers who had just recently came to the unit straight out of AIT. Seeing them deploying less than a year after AIT made me reminisce back on the days when I too was in their shoes when I went to Iraq in 2003. Of course, there were quite a few major differences between the two deployments but the emotions running through their minds were dead real and I understood that. In addition, it was a little harder for them to deal with some of the corruption and harsh treatment that was taking place within the unit because of their age. They weren't desensitized by previous experiences like SSG Tisby or I was; they were looking at this entire situation through completely fresh eyes. For the Lanuzas, they had a few problems with the unit right from day one. They had been dating since AIT and they felt that the unit was trying to throw an axe into their relationship. Things came to a head when they got into trouble for sleeping in the same room overnight. On a deployment that is strictly forbidden unless you are married. In their own minds they were in love and since they were together for a while by now they decided to get married without the unit knowing. After all, it really isn't up to your unit to "approve" your marriage. That is an incredibly personal decision and it was real funny to watch the First Sergeant get pissed off because the Lanuzas decided to get married. It wasn't her situation to try to control so I don't know why she tried in the first place. I guess you can't stop true love.

Aside from all of the working out I was doing I knew that I really needed to find another extra-curricular activity to fill some of my free time while I was there on COB Adder. Some of the days would just seem so mundane and I needed to give my mind something new to focus on. Granted, I loved working out and I had made a ton of progress towards my weight loss goals on the deployment thus far but I knew I needed more. The gym there had a bulletin board set up that advertised different activities that took place along the base. Upon taking a look at what was going on I found that there was a martial arts class that took place right there at the same gym that I worked out at on Tuesday and Thursday evenings. I saw this as an opportunity to not just relieve some frustration that I was having but to also reconnect with my past. I hadn't practiced martial arts in an extremely long time and it was high time that I got back to it.

My first class there was really fun. The class was in Escima, a Pilipino style of martial arts that involves stick fighting. By stick fighting I am not referring to a long Bo Staff but instead a pair of short bamboo sticks. A well trained Escima fighter can break almost any bone in your body with one of those sticks. There were many occasions that I took a solid hit across the hands while studying Escrima. Each and every time it hurt like hell. Sometimes we would get hit in the arms and legs as well. None of us would ever complain because that comes with the territory. You can't expect to become a great boxer unless you've been punched in the face a few times; therefore you cannot expect to become great at Escrima unless you get hit with a stick a few times. It's just common sense. The style is based on a 12 strike system that graduates to various different flow drills as you continue on with your training. The 12 strike system isn't really based on specific hits so to speak, but rather angles of attack. Learning that type of style puts a different perspective on Martial Arts as a whole. The flow drills are designed to not only teach coordination (with speed) but to also build upon your reflexes. Often times in a fight you don't have the time to think things out, but rather to react. A good fighter reacts to the situations that are put in front of him, he does not stop to think it out because while he is standing there thinking he will most certainly be killed in the heat of battle. The flow drills also look and sound very good at conventions. Sometimes you will stumble upon two great Escima masters who are putting on a show for a crowd. The constant "clicking" sound of bamboo hitting bamboo combined with the amazing movements is simply mesmerizing. If you can't watch a live Escima contest then I highly recommend looking one up on YouTube. You will not be disappointed. From a combat standpoint, Escrima is also one of the most "common sense" martial arts styles to learn. If you think about it, how many items do you encounter on a day to day basis resemble the shape of a stick? Everything from a pipe, to a crowbar, to a plank of wood fits the bill. So if you had to defend yourself in a life and death situation you are more likely to stumble upon something that resembles a bamboo stick as opposed to a katana blade. (Not that fighting with a sword is bad, I can do that too.) When it came right down to it, learning Escrima while I was deployed was a great idea. Our class had an extremely knowledgeable teacher who had over 25 years of Escrima experience. He always had stories to tell of different situations that he was involved in, both real life and training/ convention related. The experience was definitely one of the better ones of that deployment and helped the time fly by that much quicker. Since things were so bad at the unit it was nice to be able to get away from the company twice a week in the evenings and learn a style that I not only enjoyed doing but can also save my life one day.

After a few months of living on COB Adder in our luxurious two man CHU, myself and SGT Cappe were "blessed" with a third roommate. I also need to note that I am using the term "blessed" lightly. In fact, I'm using that term sarcastically now that I think about it. There was an NCO from one of the outer lying detachments that had apparently made a bad impression or two at his own unit and thus was recommended to come up to Tallil and work at the Headquarters detachment with us. Initially we didn't really see too much of a problem with any of this, until we got to know him. The man seemed to have a severe personality defect. While he got along with us most of the time, he seemed to not get along with many of the Soldiers and NCOs in the unit. I guess he had no choice but to get along with us considering the fact that we lived with him. It's never a good idea to piss off your roommates. He would get into random altercations with some of the Soldiers, but the worst of them all were the altercations with his supervisor (who just happened to be the same NCO that I had to take to the Navy doctor at the beginning of this chapter). The funny thing about that situation was the fact that he was effectively working for someone who had just as bad as a personality issue as he did. They were like two peas in a pod, and it reflected when they would break off into shouting matches against each other. Every single day he would come back to the room complaining about his supervisor, but he never realized that he and his supervisor was basically the same guy. They were so similar to each other that you could hardly tell the difference. Cappe and I used to get a laugh out of all of that, even though that wasn't even the funniest part about living with the guy.

With as many personality defects as he displayed at work, one would assume that his impressive character traits would carry on into his home life as well. Just as we assumed, this was 100% the case. He would come home to the room after a long and frustrating day of work, vent to us about it (as if we didn't hear it all happening down the hall) and then get on Skype and start yelling at his family. At first I didn't see it as too much of a problem considering the fact that all marriages have problems, but when his yelling and screaming was keeping me up until midnight or even 1 am it started to become a problem. Despite the fact that we had to miss sleep over his arguments they still brought us laughter due to the insane things that would come out of his mouth. He wouldn't have normal arguments with his family; they all seemed like arguments that you would see in a movie. He would scream at his wife out of the blue;

they would be having a perfectly normal and quiet conversation and the next thing you would hear was, "GODDAMIT!" He would treat his kids in an equal manner as well. Sometimes he would get on the line with his son, who was apparently acting up at the house and yell "LISTEN! I . . . AM . . . YOUR . . . FATHER!!!" He was yelling it in almost the same manner that Darth Vader said those same words in Star Wars. Every time he would do that I would look over at Cappe and see that he was either smirking or silently laughing. Of course, mine and Cappe's antics couldn't be seen by our new roommate because of the fact that he insisted on hanging blankets and curtains around his bed the second he got there, almost like he didn't want to look at us or something. That's ok; we really didn't want to look at the guy anyway. As if the constant shouting and the "I AM YOUR FATHER" speeches weren't enough, he also had a bit that he liked to pull where he would shout his own last name at his kid and then force him to repeat it back to him. That had to be degrading on so many levels. He would then go on to say things like, "in a court of law you're my son!" which was an obvious reference to a custody battle that he was sure to fill me and Cappe in on at least 12,000 times over the course of that year. Finally, the funniest of his antics came in the form of "smoking" his children over Skype. Yes, you read that correctly. Often times when a junior enlisted Soldier makes a minor mistake a Sergeant will force that Soldier to do push-ups and various other exercises while he explains to him or her their mistakes. This is done in an effort to teach the Soldier to act better and thus correct his or her mistake. I know that it may sound a bit inhumane, but it isn't when you compare it to the alternative, which is paperwork in the form of judicial or non-judicial punishment. As a general rule of thumb, you would rather be "smoked" then receive punishment in the form of paperwork because punishment in the form of paperwork usually involves loss of rank or money. While this technique normally works for Soldiers, I can't see why it would be sensible to apply the same technique to children. Granted, it probably got our roommate the results that he wanted, but the question really is what is the alternative to "smoking" his kids? Did he too have a set of paperwork ready for his kids? Considering this man's apparent issues I am almost afraid to know the answer to that question. He did this to his kids often, and there was even a time when he started telling his kids to get down into the front leaning rest position (push up position) and Cappe quietly got out of his bed and did it out of pure sarcasm. While our roommate was oblivious to the fact that this was happening because he was surrounded by his "blanket fort" I could clearly see what was happening and I couldn't stop myself from laughing my ass off. Ultimately, living with him created more problems than comedy (we almost came to blows one day over a door slamming dispute) but there was enough comedy involved with his actions to make the deployment somewhat bearable. Today, when I call Cappe on the phone we still joke about the whole thing; ill sometimes greet him with a "GODDAMIT!", or an "I AM YOUR FATHER!" I'll never forget living with that maniac.

Sometimes during the hot summer the power would go out. This was reminiscent of the "old days" in 2003 when the generators would go out and we would have to make do without electricity. For some reason it seemed so much worse now. I think that's partially because of the fact that it is "happening now." It always seems that the past events of your life always seem better than what's happening now when you look you look back on them. That's where such terms as "the good old days" or "back in the day" or even "the golden years" come from. Your memory always makes your brain reflect on the past in a better light than it really was, even if things weren't that good. Thus, the days that we lived in a tent and the power went out somehow looked better than living in a CHU with the power out because human memory became slightly distorted over the course of six years. In reality, things were actually slightly worse when power would go out in the CHUs because the CHUs cannot "breathe" the way that a tent can. A tent is made of fabric, and as we know fabric is cloth that is sewn together. Even though we can't see holes in it, there are plenty of them there. A CHU on the other hand is nothing more than a miniaturized trailer. It's like living in a trailer park without air conditioning. There's a good chance that sucks. This happened to us a few times while we were out there and each and every time it was pure misery. That's really the only way to put it.

The Soldiers in our unit were tasked with a special duty called VCC duty. VCC stood for "Visitor Control Center," which was the place where Iraqi contractors came into the gate every morning on the way to work at their job sites which were spread out among the base. This was the exact same duty that I had to pull in 2003. Iraqi contractors were trusted to come onto the base and work all day in the heat for the lowest of wages, and while doing so they were being watched over by a pair of US Soldiers. At times the duty seemed extremely mundane but at the same time you still have to be on your toes just in case these workers get out of hand. There were usually 15 to 20 workers per two US Soldiers. Get the picture? You HAVE TO stay alert. Sometimes there would be reports of incidents where the Iraqis would try something while a Soldier was watching them on VCC duty. Sometimes, it would get violent. There was really no way around this, whoever screened the workers before they came onto the US Camps wasn't able to fully gage what they would do. Incidents would be few and far in between, but they were still incidents. It wasn't like incidents were going away. We would often work long hours in the sun, trying our best to not only stay hydrated but to also watch and make sure that they Iraqis didn't try anything. When you have this type of responsibility on your hands and you still have the thoughts of missing home and your responsibilities in the office on the other side of the airfield on your mind it could tend to be a lot. I know that it may not sound like it could be a lot, but believe me things can tend to weigh on you when you encounter these types of situations. You are far away from home; in fact you're homesick. You are being ridden everyday by an overbearing and micromanaging boss, and now you are stuck with the responsibility of watching over 15 Iraqis and making sure they don't try to bomb the camp. It's just not easy. Nowadays when I think back on my first deployment and compare it to this one, I often think about how we were almost like a family on the first "go-around." Even on the days that I would fight and argue with Cursey in 2003, we would still find a common ground for the greater good. After all, that's what friends do, and in a weird way Cursey and I really were friends back then. If you fast forward to 2009, that unity just wasn't there. Sure, I had a few friends, but it wasn't like before, and the leadership sure as hell wasn't taking care of us in the way that the previous leadership had. What had changed? Why was the Army that I loved so much was undergoing such a change? I didn't get it. I had done everything that I was supposed to do, and even still I was on edge when performing a single task of watching Iraqis. If there was ever a time that I realized that most of us were "on our own" out there, this was it.

The different projects that had to be handled on VCC duty varied from day to day. There were a lot of different Iraqi contracting companies that worked on the camp and each company usually had a team of Iraqis come in every morning and do the work. There was only one duty that didn't involve watching Iraqis which I ended up having to pull one day while I was there. That duty was burn pit duty. All of the trash from the entire camp was taken out to this huge burn pit. It was honestly the biggest landfill that I had ever seen, and I was surprised that the flames didn't get out of control from time to time. The garbage stunk so badly; and if you inhaled the fumes for any more than ten seconds you would start to gag violently. It was terrible. Even though this duty sounds terrible so far, there was one very special experience that I endured that day. The garbage (as well as the ash) inside of the dump needed to be constantly pushed into the fire with a bulldozer. Usually there was an NCO that worked there who was in charge of doing all of the bulldozing and the VCC Soldiers weren't required (let alone authorized due to lack of licensing) to drive the bulldozer. This day ended up being different. The NCO was out there in the sun for a long time and apparently had enough. He got out of the bulldozer and looked at me and asked, "Wanna give it a try, Sergeant?" I thought about it for a second. I knew that I didn't have to do it, but at the same time how many chances am I going to get to drive a bulldozer in my lifetime? Plus the other NCO legitimately needed to get out of the heat for a while. I agreed to do it, and after he gave me a quick five minute block of instruction I caught on and started driving. I was amazed at how easy the machine was to operate, considering the fact that it was nothing like a car and this was my first time. I ended up working with the bulldozer for a few hours and when the day was over I was actually proud of myself for doing something new, and doing it well to boot. Later that evening I emailed a number of my friends at home, including Josh, about my new accomplishment. This resulted in a new collection of bulldozer related jokes over the next few months, which was fine by me.

As time went on things in the unit got worse. Things started to really get bad about halfway through the tour for so many reasons. The company just wasn't being run correctly on so many different levels and as a result the morale of almost all of the junior Soldiers and NCOs was in the gutter. One reason that this was starting to happen was the First Sergeant was starting to pick favorites amongst the Soldiers. There were certain Soldiers that she liked more than others, (for whatever reason) and as a result that took its toll on the morale of others. It wasn't as if it was hard to notice or anything; it was so blatant that everyone took notice. It got to the point where those Soldiers who were "favored" couldn't even get punished by some of the NCOs without the First Sergeant coming back and yelling at the NCOs involved. She would treat the NCOs like they were the ones who did something wrong; and as a result certain Soldiers escaped having to do any form of corrective training. It wasn't right and to be honest it was starting to give me a bad impression of the Army. It was like the Army that I knew was dying and was being replaced by this pitiful excuse of a unit. Back when I was at Fort Campbell people couldn't get away with this sort of thing. Furthermore, leaders had more integrity then to sit there and favor certain Soldiers over others. You may think that witnessing something like this doesn't have much of an effect on morale; but believe me it took a toll on everyone there, including myself. It was just another reason why I couldn't wait for the deployment to be over.

Another problem that I ran into was that the First Sergeant now required that all of my weigh-ins would be supervised by her. Now, I had spent the first half of that deployment busting my ass and by now I had lost about thirty pounds, which was considered excellent progress but it wasn't good enough for "her standards." She felt that my tapings weren't "being handled correctly" and there was "just no way" that I was losing the amount of body fat that the NCOs who were taping me would claim that I did. So she now started to supervise my tapings and would scrutinize every little aspect of them. Sometimes she would yell at the NCOs for allowing me to "suck in," even though most units do allow "sucking in." In most of the units I was in I was allowed to do it, so why not here? There were even times when she would force me to repeat my Social Security Number while my waist was being taped just to make sure I wasn't "sucking in." Trust me; that was a bit degrading. The thing that really upset me was that none of the other Soldiers in the unit who were enrolled in the weight control program were subject to the same treatment. It was just me. Now, put yourself in my shoes for just a second: you know that the only thing that has been holding back the progression of your career was a minor weight problem. You start working extremely hard to overcome that problem but you have an overbearing boss that can't stand you. Now, your boss is supervising your weigh-ins, knowing that it is a sensitive subject for you. As you can probably imagine, I wasn't happy about any of this. It put an undue pressure on the weigh-ins and made them take a lot longer than they really needed to take. Considering the fact that I have probably been weighed in well over 100 times in my career I think I would consider myself an expert in the subject. By interfering with my weigh-ins the First Sergeant nearly made it impossible to make tape. Under her new strict guidelines I was coming in at 3% more than what I was last month, even though I had lost eight pounds since the previous month. That just didn't make sense. And of course all of this made me emotional. No one wanted to be in that company whatsoever because the First Sergeant was making our lives miserable. It always seemed to me that my life was the worst because everyone else took notice. It was past any idea that perhaps I was biased because I was the one involved; everyone would mention what was going on between us. Our feud transcended any other feud within the unit and it made my life a living hell. Controlling my weigh-ins just made it all worse because it not only seemed to make the days go by longer but it also made it seem like there wasn't a "light at the end of the tunnel" when I would return to Fort Drum.

The weigh-ins weren't the only part of my training program that she took control of (and subsequently messed up). As if she wasn't being strict enough to begin with, she now decided to pull me out of unit PT sessions in the morning and force me into doing a special PT program with her in the morning. She used the excuse that since she hadn't enforced a true Special Population PT program in the unit that she would "right the wrongs" and take control of my PT program. I found it absolutely pathetic that she was using my PT time to try to cover up her failures as a leader, but I had no choice but to go with it. Just like my ever-so-scrutinized weigh-ins, I was the only one whose PT program she took charge of. None of the other overweight Soldiers (there were a few of them) were subject to this kind of treatment. So it was clear that this was a personal attack. What was even worse was the PT "program" that she put me on wasn't even a real program, it was some bullshit exercise routine that she pulled out of a women's health magazine, designed specifically for women. I would do the exercises that she forced me to do, and get absolutely nothing out of them. I may have left the morning sessions sweating a little but that was more because we were in Iraq where it was hot to begin with; not because she actually gave me a good workout. I would have been better off if I stayed in unit PT sessions, at least then I would still get something out of it. So now I knew that if I wanted to keep losing weight I would have to work out even harder in the evenings, which means I would have to make for this loss of productivity during my personal time. Once I got a true feeling of the program that she put me through it sent me a clear message: she was indeed setting me up for failure, no question about it. If someone intentionally makes your weigh-ins harder to pass and then limits the activity that you are doing and so you are now losing less weight, how could you now assume that the person is setting you up for failure? If

I thought for just one second that the First Sergeant was EVER on my side I would have been a fool. This was personal, and as bad as it was I knew I had to keep fighting back. First and foremost I had to keep working as hard as I could in the gym in my spare time. Secondly, while at the office I had to be extra careful not to make a mistake. I had to triple check my own work, as well as Cummings' work just to make sure that I didn't give the First Sergeant an excuse to try to come down on me. Sometimes when I would find out about specific incidents where the First Sergeant was trying to screw with a Soldier I would take the time to look into it. If I found that the First Sergeant was doing something to someone that was outside of regulations I would go into her office and fight her on it, effectively standing up for the Soldiers. She hated it when I did this. It didn't even have to be anything serious; it could have been a simple matter of flagging a Soldier without the proper paperwork. Sometimes she would ask me, "Why do you have to fight me on everything?" I would just glare at her and tell her that as the S1 I have to uphold the regulations. I could tell by looking into her eyes that by fighting against me all the time she was also spent. It was starting to tire her out because she knew I wasn't going to go down without a fight. I was fine with making her feel this way. After all, she started it by making it personal. If she wasn't going to cut me any slack, then I would be damned if I was going to cut her any slack in return. It was just that simple. The remaining months of that deployment were so hostile, and I just dealt with it the best I could. One thing was for sure, I wasn't about to let her slow me down in the gym at night. I was going to accomplish my goal, or damn near die trying.

Since I didn't get to leave COB Adder over the deployment to go on any convoy missions like last time I was in Iraq I was absolutely dying to get off of the camp and just breathe. I would have taken any mission that came my way to just get a break. I didn't care where it would be. I knew that I was going to be afforded the opportunity to go on a pass to Qatar in October which I was really looking forward to. Even still, I needed to do something sooner. I felt like I would lose my mind if I stayed there any longer. Things were just so monotonous on Adder. Life was the same routine every single day and I was getting sick of it.

Months before my unit deployed to Iraq our unit sent two other detachments to other parts of the theater of operations, on orders from Department of the Army of course. Due to the new structure of deployments (which involved units not actually falling under their home headquarters while deployed) one of these two detachments ended up falling under a command based in Kuwait, and therefore they were deployed to Kuwait. Even though they weren't really our responsibility out there, our command team insisted that we checked in on them from time to time. What that meant for me was that I would occasionally have to process some of their promotion packets and other paperwork. They couldn't rely on their S1 to do the right thing very often. This had actually been expected, my level of expertise usually wasn't matched by others very often so most other S1's would end up paling in comparison to my ability. The time finally came when the Command team planned a trip down to Kuwait to visit with that Detachment. Even though the First Sergeant was going on that trip, I still wanted to go because I knew it would be a break from the day to day monotony in Tallil. Also, I had friends down in Kuwait that I missed dearly and there was a lot to do down there. Since it was technically a garrison post you could even wear civilian clothes. That idea in itself would make the trip worth it. Knowing that I could be out of uniform for a week was just too good of an opportunity to pass up.

When I got down there to Kuwait I was so glad to be there. The detachment was deployed to Camp Arifijan, which I already knew was nice from my previous visit in 2004. Even in all of its luxury there were enough new additions to the camp to make it feel like a new experience again. I'll never forget my arrival there to greet the troops. First, the Company Commander walked in. Someone called the room to the position of attention, which is custom when your commanding officer enters the room. After he told the room to carry on a few of the Soldiers went to greet him, but it was still a lukewarm greeting at best. Then, the First Sergeant walked in. She immediately started grilling a few Soldiers, living up to her reputation of being completely rude to everyone at the absolute worst times. I stood out in the hallway and listened to what was going on, and aside from hearing her voice the rest of the room was silent; so silent that you could hear a pin drop. Then, almost on cue I walked in. The Soldiers all looked at me and erupted. A few of them shouted, "Oh my god it's Sergeant Conklin!" Most of them ran up to me and shook my hand and immediately started asking me if I could do things for them. They were all telling me how bad the S1 was there; so much so that a few of them jumped the gun and asked if I was going to be staying there permanently. Obviously I couldn't, but I did tell them that I would do whatever I could for them while I was there. I also pledged to them that

I would stay in touch better via email and help them as much as I could from Iraq. I was amazed at the reception that I got by visiting them; they made me feel like I was on one of those USO "support the troops" morale tours. Only instead of being a celebrity I was a fellow Soldier. The First Sergeant actually took exception to all of this. Apparently she didn't like the fact that everyone was so happy to see me yet they hated seeing her. She tried going on a power trip, telling a few of them that they couldn't ask me for things without going through her first. Sensing that I had the upper hand I immediately shut that idea down; not only in front of her but in front of the other Soldiers and NCOs. Face to face I said to her, "These things would be done quicker if they were sent to me directly. If they are sent to you first they may sit in your inbox for a few days, after all you are a very busy person, aren't you First Sergeant?" As I made that statement with a sense of sarcasm in my voice all of the NCOs in the room rallied behind the cause and agreed. Finally she gave in. On a professional level it did make more sense to send the work directly to me. On a personal level however it felt really good to "shut her up" in front of the whole room. It was a small victory, but still a victory nonetheless.

I also made sure to meet up with an old friend of mine in Kuwait as well. Josef Smith, a Sergeant First Class from the unit had become one of my closest confidants over the past few years at Fort Drum. Josef was a good man who was always willing to listen to my concerns when I needed a "shoulder to lean on." Since we were in the same unit for a while he had witnessed many of the corrupt actions that took place in the unit and certainly felt my pain. He also had a lot of respect for my work ethic in the office and wouldn't hesitate to turn any of his Soldiers in my direction when they needed help. It was nice to have at least one friend amongst the senior NCOs in that unit. There was so much crap going on by this point that I really couldn't rely on any of the senior leadership whatsoever. Unfortunately I hadn't seen Josef in a number of months since he was on the Kuwait rotation, so a trip to Kuwait was a good opportunity to meet up with an old friend.

At the end of the duty day we decided to grab a smoke and have a heart to heart conversation about some of the things that had been going on. Like usual I had one of my cigars and he of course was a cigarette smoker. We traded stories of what we had been through over the past few months on our respective deployments. The funny thing was that most of our stories were bad ones. Even though the Soldiers in Kuwait were living the life of luxury the mood was ruined by an abundance of bureaucratic rules that mostly made no sense. It was so bad there that it made the Soldiers miserable. Over the years I could never understand why the Army does that to its Soldiers. Anytime that conditions greatly improve for Soldiers there seems to be a sudden influx of new rules that don't seem to make any sense. Sometimes the rules are made for "safety reasons" but on most cases the result is Soldiers being treated like little children. What's even worse is that the Army is the only branch that does that to its troops; the Marine Corps and the Air Force do not treat their troops like kids, so why does the Army have to? Hearing some of Josef's stories about the crap that they went through in Kuwait shocked the hell out of me and made me just a little bit grateful that the rules in Iraq weren't that bad.

I also went into detail with Josef about some of the things that the First Sergeant was putting me through. He congratulated me on the extreme amount of weight that I had lost and he just couldn't understand why the First Sergeant was micromanaging my PT and weigh-in programs to such a high degree. He really didn't agree with that and it boiled down to the same mentality that I was being treated like a kid in a lot of ways, which was somewhat similar to what was happening in Kuwait with his detachment. He did give me some good advice though; to keep my head up and continue working hard in all aspects of my life. He told me that if I kept on working that no one could fault me. In other words, with enough hard work I could rise above any amount of challenges that were being thrown in my direction. There was one final thing that he said to me before I left; something that he had said to me over the years on more than one occasion that I still take to heart. He said, "Ken, be good to yourself." I'll never forget that. If you really think about it, despite it being a short and simple statement it makes all the sense in the world. You have to be good to yourself in this world because there is no guarantee whatsoever that the people you encounter in your life are going to be good to you. Therefore, since we all have a need to feel good at times, we have to take it upon ourselves to make ourselves feel better, to do good for ourselves.

Before I knew it, it was time to fly back to COB Adder. The trip had proved to be extremely refreshing for me on so many levels. Just getting away from Adder for that week was good enough, but meeting up with an old friend made it even better. On a professional level I now had an idea as to just how much Human Resources support that I was going to have to provide to them for the remainder of the deployment. It almost felt like

I had to carry multiple units on my shoulders due to the lack of support that they were receiving from the other S1s. I didn't mind doing it because I took a lot of pride in my job. I knew that if the careers of those Soldiers were in my hands that they would be taken care of, no questions asked. Even still, I was starting to get tired. I just wanted the deployment to be over already. It had been a long seven months jam packed with mundane bullshit. Things were absolutely nothing like they were back in 2003 and as a result the excitement of deploying; the "butterflies in your stomach" so to speak just weren't there. So I just resorted to falling back into my same old routine in an effort to get this tour over with.

In October 2009 there was an incident that changed the way I looked at the deployment in general. We hadn't had too many rocket attacks over the year, just a few which obviously paled in comparison to the amount of attacks that we sustained in 2003. One day there was an attack extremely close to our living area on COB Adder. Four rockets had impacted in an area near a huge generator that was next to our CHUs, and in fact one of the rockets actually hit the connex-sized generator. The rocket didn't do enough damage to blow the generator up but it did do enough damage to blast quite a few pieces off of it and cause it to leak fluids all over the ground. There was also a lot of smoke in the air from the impact which signaled that some part of the generator (possibly the fluids) caught on fire. All of this amounted to an extremely dangerous situation.

When rocket attacks like this take place the unit in that is closest to the impacted area is supposed to send a team called a PAR team (which stands for Post Attack Reconnaissance) to survey the area and make sure that all munitions are cordoned off, as well as recover all shrapnel and bring it back to headquarters. This is an extremely dangerous activity because you never know what you may find; you may stumble upon a rocket that hadn't exploded yet. As a result anyone on the PAR team has to not only be fully alert at all times, but also needs to be fully trained in the proper procedures concerning this activity. Anything less is unacceptable because the lives of everyone on the team are on the line. Every unit that is deployed is required to identify specific Soldiers who will serve on the PAR teams. Those Soldiers receive the training and it becomes their duty to perform the reconnaissance every time there is an attack. Units are even required to send alternate Soldiers to the training as well in case any of the primary Soldiers are on leave when there is an attack. As you can see, this system was put into place to ensure that there was always a trained and qualified PAR team available at all times. That just makes the most sense.

So the day came along when this fateful attack took place on COB Adder and as it turned out, both the primary and alternate NCOs who were supposed to run the PAR team (one of which was SGT Cappe) were on leave. There were no other NCOs available to fill the spot, so I was ordered to go out there and take charge of the PAR team even though I never attended the training. Despite that crucial fact I wasn't about to protest; after all this was a time of crisis and those Soldiers needed a leader. There was simply too much at stake for me to stand up and complain about a technicality. Granted, the unit leadership should have planned a lot better and sent a few more NCOs (perhaps even me) to the training but that wasn't something that could be changed now. I had to go out there.

It was so hot out that day, easily 110 degrees which seemed a lot hotter while wearing our helmets and flak vests. I had the convenience of leading the Soldiers from my squad (the Lanuzas and SPC Daily) on the reconnaissance mission. That actually helped me out a lot because I dealt with those Soldiers on a day to day basis and it is always better to work with people that you are more familiar with. We scanned the entire living area looking for any signs of shrapnel, unexploded munitions, or even worse, casualties. We found nothing until we made it to the exterior part of our living area, which is where the generator was located. As we approached the generator we saw that a huge hole was blasted on one of the upper corners where the rocket had impacted and subsequently went inside of it and possibly exploded. A large chunk of the generator had flown off and hit one of the nearby cement walls and was now lying on the ground along with a few large chunks of cement. There were puddles of fluid along the outside of the generator, some of which looked like motor oil and some looked like antifreeze. The combination of the intense heat and the puddles of potentially flammable chemicals gave the air a horrible odor. There was plenty of smoke in the air too, which didn't help matters much. There was a lot of shrapnel on the ground surrounding the generator which I immediately started picking up. I put all of it into Dexter Lanuza's backpack since part of our mission was to retrieve as much of the shrapnel as possible. Over and over again the Soldiers kept asking me if I needed help, to which each time I replied with a simple, "No." I was not about to let any of these young Soldiers take the risk of cutting themselves picking up all of this shrapnel. Every piece was extremely jagged, and since they were all young I didn't really see the point of risking any of them getting hurt. After all, I was their leader. If anyone was going to get hurt, it should be me. A leader should always make sacrifices for their Soldiers, regardless of the situation in which they find themselves in.

Once all of the shrapnel was picked up from the outside of the generator it was time to look inside of the generator. It was a huge, connex-sized generator with a box-shaped hole built into it large enough for a technician to climb into it and perform maintenance on it. I stepped around the massive puddles of oil and gazed inside the generator to see if there was anything in there. All I could see in there were some parts of shrapnel, but I couldn't get a good glimpse of what was in there without getting closer. I called headquarters via the radio that we were issued and I was specifically told that all pieces of shrapnel had to be retrieved. It did not matter if the shrapnel was inside of a potentially dangerous generator or not. I thought about it for a second; if this absolutely had to be done there was no possible way that I could ask one of my subordinates to do it. They were all young, no more than 19 years old. There was smoke everywhere and there was no way of telling if there was something inside of that generator that hadn't exploded yet, meaning that by just climbing inside you would be risking your life. The bottom line was that despite the risk, someone had to climb in there. I looked back at the Soldiers, who were just looking at me with a blank look on their faces. They had heard my conversation on the radio and they knew that someone was going in there. As they all contemplated their fate, I just looked at one of them and handed them my rifle and simply said "hold this." I then climbed into the smoking generator and found the shrapnel. When I climbed out into the sunlight I was able to see the full size of what I had retrieved: it measured about a foot in length and was jagged on all ends. It was clearly a part of the rocket that had hit the generator. Needless to say, I was glad that the rocket hadn't exploded while I was inside of the generator, because I obviously wouldn't have lived to write this book. All of the Soldiers looked at me and told me that I was a "bad ass" for having the guts to do something like that. I could tell from the tone in their voice that I earned their respect by doing this. To be honest, it was never about earning respect or being viewed as a "bad ass." It was always about protecting those Soldiers and looking out for them. What if the generator did explode with one of them inside of it? There's no way that I could live with myself if that happened.

I was their leader, plain and simple. You can either lead from the front or lead from the rear. Leading from the rear is for cowards.

When we got back to the company to get debriefed by the Officer in Charge of the PAR team he thanked us for a job well done. He also thought that what I did was extremely heroic and deserved some recognition. After everything that had happened I actually expected this, but I didn't expect what happened next. I was called into the First Sergeant's office to discuss the events of the attack. She actually had the nerve to tell me that what I did was stupid, and that I should have sent one of the junior Soldiers into the generator. I attempted to reason with her, explaining to her my motives for climbing in myself. She didn't want to hear any of it, and tried giving me a line about being "more valuable" than the other Soldiers due to my rank. She tried telling me that as a leader I should order them around and make them do the hard work. I really didn't agree with this. The tone of the meeting sharply changed when she looked me dead in the eyes and said, "If it were me and you out there, I would send you in because I am the First Sergeant, you're just the Sergeant. You should have sent a Private in there." That's when I lost it. I shouted at her, "It's nice to know where I stand!!! I'm glad to know that if it was just us that I would be the one climbing in there! That's what I love about this unit, your GREAT fucking leadership!" I just couldn't take it. I didn't care about the fact that my outburst could result in some sort of non-judicial punishment. I had it with her constant issues with me. The entire deployment she had given me a hard time, and now I was being told that looking out for young, inexperienced Soldiers was a bad idea. I couldn't take that. As it turns out, I never got busted for my outburst, which was obviously fine by me. Even still, I was absolutely sick of having to work for such a horrible leader. It furthered my level of disrespect for her, and fueled my hunger to get the hell out of that unit when the deployment was over.

Later that night one of the Soldiers came by my CHU to thank me for what happened earlier. I didn't feel that the act needed thanking but it was still nice to know that it was appreciated. I shared the story of my experience with the First Sergeant and the Soldiers couldn't believe it. I really didn't care about that though, I had earned the respect of the troops and that in itself was good enough for me. I had come to expect terrible leadership from the First Sergeant by now, so by now this type of thing was the status quo. Granted, I lost even more respect for her because of this but when I look back on things I know that I should have expected it. At least everyone else saw her flaws and it wasn't just me.

In the upcoming weeks all of the Soldiers that were in the unit were recommended for a Combat Action Badge. A Combat Action Badge, (also known as a CAB) is an award given to support Soldiers who are either engaged by the enemy or are forced to engage the enemy in a combat zone (such as Iraq or Afghanistan). The award was created as an award that support Soldiers can receive since they do not qualify for the Combat Infantry Badge, which is almost the same award only it is specifically for Infantry Soldiers. Over the years the requirements to receive the CAB have been adjusted and as a result you can now receive one if there is a rocket attack within your vicinity, even if you sat in your office and had nothing to do with anything else involved. I understand the reasoning because of the fact that the rockets did technically put your life in danger, but believe me there are quite a few people (including leaders) within the unit that felt that none of the Soldiers in our company deserved the award. When it came right down to it, I felt that due to the actions of myself and my team that we certainly did deserve it. We weren't sitting there in the office when it all happened, we were right out there. To insinuate that we didn't deserve that award was simply asinine, but that didn't stop anyone from bringing it up. For the remainder of my career I wore the badge proudly on my chest, knowing damned well that I earned it.

October came to a close soon enough which was a sign to me that the deployment was going to be over before I knew it. Just a few more months and I knew that it would be time to go home. The holidays were around the corner and I knew that being there for them wouldn't be any easier than it was on any of my previous deployments. With that said, it had been a long deployment thus far and I needed a break. My leave seemed like it was so long ago, and in a lot of ways it was. I ended up getting to go on a 4 day pass to Qatar, which was great for me because I knew that Qatar was a good way to relax. I had been there so many times in the past so I knew exactly what to expect on one of these trips. Also, I wasn't going to be on the trip alone, as the unit was sending SPC Daily down there with me. It's always nice to go down there with someone, because in the rare occasion that I don't make any new friends at least I have a friend from my unit with me.

The trip ended up being a lot of fun. Of course we partook in our customary three beers a night just like the other times that I had been to

Qatar. On the nights that we partied on the camp I made a lot of new friends which was also pretty cool. It's always nice to make a new friend or two, even in such short circumstances. We went on a number of trips too, to include an SUV ride through the sand dunes of Qatar which culminated in a stop at a small resort on the Persian Gulf. The resort served a lunch selection of Kabobs and other assorted dishes, but what made the stop even more memorable was the fact that you could actually go swimming in the Persian Gulf. Now, I am not a person who swims (in fact it is one of the things that I actually do fear) so instead of swimming I took a walk in the Persian Gulf. That's right, you read that correctly. I WALKED in the Persian Gulf. I walked into the water until it was about waist-high and I looked down to see numerous jellyfish in the area. We were told about the jellyfish in our safety brief prior to arrival so they were no surprise to me, but it was still funny to look out into the landscape and see some of the other Soldiers flipping out over the jellyfish. A few of them even got bit and they had to rush out of the water. I on the other hand didn't fear the jellyfish, the water itself was enough for me to handle. After enjoying the trip for a while I decided to go sit on the beach with a few friends and enjoy a Hookah and trade stories. That was actually better than getting stung by a jellyfish when you really think about it.

Another trip that we took in Qatar was a trip to the Souqs. The term Souqs refers to the market section of town. The Souqs are obviously broken down into different sections, there are the clothing Souqs, the Jewelry Souqs and so on. I had made it my goal on this trip to finally break down and buy a nice necklace. I had an idea in mind that I would buy a chain that was either made of gold or silver. Both of which would be somewhat expensive had they been purchased in the United States. The appeal was the fact that buying them in Qatar was actually a lot cheaper than buying them at home. I had always heard stories of Soldiers who bought a gold chain for $500 that would have been valued at $2,000 in the US. I wanted to take advantage of this myself, so I went shopping. After passing through various jewelry shops I finally found what I was looking for, the perfect gold chain necklace that I could buy and wear proudly when I got home. Upon hearing the price of the item, which was a whopping $1500, I realized that it was a bit steep for me, with or without the sale. I reluctantly decided to pass on the gold chain, even though I wanted one so very badly. It was then that I noticed something off to the left. It was the case of silver jewelry. Everything there was so shiny and beautiful. A silver chain necklace similar in design to the gold one caught my eye and so I decided to try it on. It was one of the nicest chains that I ever saw, and it was 100% silver. While I will not disclose the price of the necklace here, I will tell you that it was not only considerably cheaper than the gold necklace but it was also cheaper than a Silver chain of equal size and weight in the US. Therefore, I looked the shopkeeper in the eye and said, "Well, silver is the new gold anyway, right? I'll take it." And so I bought the chain.

Our final destination that evening was a bus ride to a Moroccan restaurant. Everyone filed onto the bus in the middle of the city and awaited the bus driver to show up and take us to go eat. Suddenly, a local citizen came up to the bus holding a few bags in his hand. After looking closely, I realized that the man had freshly roasted chickens in these bags. He looked at us and spoke in his broken English dialect, "Chicken? Chicken for you?" He was trying to sell us the chickens that he had in the bag. Now, we were all hungry but since we were getting ready to ride to a restaurant we really didn't want the man's chicken. So, like any consumer we all said, "No." If that was the end of it, everything would have been fine, but the chicken salesman decided to try to push it a little further. He came back onto the bus, and started proclaiming for the world to hear, "Chicken, its good chicken. You, mister, you want chicken!?" Once again, nobody on the bus wanted this man's chicken. Feeling defeated, the man left the bus and this time was followed by the bus driver. I remember thinking to myself, "Finally the bus driver made it, now we can get out of here and head to dinner." Just as we thought the bus was about to pull away, we were interrupted by one last visit from the chicken salesman. He stormed onto the bus, and started shouting at the top of his lungs, "CHICKEN! CHICKEN! CHICKEN! CHICKEN! CHICKEN!" Obviously he was adamant about selling his chicken but the difference was this time his actions caused the whole bus to break out into laughter. As we all shared in the laughter, the bus driver started yelling at him and threw him off the bus. Apparently he wasn't in the mood to deal with the chicken salesman. Either way, it was one of the funniest things that I saw on that deployment and it was a nice way to end our final night in Qatar. To this day every time I see a roasted Chicken I think back on the memory of that crazed man storming the bus in one final effort to sell some roasted chicken.

The holiday season came along soon enough just as I knew it would. It was a positive thing because it was a sign that the deployment was coming to an end soon, but at the same time it was still a negative because it's always hard to be away from home for the holidays, especially if you're in a unit where you are absolutely unhappy. Throughout all of the negativity the one thing that helped me keep my head up was the idea of going home. Also the unit was informed that we would be going home a few weeks earlier than we had planned, which was probably the best news of the entire deployment. The reason for the early departure was the fact that President Obama had ordered a drawdown of the troops in Iraq. The United States of America had been conducting operations in Iraq since 2003 and it was time to start bringing the troops home. The process had actually started over the summer when combat brigades were pulled out of the major cities and put into the outer lying camps that were far away from the general population. COB Adder was one of those camps. It didn't make things in the country any less dangerous, it was just time for the US to start "wrapping things up." Eventually all US Soldiers would eventually pull out of Iraq and turn all operations over to the Iraqi Soldiers/Police forces. It was only a matter of time. In the big picture, our unit had a relatively small role in in the theater of operations so there was no reason why we needed to stay much longer. It just made sense for our unit to go home earlier.

The idea of going home early did make the week of Christmas a little easier to get through. There was also a USO tour like most years. This year's guest was UFC Fighter Tito Ortiz. He gave us a speech and told us that the second that the USO approached him with the possibility of coming overseas that he jumped all over it. He had a lot of heartfelt words for us, and told us that he views the Military as a second family. He even had an American Flag that he had flown over a Navy Base that he was going to carry to the ring for his next fight. What I found amazing about all of this was that as a UFC fan, I have heard a lot of people bash Tito Ortiz for being a little bit of an asshole and having an attitude problem. As far as I am concerned, that is all just for TV because he came off as one of the nicest and most humble celebrities that I ever had the chance to meet. He took the time to answer plenty of questions from anyone who had something to ask. He also took the time to take pictures with everyone. I feel he was a total class act and I still have my picture that I had taken with him. When you look at the big picture, it takes a lot of guts for someone who isn't a trained Soldier to come over to Iraq. As a result of this meeting I'll never have a single negative thing to say about Tito Ortiz.

Another thing that made that week special was receiving a package from home. A couple of weeks earlier I had told my dad that I really needed a "taste of home" for Christmas. Every year we make Christmas cookies at home and I was really in the mood to have some of them this year. Even though the DFAC there was state-of-the-art and would have a complete spread for Christmas that just wasn't going to be good enough for me. My dad understood my feelings on the subject so he made some Christmas cookies and sent them out to me. Once the package was in the mail he told me that the kids put something special in there for me that they were sure that I would like. I waited in anticipation for the package to arrive, just wondering what the kids sent me. When the box finally came in, I was careful to open it privately in my room because I knew there would be cookies in the box. Even though I had lost a lot of weight, I still hadn't made tape yet under the strict conditions that the First Sergeant set forth. The last thing I needed was to be caught eating cookies from home. That would have caused her to harass me even more, even though it was the holidays. I really wish that I was exaggerating right now, but believe me the First Sergeant was so damn heartless that it wouldn't have mattered if it was the holidays or not.

It ended up being a good decision to open the package in my room because just seeing the contents brought me to tears. And just to clarify, it wasn't the cookies that made me cry, it was what the kids sent me: they took the time to draw a huge picture of the living room and all of its contents, (including the Christmas tree and some of my dad's swords that he keeps on the walls) with crayons. Then there were quite a few other pictures and all of them said "We love you and miss you Kenny." Seeing all of these pictures meant the absolute world to me and I made sure to go back to the office later that evening to call home and thank them. Today I am not sure my little brother and sister realize just how much that meant to me, but I still have those pictures. I'll keep them forever. Overall it was the best care package that I ever received on all of my deployments and I don't think anything could ever top it.

Any hope of having a great holiday would soon be crushed. As per the duty roster, (which was created by the First Sergeant) I was set to pull VCC duty on Christmas day. I guess I should have known better than to think that I wouldn't have to pull some sort of bullshit duty on a holiday, after all the exact same First Sergeant did this to me last New Year's Eve when we were still at Fort Drum. The only difference was that we were deployed, so I wasn't about to complain about pulling the duty because if I actually did get pulled off of it then someone else would have to do it. It wasn't like our duty requirements went away on the holiday, so in the interest of the other Soldiers I didn't say a word about it. It would have been wrong for me to throw one of them under the bus and make them work on a holiday. Just because I was being treated a certain way didn't mean that I was going to treat others that way. That just wouldn't be right. I did a little bit of reflecting on Christmas day about this very subject however. I had been treated so badly for so long, and I asked myself, "Just how much longer is this going to go on for? How much longer am I going to be treated like this?" On this deployment I had made vast improvements in my physical fitness and my stellar job performance spoke for itself, yet I was still treated this way. It all made me feel like I could do nothing right in that unit, as long as that one particular person was in charge my life was going to be difficult. I resorted to looking at the bright side and looking forward to the future. This deployment was almost over and I was ready to go home. Now I just had to get through the next two months.

2010 came roaring in with a lot of thunder. There seemed to be a lot to do around the office, not just from a normal work standpoint but also because there were no replacements coming in because of the drawdown of US forces. That actually made things harder for us because now we had to turn in all of our equipment and our office buildings to the base operations. From there they would most likely be turned over to an Iraqi unit. The process showed that BASEOPS was a lot stricter on their requirements. Everything started to pile up and the work days sucked more and more as time went by. The closer we were to going home the harder things seemed to get. At this point everyone just wanted to go home. Enough was enough. Even through all of the crap that we had to get done the First Sergeant was still riding her "high horse" and still making everyone miserable. She still supervised and controlled my weigh-ins, and by February 2010 I was down to weighing 186 pounds, which was the lowest I had ever weighed in my entire career. When you compare that to weighing 233 pounds when the deployment started, I would say that I made some excellent progress. I actually should have made tape on this weigh-in because I knew how my body functioned. At any time in my life that I weighed anything less than 195 pounds I would be not only meeting the standard, but exceeding it as well. None of that mattered however because as long as she was rigging my weigh-ins to my disadvantage I was never going to make tape there. I could have showed up weighing 160. It wouldn't have mattered; she would have found something wrong. Hell, at 186 I could look myself in the mirror and see some definition in a lot of places. I had taken off so much body fat that the only way that I could possibly fail a weigh-in was if it was rigged against me from the start. As much as this hurt me on a personal or professional level I was still proud of myself for all that I accomplished. Losing 48 pounds was no easy accomplishment and I knew that by doing it I not only looked better but I greatly improved my own health as well. My achievements finally came to a head in February when I signed up to run in a half marathon that took place on COB Adder. I had ran many of them over the course of my life so I was confident that I could complete the race with no problem, but there was still "something 'special" about the idea of completing a half marathon after spending an entire year working my ass off. It made me feel like it really was all worth it. One of the senior NCOs in the unit forced many of the Soldiers to sign up and run in this race, which I didn't agree with, you should only compete in one of these events if you really want to. I, on the other had didn't need to be forced, I planned on running anyway. What made the race extremely difficult for some Soldiers was the fact that it took place the day after our unit held a record PT test. Most Soldiers complain about having to take a PT test, so I can't even imagine being upset about doing both . . . I had never shunned a PT test in my entire career nor had I backed out of a long distance run. While some of the Soldiers there were griping and complaining about this situation I decided to embrace it. On the day of the PT test I went out there and scored a 290 out of 300 points, scoring the best in the company. The following day I ran the race and I killed it. I do not remember my time for completing the 13 miles, but I do know that I beat a majority of the Soldiers in that as well. I held my head high that day, knowing that I had accomplished something. Doing that well on both of those events on back to back days should have sent the chain of command a message, but at the end it didn't matter. Despite my achievement I still had to be weighed and taped in the unfair manner that I was. I wasn't going to be given the option of a different NCO to conduct the weigh-ins. That's just how it was. Even still, it felt good to look my oppressors in the eye, knowing that they couldn't achieve what I could, even if they had tried.

As the deployment finally came to an end I sat back and did a lot of reflecting. For one, I knew that despite being the victim of personal attacks on the part of bad leadership I still achieved a lot. Everything I did in the office was great and everyone who needed my help never left my office unhappy. That in itself was an achievement. I had learned some valuable Escrima skills that I knew could save my life one day. You just can't put a price tag on that type of experience. I also felt a certain feeling deep down that this deployment was the end of an era due to the fact that all US Forces were being pulled out of the country. I found it almost ironic that I was part of the initial invasion in 2003, and years later I was part of the drawdown in 2010. Thinking about that not only made me feel old, but it also made me realize just how much I had experienced over the years. So much time had flown by in my life and so many things have changed in the world. Who knew what tomorrow's Iraq would look like? Would it stay peaceful without the presence of US Soldiers? Only time would tell. Either way, I was extremely happy about the fact that it was time to go home. We went through so much out there and because of that I had so many mixed feelings. Ultimately I kept a positive outlook on the future. For one, I was about to go home and see my family and friends again. I missed everyone back in Saint Johnsville so much. I was also hopeful about the possibility of being taped by someone else without First Sergeant's supervision. I knew that might have been a long shot, but I also knew that if I was given a fair shot I could make it. Ultimately I knew one thing above all else: this was indeed the worst deployment out of my three. It was great to know that this bumpy ride was over. It was time to go home.

On our way back to Fort Drum we had to pass through Baltimore, MD just as we had on the way over to Iraq in the first place. For some reason the Battalion leadership made a mistake when our flights were booked out of MD and as a result we were not all on the same flight back. I was put into a group that took a connecting flight into Philadelphia, PA while some of the other Soldiers flew into Syracuse, NY. Our problems were complicated when we arrived to Philadelphia when we realized that there weren't any flights leaving for Syracuse until the next morning. This was obviously due to a flaw in the planning process but it wasn't a reflection on us. We were given a hotel room in Philly for the night. At first this seemed like a bad idea but then I realized that a long lost friend of mine, Jason Mays lived there. I hadn't seen him since I left Fort Campbell in

2004 (considering he didn't go to Duke's yard for the wrestling reunion) but we had stayed in touch over the years. So I called him up and we went out and grabbed a couple of six packs of Heineken and went back to the hotel. It was almost like old times again, except there was one thing missing, and that was AJ. (He wasn't from Philadelphia so he obviously wasn't there.) As we drank our beer we decided to give AJ a call and put it on speakerphone. He was actually jealous that we were able to meet up by chance and do something like this. We vowed to him that one day again the three of us would get together, just like the good old days. The next morning I boarded my plane enroute to Fort Drum. I was so ready to get home already but I still considered it a blessing that I was able to reunite with an old friend, even if it was just for one night only. It reminded me of the old saying, "It's a small world after all." You never know when you are going to come across an old friend in your travels. They say that you should never burn bridges because you don't know when you're going to have to cross them again. I would say that's accurate.

CHAPTER 13

THE BEGINNING OF THE END

When I finally arrived back to Fort Drum I found out that we would be authorized to take a pass just like my previous deployments, however it was only going to be a two day pass. I couldn't believe that. Even though I was extremely happy to be back on US Soil, I felt that we deserved more than two days off after a long year. On my first deployment my unit was granted a four day pass. Years later when I returned from my second deployment I thought it was a little unfair that we were only getting a three day pass, but I dealt with it. Now that I was only getting a two day pass I felt that the Brigade was crossing the line with the lack care for its troops. Granted, I knew that we would be permitted to take 30 days of leave when we were finished with our in-processing (which took place after the two day pass) but that didn't change the fact that we should have been given a minimum of three days off upon returning. What could be the possible motive for doing this? Was the Brigade (and subsequently the Battalion) Headquarters in that much of a rush to get the Soldiers back to work? It made no sense to me and it came off as a very heartless action on the part of the leadership.

When I got home for the pass I wanted to start partying right from the start. I took my family to Applebee's for dinner on my first night and then headed over to Josh's to drink some beer with him and the rest of the gang. Of course no night with Josh would be complete without a few "Loyalty over Victory" toasts. Even though it was a week night a few people still came out since it was my first day back, which I appreciated. It was so good to see everyone and made me even happier to be back at home. After a long year of hell it just felt good to be appreciated. God knows I wasn't really made to feel appreciated at the unit while I was deployed, that's for sure.

Even though the two day pass flew by relatively quickly I still was able to spend a lot of time at home for the few weeks prior to leave beginning. For one, I could go home on the normal weekends. Also, there were a lot of days that our training and reintegration classes would get over by 9:30 AM, so most days I would just get on the road and drive home and then go back to Fort Drum early the next morning. I just wanted to spend as much time with the people at home as possible. I really had no desire to sit around at Fort Drum during the week since I had just spent an entire year with most of them. All I really wanted was to be home. While going home all the time I obviously spent a lot of time hanging out and partying with Josh but I also went to a few concerts. I had a passion for live music so I figured I would take advantage of all of my free time by going to a few. I took my brother Jason to a Breaking Benjamin concert in Utica, NY along with a few other friends and I also went to a Killswitch Engage concert with Josh and a few others at a place called Northern Lights, located in Clifton Park, NY. I had a great time at both shows and I realized then that there is only really one way to live your life; by living it to the absolute fullest.

Things at the unit during these first few weeks were still an absolute mess. The First Sergeant was still in charge, which was a detriment to the Soldiers because she didn't know what she was doing half the time. She would sometimes go out to the formation and go on a power trip, or she would come out and say something that everyone knew was factually wrong, which just made her look that much more incompetent. Ultimately most of the Soldiers tried their best not to care; to ignore what she was doing because they all knew that our time to finally go home on leave was rapidly approaching. Since so many of them lived far away in other states they hadn't had a chance to go and see their family for the most part. I was a unique case; being stationed so close to my hometown gave me a distinct advantage over everyone else in the unit. I could literally take a quick, two hour road trip any time I was feeling homesick. It was just that easy. While I did feel bad for some of the Soldiers there, I had to keep reminding myself that it wasn't really my problem; there was nothing that I could do to get those Soldiers closer to their homes. If anything, they should have tried to call their branch managers like I did years ago to get stationed near their homes.

So my 30 days of leave began and I was more than happy to leave that "mess" of a unit behind for a whole month. I wanted nothing to do with it when I was on leave. I wanted that unit to be the very last thought that would be on my mind. That was the only true way to free my mind. Every day I tried to do something that I enjoyed, whether it was just hanging out at Josh's house, going to the local bar, or by going to more live shows. I even had a chance to go and see my good friend Jeremy Carter's band, The Cast Before the Break live for the first time. I must say it was a great show and if you ever have an opportunity to go and see that band live in person or buy one of their albums I highly recommend doing so. You will not be disappointed.

Even though my leave went by fast and I had a good time, I still found out some bad news while relaxing; that being that the Army put me on orders to Fort Leonard Wood, Missouri. Even though I was desperate to leave Fort Drum, I knew that I didn't want to go to Missouri. From what I have heard there isn't much to do there and the post is surrounded by small towns with no businesses or anything to enjoy yourself with. Fort Leonard has always had the nickname, "Fort Lost-In-The-Woods" and rightfully so. Being stationed there would be no different than being stationed near a town the size of Saint Johnsville. On a normal basis that doesn't really interest me. I am a person that needs to be in a booming environment with lots to do. Saint Johnsville was bearable to me because I knew everyone. That is how I can tolerate the small town atmosphere that the town promotes. I love life at home in Saint Johnsville, but I couldn't imagine how bored I would be if I had to live there and had no friends and knew no one. It's just like I said earlier: the place doesn't make the place, the people make the place. Fort Leonard wood just seemed too unappealing to me because there wouldn't be any people there. I had to figure out a way out of that assignment and into a new one. There were a number of places that I wanted to go, and I made it my personal mission to start making phone calls for a new assignment the day I got back to Fort Drum.

When I got back to the unit, I was surprised with a very unpleasant surprise: a good old fashioned weigh-in. That's right, you read that correctly. I was forced into a weigh-in on my first day back at Drum. There was no talking the First Sergeant out of making me go through with it; she had made up her mind. What was even worse was the fact that I was the only one who was weighed in that day. Nobody else from the unit, to include other overweight soldiers was weighed in. This all resulted from the same motives that existed back on the deployment: a personal vendetta. It was obvious that I had gained some weight on leave. I was on vacation for 30 days and pretty much doing whatever the hell I wanted. I knew deep down that the First Sergeant knew that this was going to happen and that was part of why I was weighed in right on the day I came back. I wasn't even allowed to try to take a week or two to drop a few pounds and redo the weigh-In. If I was given that opportunity I knew (and everyone else knew) that I would have had a much better showing but as I stated before it wasn't like the First Sergeant wanted me to have a good showing. I could slowly start to see the "writing on the wall." This weigh-in took place for a reason, and a very sinister one at that.

Just before we took our leave there was a formation at the company where the Commander and First Sergeant congratulated us on a job well done and thanked us for all of our hard work over the course of the deployment. It was during this same speech that we were told to "have fun" and the First Sergeant herself said, "I know ya'll are gonna be hitting up the bars and restaurants for the next month so make sure you enjoy it because you all deserve it!" Fast forward 30 days and I am not only being singled out and weighed in but when I brought up that "speech" after the weigh-in everyone acted like it didn't happen. That obviously pissed me off to no end. How could they do this to me? How much hate could you possibly have for a person if you are starting with them on the first day that they get back from leave? It was during this same conversation that I mentioned the "bars and restaurants" speech that the First Sergeant immediately started bringing up the subject of chaptering me out of the US Army. Now that was an idea that really didn't interest me whatsoever. Over the years I had come to love the Army. I valued my experiences and I cherished the idea of one day earning a retirement after 20 years of service. There was just no way that I could handle the idea of losing all of that. I was one of the best Soldiers that the unit had; not only had I done my job exceptionally well over the years and deployed numerous occasions but I also scored among the highest PT scores in the entire company. It just didn't seem conceivable that I could be chaptered out, but now I was being presented with the idea as if I had no choice in the matter.

Even with the odds suddenly against my favor I had to keep my head up and return to my duties as the unit S1. Things were not looking good for me whatsoever but I still worked hard in the office because that was my job and I loved my job. The careers of every Soldier in that unit were in my hands and I wasn't going to let those Soldiers suffer. It was the exact same way on the deployment; I would shine in times of desperation. I had no choice. I didn't know any other way. Every single day the subject of my chapter would come up, whether it was in a meeting or if it was just brought up in passing. And every time it was brought up, it damaged my morale that much more. It was starting to affect me on a psychological level, and every time this happened I would ask myself, "What about all the sacrifices that I made? Why isn't any of this being taken under consideration? Were all of my sacrifices in vain? Didn't I deploy years ago under a six hour notice?" As you can probably imagine, attempting to balance a full workload in the office and an emotional workload like this at the same time just isn't easy. It was apparent that I could perform in the gym if given the chance but none of that was going to help me now since I wasn't being given the chance. I had to figure something out.

I knew that despite the threats and constant reminders that the unit was going to initiate chapter proceedings I was still on assignment to go to Fort Leonard Wood. I started to look at the possibility of "beating the clock," meaning that maybe I could leave Fort Drum on those orders before the chapter paperwork was initiated. I had that one advantage working in my favor; the fact that paperwork hadn't actually been initiated yet, it was more or less a bunch of threats on the First Sergeant's part. As long as she continued to make empty threats I believed I still had the chance to get out of there.

While I was now being faced with the problem of a possible separation from the Army I still had the problem of Fort Leonard Wood to deal with. Simply put, I didn't want to go there. So I decided to call an old friend for a favor. Chief Broadbent, (who had left Fort Drum years ago to go to Korea) was now working in a position where he could help me out. I asked him if he could do me a favor and contact my branch manager to have the assignment to Fort Leonard Wood deleted and replaced with an assignment to Korea. I really wanted to go back to Korea badly. There were just so many reasons to go. For one, I missed being there. The 13 months that I had spent there was one of the best times of my life. Not only that, but with Chief Broadbent working in the position in which he was working he could ensure that I worked directly for him. I've always found that if you like your boss you will perform a lot better than if you despise them. Let's be honest, by this point I had plenty of experience working for both "types" of bosses and I was certain that I would much rather go and work for an old friend again as opposed to stay on the path that I was on.

Soon enough I verified that my new assignment was posted online to Army Knowledge Online account. Knowing just how badly I wanted to leave Fort Drum I viewed this as a "light at the end of the tunnel." This gave me a new hope; a hope that I really could beat the system and be given a second chance, a hope that I could overcome all of the adversity that had been thrown in my direction over the past few years. My journey had been a long and hard one, and it was nice to know that I was finally going to gain some ground. Feeling confident and strong I continued forward, working hard every day in the office, believing that I wasn't going to get chaptered out. It felt great, but unfortunately these feelings weren't going to last.

In just under two weeks, I received a heartbreaking email from my branch manager that stated that my new assignment to Korea was deleted. I would not be allowed to leave Fort Drum after all. As a sign of courtesy and respect, my branch manager did give me an explanation as to why my assignment was deleted. The message indicated that individuals from my unit had contacted branch to inform them that they had initiated separation paperwork. Due to this fact, my branch manager had no choice but to delete the assignment. It was nothing personal on branch's fault; they are more or less obligated to respect the wishes of a unit when it comes to matters concerning one of their Soldiers. At the bottom of the email I could see that the branch manager had included the email traffic that came from my leadership as well. This really helped me out because by reading this I could pinpoint exactly who (if anyone) was assisting the First Sergeant in my chapter process. Upon reading the message I found that she wasn't acting alone; she had the assistance of the Brigade Sergeant Major. Apparently he was guiding the push to get rid of me. While the First Sergeant wanted me gone, she was an extremely incompetent leader and couldn't quite figure things out on her own. The Brigade Sergeant Major on the other hand was extremely competent and with his guidance the First Sergeant could actually gain some ground against me in the paperwork department. What made all of this worse was the fact that the Brigade Sergeant Major had a major attitude problem and didn't come off as the nicest guy in the world. While he was the type of leader who was big on enforcing standards, he was also the type who didn't want to hear any excuses about anything, to include injuries. He had a reputation for being "too hardcore" even when it was absolutely unnecessary. He would often hold meetings with all of the company First Sergeants in which he would scrutinize every Soldier assigned who was either overweight or had an injury. He was of the mentality who would believe that anyone who was hurt was possibly lying and anyone who wasn't up to standard was lazy. He would not take the time to meet the Soldiers and realize that some of them had flawed leadership. He would sometimes come down on the Sergeants in the unit who were bad leaders, but he wouldn't take any time to actually correct the problem. He would instead hold long "meetings" with the NCOs where he would yell and talk down to people, never taking the time to actually teach anyone anything. Even still, with his expertise fueled by his bad attitude I knew that I now had another "enemy" working against me who was going to do his very best to ensure that my chapter packet was signed. I now had to figure out a way to fight back, and I needed to do it fast.

The very same day that I received this email from my Branch Manager I was called in to meet with the First Sergeant. I believe that she was under the assumption that I hadn't read the email yet because she broke me the "news" about my assignment being deleted in a manner that came off as if she had the "ball in her court." She told me that under no given circumstances would I be allowed to leave Fort Drum and that I will not be able to get out of the chapter proceedings. She then told me that I had better not try to fight the chapter because it would just make things worse for me. She told me that there was just no way that I could win and by fighting it I would risk losing my Honorable Discharge and thus having it reduced to a General Discharge. Obviously, after all of my years of service the last thing that I wanted was to lose out on an Honorable Discharge. For one, I had always served with honor and dignity and my work ethic carried with it a certain level of distinction that wasn't found with many other Soldiers. Furthermore, an Honorable Discharge carries a certain amount of benefits with it, to include the ability to go to college and earn a degree under the Post-911 GI Bill program. The most logical choice for me would be to go to college if I had to leave the Army. After all, I would already have an impressive resume considering I had not only served in the Army but also because of the fact that I worked in Human Resources. Deep down I always wanted to own another business, so I figured that if I went to school and earned a degree in Business that I would be able to achieve my personal goals without a problem. After contemplating all of these ideas I realized that if what the First Sergeant was telling me was true then I should just lay down my arms and not fight the chapter. Risking the loss of an Honorable Discharge would damage my future and thus would be a dumb idea. In one final act of defiance, I told the First Sergeant at the end of the meeting that I had already seen the email from branch, and that everything she told me I already knew. She looked at me with a pissed off look on her face, feeling as if I took her moment away from her. I was perfectly ok with that, considering the fact that she was trying to take my career away from me.

Things started to get a lot rougher for me over the next few weeks, especially from an emotional standpoint. I now hated going to work more than ever. Just the idea of knowing that there was no light at the end of the tunnel; no hope to get out of Fort Drum (in a positive manner) was killing me. I no longer wanted to be there and what made things worse was the fact that many of my friends had left since we returned from the deployment. I was running out of allies, people who I could talk to and I knew I needed to make a few new friends. Finally one day at work, I made that new friend that I needed so badly. Her name was Brenda, and she was assigned to the same unit as me. She came into my office needing help getting her promotion packet updated, which was my job after all. I don't know how it happened, but we ended up talking after that and became great friends. She had to go on a training exercise with the rest of the unit for a few weeks and while she was away we were able to stay in touch and get to know each other a little better. Over the next few months we did grow closer and day after day we would call each other. While things were starting to get a lot worse for me in the office Brenda would always be there for me. Every day she would listen to my problems and offer me advice on what she thought I should do about my situation. It was extremely comforting to know that I had a new friend that was not only willing to lend an ear, but also willing to sympathize. She agreed with the fact that I had been singled out and mistreated, and that my situation was certainly an unfair one. Ultimately that was what I needed, someone to be there for me. There were some days that things seemed so hopeless for me in that unit and all I needed was someone to talk to. Considering the high amount of stress that I was under and the fact that I would have to work in a room full of people whose sole purpose in life was to kick me out of the military. I am not sure how much worse things would have been for me if I didn't have someone to vent to. Over the duration of the year she was always there for me until she had to deploy to Afghanistan in early 2011. Although I was sad to see her go I understood that it was the very nature of the Army for Soldiers to have to deploy at a time of war. Throughout the deployment we still stayed in touch, as she was interested in what the outcome of my situation would be. I was always thankful for the fact that she helped me through this incredibly tough time, and to this day I do not know if she realizes just how much she carried me. To say the least, my final year in the Army was my hardest one on an emotional level and I appreciated her friendship.

Every single day at the office my chapter was brought up in some manner. Whether it was through being forced to update a slide show that had a slide dedicated to my own chapter, or if it was the First Sergeant just bringing it up to me in conversation (as if I really wanted to talk about it). I didn't matter how or in what fashion it was brought up, it still hurt me every time and put a considerable amount of strain on my duty performance. How could anyone operate under these conditions? I was still being given constant work-related tasks, as if I was still "part of the team." I tried my best to work out and lose the weight, but even that didn't matter because I was told that even if I did lose the weight it wouldn't help because the paperwork was already initiated. They wouldn't rescind the paperwork just because I met that standard, which as far as I was concerned was illegal. In fact, that wasn't the only thing about the situation that seemed "sketchy" to me. I knew deep down that the true reason that this was happening was because they wanted to get rid of me. I had a consistent record of proving some of the leaders wrong on certain things that came up over the years. I knew that I was viewed as a troublemaker and in reality a chapter for overweight was just an excuse to get rid of me. It could have been any reason when you really think about it; had I received a DUI on a Friday night the chapter would have been for drug and alcohol abuse; at the end of the day it didn't matter. The proceedings were started due to a personal issue; weight control was just an excuse.

Because of the constant pressure and everything else that was going on, I started to document everything. I kept a file on my computer which I annotated every single thing that was said to me in reference to my chapter. I also annotated every time that I was weighed in. I didn't understand why I was even being weighed in. I had already been told that

I wasn't going to be allowed to stay in the Army, so why were they going through the procedures of putting me on a scale to see how I would do? I choked it up to the fact that most of the leadership didn't really know what they were doing for the most part. Things got even weirder for me as the days went by. There was a day when I was called into the First Sergeant's office to discuss this chapter for what had to be the 100th time. I was really getting sick of talking about it day after day, but on this one particular day something was brought to my attention that gave me just a little bit of hope. The First Sergeant said to me, "Your packet is in one of the review stages by JAG. There was a problem concerning your counseling statements. JAG needs to see a counseling statement for each and every time that you were weighed in over the years, and I didn't include them because I lost half of them. I know that every time we weighed you in that you were given a copy of these counseling statements, so I was wondering if you wouldn't mind providing us with your copies so we can expedite your separation packet." Stunned, I just looked at the First Sergeant in silence for a moment. Before I said anything, I really needed to contemplate what she just told me. By telling me that she lost half of the documents that are needed for my own separation packet, she effectively "showed me her hand." Why would she do this? Did she really think that I would facilitate my own demise? Knowing that I didn't want to leave the Army she must have known better than to ask me such a stupid question. I finally spoke, "Well First Sergeant, I never keep my counseling statements. I usually just throw them away. I was never really required to keep them, so why would I keep a document that told me I was a little overweight? Don't you think that I would find that a bit degrading, First Sergeant? Furthermore, if you know that I don't really want to get out of the Army why would you ask me to help you out?" For a minute she just looked at me, almost puzzled for a second. She finally said, "I had a feeling that you were going to say that. That's ok; I'll just talk to the Brigade Sergeant Major. There has to be a way to push this packet forward without those counselings. Thanks anyway." With that I left her office, realizing that even in my "opponents" stronger moments they were still weak, still making mistakes. They really had me reeling for a while, thinking that I had no hope to stay in the Army. Now that I knew that they had made a mistake of this magnitude I knew that at a minimum I had a little more time on my hands. Above all else I knew one other thing; the fact that I needed to finally buckle down and speak to an attorney about this matter. In all of my dealings and conversations with the First Sergeant on this matter things never really seemed "right" and by finding out that there had been a number of lost documents I realized that I may actually have more rights then I realized. I made an appointment to go see an attorney at Trial Defense Services (the organization that provides defense attorneys for accused Soldiers) the following morning. Excited about the appointment the next day, I went to sleep that night knowing that the next morning I would finally get some real answers.

I arrived at Trial Defense Services (also known as TDS) the next morning with mixed feelings of hope and nervousness. I knew that this day would prove to be that day that I either found out that the leadership was 100% correct in all of their procedures and therefore I had no ground to stand on, or I would come to find out that I really did have some hope. I met with an Army defense attorney and ran down my whole situation for him to ponder. Right off the bat he let me know that since this was a walk-in appointment that it wouldn't count as "official counsel." He also told me that he would explain to me exactly what "official counsel" meant. In effect there was a certain set of procedures that had to come into play when it came to separation proceedings, and therefore once the unit initiates certain steps, a Soldier is fully entitled to "official counsel." What this more or less meant was that I was receiving some guidance from an attorney now, and that I would still be allowed due process when the process was actually initiated. By coming to an understanding with that very topic I now knew that I actually had more time then I realized. He also told me that most of what I had been told by the First Sergeant and other members of the unit were outright lies. First of all, since I had more than six years of service (I had over nine years to be exact) I had the legal right to challenge the discharge, which meant that I had the right to fight back after all. I was told that I could challenge the chapter and have it sent to an administrative separation board and they would hear the case. The board would operate very similar to a trial, in which I would have the right to an attorney (the one I was speaking to) and I could call forth as many character witnesses as I wanted to voice to the board members that I shouldn't be separated from the Army. I would also be allowed to make statements on my own behalf, and my attorney would obviously present evidence and speak as well. Hopefully, the board members would see my side of this and overturn the unit's decision. In contrast, the unit would send a prosecuting attorney who would argue for my separation, and would have the same rights to present evidence and witnesses that I did. The three board members would effectively serve as both judge and jury, which is the major difference between an administrative separation board and an all-out trial. Even though it would feel like and be run like a trial it wouldn't actually be a trial which is a major difference. Another thing that the attorney advised me of was the fact that in most cases when a Soldier is recommended for a discharge under these conditions they don't usually fight back. They usually just take it lying down. I obviously wasn't like everyone else, I was a man of principle and I believed in fighting for what was right. He then went on to tell me that by standing up and fighting for myself I may end up creating some enemies in my unit, to which I replied by telling him, "I'm not worried about that because the people who are initiating these proceedings are my enemies regardless." It was at this point that I fully explained to him that although I am being recommended for a discharge under the Army Weight Control Program that it all stemmed from a personal issue; this was just an excuse to get rid of me. When asked if I could actually prove that in court, I did let him know that there were a number of witnesses at the unit who have seen it happen and I would ask them to testify on my behalf.

The longer this meeting went on the stronger I started to feel. What this ultimately meant to me was that I had the chance to create an even playing field, once and for all. I knew that I had worked hard over the years and made a lot of friends, allies if you will, who would be willing to speak on my behalf. I had done so much good in my career that I would just have to start calling in favors for people to testify at my board. This wasn't the only lie that the attorney filled me in on; apparently when I was told that I would lose rights to an Honorable Discharge if I fought the chapter I was lied to. The only type of discharge that you could receive for an overweight chapter was an Honorable Discharge. I don't care what anyone says about this subject, be it a civilian or a member of the military but there is absolutely nothing dishonorable about being overweight. Granted, it is against regulation but it isn't dishonorable. I just wish that more leaders in the Army understood that concept. I was even lied to on the approval process of the separation. I was once told that I would suddenly just receive orders one day; as it turned out I actually needed to be served papers in a formal manner since I was attending a board. Just like a trial, there was a whole set of procedures that had to be followed and one of those procedures was that I had to be served papers a minimum of

14 days from the day of the trial. The attorney told me that a better way to look at it is to think as if I have 14 days left in the Army at all times and not to let anything the unit leadership says to me effect my morale or psyche. As long as I kept a level head through all of this I could mount a good enough defense and hopefully win at the board. When it came right down to it I was lied to on so many levels and it felt great to finally receive some advice from someone who knew how to fight the unit. I remember feeling so full of life when I left the attorneys office that day. I rushed home and called Brenda and told her the great news. She was glad to hear that no matter what the unit couldn't take away my honorable discharge. It felt even better to share this great news with a friend. I was so full of energy, and it turned out to be one of the most positive days of that era for me. I went to bed that night knowing that the next morning I would walk into the unit a proud man, ready to fight back. I knew that there was a chance that I still wouldn't win, but at least I knew deep down that I wasn't going down without a fight.

The next day I was called into the First Sergeant's office. By now I was used to the constant harassment and the mentions of my chapter. The only difference was this time her shenanigans weren't going to bother me. She had heard that I went to see an attorney, and didn't seem too pleased about it. She acknowledged that fact that I did have rights, but was confused as to why I would even want to fight back. She couldn't understand why I wouldn't just take it and get out. I maintained my composure in this meeting, trying not to "show all of my cards" and lose my composure. I knew that through the remainder of this process I had to be smarter than my enemies. That was the only way I could win. Before I left her office, she informed me that the real reason that I was being called in there had nothing to do with discussing my meeting with an attorney, but instead the reason was to inform me that I was now being relieved of my duties as the S1 for the unit. She told me that since I was going to lose my case (as she thought) that there was no reason for me to be the S1 anymore and I would be replaced next week. As far as I was concerned the First Sergeant was crossing the line on this one. She knew I loved my job with a passion and by taking my job away it was an attempt to destroy my morale once and for all. I was greatly affected by this and it certainly hurt me. I also viewed this as a way to punish the Soldiers in the unit. Over the years I had provided the unit with top notch, five star services as the S1 and now that they didn't have me doing that anymore their careers were going to suffer in some way, shape or form. While I didn't know who my replacement would be just yet, I knew that there was almost no way that they would put forth the same effort that I did. Furthermore, I treated the Soldiers in that unit with respect, there was a good chance I would be replaced by an asshole which wouldn't really make anyone happy. It bothered me a lot but it wasn't enough to destroy my motivation as a whole. I was still riding the positive feeling from the meeting with the attorney and therefore this didn't change the fact that I was a man on a mission, willing to stand and fight. It's just a shame that the unit gave up on me so quickly. By relieving me of my duties they proved that they not only wanted me gone, but were also willing to cut their losses and move on. What a shame.

I ended up being replaced by a Specialist that was not only bad at doing the job itself, but she was utterly disrespectful to most of the Soldiers in the unit, to include her superiors. There were so many problems with this Soldier, ranging from a long turnaround for submitted work (because she would let work sit on her desk for weeks), to refusing to listen to Soldiers' problems. When she would finally complete some of her work it would come back with many errors and need correcting. Now, in comparison to the quality of work that I put forth, (I always got things done on time, if not early and my work was ALWAYS mistake-free) this Soldier's efforts were simply unacceptable. Sometimes the Soldiers in the unit would come to me late at night in the barracks and complain about the new S1. We used to hold mock "hallway meetings" in which they would voice to me their concerns and I would do my best to console them in any way I could. Sometimes I would tell a few jokes; sometimes I would offer them advice on what to do to overcome some of their problems. It got to the point where each and every night somebody was complaining about the overall conditions in that unit and it truly hurt me that the most that I could now do was offer some advice. I had no authority to step in and do anything about it. I now had no job, all I was supposed to do was come to accountability formation in the morning and then I would be "off" for the day. None of the leadership wanted me around the unit area anymore. I took this as a terrible insult and a smack in the face considering just how much I loved my job. I had such a raw passion for doing my job that by not being allowed to do it anymore I was genuinely hurt inside, and the worst part was that the leadership KNEW that. There were all sorts of speculation amongst the disgruntled Soldiers within that unit that the true reason that I was relieved of my duties was because it would directly hurt me. And who could blame any of them for being disgruntled? They were now being cheated out of top-notch, first class support by one of the greatest S1's that they had ever come across. The whole situation not only hurt me, but hurt those Soldiers as well. When it came right down to it, I was replaced by a disrespectful, lazy, "garbage" Soldier who didn't give a crap about anyone, while I no longer had a job. All of this just continued to "fuel my fire." I was going to try my hardest to win at my separation board, no matter the cost. What made it all worse was that no one seemed to know when the board would be. Granted, that gave me more time to prepare even though the lack of a solid board date (or even proper paperwork for that matter) was just another sign of how disorganized that unit had become.

Even though things were steadily getting worse in that unit, there was a "light at the end of the tunnel" so to speak. The First Sergeant had requested a retirement after over 20 years of service and finally the week had come where she would start clearing and go on retirement leave. That meant that her time here was done and some of my suffering was over. I really wasn't exactly sure what sort of impact this would have on my chapter packet. Would the new First Sergeant (who I hadn't met yet) consider revoking the packet and give me another chance? Or was the packet too far along at the Battalion level? Only time would tell. The only thing that I knew for sure was that I obviously had no personal issues with the new incoming leadership and there was no reason to create any. The idea of my nemesis leaving did give me a slight ray of hope, and it also strengthened my pride as well. Since the First Sergeant had made it her personal mission to get rid of me, I knew that every time that she saw me was just as painful for her as it was for me. I wanted nothing more to be in the office on her final day, knowing that she was gone and never coming back, even though tomorrow morning I would still be around. Even if I was chaptered out the following week, I didn't care as long as I knew deep down that I outlasted the First Sergeant. That would make me feel really good to say the least.

As I kept "waiting out the clock" for the First Sergeant's final day to arrive I continued to see things in the unit fall apart. Everything seemed to be in disarray. There was a Captain who was temporarily in command of the company until our new commander arrived, and he kept on losing documents, fumbling his words in front of formation, and even waited until the last minute to make every one of his decisions. This guy was even worse than the departing First Sergeant, except I didn't have a personal issue with him, he was just disorganized. I just couldn't understand why this place was falling apart so quickly. I asked myself, "How bad is this unit going to get?" I wondered what had happened to the Army that I had grown to love so much. Where did it go? What happened to the days when this unit felt like a mighty empire under the hand of 1SG Gudger? Was it really all him the whole time? As time went by, I witnessed the quality of the senior NCOs in that unit start to deteriorate. Sure, there were still a few good ones, but for the most part the other ones were just carbon copies of the First Sergeant, just without as much power. I didn't get it. There was no real logical way to figure out what had happened, all I could really do was sit back and watch the show. Only it wasn't an entertaining show; it was a sad, depressing, low-quality sitcom at best.

During the First Sergeant's final week there were a few interesting things that happened. First of all, our unit was greeted by the presence of a true leader. The legend himself, 1SG Gudger had returned to Fort Drum for that week. While he wasn't there full time to retake his old position, (he was actually called up to testify in a trial) he still had some time to stop by his old stomping grounds to visit everyone. Even though the unit had acquired quite a few new faces since he left, he was still able to come over and see a few familiar faces, specifically Cappe and I. We had a lot of stories to fill him in on, to include the circumstances of my chapter. He was disgusted to see what the unit had become, things were so much better here when he ran the unit and it was a shock for him to hear some of the stories of the corruption that had taken place, not only at Fort Drum but in Iraq as well. It didn't take long to convince him of the problems that we had suffered since he left, and even though he couldn't really do anything about it at the time he could still offer us his advice and condolences. He continued to pop into the office over the next few days, checking in on us and seeing if we needed anything. It was so good to have him around; he seemed to breathe a new life back into the place. In a lot of ways the unit "died" when he left, and now that he was back (albeit temporarily) things really started to feel better around there. I will never forget the day that he and his replacement (my nemesis) came face to face for the first and only time. She was standing in the hallway of the company area telling her replacement that the company was currently in "such great shape" and that when she inherited it from 1SG Gudger that the place was a complete wreck and there were countless problems.

She then continued to run down 1SG Gudger's legacy, saying all sorts of things that just weren't true. She even labeled him as a bad leader. What she didn't realize was that while she was going off on a rant of how bad she thought 1SG Gudger was, that he was standing directly behind her and heard the entire thing. That was the funny part. Over the years 1SG Gudger used to claim that he was a man who liked to use "colorful words," meaning that he would use whatever foul language that he needed to in order to get his point across. While I cannot remember exactly what he said to her upon hearing her disparaging remarks, I do know that he not only "put her in her place" but he also used quite a few of his "colorful words." For the rest of the time that he was there she avoided him and didn't say another word to him after that incident. As far as I was concerned she deserved that treatment. 1SG Gudger was (and forever will be) heralded as the greatest leader that the company ever saw, while she was the absolute worst. Given those conditions you would think that she would show a little bit of respect, but considering her rambunctious personality that just wasn't the case. She deserved what she got on that day, 1SG Gudger made her feel "small" and rightfully so.

The new First Sergeant took over, and within the first week she wanted to have a conversation with me concerning my issue. She made sure to inform me of the fact that her and 1SG Gudger had been friends for a long time, and that 1SG Gudger had spoken highly of me to her. So, with that said I proceeded to inform the new First Sergeant of everything that had happened in regards to my situation since the very first day that I was informed of the chapter. I told her about the botched and biased weigh-ins. I told her how her predecessor had a very serious issue with me, and I was brutally honest about exactly why that issue came to fruition. Over the course of the conversation things started to seem very positive, and thus the new First Sergeant told me that she couldn't really guarantee anything, but she would see what she could do about putting my chapter on hold. She first needed to see the packet (which I understood). The sad part was that since I was left out of the loop I really had no idea where my packet was, so I couldn't point her in the right direction. I would have to bide my time and wait, but overall the meeting was positive and I left that day feeling as if there may be some hope for me after all. God knows that I needed it, because the past few months had been an extremely tough time for me.

Even though the new First Sergeant took over, my nemesis would still be around for a few more days finalizing her out-processing paperwork. This was typical protocol that every Soldier had to go through, but it was still agonizing to have to see her for any longer. I just wanted her to be gone already. We had been through so many disputes and arguments that I was just ready to get her out of my life and move on. I can still remember the day she left, clear as day. There was an officer that had an office next to my old section, and I stopped in to talk to him for a few minutes while I waited for my replacement to show up and unlock the door to my old office. Even though I didn't work there anymore, I had left some personal things behind and I wanted to clean my desk out and take my stuff home. While waiting in the office next door I noticed a half busted sledgehammer in the corner. For some reason, it caught my eye and I asked him why it was there. As it turned out, the motor pool had replaced the hammer since it was slightly (but not too severely) broken and they were just going to throw it away. The officer decided not to throw it away, and instead took it back to the company figuring that someone could get some sort of use out of it. I looked at it again, and I asked him if anyone had claimed it yet. No one had, and so he offered it to me. Now, considering the fact that I had no real job at this point, let alone any responsibilities to speak of there was no real reason for me to take the sledgehammer, but I did anyway. It just felt cool to have my own sledgehammer. For the rest of the day I walked around the office with that sledgehammer, as if I was the wrestler known as Triple H. There were even a few Soldiers that called me Triple H that day, which I thought was even funnier. Soon enough, the time came when my nemesis, the former First Sergeant, had to come into the office to say goodbye for the last time. I didn't say a single word to her, knowing that she still held her rank I didn't want to get busted for any sort of UCMJ punishment on her last day. I still had an obligation to respect her rank, so I just let things go . . . until she approached me. She tried to talk to me, in which I didn't really say much back to her. I stood there, face to face with her, with the sledgehammer lying on my shoulder. I didn't mean to put it up there, and it wasn't being done in any sort of threatening manner. In fact, it was all coincidental; when she approached me I had already had the sledgehammer perched upon my shoulder. Realizing that I wasn't really trying to make small talk with her, she looked at the hammer and said, "You probably want to hit me with that, don't you Sergeant Conklin?" I really wish that I was making that up, but I am not, she really said that to me. Sensing that she was testing me, I didn't say a word; I just looked at her and smirked. She then did something that I didn't expect. She offered her hand in an effort to shake my hand and said, "You stay out of trouble Sergeant Conklin." I shook the hand of my nemesis and I looked her dead in the eye, still holding my mighty sledgehammer, and said to her, "You should probably try to do the same." With that, she just looked at me puzzled, grabbed her things and walked out of the building . . . for the final time. On that day, I achieved the minor goal that I wanted to achieve: outlasting my enemy. If you notice, we didn't part on a "goodbye." We parted on more of a mutual feeling of where the other person stood. Today, that sledgehammer sits on my father's back porch, and that is where it will stay.

With my old nemesis out of the way, I was hoping for a new beginning under the new First Sergeant. I knew that the very tone of the company was about to change, things were going to be different from now on. I waited, hopeful that I would receive some word that my chapter packet was going to be put on hold and that I would be given another chance. That's all I really needed, a fair chance. I knew that if I was given about six months and I was taped fairly I could make tape and be allowed to stay in the Army. Out of nowhere, I had a family emergency and I had to take leave for a week. I had absolutely no choice but to go on leave, and just like all of the other times that I had an issue Brenda was there to lean on. I will never forget that, and she knows that. Prior to going on leave, the new First Sergeant called me into the office and told me that there was nothing for me to worry about, that the unit was going to let me stay in the Army. I could go home on emergency leave worry free and not worry about a thing. My Army career wasn't going to come to an end. I wanted to rejoice so badly, but the emergency that I had to deal with consumed me so much that it was the only thing that I worried about. I knew that later on I would have the chance to celebrate this great news, but now just wasn't the time.

I went on the week of emergency leave and took care of business. Before I knew it my leave was up and it was time to go back to the unit. I returned there with the most optimistic feeling that I had felt in a long time. My family had overcome a serious emergency and now I was going to get to go back to Fort Drum and stay in the Army. Deep down I knew that it was only a matter of time before I would be allowed to reclaim my position as the S1 of the unit. That wasn't just something that I wanted,

I knew that all of the Soldiers wanted that as well. If I was able to reclaim my position I could not only "right the wrongs" but also re-institute some of the order in the unit that had been lost. The Soldiers there needed someone to look up to, and in the past that someone was me. I was ready to become that "someone" again. I would not fail them and I would never turn my back on them. I don't mean to sound self-righteous, but in a world where most of the leaders are corrupt, someone has to stand up for the junior Soldiers, the "little guys" if you will. I was always the one who did that, and I was more than ready to do it again.

On my second day back, things just didn't seem right to me. All day long I couldn't quite put my finger on it but I knew that something was "off". At the end of the day I was called into the Commander's office. I had a funny feeling that this wasn't going to be a good meeting (after all what meeting with your commander is a good one?) and that everything that I was told in reference to being allowed to stay in the Army was bullshit. It was just this feeling that I had, and unfortunately it was true. My Company Commander told me that my packet was "too far along" and there was "no way to stop it." The Battalion leadership already had visibility on the subject (thanks to my former nemesis) and because of that my chapter was not a dead issue after all. I then went on to explain that I was told prior to taking leave that it was a dead issue, to which he replied with "I don't know why the First Sergeant told you that." Obviously, this crushed my morale. I now had to continue to fight this issue. I really believed that since the previous First Sergeant had left that I would be able to get out of this. Now I was thrown off a little. How could I possibly fight a battle against people I hardly knew? They didn't have a personal problem with me, so that argument may not stand at my hearing. Seeking answers, I went back to see my attorney again the next day.

Upon meeting with my attorney, he reminded me of many of the things that he told me in our previous meeting, which by now had actually happened months ago. He also told me that he was never informed that I wasn't being chaptered out, so it was most likely a case of misinformation or an outright lie when I was told that. So with that said, I was forced to switch back into "trial mode." I knew without a doubt that I was going to have to stand before that board, so it was time to get ready. I started calling as many of my character references as possible. I knew that I needed all the help that I could get, so I called everyone that I could. I called Colonel Alvarado, who by now had not only been promoted from Lieutenant

Colonel (O-5) to Colonel (O-6) but was also now serving as the Chief of Staff for the state of New Jersey. I knew that he had a lot of pull because he was in a very high position. Maybe that pull could help me. Perhaps the board would take the fact that an officer of his standing was willing to speak up for me. I also called other friends from my past. Josef Smith, who by now had left for Korea was willing to testify for me. I called Kathy, who was now a Warrant Officer in the New Jersey National Guard. She would also testify for me, and was willing to not only mention my work ethic in the office, but was also going to talk about the fact that she knew me for years and that she personally witnessed me score high on army PT tests. That was important, everyone who was on my side felt that my PT tests shouldn't be ignored. I called Maria, who by now was a Staff Sergeant serving in an AGR position in the guard. She was more than willing to testify to the fact that I was influential on her career. Chief Broadbent was also willing to testify. After all, he was a mentor of mine in the past and he really knew what I was capable of. Knowing that I needed all the help I could get, I called Jason Mays as well. Even though he was retired, he had known me as a personal friend for an extremely long time. If there was anyone that could testify to my character it would be him. I even called Cummings, considering the fact that she was the last Soldier who worked for me I figured that she would have some good things to say about me and my duty performance. Even though most of the people that I called to testify were from different parts of my career it didn't change the fact that they could help me. My experiences with each of them spoke for themselves, now it was just a matter of the board hearing what they had to say and realizing that some of the disparaging remarks that were written into my packet by my former nemesis just weren't true. All we had to do was wait for the board to be announced, which still hadn't happened even though we assumed it would be coming soon.

The routine at the unit suddenly became the same old routine as before, minus the personal issues with leadership. I was required to show up in the morning, go to formation and do PT, and then I would be off for the day. I still wasn't allowed to return to my old job as the S1/HR NCO for the unit, which still bothered me day after day. I knew that I could still contribute to the unit and I knew that it hurt those Soldiers that I couldn't come to work every day and do my job. Sitting on the sidelines was probably one of the worst experiences of my career. What also didn't make sense was the fact that the unit was still conducting weigh-ins for me every month. I didn't understand what the point was. The paperwork was still in motion; the battalion was hell bent on chaptering me out, because after all they don't like to let issues die. When an action goes to their level they almost always seek a final resolution. So why was I being weighed in? By now it seemed like a degrading task that I just had to deal with. That didn't mean I wanted to deal with it. I already knew my fate by now; why make me go through the scrutiny? I had gone through the fake "we're going to let you stay in the Army" stage, so by now my morale was pretty much dead. Before long I hated showing up there, just as much as I did before. Over the next few months there was no real effort to make me feel like I was part of the team. It was constant exclusion and alienation. Despite the hope that it would get better when the old First Sergeant left, it really didn't. By now I could definitely see the writing on the wall.

Over the course of the year I tried my best to keep my head up no matter what obstacles were put in front of me. I still went home almost every weekend and I viewed any chance to leave Fort Drum as an opportunity to relieve some stress. I wasn't partying nearly as much anymore, in fact I had significantly cut down on my drinking so most of the weekends that I was home I would end up spending a lot more time around the house with the family. There was one weekend in particular that came along in which my father did something very special for me, which helped to re-ignite my "spark" when I needed it. He was out one morning taking our dog Shadow for a walk when he approached the public library in Saint Johnsville. Upon walking by he noticed that on the right side of the library (if you are looking at it that is) there is a civil war monument with a cannon and an empty flagpole. He didn't really understand why the flagpole was empty, and it needless to say its emptiness didn't sit well with him. He asked the librarian why there wasn't a flag there, to which she didn't have a real answer for my dad. So he offered to donate an American flag to be flown there. When she agreed to accept his offer and fly the flag, he explained that it wasn't just any American flag that would be donated, it was a special one. During my previous deployment to Iraq in 2009 I had the opportunity to fly a few flags over COB Adder and send them home. I gave two of them to my dad, in which he offered one of them to the library. Upon hearing the news that the library would receive a flag that was flown over a US Airbase in Iraq, the librarian immediately set a date in late October for it to be flown. What was even better was that my dad told them that I would show up on that day in full uniform to fly the flag.

When the day finally came, I walked to the library donning my Class A uniform. All of my ribbons were in perfect order and my Combat Action Badge glistened in the sunlight. I had told all of my friends to show up to watch the presentation, to which a few of them actually did. There was a decent crowd there, (but not too big) that included my family, my old Kung Fu instructor Al Kirby, Josh Richard, Joe Carter, and a few members of the town's DPW among others. I gave a quick speech about patriotism and the United States of America, and what it meant to me to be able to donate this flag to not only our library, but the people of my town. Afterwards, I called my dad over to join me at the flagpole and we unfolded the flag just like any other military ceremony. We then hoisted it up the pole, where it will stay forever. A few pictures were taken and I shook hands with everyone and we left. I remember thinking to myself that day about just how much of an honor this was. Here I was given the opportunity to do something positive for the town and it turned out great. I think I learned a few things that day, for one I learned which friends really cared about me and the things that I was doing. I invited a lot of friends out that morning, but not all of them showed up. I also learned that no matter what kind of adversity I was facing back at Fort Drum that I still had it in me to do something right; something positive. I didn't have to stoop down to the level of the people who were trying to hold me down. I could rise above all of that and overcome things, even if it was only a matter of overcoming them in my own heart. It made me think back on a fortune cookie that I had received at a Chinese restaurant earlier that week. The fortune said, "Just because others do wrong does not imply that you are good." That message had left me thinking for the week; asking myself if I was truly correct for standing up to the corruption for all of these years. It's funny how the slightest thing could make you second-guess your own decisions. All of that no longer mattered however, after this experience I was able to re-affirm in my own heart that I was good, I was still the "good guy." A member of the Saint Johnsville American Legion post also attended the event, to which he asked me if I would consider joining the post later that evening. Considering the fact that the American Legion is an organization that likes to give back to the community and take care of veterans as much as possible I decided that joining was the right thing to do. Later that evening I took a walk up there, (still in uniform) and signed up, becoming a proud member of American Legion Post 168. I know that since I travel a lot I don't always get to make it over there, but believe me there will always be a special place in my heart for the American Legion.

I had so many positive feelings running through me from the day that I flew the flag that I decided to pick myself up and try my best to lose the weight. Over the month of November I worked extremely hard, sometimes going to the gym three times a day. Since I still didn't have a job I had the free time on my hands to do so, so taking advantage of that was probably my smartest option. When my December weigh-in came along I had lost a whopping eight pounds, which was the most that I had lost since I was notified that I was being chaptered out. Even though I knew that I would eventually have to stand before a separation board I assumed that if I got into the proper shape by the day of the board that they would dismiss the proceedings out of a legal and moral obligation. I knew the unit wouldn't back off under these circumstances, but the board would have no choice. I still hadn't been served my papers for the board, which meant that I not only didn't have a board date but I had a minimum of 14 days left in the Army (as per my attorney's guidance). I set out to work out that much harder, and knew that if I lost eight pounds in one month that I could probably do the same the next month.

It was during this time that a new Sergeant First Class (E7) came to the unit who ended up being assigned as my Detachment Sergeant. At first, I really didn't know what to think of him. I hardly knew him and the only background information that I had on him was the fact that he was a former infantry NCO. As I stated before, the Infantry Corps tends to breed leaders that are harder on people then they need to be, and usually when they cross over to a support unit they carry this "hardcore" attitude with them. Part of that "hardcore" attitude includes instantly passing judgment on overweight Soldiers and Soldiers on profile, usually without even getting to know them to really judge their work ethic. As I stated before, I have never been a fan of their mentality on this subject and it does need to change. So because of this "personality defect" as I like to call it, I started off on the "wrong foot" with this NCO right from the beginning. I remember thinking to myself, "Great, just what I need, a new enemy." I thought my days of making enemies in this unit were through, I had tried my best to maintain a low profile during formation since I no longer had a job and since my nemesis had left. There was no reason for me to start making enemies again. It's just too bad that this NCO didn't feel the same way.

What made things worse for me was the fact that this NCO was appointed the duties of being my "escort" every time that I had to go to TDS to talk about my case. As if I needed escorting (which I did not), he would make it worse for me by attempting to talk my attorney into accepting paperwork that just wasn't correct. Quite often the paperwork was turned down because whoever was processing it was just that incompetent; they didn't seem to know their job as well as I did. When this would happen, the NCO would accuse me of asking my attorney to "fudge" the documents. Now, it was a well-known fact that my attorney was on my side, but he has a legal obligation just like anyone else which meant that he couldn't "fudge" documents because he would be risking his own career by doing so. He had too much integrity to do something like that. "Fudging" documents was something that my unit did, but that didn't mean that everyone else did it. This usually worked to my advantage because every single time that the unit would mess up the paperwork it bought me that much more time, which also upset my Detachment Sergeant (once again, not my fault). I can remember riding back from one of these appointments with him, when I finally decided to break the ice. I asked him, "What is your problem? We hardly know each other, and you always act like this crap is my fault when you can clearly see that the paperwork was wrong, which isn't even in my hands." His response astonished me, but I guess I should have expected it, "Look SGT Conklin, I am a company guy. The First Sergeant and the Commander asked me to act a certain way when dealing with you and paperwork, and that's what I am going to do. I'm sure you're not a bad guy, but as far as battalion is concerned you are a bad NCO. So when it comes to your paperwork, if you have any problems take them up with the commander." I couldn't believe it. He was new here and yet he created a grudge against me based on things he was told by his superiors, who were also people that he just met. He now legitimately didn't like me, which was a shame but I now knew that I wasn't changing his mind. As long as the Battalion didn't like me, he wouldn't either. Through all of his "tough guy," infantry bravado, he was really just a "yes man" at his core. That's all he was. You never would have thought that based on what he had done in the past as an Infantry NCO, but when it came right down to it the man was not a leader; he was just appointed to a leadership position. So now I knew that when I would get into altercations with him in the future (which I was almost positive would be coming now) that they would be nothing more than a carbon copy of the arguments that were presented to him by the individuals that he answered to. Throughout all of my years as a Non-Commissioned Officer I always strived to be better than that. I always knew that being a "yes man" was wrong, and that it really wasn't what was best for those who served under me. I guess not everyone looks at it that way, and not everyone is concerned with the welfare of their subordinates. Some are more concerned with their own evaluation reports and their own promotion potential, leaving no room for the possible thought of coaching and mentoring a subordinate so they can one day reach that level. As sickening as that is, it is a real problem that exists in the Army as a whole and a problem that now added to my already complicated situation.

Shortly after the weigh-in that I displayed great progress I was notified that I would now be given a job at the unit. At first this sounded like a great idea, and I hoped that it meant that I would be reclaiming my rightful place as the S1. I knew that most of the Soldiers wanted to see me get my old job back, and so did I. Every day I was getting knocks on my barracks room door by various Soldiers who wanted to complain about how bad things were getting. Each time I just took it all in and offered counsel, almost like a prisoner who was once in power. It was an odd feeling but there were many days when I felt as if I was unofficially their leader. It was these conversations that made me want my old job back that much more. The idea of returning to work would actually motivate me even more which would obviously carry over into the gym. As it turns out, all of that was just a bad "pipe dream." My new job wouldn't be S1 at all; instead I was being put on snow plow duty at Fort Drum for the duration of the winter. Fort Drum was notorious for its vicious winters and "flash blizzards" and now I was going to have to be the NCOIC of a shift of Soldiers whose sole purpose was to keep all of the parking lots and unit areas clean. What made things worse was that I was going to be put on the night shift of this detail from midnight to 0700 hours (7 AM). This is affectionately referred to as the "graveyard shift". The main problem that I had with this was that it was a seven day a week detail, which meant that we could possibly be on call during the weekends. I really wasn't interested in missing out on any weekends at home, and I made that very clear right from the beginning. Luckily, the Sergeant First Class who was in charge of the entire detail wasn't even from my unit, and we took a liking to each other right from the beginning. He always assured me that I would never have to miss out on my weekends at home, as long as I did what was necessary during the week. I had no issues with that, and it was nice to work for a leader that was actually sympathetic for a change. Over the next few weeks I found out why he was ok with me for the most part. It turned out that he was in legal trouble too, which stemmed from a personal incident that he had in his life that involved alcohol. His retirement packet was already submitted, so I wondered if all of this would cause him problems or even worse (for him) cause his retirement date to be pushed back. Looking back, I think that he took such a liking to me because I was in some form of legal trouble (albeit for being overweight) also and that fact alone helped him relate. He would rely on me for a lot of things in relation to the mission, to include having to pull an extra hour of duty from time to time. I honestly didn't mind because the man treated me with respect from the beginning. He never judged me for my issues, which is all that I could really ask. I know that legal issues for overweight have almost nothing in common with alcohol-related incidents, but as the old saying goes, "misery loves company."

What was even better about being on snow plow duty was the fact that anyone assigned to the duty was removed from their unit for the duration of the detail . . . or so I thought. There were some days when this would work out to my advantage, there would be a serious detail or training exercise taking place at my unit and I would be exempt because I was on recovery from pulling a seven hour shift the night before. Then, there were certain days where members of the unit would ignore this rule. My good old, "yes man" Detachment Sergeant was notorious for this. I would constantly have to tell him that I was exempt (by orders of the Command Sergeant Major) from all unit activities while assigned to snowplow duty. He would always try to tell me that due to my "special situation" that I was different and that if he called me that I had "better answer my phone if I knew what was good for me." I don't know who he thought he was dealing with, but I remember always hoping to myself that he would actually try to put his hands on me. I would have beaten his ass without even thinking twice about it. I know that doesn't sound very professional, but put yourself in my shoes for just a second: the man was bothering me every day, even though he had no right to do so, claimed he was ALWAYS acting on behalf of his bosses and then had the nerve to hint at threatening me. Both his words and actions always put me on edge. Things started to get worse when he would no longer wait until a decent time of the day to call me. I would get off of my shift at 7 AM, and despite knowing this fact he would call me at 9 AM, and 1 PM, just to fill me in on pointless information that I didn't pertain to me, or to outright start an argument with me. It never mattered to him that I had worked all night and needed my sleep in order to be effective the next night on duty. This was a deliberate attempt to mess with me, and I am sad to admit that it worked. Sleep deprivation is a technique used to break someone down. It is used for various purposes, and in this case I feel that it was being done just to break my spirit. If I didn't answer my phone when he called, he would just call over and over again until I answered. When that no longer worked he started coming to my door, knocking as loud as he could until I answered. In other words, I was never going to get a full eight hours (or even four hours) of sleep after pulling a shift. This had a direct impact on my performance in the gym, and it got to the point where I had to stop going into the gym altogether because I needed as much rest as possible before my shift started. It was bad. Before I knew it, I was slowly starting to gain weight again. When you think about it, if you spend your whole night sitting down in a plow truck and then your whole day laying down in a bed you don't really have any time to squeeze in physical activity. By doing this to me, he circumvented all efforts to lose the weight. To this day I still ask myself if that was part of the plan. I think I sent the unit a clear message when I lost the eight pounds that I was not going to go down without a fight, and he was their way of "fighting back" against me. I know that I'll never "officially" know the answer, but I know that the Detachment Sergeant did have it out for me because he told me that he did to my face on more than one occasion, so what's to say that maybe he wouldn't try to stop me from dropping the weight and winning my case? As I said, I will never know the answer, but I will always know that he was a cruel, cold man who had no business leading Soldiers.

The actual snowplow duty itself wasn't that bad. As I stated earlier I had the blessing of working for someone who actually showed me some respect, but that wasn't the only thing that made the duty an enjoyable experience. I had a group of Soldiers who worked for me on the duty that were actually a pleasure to be around. That in itself was funny because all of the Soldiers there had some sort of issue back at their unit, regardless of what it was. (This furthered the idea that the Battalion only put Soldiers into this unit who were considered "undesirable" back at the unit.) There was one Soldier on duty who didn't understand English very well. There was another Soldier there who was in the process of receiving an Article 15 for insubordination. There was also a Soldier by the name of Gibson there who was actually from my unit. In fact, Gibson deployed to Iraq with me in 2009 and was always a hard worker and a great mechanic but he liked to drink almost every single day. He would always show up to formation smelling like booze. Aside from that flaw he was a good Soldier, but that didn't matter. You see, every one of these Soldiers had a flaw, and because of that they were more or less "exiled" from the unit and put on this duty. No one wants a Soldier at the unit who is drunk, or who is in trouble, or who cannot understand some of the commands that he is given. I know that sounds harsh, but that is because it is harsh. I felt bad when I finally came to the realization of exactly why they were put on the duty. I don't know if any of them realized the reasons why, but that didn't matter. The damage was done. I tried my best over the course of the winter to take care of them as much as I could, but there was only so much that I could do. Granted, I was in charge of this shift of Soldiers but I was also in the "crosshairs." The unit wanted me gone just as badly as they wanted any of them gone. I hate having to admit that nowadays but that is just how it was. We worked hard throughout the long, harsh winter and we did so with pride. I always got a kick out of riding in the truck with Gibson because he was always full of jokes, just as he was when we were deployed in the past. It was nice to see that he was able to keep his head up through all of this. It was funny, because it got to the point where I actually looked forward to my shift. Once again, the people make the place. As a whole, snowplow duty itself wasn't a bad experience, I liked the people who I worked with and I liked the job itself. I just hated the fact that I had a Detachment Sergeant who intentionally ruined my sleep on a day to day basis.

In early March 2011 I was pulled off of snowplow duty. I knew that I would miss the "good times" but like all great events in life it had to come to an end. The winter wasn't actually over yet, as it typically snows at Fort Drum until mid-April. I had no idea why I was being pulled off of the duty early, and I speculated that it had to do with my separation proceedings. I remember thinking to myself, "Maybe my papers are ready. Maybe I'm finally going to get served. Maybe my board is right around the corner." When I returned to the unit I found out that the reason that I was pulled off of duty had nothing to do with my board whatsoever, but instead had to do with the fact that the unit was going on a field training exercise for a week and they wanted to take me with them. I was a little baffled at first, and couldn't understand why the unit would waste time training an NCO who they were going to be throwing out of the Army anyway. That made no sense to me. While preparing for the exercise, one of the senior NCOs in the unit took me aside and gave me a "pep talk." He said that he had "heard through the grapevine that since it was taking so long to get my paperwork together that they would consider just throwing out the case altogether." From a legal standpoint that actually made sense. It was now mid-march of 2011 and my contract was up on March 3, 2012. Why waste time chaptering me out of the Army less than a year out, especially considering the fact that the Army would be required to pay me severance pay because I had so served for so long? In fact, the severance amount was quite substantial and when I sat down and crunched the numbers I would actually make more money by leaving early than if I stuck around and got paid for the duration of my contract. So now that it fiscally made no sense to get rid of me I had a little more hope, and that all came out during the "pep talk" that I received that day. I suddenly felt like I had a chance, and that I could contribute to the unit once again. Deep down inside I just wanted all of the hassle to go away. I wanted to be part of the team again. Sitting on the sidelines just didn't feel right to me.

When we got out to the field I tried my best to contribute, and I did a great job in my opinion. For one, the "garbage" Soldier that replaced me as the S1/HR representative wasn't going out to the field. She had figured out a way to get out of it (like she did with most challenging tasks) and so I was to role play my old position as S1. I took accountability of all of the Soldiers every morning, sent out reports, and managed the operations center. It was almost like the good old days. I was "one of the boys" again, working all day long alongside my comrades and sleeping in the bay area with the entire unit just like a deployment. I felt that I really did some good things out there, and a lot of the Soldiers were actually happy to see that I was "pretending" to be the S1 out there. Every day someone would come up to me and ask, "Hey SGT Conklin, is it true, are you the S1 again?" Every time I would have to remind them that this was just an exercise, but to "never say never." I was really hoping that my efforts would result in me getting my job back. That was all I really wanted. I felt like part of the team again, and that in itself was a priceless feeling.

This field exercise wasn't without its fair share of problems however. Even though most of the Soldiers and NCOs welcomed me out there with open arms, the Detachment Sergeant still seemed to have a problem with me. I really didn't understand where this was coming from now, since we arrived to the field the Commander was actually treating me with respect, was it possible that his hatred had switched from being born out of his status as a "yes man" to actual anguish? I really had no way of being sure. Things really came to a head one day during our personal hygiene hour. We usually had an hour to conduct personal hygiene out there and then immediately after that we would have to go and conduct preventive maintenance checks (also known as PMCS) on our Humvees. For some reason, he wanted the vehicles to be checked earlier than normal on this particular morning and like usual I was the last one to find out. (Now, I will state right now that the next portion of this story may get a little graphic, so if you do not want to read graphic stuff then please feel free to skip ahead two pages.) After I finished shaving that morning I decided to go to the bathroom. I really needed to go to the bathroom and I knew I had at least a half hour left out of our normally allotted half hour. I went to the toilets that were located directly next to the building with the sinks and showers, but I found that there was no toilet paper in there. I had no choice but to walk to the other bathroom, which was maybe a quarter of a mile away, if even that. I need to stress the fact that these bathrooms were field bathrooms, meaning that they were just a room with five toilets and a giant urinal, with no walls. This obviously creates a lack of privacy, but then again this is the Army, sometimes we all have to make sacrifices. Quite frankly, as a Sergeant who had been in the Army for over nine years at this point, the minor detail of no walls in the bathroom didn't really affect me, until this day came along. When I was sitting in there taking care of my business, my Detachment Sergeant busted in there, and started yelling at me, asking why I was taking so long this morning. It was now that he decided to inform me that we didn't have the customary hour for hygiene that we normally had, and that we actually had a mission to attend to this morning. Upon asking him why he didn't tell me that earlier, he just started yelling at me more, claiming that it wasn't my place to ask him questions. Then, he asked me why I was even in this bathroom to begin with, since there was another bathroom close to the shower/sink building. Of course, I told him the truth; that being that there was no toilet paper in the other bathroom, so I had to walk all the way over to this one. His response that followed actually shocked me. He literally began yelling at me for not having brought my own toilet paper, despite the fact that it wasn't even on the packing list. In fact, everyone was told that there would be toilet paper out there and not to bother bringing any. Yes, you read that correctly. The Detachment Sergeant apparently had nothing else better to do then to waste his time yelling at me about toilet paper. Keep in mind the fact that these bathrooms do not have walls inside to separate the toilets, therefore he was staring me dead in the eye the entire time that he yelled at me. This embarrassed me to a great degree, and obviously pissed me off. I remember thinking to myself that he must have crossed some sort of barrier, that a man shouldn't treat another man in that manner under any circumstances. It just didn't seem right that he should be able to get away with doing that to me. I was bound and determined to strike back; I just had to figure out how.

Once I was finished "conducting my business" in the bathroom, I immediately sought out the unit's Equal Opportunity Representative. There had to be some sort of complaint that I could file about this. I didn't feel right about what was said to me, or the manner in which it took place. Why couldn't he wait until after I got out of the bathroom? Did it really need to take place in the bathroom itself? He took it too far in my opinion. When I finally found the unit EO Representative I filled him in on everything that had happened. Unfortunately, there was no valid complaint that could be filed, despite the fact that what he did was messed up. Basically, this had never happened before so there was no rulebook written to cover the proper procedures when you are yelled at for no reason while going to the bathroom. As far as the EO Representative was concerned, my only choice was to sit there and deal with this. I wasn't having that; just like everything else in life I wasn't going down without a fight.

I was bound and determined to get back at the Detachment Sergeant for what he did. As far as I was concerned, he damaged my pride and I absolutely needed retribution in order to rebuild it. Since the EO Representative clearly wasn't going to help me, I decided to turn to the people; turn to the crowd if you will. I told everyone about this, in an effort to smear him. I didn't care about his image, in fact his image deserved to be tarnished after pulling a stunt like this. Later that evening, my efforts finally paid off. Everyone was in the sleeping bay, getting ready for bed. The whole unit was in there, which must have amounted to about 40 people including the Commander and the First Sergeant. Out of nowhere, Cappe stood up and announced that he had to go to the bathroom. He then looked over at one of the other Senior NCOs in the Detachment and said,

"I'm goin to the bathroom, I got my own toilet paper though, so no one has to yell at me for not bringing my own!" Once he said this, the entire room broke out into laughter, since they had heard me tell the story earlier in the day. Embarrassed, the Detachment Sergeant looked over at me with an angry look on his face. He didn't say a word, and I could tell that he was embarrassed. To capitalize on this, I looked him dead in the eye and asked him one question, "Is something wrong?" He said nothing, and just laid back down staring at the ceiling. To me, this amounted to a small victory; a victory that I rightfully deserved. After all, he started it. I feel that when dealing with enemies there are still certain rules to be followed. If you absolutely must damage the dignity of your enemy, you should never do so by striking at them when they are in a vulnerable position, such as the bathroom or the shower. Instead, you should be a man and strike at them when they are strong. Anyone can kick a man when they are down. It takes a real man to stand toe to toe against their opponent when they are at full strength; figuratively and literally speaking.

The field exercise was finally over and so we returned back to the unit area. We had to run all of the vehicles through the wash racks and then turn in our weapons. Once we were finished with all of the required tasks we would be permitted to take a well-deserved four day pass. The entire time I pondered the events of the week. Despite my altercation with the Detachment Sergeant it was still a productive week. I really loved the fact that I was able to go out there with them. As time went on, I found out that any idea that I was going to be allowed to stay was purely a lie. I wasn't going to be allowed to stay. My administrative separation board would take place just as planned, and when it came right down to it the only reason that I was sent to the field was because they needed more Soldiers. That was the only reason. It was never about "welcoming me back into the fold" or "making me feel better." As much as I appreciated going out there, finding out that I was still going to have to go before the board tarnished the entire feeling. I wasn't actually part of the unit again, and I feared that I never would be.

Ultimately there was no changing my mind on the subject of staying in. I was ready to fight for my career under any given circumstances. I would rather die than have given up without a fight. Week after week I met with my attorney and called all of my supporters to draw out my strategy. Everyone that I had asked to testify on my behalf was firmly behind me, and it just helped me to fight that much more. I didn't believe in giving up, and I would be damned if I would give this unit the satisfaction of chaptering out a proven leader such as myself. As April dragged on, I waited patiently to get served my papers. I knew that the day was coming sooner or later. Every day I woke up, looked in the mirror and told myself that I wouldn't back down from anyone, ever. I worked out every day. I would sometimes sit in my room, alone with my thoughts, anticipating the day that I would stand before that board. I was starting to get antsy, and finally the day came that I would be served. It was a day in early May. I was called into the Brigade Legal Headquarters and I was read the formal citation that comes with the paperwork. When the legal clerk handed me a copy, I saw that my administrative separation board was scheduled for May 19, 2011. That was my big day; the day that I would stand up and fight, once and for all, leaving everything on the table.

In the days leading up to my board I called all of my supporters one last time. COL Alvarado hoped that the very idea that a Colonel such as himself was willing to testify for me would be enough to send that board a message that chaptering me out of the Army was a bad idea. Kathy hoped for the best, as a lifelong friend and a person who had witnessed my expertise in the office she just knew that getting rid of me was a bad idea. Chief Broadbent felt the same way; he mentored me and he knew that I had potential. Maria shared the same sentiment; I had taught her a lot of what she knew as far as her MOS was concerned and she even credited me as one of the reasons she was promoted to Staff Sergeant, which also meant a lot to me. Cummings was ready to testify too, after working with me in Iraq she was infuriated that I was being sent away, especially after seeing other "less worthy" Soldiers allowed to stay. Overall, everyone that was behind me stood united and ready to "take up arms" for my cause. The positive impact that I had made over the years had become apparent. It was time to fight. May 19th came along, and I was instructed to drive to my attorney's office one hour prior to the actual board. We had brief meeting, ironing out the final details. Every so often I would glance up at the clock, knowing that the hour was rapidly approaching. Finally, it was 8:45 AM (0845 HRS) military time. My attorney looked at me and said, "It's time to drive over there. Since you know the way, I'll follow you." We both stood up, and I shook his hand and thanked him in advance. Like a wrestler getting ready for one last match, I took the long walk from his office to my car. I got in the front seat and put the key into the ignition and I remembered words that my dad had said to me when I was a kid,

"It's now or never Ken." As I replayed his words in my head, I reached for my IPod and played the one and only song that felt appropriate at the time. As I heard the opening chord to the song, "I am a Real American" start to play, I turned the volume all the way up and sang along with the words, "When it comes crashing down, and it hurts inside, ya' gotta take a stand, it don't help to hide. Well you hurt my friends, and you hurt my pride, I gotta be a man; I can't let it slide! I am a real American, Fight for the rights of every man, I am a real American, fight for what's right, fight for your life!" Just like every other time in my life that I listened to that song it moved me. The only difference this time was I was listening to it before an actual battle, not a staged one in professional wrestling. For a second I wanted to shed a tear, but I channeled my own energy and decided that wasn't the way to go. I was going to go in there and show those board members just who the hell Ken Conklin really was.

CHAPTER 14

YOU WIN SOME, YOU LOSE SOME

I arrived to Battalion Headquarters with my attorney, ready to get this hearing underway. We were extremely optimistic about the potential outcome. We had a laundry list of good, solid character witnesses that were going to testify on my behalf. We had some excellent documentation to submit as well, which included various character letters from even more people, my own evaluation reports and awards which all reflected me as a great leader, a few written statements that I had written myself, and of course my most recent PT card which reflected a PT score of 290 points out of a possible 300. That was going to be one of our many arguments, the fact that I was a stellar performer when it came to PT. The issues concerning my weight never actually affected my PT performance. Of course, my PT score and all of my witness testimonies were going to be just one half of my argument; I was more than prepared to talk about the fact that I was wrongfully mistreated, singled out and that my chapter was based on a personal vendetta. My attorney told me from the beginning that it would be hard to prove that, but in a circumstance like this we needed to try anything that we could. We stood on our side of the room while the prosecuting attorney stood opposite us while we waited for the three board members to order us to sit so we could begin the proceedings. The board members consisted of a Major (O-4), a First Lieutenant (O-1), and a Master Sergeant (E-8). Right from the beginning this sent me a "red flag." I could understand the idea of being judged by a field grade officer (O-4 or above) and a senior NCO, but as far as I was concerned a 1LT had no business being on that board. I was a Sergeant, a Non-Commissioned Officer with nine and a half years of service. That 1LT who was sitting there in the room probably had no more than two years in service, if that.

Did I have a legal right to take that personally? No, I didn't but that didn't stop me from feeling that way.

As soon as the board started, both attorneys gave their opening statements. I was immediately shocked by the tactic that the prosecuting attorney used. He actually painted me as a "great performer" and even went as far as to say, "no one is disputing that SGT Conklin is a good NCO, but the bottom line is that he must meet this one standard which he has failed to do for an extremely long time." I found this shocking because the prosecuting attorney worked for people who had actively plotted against me in the past, most notably the Battalion and Brigade leadership. I had meetings with the Brigade Sergeant Major where he told me to my face that he didn't care about how well I had done in any other area, as long as I didn't make tape I was a "bad NCO" as far as he was concerned. I fully expected the prosecuting attorney's opening remarks/arguments to be a direct reflection of the opinions of his superiors, yet it wasn't. I understood that he was an attorney (and a smart one at that) and by doing this he was effectively making my argument that I had been singled out and mistreated a little weaker. Think about it, how could I state that any members of the chain of command had a personal vendetta against me if their very own prosecuting attorney was willing to come out and state that I was a "Good NCO" right from the beginning? I understood the tactic, and I guess if I was in his shoes I would have opened up the hearing in the same manner.

After the opening statements took place, the board members then went on to review all of the documents that both attorneys had presented to them. Almost immediately the board members started firing off at my attorney and I with various questions about the issue. Every one of these questions seemed like they were designed to attack our argument that I should be allowed to stay in the Army. I whispered to my attorney, "Do the board members seem unbiased to you, or do they seem against us?" Instantly, he whispered back, "They seem against us." I was glad that I wasn't the only one who saw that, and to be quite frank I was a little taken back by the fact that the board members were already against us. Every question that the Master Sergeant asked us was asked in an angry tone, and she even asked the question, "Why should you be allowed to stay if you are overweight?" The two officers were asking equally condescending questions, only they didn't seem as "angry." That wasn't the way that this was supposed to work. Just like a jury in a criminal trial, the board members were supposed to enter the room unbiased. Their duty was to listen to the arguments of the prosecuting attorney as well as my attorney and then make a decision. This decision could be swayed by any number of factors and anything that either side could present to them over the course of the board. Instead, the board members came across as if they were already against us, which told us immediately that we had our work cut out for us. Attempting to convince this board that I should be allowed to stay in the Army was going to be an uphill battle to say the least.

After the board members were finished reviewing all of the paperwork that both sides had presented they indicated to both attorneys that it was now time to call any witnesses that would be willing to testify. First, the prosecution was asked if they had any witnesses to call, to which they didn't. I couldn't even imagine how much worse this board would have been if the prosecution had called in any of my enemies from the past. By not calling anyone forward to testify I felt as if I had a slight "one up" on the prosecuting attorney. It was a small bit of momentum, and I needed all the momentum that I could get.

Almost all of my witnesses would be testifying over the phone from a different location than Fort Drum. There was only one that was actually at Fort Drum, but he had out-processing appointments so he had to be called over the phone as well. Each witness would be called on speakerphone for the entire room to hear and then they would be required to be sworn in, just like in a real trial. The first witness that was called was SFC Josef Smith. At the time he was stationed in Korea so it took a few tries to get through to him, but when we did finally get ahold of him he was ready to speak his piece. After introducing himself to the board members, he went on to explain exactly how he knew me and in what capacity that we served together. I would come to find out over the next few hours that this would be the protocol for all of the witnesses that would testify. Josef explained to the board that as far as he could see, my duty performance was excellent. He then went on to talk about an era in which he was my Detachment Sergeant (for a short period of time) and how I was one of his squad leaders. As a squad leader in his detachment he was never worried about any of my Soldiers because he knew for a fact that I would go to any lengths possible to take care of them. This helped me a lot, at least from a pride stand point because I had listened to enough of the senior NCO's in this Brigade (to include the Brigade Sergeant Major) run down my leadership capability. It was nice to hear a Senior NCO tell this board that I was a good leader. He also went on to tell the board about my achievements as the unit S1, explaining that each and every single action that I was given was completed almost immediately, which is almost unheard of with S1's nowadays. After he was finished explaining my achievements as an S1, he then went on to explain my PT performance and how any PT sessions that I led left all of the Soldiers hurting from a great workout. It didn't make any sense to him that I was being chaptered out and he told the board that he would rate me overall a "10 out of 10" and that I had rehabilitative potential, if I hadn't been failed by my leaders. He told the board that he felt that the unit's attitude toward me during this whole ordeal certainly hurt my potential and that by being removed from my position as S1 the unit was hindered as well. That argument was so strong, not only because it was true but also because his argument more or less matched mine. A senior NCO saying almost the exact thing that my attorney had said in his opening remarks legitimized all of my complaints in the eyes of the board members, which is exactly what I needed.

Once Josef's testimony was complete, it was now time for the prosecuting attorney and the board members to ask him questions. My attorney had prepared me for this prior to the board. He explained that the number one goal of the prosecuting attorney would be to convince the board that I should be chaptered out of the army, and if that included "debunking" my witnesses then so be it. There was really no limit to the tactics that the prosecutor could pull out, and this was just one of them. Upon being questioned, Josef explained something to the board that I had believed in my own heart for a very long time; that being the fact that the Army Weight Control Program is not only unfair, but outdated as well based on the trends and changes that have taken place in our society. He even used himself as an example, citing that he is neither fat nor muscle-bound but because of his body weight of 183 pounds and his height of just 69 inches that he sometimes needs to be taped. Is this entirely fair? No. Part of the problem deals with "body shapes," meaning that different Soldiers have differently shaped bodies regardless of their weight. That idea in itself makes the weight control program unfair and shows that it needs to be rethought.

Next up to testify was Chief Broadbent. Since he was my mentor in the past I felt that his testimony would prove to be extremely valuable. He had taught me much of what I knew and as a result of that I knew that he would never steer me wrong and that he would do me proud during this hearing. Just like Josef, Chief Broadbent was currently stationed in Korea, so we had to go through the same process that we did the first time as far as reaching him was concerned. Once we reached him, he began his testimony. He explained that he had deployed with me in 2007 to Afghanistan and had observed my duty performance the entire time. He went on to explain to the board members that I was extremely knowledgeable and dedicated, and that was part of the reason that I was chosen to mentor some of the New Jersey National Guard Soldiers on that deployment. He felt that I was a great leader, and even went on to mention my dedication to physical fitness, and that if given the chance I could lose the weight prior to my contractual ETS date of March 2012, which by now was just less than ten months away. Just like Josef, he told the board that he believed that I had outstanding potential to rehabilitate my issues if given the chance and that there was absolutely no doubt about that in his mind. After he was finished, the board members and prosecuting attorney didn't really have many questions for him, aside from asking him to confirm that "army standards are army standards." I am not sure if that was designed to be a "trap" or a way to "debunk" what he had said, or if it was just a quick attempt to move on to the next witness because of the fact that he was a Warrant Officer. I still am not certain. As far as I am concerned, if someone is asked to confirm that the standards exist in a hearing in which I was trying to prove that I wasn't given a fair shot to begin with then the reason that they are asking this is to further solidify the fact that the only verdict here should be a bad one. As unfair as that sounds, the Army unfortunately operates in that manner.

Kathy was the next person to testify on my behalf. Out of everyone that was testifying that day, I knew her the longest, which made her a great witness. Who better to talk about my career then someone who I knew for my entire career? We were in AIT together as Privates and we were deployed to Afghanistan together as Sergeants. Now, she was no longer an NCO but instead a Warrant Officer. I had hoped that the combination of her rank and our experiences together would be enough to sway the board in my favor. She talked about my exceptional performance over the years, not just in the office but during PT sessions as well. Kathy also mentioned how I helped her get into school on the Afghanistan deployment and how I mentored many of the Soldiers in that unit. Usually, a great mentor equals a great leader; which meant that her testimony helped combat any possible thoughts that I was a bad leader. She then re-iterated what Chief

Broadbent had said, that being the fact that I needed better leadership, someone to mentor me. I hadn't had a true mentor in so long. Ever since 1SG Gudger had left the unit I was without a real leader. The fact of the matter is no matter how great you are, you can still learn something new from someone. No one is perfect; there is always someone out there that is better than you, regardless of your achievements. If I had the benefit of a true mentor at any point in those last three years I don't think I would have even found myself sitting on this administrative separation board. Ultimately Kathy's testimony proved that I was not only an asset to the Army but to the Human Resources field as well. When it came right down to it her testimony did mean a lot to me, but unfortunately the board still threw some hard questions at her, just as they did to Josef and Broadbent. This trend of trying to debunk my witnesses apparently wasn't going to go away. I just wish that it was only the prosecuting attorney that was doing that, since it was his job. I really didn't count on an "unbiased" panel of board members taking a seemingly biased stance.

Next up to testify was an NCO from the unit by the name of SGT Kibe. Kibe and I were in the same unit for a while, and since he filled the position of training NCO we had many opportunities to work alongside each other for a while. Due to that dynamic I figured that his testimony would prove useful, especially considering most of my witnesses were people who I had worked with in the past. Kibe on the other hand was someone who I worked with as recently as 2010. During his testimony he cited that our relationship was mostly professional, but that we did talk about sports from time to time among other things. Like everyone else, he explained to the board that I was a great performer, and also mentioned the fact that he observed me doing PT in my own time to try to lose the weight. He also took his argument one step further and explained that he witnessed me taking other Soldiers to the gym to help them lose the weight in my own time as well. I really appreciated that, because it furthered the argument that I really was dedicated to fitness, I just had a few issues achieving my goals. When he was questioned by the prosecuting attorney, he told them that he believed in the same ideals that I believed in; the fact that rehabilitation should be not only considered, but handled on a case by case basis because everyone is different. That is a true fact. No one person is identical to another and there are so many issues that should be taken under consideration, ranging from medical issues, to personal preferences, to a person's endurance or even what diet works on which person. One person may be able to run four miles without losing weight because they are so conditioned to run that much, while another person can drop weight off of one mile because they aren't used to running. Everyone is different, and the idea that the same old plan can work for every person is ridiculous.

Kibe also added yet another personal touch to his testimony when he mentioned my stress levels in relation to this entire process. He knew that the concept of leaving the Army wasn't something that I had welcomed and that it caused me a lot of stress. Stress, of course can be a negative factor for anyone and can contribute to weight gain or hinder weight loss. He even went as far as to mention the fact that he had often times invited me to eat lunch with him and a few of the Soldiers at the PX, but I had to refuse because I was dieting and therefore could not eat that type of food. This showed the board that my efforts to lose the weight were not only limited to working out hard, I was taking positive steps with my diet to get the job done as well. Finally, he explained to the board all of the issues that I had with the previous First Sergeant and how she singled me out. He mentioned how she wasn't supportive of me in any way, shape or form. In fact, his office was directly across from her office and there were times when he would overhear phone calls of hers in relation to my case. These phone calls were with the Brigade Sergeant Major and every one of them that he overheard came across like there was an agenda to get rid of me. The First Sergeant obviously didn't know that her conversations were being overheard by a friend of mine, but that didn't matter. By hearing this first hand, one could rule out any possibility that the claims that I had made were "conspiracy theories" or "paranoia." I was legitimately targeted and the proof was clearly in the pudding. Of course, I had been on a diet for a while and therefore hadn't had any pudding in a long time, but that is beside the point!

Following Kibe's testimony I took a brief moment to speak with my attorney. He felt that we were starting to gain some ground, and that all of the testimonies thus far were good ones. It was still apparent that the board was biased in the prosecution's favor, but that didn't mean that we were going to give up. No, we were going to keep on fighting until the bitter end. My career was worth it after all. We pushed forward and called the next witness, who was none other than Jason Mays.

Jason went on to explain to the board members that he had known me for an extremely long time and that we served together at our first duty station at Fort Campbell. He mentioned that he had the chance to observe my workplace performance in garrison as well as while deployed. He also explained that while he didn't actually observe my PT performance, he still heard about it from many of the other Soldiers. I had built up a reputation over the years for being a great performer at PT, and in an Army where "perception and image is everything" that perception should have been a little more valuable. (For the record, I do not agree with the Army's idea that image matters. I feel that what you can physically accomplish should mean more.) Since Jason was no longer in the Army, the board members didn't seem to have a lot of questions for him. Once he said his piece, he was dismissed and told that they may call him back if they needed anything else. I understood the reasons that the board did that, but when you look at it from my perspective, he knew me almost as long as Kathy did. Just like her, the testimony of a career-long friend can prove to be a valuable one. By excusing him early I feel that the board took away his potential effectiveness as a witness hurt my chances of winning.

The next person to testify was Maria. We went through the same process of my attorney first questioning her about my performance and my integrity. She explained that I was not only a true professional at all times but also that I had become an inspiration to a lot of Soldiers and thus had a great impact on them. She then went on to explain to the board that I was once a great mentor to her, and that because of me she is now able to mentor her own Soldiers. As far as she was concerned she may not have been able to get promoted to Staff Sergeant without being able to ask for my expertise on various issues over the years. This made me think back to the character letter that I had asked her to write on my behalf earlier in the year, in which she stated that "SGT Conklin should be thought of as a survivor." Those words moved me then, and they were moving me now here at the trial. She also told the panel that she still comes to me for advice and that she is usually comfortable with my answers, she has never needed to look up anything that I told her in a regulation to verify it as fact. She stated that it would greatly hurt the Army to release me, and that doing so would be a huge mistake. She testified that my knowledge and ability supersedes my weight issues and therefore I should be given another chance, perhaps under better leadership. This fell right into play with the constant theme of everyone else who testified; that being that I could get the job done with a real mentor.

It was after her testimony that the board members began to question her. As it turned out, the board members and prosecuting attorney took exception to the fact that a Staff Sergeant claimed that my weight issues should be overlooked. Maybe it was the way she worded it, because they didn't take to some of my other witnesses the way they took to her. Then again, maybe it was because of her rank. Three of the previous witnesses were senior personnel, and so if they did have some steam to let go of they wouldn't be doing it on any of them. Either way, it didn't matter, because they suddenly got ruthless with their line of questioning towards her, which I didn't think was fair whatsoever.

When she replied that she did have Soldiers that fit that criteria, my attorney immediately objected on the grounds that the questions that were being asked had absolutely nothing to do with my chapter proceedings. That was 100% true, and I was shocked when the President of the board overruled my attorney's objection and actually allowed the questioning to continue. After further questioning, she stayed firm that a Soldier should be given a certain amount of time if they had the proper amount of mentoring, which I didn't have the slightest bit of mentoring. It was almost as if they wanted to debunk every single part of her statement or attempt to get her to change her stance. That wasn't going to happen. After firing various questions at her, the prosecuting attorney took one final shot when he asked her if she had witnessed all of the terrible stories that I told her about how I was treated, or if she had just heard it from me. Of course she had heard it all from me; she wasn't even in my unit. Why would they ask her such a question? Was it in an attempt to make me look like a fool, a liar? I hadn't been given a fair shot in that unit over the past three years and many people witnessed that. Earlier that morning, SGT Kibe himself had said that he saw it first hand, so if they already had one witness testify who claimed to have seen it in person why would they waste the time to try to devalue her argument by asking her such a question? To be honest I was quite insulted at the way the board members and the prosecution handled this one, and it showed to me that they would stop at no amount of dirty tactics to achieve their mission.

Up next to testify was Colonel Alvarado. Throughout all the years he had always told me that he would assist me in any way that he could, and testifying at this board for me was just one example of that. We had both gone into the board hoping that his rank of Colonel (O-6) would carry enough weight to show these board members that keeping me in the Army was the right thing to do, that the Army would actually be hurt by separating me. He spoke highly of me that day just as everyone else had, which certainly meant a lot to me. I'll never forget when he told them that I did have a desire and a willingness to reach my goals and that rehabilitation was a dual effort between the unit and the Soldier. That in itself should have sent the unit a wake-up call, the very fact that someone of his stature was coming forward and saying that. It was one thing for Kathy, Josef or Maria to say that; they were just Warrant Officers or NCOs and the board could use any excuse in the world to dismiss their claims, even though it wouldn't be fair. Colonel Alvarado was the Chief of Staff for the State of New Jersey; there was no way that the board should have been able to ignore a word that he said. When it came time for the board members and the prosecution to question him, they kept the questioning short. I actually thought that it was funny that the prosecuting attorney acted like a "tough guy" when he was questioning Maria, yet when it came time for him question Colonel Alvarado he didn't seem like such a "tough guy" anymore. Out of the few questions that were asked of the Colonel, there were two that not only stuck out to me, but Colonel Alvarado as well. First, they asked if he had seen me since the deployment, which aside from the time that I visited New Jersey after the deployment and a Brigade ball at Fort Drum he hadn't. I felt that this was a direct reference to the fact that I had gained some weight, and that it shouldn't matter what I looked like when Colonel Alvarado last saw me. I didn't like that to be honest. I didn't feel that it was an appropriate question and I feel that by asking that question the attorney was trying to reduce the credibility of yet another one of my witnesses. The second question hurt even more than the first. The prosecution attorney asked Colonel Alvarado how many times he had been deployed. I couldn't believe it. Seriously, what was the point of that question? What bearing would that have on my entire case? Absolutely none. As I stated earlier in this book, it is a well-known fact that some members of the Active component of the Army tend to look down on members of the National Guard. It isn't right, I do not agree with it and I never will. Was the prosecutor trying to reduce Colonel Alvarado's credibility by asking that question? No one could really be sure, but the one thing that I was sure about was that the question was an extremely inappropriate one and shouldn't have been asked. Later that day I called Colonel Alvarado and we talked about that, and even he was insulted. I was still in shock that the question was asked. When you hold the rank that he holds, it doesn't matter if/when/how many times you have been deployed.

Finally it was time for my final witness to be called, who would be none other than Cummings. She talked about our deployment together, and how I was extremely proficient in the office and proved to be a good mentor. She even went on to mention that I was the best 42A that she had ever met, which really meant a lot to me. To give the board an example of my leadership skills, Cummings decided to explain to the board members that I had helped her and her roommate study for the Soldier of the month board while we were deployed. She also mentioned how the tape test is extremely flawed and how it works against a lot of people, me included. Overall, her testimony meant a lot to me because out of everyone on the list, she was the only one who ever actually worked directly for me. That puts a different perspective on her testimony because the point of view of a junior Soldier while looking at their supervisor is obviously different than that of a fellow NCO or one of my former Commanders. I had hoped that by asking her to testify that it would give the board members a complete picture of exactly who I was, that I was known as a good Soldier, leader, technician, and mentor at all levels. When she wrapped up her testimony, I was shocked to see that the board members didn't have any questions to ask her whatsoever. I wasn't exactly sure why, maybe it was because we had dragged the board out all morning long and they just wanted to get it over with. Either way, all of my witnesses had spoken their piece, and it was now time to move onto the next step.

For the first time during the board, I was going to be given the chance to stand up and speak on my own. I had the option to make either a "sworn statement" or an "unsworn statement." The difference between the two statements is really simple: a "sworn statement" is subject to critique and questioning by the board members, meaning that they could try to take apart my statement in the same manner that they did to all of my witnesses. An "unsworn statement" on the other hand meant that the board would have no legal right to try any of that, which meant they actually had to listen to what I had to say and actually think about my message. So, in hopes that I could influence the board members, I decided to give an unsworn statement. (Also, it felt good to be able to stop them from throwing out more of the inappropriate questions that they had been coming up with all morning long.)

I stood up and began my speech, "Over nine years I have served our country and this Army with honor. During that time I went on three deployments. I was part of the invasion of Iraq in 2003, and in 2006 I deployed with six hours' notice. Can you believe that? Throughout the years I have always tried to contribute everything that I had, and as you all saw by looking at my Evaluation Reports, I did just that. Now I stand before you, being judged for something that I shouldn't be judged for. Notwithstanding the flaws in the Army Weight Control program that have been pointed out to you by everyone that spoke out on my behalf today, let's look at the rest of the picture. It has been documented by various individuals including myself, that I did not receive a fair chance at this. Why is it that when I returned from Iraq the first order of business was to initiate my Chapter Proceedings? Why is it, that I was kicked to the curb on my own, with not one member of my chain of command standing up to help me? Where does such treatment end? I can guarantee you that with the right guidance and enough time I can make this happen. I know that I stand before you as an NCO who isn't meeting a standard, but do not forget the other side of that coin: I stand here as an NCO who is part of a unit that fostered such a condition. So the question remains, will you allow me to stay, or send me away? I promise you that it will hurt the United States Army to send me home."

The board members just sat there, puzzled. I don't know what they thought I was going to say, but I knew that this was my final shot. I needed to make it count so I gave the best speech that I possibly could. My attorney whispered to me, "Great Speech! I think that helped our case." Before I knew it, it was time for the prosecuting attorney to give his closing arguments. After today's display, who knew what he would come out and say? He ended up rehashing his opening statement, citing that "No one is questioning SGT Conklin's work ethic; but at the end of the day we have to ask ourselves if we are going to choose to follow the standard, or not." With that, he closed his final argument. I had to admit, he certainly made it hard for us. Finally, it was time for my attorney to stand up and give his closing arguments. He said to the board, "Today we heard various testimonies from various Soldiers of all different ranks, from all different locations. All of them said the same thing; that SGT Conklin is a great NCO and it is in my belief that chaptering him out of the Army is a bad idea. His records speak for themselves, impeccable NCOER reports, character letters and a great PT card. With that said, it was stated earlier that he only has a little over nine months left on his contract. Therefore I ask you today, what is the harm in letting SGT Conklin stay and fulfill the remainder of his contract? Nine months isn't really a long time in the grand scheme of things, but it is enough time for SGT Conklin to still contribute to this great Army of ours."

I couldn't believe how good my attorney's closing argument was. It actually moved me. I guess that's why attorneys do what they do, because they have the ability to. Now that everything was said and done, and "all the cards were laid out on the table" so to speak, the board members had to make their decision. It was nearly noon, and so they dismissed everyone for lunch until 1400 so they could discuss their decision over lunch. I remember thinking to myself that two hours shouldn't be enough time to come to a decision considering everything that was put in front of them today. Before we broke for lunch, I took my attorney aside and asked him, in his professional opinion if he thought we had a chance. He was optimistic about our chances, and told me that even though we started off against a board that was seemingly against us we had gained a lot of ground and did an excellent job explaining our side of things. He also felt that I had "knocked the ball out of the park" with my speech and he believed that it was one of the stronger parts of our case. I guess that's what happens when you really pour your heart into something. With that, we shook hands and parted for lunch. The next two hours proved to be the longest two hours of my entire life. After everything that had transpired that morning the only thing I really wanted was my verdict. I just needed to know what the board's decision would be. During those two hours I didn't even eat lunch. Instead, I just went to my room and stared at the wall, reflecting at all of the events of my career. I knew that I had to prepare myself for the worst. I came to terms with the fact that even though I wanted to stay in the Army, things would not be so bad for me if I did have to leave the Army. For one, I would receive an honorable discharge, which is invaluable. After all I did over the course of my career, I would accept nothing less. I was still baffled that there were those that once believed that I would receive less than an honorable discharge for an overweight chapter. That just wasn't true, nor should it ever be true. In addition to the honorable discharge, I would be receiving a sizable severance package which would definitely help me in my future endeavors. After all, who couldn't use a little extra money? If I did have to leave the Army, I would also have the option to join the National Guard or Reserves if I ended up losing the weight after discharge. Ever since I was deployed with the New Jersey National Guard I had always dreamed of moving to New Jersey and the idea of joining the guard had always appealed to me. Members of the National Guard (to include Colonel Alvarado) have always voiced to me their interest in me joining the guard, so I knew that if I were to get chaptered out that I could consider that an option. Above all else, I also would receive full education benefits under the Post-911 GI Bill program, which would allow me to pursue a Master's Degree. By doing this I would certainly be bettering myself. I decided that the best thing to do would be to set out to become better than I had ever been. No matter what happened, I knew that Ken Conklin could be far better than Sergeant Conklin.

After what seemed like forever, my two hour break was finally up. It was time to hear my verdict. I met my attorney outside of the room in which the hearing was conducted in. He asked me if I was nervous, and even though I was I just replied with, "I will be fine." We filed into the room into our respective sides, us on the left side of the room and the prosecution on the right side of the room. The President of the Board read over a quick summary of the morning's proceedings. It was at that moment that the President of the Board said to me, "Sergeant Conklin, please rise to receive your verdict." Just like an accused criminal in a trial, I stood up alongside my attorney. It was then that the President of the Board read the following words off of a piece of paper, "Sergeant Kenneth B. Conklin, this Board finds that you under the provisions of AR 635-200, failing to make satisfactory weight loss progress over a two year period while enrolled in the Army Weight Control Program, did not make satisfactory progress. In view of the findings, the board recommends that Sergeant Kenneth B Conklin be separated from the United States Army before the expiration of his current term of service in accordance with AR 635-200, Chapter 18, Failure to Meet Body Fat Standards. This board further recommends that Sergeant Kenneth B Conklin receive an Honorable Discharge." With that, the board adjourned. After a long battle I finally had my verdict. I would be going home. I could have taken this opportunity to start running my mouth, but what would be the point? I stood my ground, fought my battle, and I lost. Had I not stood up for myself I am not sure if I could live with myself, but since I had I honestly didn't have many complaints. Despite losing, I decided to take the high road and I offered my hand to the prosecuting attorney. He was taken aback by this for a second until he finally shook my hand. When he took my hand I said to him, "Good showing." He wished me luck in my future endeavors, and I left the room, never to see him again. I am not sure how many people did what I did, but I felt that going out the classy way and taking the high road was the better thing to do. There is a huge difference between being unhappy about the outcome of something and being a sore loser. I wasn't about to be a sore loser, especially in front of these people. Granted, the board was against us from the very start, but I was still going to leave with my head held high.

My phone had been going off like crazy for the past hour. Everyone that I knew, including family, friends, fellow Soldiers at Fort Drum, and of course everyone who testified on my behalf wanted to know the verdict. The first thing I did was send a mass text message out to everyone who testified. That way they could have a quick answer. I received a flow of messages from people saying "this is probably for the best" and "at least you stood up for yourself." One text message said, "You're better than that place anyway Ken." I received a text message from Maria that read, "Welcome to the National Guard." I received that message almost at the exact same time that I received one from Colonel Alvarado that read, "There's a home for you in the New Jersey Guard." It was nice to know that I was wanted somewhere, that this wouldn't be the end of my life. I am a man who can stand on his own two feet, and I was bound and determined to do just that. Over the next few hours I made many phone calls to everyone who testified, thanking each one of them personally. To this day I am still grateful for the help of those who stood by my side in one of my darkest hours. We didn't win, but we gave it our best shot anyway. That's all I can ask. Over the next few weeks I would sit and wait for my separation orders. With just a few weeks left until the official end of my Army career, who knew what else could happen. Was it going to be smooth sailing from here on out? Or did I still have one last challenge in front of me?

CHAPTER 15

FINAL DISCOVERIES

Now that the board was complete the only thing that was left for me to do was to await my orders and then out-process from Fort Drum. The entire process would only take about a month, and when I reflect on my final month in the Army today it all seems like it was just a blur. Of course back then it didn't seem like a blur, in fact every day seemed to drag by. I knew that I would miss the Army a great deal, but in an effort to stay positive about the situation I really just wanted to get out of there so I can get started on my future plans. For one, I had enrolled in a college in New Jersey, so I really wanted to go there a few times over the summer to not only visit some old friends, but to also find an apartment as well. Furthermore, my brother Jason had moved to Georgia the prior year and I really wanted to go and visit him for a few days. Since I had the whole summer ahead of me before the fall semester would start, I figured that the summer vacation that I had in front of me would be the perfect time to do everything that I wanted to do.

Despite my positive outlook, the entire process of leaving the Army combined with the negative atmosphere on Fort Drum had left a bad taste in my mouth. Many of the Soldiers that I was friends with in the unit voiced their disapproval with the decision to send me home; only they didn't voice it to the chain of command, they voiced it to me. It was obviously nice to know that I had that many supporters amongst the junior enlisted ranks, but all in all I really just wanted to focus on the future. Every time that the subject was brought up to me it would make me think back on how upsetting it truly was. I didn't really want to leave the Army, but by now the best thing for me would be to get out of there. Even still, I knew that I would miss a lot of the friends that I had made over the years and I vowed to stay in touch with all of them. I never believed in saying goodbye, and this time was no different.

Friends and family at home in Saint Johnsville were just as displeased with the results. My Dad was upset that I was forced out of the Army against my will and did not agree with the way that I had been treated. My friends shared the same feeling; when I would come home for these few weekends they would all tell me that they were sorry about how things turned out, but they were at least happy that I had a plan and I wouldn't end up doing nothing with the rest of my life. Just like the friends that I had at Drum, my friends at home were vocal about the situation and I truly appreciated the support. I will never forget the people that were there for me during this very dark time of my life. Now it was time to stop looking at the dark times and instead to begin looking forward to the bright times, the good times that I was sure that my future would bring. The bottom line was that I was not going to let this loss destroy me. I would come out better, stronger and most importantly, smarter.

Memorial Day weekend 2011 came along shortly after my separation board. As a member of American Legion Post 168 I was asked to march in that year's parade, to which I was honored to do so. I wasn't out of the Army yet, I still had a few weeks left and there was no reason why I couldn't still serve and do honorable things. It doesn't matter if it was back at Fort Drum or in my hometown in Saint Johsnsville, service is service. When you march in a parade on Memorial Day you are honoring the memory of those who have fallen and I consider that to be one of the most honorable things that one could do.

I wasn't just going to be marching in the parade either; I would be carrying the nation's colors at the front of the parade. To me, carrying our nation's great flag was one of the greatest experiences of my life. You cannot put a price tag on it. It is probably one of the most patriotic things that one could do. So the parade began under the hot sun. It was over 90 degrees that day and it only took a matter of minutes for me to break into a sweat. I would not allow the heat to break my composure however. I gave my word that I was going to carry the colors, and I wasn't going to falter. The parade marched to the Saint Johnsville Nursing Home, in which we paid tribute to all of the veterans who live there. It was quite a sight to see how many of them were there, and I guess when I think back on that day it must have been quite an experience for them to see all of us. We had a huge parade which really was a sight to see. We also marched down main street to Bridge Street (for those of you reading this that have never been to Saint Johnsville, bridge street leads to a bridge which crosses over the Mohawk River). When we arrived at the river, the oldest veteran in town approached the bridge and threw a special wreath into the Mohawk River. This is a part of the ceremony and it was my first time witnessing this custom. I have to say that I found it touching. Following the ceremony at the bridge, the parade marched to the library, in which another wreath was set up near the civil war monument (which happens to stand next to the flagpole in which I flew my flag in October 2010). Once again, it was a sight to see.

Overall, the parade was a great experience, and even though it took a couple of hours to complete under the hot Saint Johnsville sun it didn't matter. I not only loved being a part of it, but I was honored as well. It was nice to be able to do one last positive act in uniform before I left the Army. I knew that I only had a couple of weeks left in the Army, so I viewed this as my "last hurrah" if you will. Today, as a member of American Legion Post 168 I can march in the annual parades, proudly wearing my uniform just as I did on that day.

I finally received my discharge orders during the first week of June. The orders read that my final day in the Army would be June 17, 2011, however if I finished my out-processing sooner I could would be permitted to leave early. I had a lot of mixed feelings on the subject, but at the end of the day the facts were the facts; reality had to set in. It was time to wrap up this nine and a half year adventure. As the next few weeks went by I reflected on all of the things that I had done over the years. After three deployments, a tour to Korea, and being stationed with two of the Army's most well-known combat divisions it was hard to believe that it was finally over. I had learned so much over the years and made so many friends. I really didn't want to say goodbye to any of them. By now, many of them were like family. It killed me that a lot of them (including Brenda) were either deployed or had left Fort Drum recently. Not only that, but my detachment had to go on a training exercise on the other side of the country during my final two weeks there, which meant that I wouldn't get to say goodbye in person to a lot of them. Cappe was included in that group, and it killed me that he couldn't be around when I left. After spending a year as his roommate in Iraq I felt as if he was one of my best friends in the Army. It just didn't seem right that things had to end this way. Sure, I knew some of the Soldiers who were left behind and had a few friends among them, but many of them were new Soldiers who had no real idea who I was. They weren't "my group" so to speak and I felt that it took away from something that could have been one of the more meaningful times in my career. In an odd way, I felt somewhat lonely and I couldn't wait to get my out-processing over with so I wouldn't have to feel that way anymore. I could go home to Saint Johnsville and be around all of my friends and family there, who I obviously knew for years. It's weird in a way because I didn't realize just how close I was with some of my fellow Soldiers at Fort Drum until these last two weeks really settled in. As the old saying goes, "you don't realize what you have until it is gone." How true that is.

Since I had no way to say goodbye to most of my friends face to face, I decided that the best way to accomplish this was through the use of Facebook. Yes, I know that may sound a little cliché, but let's be honest for just a second; everyone is on Facebook nowadays. It is a fact of life and it isn't changing anytime soon. During my last deployment to Iraq in 2009 I had fully harnessed the power of social media. Without the use of MySpace and Facebook I would have lost touch with many of my friends, who are people that mean a lot to me. By using these applications while I was deployed I was able to create a feeling that I was still home. Sometimes Josh would post pictures of parties that were happening in Saint Johnsville, parties that I would have been at if I wasn't deployed. By messaging everyone and looking at the pictures it made me feel a little bit better about being away from home. Granted, you will never get the same feeling out of the internet that you would have if you were there in person, but trust me when you compare Facebook to the "snail mail" that I had to use in 2003 it is a lot better. So, I applied the same principle to my farewell from the Army. For those of my friends that I was able to say goodbye to in person it worked out fine, but for everyone else I decided to write a "note" on Facebook and "tag" everyone on my friends list that was in the Military. I didn't even realize that I had well over 150 people on my list that I had served with over the years, but I guess that's what happens when you spend over nine years traveling the world. When writing this "note" I let pure emotions flow and therefore everything was straight from the heart. After all, why shouldn't it be? This was in effect my farewell speech so the only option that I could see was to make it as good as possible. So, without any further ado, I have decided to include the "note/speech" in its entirety right now:

Positive reflections of my 9 ½ years in the Military

"As many of you may know by now, I am going to be leaving the Army in 5 days, on June 17th, 2011. I have a lot of mixed emotions about this subject that I feel the need to bring to light. I first entered the Active Army on November 6th, 2001. I have a lot on my mind concerning this and I feel that the best way to express how I am feeling right now is to send this out to everyone. The purpose of this is to solely reflect on the positive experiences I had in the military and how they helped shape me as the man that I am today. I do not place sole credit on the army for me being who I am today, as I feel that I was blessed with great friends, a great father, and great family in life as well. There is no room for negativity in this message, as I truly hope to simply leave all the negative feelings and memories behind and remember just the good ones. I know that isn't actually humanly possible, but I guess what I am trying to say is that one shouldn't hold onto the bad experiences in life. Many of you are probably aware that over the past 12-24 months I have had quite a few negative experiences. Those negative experiences are not what this is about. I also want to send across the simple message that the individuals I served with in the military, as well as individuals that I know in the military, whether they served in the past or currently serve now, will always hold a special place in my heart. I went as far as to tag every one of my friends that I have known in the military in this note, to ensure that all of you get a chance to see it. Also, please note that if you are in the military and you happen to be on my friends list, that means I truly do consider you a friend. I am not one of those individuals that feels the need to send an add request to everyone that they know, work with, met on the street, etc. So understand that if your here and able to read this, you were my friend. Over the past 9 1/2 years, I built many bonds with some of the people I met/encountered in the military. I've also had the blessing of being able to travel

the world. Over the years, I had the opportunity to travel to 14 countries, as well as over 20 states. I gained some excellent work experiences, skills, and most importantly memories. In March 2003 I deployed as part of the initial invasion of Iraq. I was stationed at Fort Campbell, KY and I was in a good unit with some great friends. I was only 19 years old on this deployment, and the things that I saw and experienced I'll never forget. Let's also not forget that the invasion of Iraq has historical significance, and therefore any of you that may have served over there technically lived through history. That event will be taught to children in social studies/US history in years to come, just as we all learned about the civil war, WWI, WWII, etc. I am truly proud of going there. In late 2004 and most of 2005 I had the blessing of serving a year in Korea. Simply put, my time in Korea was some of the most fun I've had in my entire life. Not only did I get to see a lot of the country, (which is a beautiful place mind you) but I also made some great friends and had a lot of fun partying with my fellow US Soldiers, as well as some of the KATUSA Soldiers as well. And those KATUSA Soldiers, they became great friends of mine as well. To this day I still tell people of the good times I had in Korea. I'll never forget those days. By late 2005 I went to Fort Drum, NY, where I was able to go and visit home every weekend. It has been great being able to go home on the weekends and see my family as well as the friends that I went to high school with. A lot of Soldiers don't get that privilege and I guess I was lucky in that aspect. But just because I was going home often, doesn't mean I didn't forge bonds at Fort Drum as well. I also deployed 2 more times out of Fort Drum, once to Afghanistan from 2006-2007 and one more time to Iraq in 2009. Afghanistan was a great deployment, as I found myself, an active duty Soldier attached to a National Guard battalion out of New Jersey. I learned many things serving with that unit; most notably that the Soldiers in the National Guard are indeed hard workers, great soldiers, and great people. I made so many close friends on that deployment and they are the sole

> **reason I am deciding to attend college in New Jersey this fall as well as eventually join the New Jersey National Guard as well. To all my New Jersey friends, you all have done far more for me than I have done for you, and I thank you. Serving alongside all of you made me a better person, and I mean that. As far as my deployment in 2009 to Iraq, I will simply say that it was not the same Iraq that it was in 2003. Those of you who may have served a couple of tours there know exactly what I am talking about. So anyway, to close this note, I wish to state to all of my military friends, thank you. Thank you for being a friend, and more importantly thank you for serving. I firmly believe that people take a lesson, an experience from everyone they encounter in life. Those lessons help shape the person that you are. I know that I served with no regrets. I may have made choices that others disagree with, but that's the nature of life, isn't it? If any of you ever need anything, you know how to reach me. I always tried to give every one of you, as well as the Army itself, my very best. Thanks again. I love you all and I will never ever forget any of you. Experience is the benchmark of maturity."**

With that, my "farewell speech" was complete. I received an overwhelming response to this since all of my military friends were "tagged" in this they all received an instant notification when it was posted. Some of their responses made me laugh, some made me cry, all of them brought a smile to my face. I always tried my best to not only help others but to also positively influence everyone that I encountered. I believe that it is crucial that we all live as strong human beings, but I also understand that not all of us have it in us to be that way from the start. Sometimes we need a little help, a "boost" if you will. The fact of the matter is that there is nothing wrong with that. No one can be perfect from birth. We all need help along the way. Elvis had to learn how to sing from someone. Somebody had to teach Bruce Lee how to fight and Ronald Reagan needed to be inspired by someone before he eventually became President of the United States, in which he was then the one giving the inspirational speeches. With that said, I may have fought the good fight, but I couldn't have gotten there on my own. Without my father raising me the way that he did I never would have been able to stand on my own two feet and therefore I would not have had the strength to leave my home (which I loved) in order to join the Army. Without SGT Michael Ramos, SSG Maurice Stewart, and CW3 Brandon Broadbent I would not have been able to rise through the ranks and become the absolute best Human Resources NCO that I could be. Without the Soldiers of the New Jersey National Guard I would not have realized that I was "too much" of an asshole and needed to change my ways. Without my good old roommate SGT Cappe I may not have been able to make it through Iraq in 2009 with a clear head. Without Josh and the gang in Saint Johnsville I may not have been able to "recharge" enough on the weekends to keep on "fighting the good fight" back at Drum. The point that I am trying to make here is that no one is invincible, no one is Superman. Everyone needs someone. Just like Elivis, Bruce Lee, and Ronald Reagan I needed some help along the way. After all, we all do from time to time. I am just thankful that I met people along the way who were willing to help me out. In my opinion, that is part of what the Human Spirit is all about, helping one another and standing up for yourself in the face of adversity. With that said, I was fully prepared to finish my out-processing and head home. I poured enough emotion out in that note that I posted, so now there was no more "stuff in the basement" if you will. It was time to go home.

The final days of my out-processing started to dwindle down quicker and quicker. Since the unit wasn't going to make me a farewell plaque I took it upon myself to do so. Usually, it is customary to make a Soldier one on their way out of the Army, but since the unit was gone I don't think anyone even thought of it, so I did it myself. I had a nice shadowbox made with all of my old unit patches, my name tapes, rank, all of my Class A ribbons and of course my Combat Action Badge. I was extremely proud of all of my accomplishments in the Army and I wanted to immortalize those achievements in trophy form. I still have the shadowbox and it hangs on my living room wall in my apartment. I remember Colonel Alvarado telling me that soon enough I would be able to make a new one to showcase all of my National Guard achievements. I think he was right when he said that. I guess only time will tell.

With that, my final day in the Army finally came along. I feel the need to include a slight disclaimer right now, so here goes: my last day in the Army turned out to be the worst day of my life. What you are about to read may be considered graphic by some readers, so if you do not want to read a graphic story, or if you are weak at heart, feel free to skip to the epilogue. What follows this paragraph can be considered graphic. When it came down to deciding whether or not this should be included, I decided that it was best that it was, because it not only had a profound impact on me, but the rest of my life as well. Furthermore it happened, and in the interest of full disclosure of the events of my life this story should be included. With that said, you have been warned, so read the remainder of this chapter at your own risk.

It was 6 AM on my last day in the Army. The housing department at Fort Drum was scheduled to come through my barracks room at 10 AM to clear my room and give me the approval to final clear Fort Drum. Sometime after that I would report to Clark Hall and finalize my clearing. Even though I had four hours to kill before housing showed up I finished cleaning my room because it did need to be done. I gathered up the rest of my trash, and proceeded to walk down the hallway to exit the building and throw it out. It was then that I encountered a Soldier (who happened to be a friend of mine) who asked me a question. He said, "Hey SGT Conklin, since housing is coming through your room at 10, do you mind putting in a work order with them so they can unlock the bathroom door so we can clean it? There's a nasty smell and since the door is locked I can't clean it." Since the Soldier was a friend of mine I had no problem fulfilling his request. Upon walking up to the door, I noticed that there was an odd smell coming from there. It could have been from anything, perhaps the toilet had overflowed or maybe a Soldier dumped their garbage in there and locked the door as a prank. Either way, I figured that it was the best bet to take care of the situation. Even though it was my last day in the Army, my last official day as a Sergeant, I decided to still do the right thing. I first exited the building to get rid of my own trash and then I returned to the duty desk. I asked the duty NCO (who was a fellow Sergeant) if he had the phone number to put in a work order. It took him a few minutes, but after a while he was finally able to dig out the number. With him standing there, I called the public works office (housing) and put in a work order to have that bathroom lock opened so the Soldier could clean it out. After we talked, the housing representative informed me that it would take about two hours to arrive and take care of the issue. At this point I felt that my job here was done, but upon hearing that it would take housing two hours to arrive, the Duty NCO decided that we should just fix it on our own. I can still remember him saying to me, "We can probably pick the lock on our own, clean the bathroom and get out of here in under 20 minutes. Were NCOs aren't we? Let's just get this shit done." As a fellow Non-Commissioned Officer, I admired his spirit. He possessed that same spirit that has allowed the NCO Corps to persevere all of these years. As a Human Being, I understood why he wanted to get the job done now. He had been on duty for 23 hours, which meant that he only had one more hour to go. He was probably dead tired; why would he want to wait two more hours for housing to show up? The logic made sense; the sooner he fixed the problem the sooner he could go home and go to sleep.

We walked upstairs to approach the bathroom door. First, he tried to open it, which he couldn't. Then, I took a crack. I also couldn't open it. The only thing that remained constant was the fact that there was a strange smell coming from behind the steel door. Eventually the Duty NCO realized that this was an old lock, and based on the style of the lock he could probably pop it open with his Gerber tool. He took about two seconds to inform me of this very fact, and then he broke out the tool. There was a tiny hole on the doorknob that he stuck the tool into. After he shifted the position of the tool a few times we finally heard the lock pop, which meant that we could get into the bathroom. As I stood behind him, he turned the doorknob and pushed the door with his hands, yet it still wouldn't budge. He then looked at me and said, "Something here isn't right." I immediately had a bad feeling deep down in my stomach, as if something terrible was about to happen. Something felt wrong all of a sudden. To this day I still can't put my finger on it, but I just knew something was wrong. The Duty NCO then decided to turn the knob again, but only this time he put all of his body weight on the door and pushed with all of his might. For an NCO who was six inches taller and 30 pounds heavier (surprised he wasn't chaptered out like I was) I actually expected more, but in all of his efforts he was only able to push the door about four inches, just enough to turn a light on and squeeze his face between the crack of the door and the wall.

As the door was pushed open a putrid smell filled the barracks hallway. It was worse than anything that I had smelled in my entire life. The smell was so bad that I could nearly taste it. I had no idea what it was, the only thing that I knew was that it was far worse than what we had smelled when the door was still closed. The duty NCO peered his head into the small gap between the door and the wall, and he shouted, "OH MY GOD! IT'S A BODY!" He immediately pulled the door shut, and looked me dead in the eye and said, "There's a body in there, a Soldier!" I was shocked. I had no idea what to say, and to be honest there was nothing that I really could say. By now the smell was so pungent that I couldn't escape it, even with the door closed. I am not sure if it had to do with the psychological effect of knowing what was actually behind that door or not, but either way it was bad. I wanted to double over and collapse and start puking, but I couldn't do that. The Duty NCO then told me to stand in front of the door and ensure that no Soldiers went near the door while he went downstairs to call 911. Sensing that there was no other choice, I did as I was asked.

I knew that since the Duty NCO called 911 there would be Military Police there before I knew it. They never treat a deceased person lightly. Even still, it felt like an eternity before they arrived. The entire time I had to stand directly in front of the door, knowing exactly what was lying behind me. That wasn't easy to say the least. Not only did it smell bad, but knowing exactly what the cause of the smell was had a significant impact on me. Over the next few minutes the Soldiers that lived in the barracks passed by since they had to go to work. Since many of them were friends of mine they all greeted me with such words as, "Yo! SGT Conklin your still here?" or "Hey Hey SGT Conklin make sure you don't leave without saying goodbye." One Soldier even stopped and tried to hold a conversation with me, totally oblivious to what was in the bathroom behind me. Each and every time I swept them away, telling them to go on and that I would talk to them later. I know that this seemed a little "out of character" for me, since I had always made an effort to hang out and make conversation with the Soldiers as much as possible. Today was different however. Not only was I mentally distraught, but I had to protect the secret of what was behind me until the police arrived. It was such a hard time for me. This was the first time in my entire life that I had dealt with something like this and I really had no idea how to handle it. I wanted to puke my guts out. Finally, the Military Police as well as a few CID agents arrived. They took control of the area, and immediately asked the Duty NCO and me a few questions. The questions were all of a demographic nature; more or less the 5 W's: who, what, where, when and why. Once the Military Police Officers were finished with their questioning, I was forced to report to the CID headquarters on Fort Drum to answer a lot more questions. There was a huge difference however, that being the fact that the questions at CID seemed a lot more condescending, almost aimed in a way that would point blame at an individual. I knew that I was innocent of any wrongdoing, so I didn't let this tactic bother me despite how much they tried. At one point they asked me if I actually saw the body, to which I didn't. There was only a small gap between the door and the wall, and since the duty NCO was so big I didn't see any of the body whatsoever. So, my answer was such that I didn't see the body, which was true. Then the CID agents asked a few more questions, which I answered them all as accurately as I could. I thought everything was going well, until they asked me the question, "So when you saw the body, what did it look like?" I immediately got mad at that question, but didn't show it because I knew that it would give them more reason to mess with me. Why did I get mad you ask? Well, think about it, the opening question was, "did you see the body?" Then after a number of questions, I am suddenly asked, "When you saw the body, what did it look like?" Considering the fact that I answered "no" to the first question, why would you think that I would have any answer to the other question? It was ultimately a tactic to try to catch me in a possible lie, had I been lying. After a couple of hours of questioning and fingerprinting I was finally let go. At this point I was a broken man. This was the worst day of my life, period. I had never experienced this before, and needless to say it wasn't a good experience. I decided that the best thing to do was to go to Clark Hall and finish my out-processing. After everything that I had been through I just wanted to get things over with. The circumstances surrounding my chapter had been bad enough, but I finally grasped them. I was ready to go home and accept what had happened, but then this happened and there was just no telling how long it would take me to get over this. It was a terrible circumstance. Finding the body had a terrible impact on me, for so many reasons. For one, it would end up keeping me up at night for a while. The whole situation was messed up to say the least. In addition, I thought about the family. What would the Army tell them? It couldn't be the truth since the Army didn't actually know the truth. If they knew the truth I wouldn't have been questioned in the manner that I was. The bottom line was that this was an absolute terrible situation that I had the misfortune of being tied up in. When it was all said and done, I was finally released from Fort Drum to go home. I rode home, tired and defeated after the events of the day. All I really wanted to do was break down and cry. The triumphant feeling of standing up for myself in my darkest hour was replaced by the dark feeling of this discovery. I was no longer excited, happy, or celebrating. Instead I felt sad and destroyed. I discovered a dead Soldier during my last day in the Army. I had no real details; just that he had been AWOL for a while. Other than that I had nothing. As CID was done with me I stumbled over to the transitions section at Clark Hall where I would out-process. The entire process would end up taking a few hours, and the whole time I wanted to cry. It was next to impossible to hide my feelings on the entire situation. When it came right down to it, the whole thing was a shame. Why couldn't anyone have discovered this sooner? Why me, and why on my last day? I asked myself earlier in my career, "what had happened to the Army that I loved so much?" I couldn't help but to think that under that Army this wouldn't have happened. Yet, I was stuck with the heartbreak of this Soldier, a man who I had never met. All of this passed through my head as I out-processed Fort Drum. When I was finished, I got on the road to drive home to Saint Johnsville. I still felt messed up inside. There was only one thing left to do in order to get over this, so I decided to do it. I picked up my Blackberry, and I searched for the name, "Dad cell." As he picked up the phone, I told him that I was on the way home, but things weren't ok. As he asked what was wrong, I said, "I found a dead body today. This is the worst day of my life." With that, my Dad replied, "I've been there. I know what you're going through." My dad, a career caretaker in a cemetery was the best person to advise me at this point. It wasn't an Army chaplain, an Army doctor, or a fellow Soldier. It was my Dad. When it came right down to it, the same man who saw me off as a young 18 year old kid on November 6, 2001 was the same man who saw me return on June 16, 2011. After all of my achievements and all of the suffering I was certainly a different man, but he was the same Dad and I will forever be thankful for that. Some prefer to focus on the past, while others prefer to focus on the future. I am here to tell you that unless you learn from the past that you can NEVER change your future.

EPILOGUE

For me, writing this book was an absolute must. For one, there was the fact that many people over the years voiced to me that they thought that I had an interesting story to tell, one that would give us support Soldiers a voice in the world. As I mentioned in the Prologue, every Army related story told seems to cover combat. I hope that in this writing I was able to convey to the world that the Army is more than just the "bombs and bullets" that the media tends to portray and that the sacrifices that support Soldiers make are very real. Take under consideration the fact that sacrifices made are relative to who is actually making the sacrifice, meaning that something that is easy for one person may be hard for another person and vice versa. That's just some "food for thought" so to speak.

In writing this book I was able to take a legitimate step down memory lane, which ultimately led me down a path of self-reflection. Through this process I have gained a newfound respect for authors. The task of writing this book wasn't exactly an easy one and I must say that the only way to appreciate the lesson learned through this process is to actually experience it.

Today I often reflect on the things that I did while I served. I stay in touch with many of the friends from the Army and I always will. I am thankful for their friendship and they will always be my brothers and sisters in arms. I have found that even in my civilian life that some of them do still call me for help, usually guidance in relation to Human Resources issues. Every single time that I can help I do, not only because I want to help but also because I miss the Army that much. I live a much happier life now in New Jersey but even though I am happier now I try to live my life to a certain standard. The following is a set of "guidelines" so to speak, rules that I live by today. Perhaps these "rules" can help others to lead better lives, so I decided to include them here:

1. Don't Judge a book by its cover. I mean that in a literal sense and a figurative sense. In a world where "first impressions are everything" we often forget to look past what is on the outside and look to the inside. For instance, I was judged in an unfair manner even though I was an extremely hard worker. I learned an important lesson in life from that experience, that being that being judged doesn't feel good. You should never pass judgment on other people, especially if you haven't really had a chance to see what they are all about.
2. Be positive. I stress to people all the time that they should try to be positive as often as possible. I understand that every one of us has problems, we are human beings and none of us are perfect, however we do not realize just how much self-loathing can make our problems worse. If I sat around and felt sorry for myself during a majority of my career I probably wouldn't have been able to achieve what I did, and I probably wouldn't have had the guts to stand up for myself. Positivity breeds Confidence. If you are negative all day long you will just continue to breed other negative feelings. If something is getting you down, just turn your focus to something positive. It has worked for me all of these years, so I know it can work for others. Nothing makes me sadder then hearing people complaining about going to work on a Monday morning, even though the unemployment rate is currently at an all-time high. You may have a job today while your friend does not, yet you may choose to complain about having to go to work. To me, that makes no sense. By being positive we can also contribute to society. Personally I love helping others, and everyone should. You can't help anyone if you're walking around complaining all day.
3. Seize the day; every day. Make it your mission to achieve something every day, regardless of how big or small your achievement may be you will find that you lead a happier life by giving it some sense of purpose. It could really be something as small as reading a book, or working out at the gym. The term "seize the day" is twofold as well, meaning that we should try our best to live our lives to the

fullest. There is so much out there for us to enjoy, so go out and enjoy it.

4. Always stand up for yourself, especially if you feel you're correct. If you believe in your stance, then by all means you should stand up and fight for it. Do not back down from a challenge, regardless of what it is. As the saying goes, "It's not about the size of the dog in the fight; it's about the size of the fight in the dog." When I was a kid, my dad once told me that if I ever found myself surrounded by a gang that wanted to kick my ass, to make sure that I went after the biggest, baddest guy. The morale of the story is you will most likely get your ass kicked, but the rest of the gang will think twice about coming after you because you were crazy enough to challenge the biggest one. Even though I lost my trial, I still stood up for myself and because I had the guts to stand up against the system I now have the confidence to take on any challenge that comes my way. Think about it, what could be worse than what I already went through? I feel that everyone should apply this principle to life. Simply put: don't back down.
5. Always help others when you can. The world is so much bigger than you or I. We shouldn't be so arrogant (or ignorant for that matter) that we can't help one another out. There is a lot of selfishness in the world today, and it doesn't have to be that way. There is really no other way to say it than that.

With that said, I hope that you too can apply these principles to your life. I hope that anyone who had read this can apply some of the lessons that I learned during my career in an effort to better their own lives. I will always be thankful for everyone who helped me out along the way. To all of my fellow Soldiers, thank you for your service. It was an honor serving with you all. I have a feeling that this isn't the end of my journey; in fact it is just the beginning. Upward and onward.